THE
HISTORY
OF PRINTING
IN AMERICA

Peale Pinx.t   W.R. Jones Sc.

THE
HISTORY
OF PRINTING
IN AMERICA

with a Biography of Printers

& an Account of Newspapers

BY Isaiah Thomas LL.D.

Edited by Marcus A. McCorison
from the Second Edition

WEATHERVANE BOOKS
NEW YORK

TABLE OF CONTENTS

PREFACE TO THIS EDITION

THERE are very few books of a historical nature which deserve republication after 160 years of existence. Isaiah Thomas's *History of Printing in America* is one of them. His book is still the beginning point for most investigations into the history of American printing, for he provides the tantalizing clues from which his successors have built their own studies. Further, his personal knowledge of many of the people and events which he describes in a frank and unadorned manner makes excellent and often amusing reading.

It would be folly to pretend that the book is not outdated. More recent work by numerous scholars has made that abundantly clear. Even in his own day, Thomas received several lengthy memoranda from William McCulloch which measurably improved his information about Pennsylvania printing. McCulloch's contribution was not published until April 1921, when C. S. Brigham edited it for the *Proceedings of the American Antiquarian Society*. However, and with whatever disclaimers are required, *The History of Printing in America* retains the essential beginnings which lead the reader into fascinating byways of American history and the craft which in such large measure perpetuated it.

The History of Printing in America first appeared in 1810 and was based on Thomas's long fascination with his trade as well as upon his very extensive library of books and newspapers which he had collected to prepare such a history. Two years later his collection became the foundation of the library of the American Antiquarian Society. He continued to make notes and corrections in his copy of the history with the intention, unfulfilled at his death in 1831, to prepare a second edition. His wish was fulfilled in 1874, when the American Antiquarian Society published the second edition based on his notes and the extensive knowledge of Joel Munsell, the printer of Albany; Samuel Foster Haven, the librarian of the Society; and John Russell Bartlett, John Carter Brown's librarian. The text of that edition has been followed in this version of the book.

Isaiah Thomas was the leading American printer and publisher of his day. He was born on January 19, 1749 (O.S.), to an old but poor Boston family. His father, Moses, abandoned the family and in 1756 Isaiah was bound out by the Overseers of the Poor of Boston to a shiftless printer named Zechariah Fowle. Thomas stayed with him for ten years before running away, first to Halifax, Nova Scotia, and then to Charleston, South Carolina. His vagabond days were exciting and he found himself frequently in difficulty with his employers and the civil authorities. He returned to Boston in 1770 with the first of his three wives and in July went into partnership with his old master, Fowle. In Boston he continued to harass the authorities and on the night of April 16, 1775, he fled to Worcester, Massachusetts, with press and types.

The next year he leased his newspaper, *The Massachusetts Spy,* and went to Salem in an effort to improve his shaky fortunes. He returned to Worcester in 1778 no richer and without his wife, who had run off with Benjamin Thompson the Tory, later Count Rumford.

In the succeeding years Thomas's fortunes did improve. At the height of his prosperity he employed 150 people in a printing office containing seven presses. In addition, he owned a paper mill, a bindery, and eight branch offices scattered about in Massachusetts, New Hampshire, Vermont, New York, and Maryland. His other business interests included real estate in Boston and other places, as well as shares in a number of Worcester enterprises. When he retired from active business in 1802 he was a wealthy man.

Thereafter he devoted himself to his book collecting, *The History of Printing*, and the American Antiquarian Society, which he founded in 1812. Thomas died on April 4, 1831, full of years and honors. Excellent accounts of his life by his successors in the American Antiquarian Society may be found in R. W. G. Vail's brief essay in the *Dictionary of American Biography* and in C. K. Shipton's *Isaiah Thomas* (Rochester, N.Y., 1948).

Quite obviously, in dealing with a work of this nature, several difficult editorial decisions had to be made. The present editor is fully aware of the pitfalls attendant to these judgments and can only hope that the larger good will be served by his choices.

Certain deletions have been made. The portions dealing with Spanish (or South) American printing were excised. In fact, the editors of the 1874 edition found Thomas's treatment so imperfect that Mr. Bartlett wrote a new essay for the book. Also deleted were several lengthy appendices which contained material easily available elsewhere and which were tangential to American printing history. Other appendices have been incorporated directly into the text where the weight of the information was deemed sufficient to warrant it. Further, the lists of imprints have been eliminated because they have been superseded by other publications, although a number of Thomas's comments on particular books, taken from those lists, have been incorporated into this text. With these exceptions, the text is inclusive.

In the matter of arrangement, a major change has been effected. Thomas published his book in two volumes. The first dealt with the biographies of printers and the history of printing by towns within states, with subsections on booksellers, etc. The second volume was addressed to the history of newspapers by towns within states. We have merged the two volumes into one, placing the histories of newspapers as another section within the general treatment of printing by states. Thus, all material on Massachusetts, for example, will be found within one chapter.

Corrections and emendations have not been made. To have attempted them would have resulted in a new, multivolume work. This was not within the intentions of the publisher or editor. Since Thomas's day a good many books and articles on American printing have appeared which have greatly enlarged the knowledge available on our subject. In the mid-1930's Douglas McMurtrie attempted to produce a four-volume history which would fill this very important gap in modern American historiography. He published volume two on the Middle Atlantic states but no other volumes were issued, although volume one was in galley proof. The point of this digression is to make clear the problems involved in trying to rewrite Thomas as well as to emphasize the great desirability of a thorough, modern history of American printing. This volume is not intended to be that. We have thus taken Thomas as edited by the 1874 committee. The present editor has improved bibliographical citations and has noted the more recent books or articles dealing with the topic under discussion by Thomas.

In the matter of footnotes, we have left Thomas's in place, using old marks (*, †, ‡, etc.). The notes of Haven, Munsell, Bartlett, Trumbull, Jones, and McCorison have been numbered and placed at the end of each chapter.

The editor would like to thank Isaiah Thomas, the 1874 editorial committee of the American Antiquarian Society, Alden Johnson, and Roderick Stinehour for making this book possible.

M. A. McCorison

American Antiquarian Society

PREFACE TO
THE SECOND EDITION

THE Committee appointed to supervise the republication of Thomas's *History of Printing in America*, have endeavored to carry out, as nearly as practicable, the intentions of the author, disclosed in a corrected copy, left by him for a new edition.*

Mr. Thomas made omissions and alterations in the text of an interleaved copy, and provided material for insertion not always entirely digested; but his ideas in regard to the manner of preparing the work for republication were sufficiently indicated by what he had already accomplished. He says, in a memorandum, that he proposed to take another copy, and make all the alterations, etc., in that, with more care; adding the request: 'If I should not live to fulfil my intention, and the work should be again printed, I hope some friend will do it.'

The expediency of omitting his preliminary account of the beginning and progress of printing in the Old World, has been determined by the circumstances of the case, rather than by an intimation of the author's wishes. Mr. Thomas had, indeed, bestowed considerable labor on a revision of that part of his book; but, though very desirable at the period when he wrote,

* The first edition appeared in 1810 and the second in 1874.

XV

it has been viewed by the Committee as less adapted to the present state of information on that subject, as requiring too much modification and enlargement, as occupying space demanded for additional matter of an important character, and as not essential to the special object of presenting a history of the *American* Press.

The American Antiquarian Society are gratified in being able to reproduce the *History of Printing in America*, Mr. Thomas's great and distinctive enterprise, after his own revision, as an appropriate memorial of their honored Founder and first President.

The original book is rarely met with in the market, and large prices have been paid for copies occasionally found. A desire to reprint has often been manifested by prominent publishers, but has usually been connected with some project impairing the identity of the work, and involving a continuation of the history of the art, and the biographical notices, to a later period.

Mr. Munsell, who [printed the second] edition, had long held a similar purpose in mind, and had made collections with reference to it; but since the Antiquarian Society, of which he [was] a member, decided to put to press the revised copy left in their possession, he [gave] the advantage of his information and judgment to that object, being joined to the Committee in charge of the publication. Mr. Paine, the Treasurer of the Society, has served faithfully on the Committee from the beginning. The principal responsibility and labor have, however, necessarily devolved on the chairman, with whatever accountability belongs to that position.

The first edition of the *History of Printing in America* was dedicated to '*The President and other Officers and Members of the*

American Philosophical Society *in Pennsylvania*, and *The President, Counsellors, and other members, of the* American Academy of Arts and Sciences *in Massachusetts.*' If the new edition had come from the hand of the author there is the best reason for presuming that it would have been inscribed to the society of his chief interest and affections, the American Antiquarian Society, whose later birth and infancy had been so largely the object of his care.

The following extracts from the original Preface are all that may suitably be repeated in this place.

'Amidst the darkness which surrounds the discovery of many of the arts, it has been ascertained that it is practicable to trace the *Introduction* and progress of Printing, in the northern part of America, to the period of the revolution. A history of this kind has not, until now, been attempted, although the subject, in one point of view, is more interesting to us than to any other nation. We are able to convey to posterity a correct account of the manner in which we have grown up to be an independent people, and can delineate the progress of the useful and polite arts among us with a degree of certainty which cannot be attained by the nations of the old world, in respect to themselves.

'I am sensible that a work of this kind might, in other hands, have been rendered more interesting. It has a long time been the wish of many, that some person distinguished for literature would bring it forward; but, as no one has appeared who was disposed to render this service to the republic of letters, the partiality of some of my friends led them to entertain the opinion, that my long acquaintance with Printing must have afforded me a knowledge of many interesting facts, and pointed out the way for further inquiry, and that, therefore, I should assume the undertaking. Thus I have been, perhaps too easily, led to engage in a task which has proved more arduous than I had previously apprehended; and which has been attended with much expense.

'It is true, that in the course of fifty years, during which I have been intimately connected with the art, I became acquainted with many of its respectable professors; some of whom had, long before me, been engaged in business. From them I received information respecting the transactions and events which occurred in their own time, and also concerning those of which they received the details from their predecessors. By these means I have been enabled to record many circumstances and events which must soon have been buried in oblivion. My long acquaintance with printing, and the researches I made in several of the colonies before the revolution, certainly afforded me no inconsiderable aid in this undertaking; and, to this advantage, I may add, and I do it with sincere and grateful acknowledgments, that I have received the most friendly attention to my inquiries from gentlemen in different parts of the United States; among whom I must be permitted to name the following, viz. —EBENEZER HAZARD, esq. and judge J. B. SMITH, of *Philadelphia*; the hon. DAVID RAMSAY, of *Charleston*, Southcarolina; rev. doctor MILLER, of *Newyork*; rev. AARON BANCROFT, and mr. WILLIAM SHELDON, of *Worcester*; the rev. THADDEUS M. HARRIS, of *Dorchester*; the rev. doctor JOHN ELIOT, of *Boston*; and the rev. WILLIAM BENTLEY, of *Salem*; Massachusetts. To these I must add, among the elder brethren of the type, WILLIAM GODDARD and JOHN CARTER, esqrs. of *Providence*; and mr. THOMAS BRADFORD, and the late mr.

JAMES HUMPHREYS, of *Philadelphia*. Many others belonging to the profession, in various parts of the union, have laid me under obligations for the information they have given me.

'Through the politeness of various gentlemen, I have had access to the ancient MS. records of the counties of Middlesex and Suffolk, in Massachusetts, where Printing was first introduced to this country; to those of the colony of Massachusetts, and of the university of Cambridge; and, also, to those of the United Newengland Colonies; all of the seventeenth century; —likewise, to the records of several of the southern states; and, to many of the principal libraries in different parts of the United States. From these documents and institutions I have obtained much valuable intelligence.

'Yet, nothwithstanding all these advantages, I have experienced much difficulty in collecting, through this extensive country, the facts which relate to the introduction of the art of Printing in the several states. These facts were all to be sought for, and the inquiry after them had so long been neglected that the greater part of them would soon have passed beyond the reach of our researches. Most of the printers mentioned in these volumes have long since been numbered with the dead, of whom many were but little known while living; yet, the essential circumstances respecting them, as connected with the art, will, I believe, be found in the following pages; although I cannot flatter myself that they will be entirely free from unintentional errors or omissions.

'The biographical sketches of printers are principally confined to their professional concerns, and to such events as are connected with them.

Preface

'Newspapers are placed in the proper order of succession, or agreeably to the periods in which they were established in the various cities, towns, &c.

'The narratives respecting such persons as remained in business after the American revolution, and such newspapers as were continued after this event, are brought down to the time when those printers quitted business, or died, or these publications were discontinued. From the settlement of the country to the establishment of the independence of the United States, few Printers, and not many Newspapers, have, I believe, escaped my observation; and, I may venture to assert that the data respecting them are as correct, as can, at this period of time, be obtained by the researches of an individual.

'The history of printing in America, I have brought down to the most important event in the annals of our country—the Revolution. To have continued it beyond this period, all will admit would have been superfluous.

'From the consideration that the press, and particularly the newspapers to which it gave birth, had a powerful influence in producing the revolution, I have been led to conceive there would be much propriety in giving accounts of the prosecutions of printers for publishing Libels, which occurred under the several colonial governments. Articles of this description, will be found in such parts of this work as contain memoirs of the Printers who were prosecuted, or descriptions of the Newspapers in which the supposed libels were published.

'With a view to gratify the admirers of typographical antiquities, I have, in several instances, given, as accurately as the nature of the case would admit, representations of the titles of the most ancient Newspapers; from which a tolerable idea may be formed of the fashion of the originals.

'Although a work of this nature may be principally interesting to the professors of the typographic art, yet the facts relating to printing are necessarily connected with others which I have thought it proper to enlarge upon. This circumstance may render these volumes amusing to the man of letters, and not altogether uninteresting to the antiquary.

'I devoted sometime to obtaining a correct account of the booksellers in Boston; it having been my intention to take notice of all who were in the trade from the first settlement of each colony to the year 1775; but I discovered that particular information from other states respecting many, who, in this character, have passed over the stage of life, could not be procured, therefore, the statement is not so complete as I intended it should be. But supposing that the particulars which I have collected may afford some gratification, I have annexed them to this work.'

It only remains to be stated that the notes in this edition, are those of Mr. Thomas unless accompanied by an initial letter or other indication of different authorship. Thus B is for Hon. John R. Bartlett, H is for the chairman of the Committee, [Samuel Foster Haven], and M is for Mr. [Joel] Munsell. The notes respecting Paper Making, etc., in Pennsylvania, communicated by Mr. H. G. Jones of Philadelphia, bear his name or initials.

THE
HISTORY
OF PRINTING
IN AMERICA

* I *

ENGLISH AMERICA
NOW THE UNITED STATES

THE early part of the history of the United States, is not, like that of most other nations, blended with fable. Many of the first European settlers of this country were men of letters; they made records of events as they passed, and they, from the first, adopted effectual methods to transmit the knowledge of them to their posterity. The rise and progress of English America, therefore, from its colonization to the period at which it took a name and place among sovereign and independent nations, may be traced with the clearness and certainty of authentic history.

That art which is the preserver of all arts, is worthy of the attention of the learned and the curious. An account of the first printing executed in the English colonies of America, combines many of the important transactions of the settlement, as well as many incidents interesting in the revolutions of nations; and exhibits the pious and charitable efforts of our ancestors in New England, to translate the sacred books into a language which, at this short distance of time is, probably, not spoken by an individual of the human race, and for the use of a nation* which is now virtually extinct. Such is the fluctuation of human affairs!

* Part of the aborigines of the country.

3

The particulars respecting the printing and printers of this country, it is presumed, will gratify professional men; and a general history of this nature will certainly preserve many important facts which, in a few years, would be irrecoverably lost.

Among the first settlers of New England were not only pious but educated men. They emigrated from a country where the press had more license than in other parts of Europe, and they were acquainted with the usefulness of it. As soon as they had made those provisions that were necessary for their existence in this land, which was then a rude wilderness, their next objects were, the establishment of schools, and a printing press; the latter of which was not tolerated, till many years afterward, by the elder colony of Virginia.

The founders of the colony of Massachusetts* consisted of but a small number of persons, who arrived at Salem in 1628.[1] A few more joined them in 1629; and Governor Winthrop, with the addition of his company of settlers, arrived in 1630. These last landed at the place since called Charlestown, opposite to Boston, where they pitched their tents and built a few huts for shelter. In 1631, they began to settle Cambridge, four miles from the place where they landed. They also began a settlement on the identical spot where Boston now stands. In 1638, they built an academy at Cambridge, which in process of time was increased to a college: and they also established a printing house in that place. In January, 1639, printing was first performed in that part of North America which extends from the gulf of Mexico to the Frozen ocean.

* The reader will observe that I am here speaking of Massachusetts proper, not of the colony of Plymouth, where a settlement was made in the year 1620. That colony has, however, long since been incorporated into that of Massachusetts.

For this press our country is chiefly indebted to the Rev. Mr. Glover, a nonconformist minister, who possessed a considerable estate, and had left his native country with a determination to settle among his friends, who had emigrated to Massachusetts; because in this wilderness, he could freely enjoy, with them, those opinions which were not countenanced by the government and a majority of the people in England.

Another press, with types, and another printer, were, in 1660, sent over from England by the corporation for propagating the gospel among the Indians in New England. This press, &c., was designed solely for the purpose of printing the Bible, and other books, in the Indian language. On their arrival they were carried to Cambridge, and employed in the printing house already established in that place.

Notwithstanding printing continued to be performed in Cambridge, from a variety of causes it happened, that many original works were sent from New England, Massachusetts in particular, to London, to be printed. Among these causes the principal were—first, the press at Cambridge had, generally, full employment; secondly, the printing done there was executed in an inferior style; and, thirdly, many works on controverted points of religion, were not allowed to be printed in this country. Hence it happened that for more than eighty years after printing was first practiced in the colony, manuscripts were occasionally sent to England for publication.[2]

The fathers of Massachusetts kept a watchful eye on the press; and in neither a religious nor civil point of view, were they disposed to give it much liberty. Both the civil and ecclesiastical rulers were fearful that if it was not under wholesome restraints, contentions and heresies would arise among the people. In 1662, the government of Massachusetts appointed licensers of the press;* and afterward, in 1664, passed a law that 'no printing should be allowed in any town within the jurisdiction, except in Cambridge;' nor should any thing be printed there but what the government permitted through the agency of those persons who were empowered for the purpose. Offenders against this regulation were to forfeit their presses to the country, and to be disfranchised of the privilege of printing thereafter.† In a short time, this law was so far repealed as to permit the use of a press at Boston, and a person was authorized to conduct it; subject, however, to the licensers who were appointed for the purpose of inspecting it.

It does not appear that the press, in Massachusetts, was free from legal restraints till about the year 1755. *Holyoke's Almanack*, for 1715, has, in the title page, 'Imprimatur, J. Dudley.' A pamphlet, printed in Boston, on the subject of building market houses in that town, has the addition of, 'Imprimatur, Samuel Shute, Boston, Feb. 19, 1719.' James Franklin, in 1723, was ordered by the government not to publish *The New England Courant*, without previously submitting its contents to the secretary of the province; and Daniel Fowle was imprisoned by the house of representatives, in 1754, barely on *suspicion* of his having printed a pamphlet said to contain reflections on some members of the general court.‡

For several years preceding the year 1730, the government of Massachusetts had been less rigid than formerly; and, after that

---

* Gen. Daniel Gookin, and the Rev. Mr. Mitchel, of Cambridge, were the first appointed licensers of the press in this country.

† See this stated more at length in the account given of Samuel Green, printer at Cambridge, Massachusetts.

‡ See Franklin, and Fowle.

period, I do not find that any officer is mentioned as having a particular control over the press. For a long time, however, the press appeared to be under greater restrictions here than in England; that is, till toward the close of the seventeenth century.

In the course of this work it will appear, that the presses established in other colonies were not entirely free from restraint.

The rulers in the colony of Virginia in the seventeenth century, judged it best not to permit public schools, nor to allow the use of the press.* And thus, by keeping the people in ignorance, they thought to render them more obedient to the laws, to prevent them from libelling the government, and to impede the growth of heresy, &c.

The press had become free some years previous to the commencement of the revolution; but it continued for a long time duly to discriminate between liberty and licentiousness.

Except in Massachusetts, no presses were set up in the colonies till near the close of the seventeenth century. Printing then was performed in Pennsylvania, 'near Philadelphia,' and afterward in that city, by the same press, which, in a few years subsequent, was removed to New York. The use of types commenced in Virginia about 1681; in 1682 the press was prohibited. In 1709, a press was established at New London, in Connecticut; and, from this period, it was gradually introduced into the other colonies; as well as into several of the West India islands, belonging to Great Britain.

In 1775 the whole number of printing houses in the British colonies, now comprising the United States, was fifty.

Till the year 1760, it appears that more books were printed

* George Chalmers, *Political Annals of the Present United Colonies* (London: Bowen for the author, 1780), I, 32 and 345.

in Massachusetts, annually, than in any of the other colonies; and, before 1740, more printing was done there than in all the other colonies. After 1760, the quantum of printing done in Boston and Philadelphia was nearly equal, till the commencement of the war. New York produced some octavo and duodecimo volumes. The presses of Connecticut were not idle; they furnished many pamphlets on various subjects, and some small volumes. Some books were handsomely printed in Virginia and Maryland; and folio volumes of laws, and a few octavos and duodecimos, on religion, history and politics, issued from the presses of Carolina, Rhode Island, New Hampshire, &c.

Before 1775, printing was confined to the capitals of the colonies; but the war occasioned the dispersion of presses, and many were set up in other towns. After the establishment of our independence, by the peace of 1783, presses multiplied very fast, not only in seaports, but in all the principal inland towns and villages.

NEWSPAPERS TO an observer of the great utility of the kind of publications called newspapers, it may appear strange that they should have arisen to the present almost incredible number, from a comparatively late beginning. I would not be understood to intimate that ancient nations had no institutions which answered the purposes of our public journals, because I believe the contrary is the fact. The Chinese gazettes may have been published from a very remote period of time. The kings of Persia had their scribes who copied the public despatches, which were carried into the one hundred and twenty-seven provinces of the Persian empire 'by posts;' and, it is probable, they transmitted accounts of remarkable occurrences in the same manner. The Romans also adopted the custom of sending into their distant provinces written accounts of victories gained, and other remarkable events, which took place in that empire.[3]

In the year 1531, a newspaper was printed at Venice, for which the price charged was a Venetian coin called *gazetta*; and hence is derived our word gazette; the name of the coin having been transferred to the paper.*

The first newspaper produced by the English press, was entitled *The English Mercurie*, printed and published on the 28th day of July, 1588, in London, by Christopher Barker, who was printer to Queen Elizabeth. A copy of this paper is preserved in the British Museum.[4]

Another paper was printed in London, anno 1622, the title of which was *The Weekly Courant*. In 1639, a paper was printed at Newcastle upon Tyne, by Robert Baker. The Mercuries succeeded, being first published August 22, 1642, and continued occasionally through the protectorate of Cromwell, and after his death. One was entitled *The Mercurius Rusticus*, or 'the Countrie's Complaint of the Barbarous Outrage began in the year 1642, by the Sectaries of this once Flourishing Kingdome;' edited by Bruno Ryves. These papers were generally in quarto, and sometimes contained two sheets; but neither of them obtained a permanent establishment.

* I will here take leave to remark, that the statement of facts respecting the *origin* of newspapers, as published in the introduction to the History of Newspapers in the first edition of this work, was taken from writers whose authority I considered unquestionable. Among the works I consulted was the British Encyclopedia; but farther researches convince me that the encyclopedists made some erroneous statements on this subject. These errors I discovered, and corrected in their proper place.

The oldest English newspaper I have seen, is one now in my possession, which was published weekly on Thursdays, anno 1660. The title of it is *Mercurius Publicus*, 'Comprising the Sum of Forraign Intelligence: With the affairs now in agitation in England, Scotland, and Ireland, For Information of the People. Published by Order.' This publication was begun that year; it contained two small quarto sheets. A number of books and medicines for sale, by various people, are advertised in that paper, which was printed in London 'by J. Macock and Tho. Newcomb.' I cannot determine if any other periodical work was published in England at that time; but Sir Roger L'Estrange published a paper called *The Public Intelligencer*, in 1663.[5]

The British Encyclopedia, and other works, state, that 'the *first* gazette in England was published at Oxford,' the court being there on account of the prevalence of the plague in London. It was 'in a folio half sheet, Nov. 7, 1665. On the removal of the court to London, the title was changed to *The London Gazette*.' The publication of newspapers and pamphlets was prohibited by proclamation in England, anno 1680, but although this was done away during the revolution in that country, newspapers were afterwards made objects of taxation.

In 1696, *The Athenian Gazette* was published in London, by John Dunton, whom I have had frequent occasion to mention. In that work Dunton states, that only nine newspapers, the *Athenian Gazette* included, were then published in England. Newspapers were not published in Scotland till after the accession of William and Mary to the throne of England. In the year 1808, the newspaper establishments in England amounted to one hundred and forty-five. Of this number forty-seven were published in London, viz: nine morning, and seven evening, daily papers; nine were printed three times, and one twice a week; and there were nineteen weekly, including eleven Sunday papers. Ninety-eight were printed in all other parts of England. The same year, nineteen were printed in Scotland, and thirty-five in Ireland, making the whole number published in the United Kingdoms of Great Britain and Ireland, one hundred and ninety-seven.

The celebrated Horace Walpole observes, that a Gazette was published in France, anno 1631, by Renaudot, a physician at Paris.[6] This was prior to the appearance of the *Journal des Savans*.

That kind of literary journals, called reviews and magazines, appears to have originated in France. The first production, of this description, was the *Journal des Savans*, which, according to D'Israeli, made its début on the 30th of May, 1665, and was contemporaneous with the *London Gazette*. It was published by Dennis de Sallo, an ecclesiastical counsellor in the parliament of Paris, in the name of the Sieur de Hedouville, his lacquey. Some suppose de Sallo adopted this method of sending it abroad in the world because he thought so humble an author as his servant would disarm criticism of its severity; or, that the scurrility of the critics would produce less effect than if directed against himself.

The *Journal des Savans* comprehended a variety of subjects. It contained an account of all books published in Europe; panegyrics on deceased persons of celebrity; it announced all useful inventions, and such discoveries as were beneficial to the arts, or curious in science; chemical experiments, celestial and meteorological observations, discoveries in anatomy, and in the practice of physic; decisions of the ecclesiastical and secular tribunals; and the author intended to publish an account of the censures of the Sorbonne, &c., &c. In the course of a few years many imitations of this journal were published in different parts of Europe.

Dr. Miller, of New York, in his valuable work entitled, *A Brief Retrospect of the Eighteenth Century*, mentions that 'in 1671, appeared the *Acta Medica Hafnensia*, published by M. Bartholin. To which succeeded, in 1672, *Mémoires des Arts et des Sciences*, established in France, by M. Dennis; in 1682, the *Acta Eruditorum*, of Leipsic, by Menkenius; in 1684, *Les Nouvelles de la Republique des Lettres*, by M. Bayle, and the *Bibliotheque Universelle Choisie, et Ancienne et Moderne*, by Le Clerc; in 1689, the *Monathlichen Unterredungen*, of Germany; in 1692, the *Boekzaal van Europa*, by P. Rabbus, in Holland; and in 1698, the *Nova Literaria Maris Balthici*; together with several others in Germany, France and Italy.' These were all of that class of periodical works which are called reviews. The first publication of this kind in England, was *The History of the Works of the Learned*, printed in London, in 1699; which was soon followed by *Memoirs of Literature*, *The Present State of the Republick of Letters*, *The Censura Temporum*, and the *Bibliotheca Curiosa*. These were published in England the beginning of the eighteenth century, but they were soon discontinued.*

The first English literary work, bearing the name of a magazine, was published in London in the year 1731, by Edward Cave,† and is continued under the title of *The Gentleman's*

---

* Samuel Miller, *A Brief Retrospect of the Eighteenth Century* (New York: T. & J. Swords, 1803), II, 235–236.

† Edward Cave, the founder and editor of *The Gentleman's Magazine*, which has been 'The fruitful mother of a thousand more,' was the son of a shoemaker at Rugby, in Warwickshire, England; at which place he received his education in the free school. His apprenticeship he served with Collins, a printer and an alderman's deputy, in London. When he was of age, he wrote for *Mist's Journal*,

Magazine, at this time. It has acquired credit not only from its long establishment, but from its usefulness, and a considerable addition was made to its reputation by the labors of the learned doctor Samuel Johnson.

The second performance of this description, was *The London Magazine*, a valuable publication, which was continued fifty years. *The Scot's Magazine*, is said to have been the third magazine published in Great Britain. *The European Magazine* was established in 1782.

There are, at this time (1810), upwards of forty periodical works, denominated reviews and magazines, published in Great Britain and Ireland. Some of these reviews are regularly reprinted and republished in the United States. A list of the works of this description, which are published in the United States, will be found in the appendix.

The British Encyclopedia, with large additions, in twenty volumes, quarto, was reprinted by Thomas Dobson, of Philadelphia. It was published in half volumes, two of which came from the press annually.

The first public journals, printed in British America, made their appearance in 1704. In April of that year, the first Anglo-American newspaper was printed at Boston, in Massachusetts Bay, by the postmaster, whose office was then regulated by the colonial government. At that period, I believe, there were only

---

and became the editor of a country newspaper. Through the interest of his wife, he obtained a small place in the postoffice; and some time after was promoted to the office of clerk of the franks. At length, he was enabled to purchase a small printing apparatus, with which he commenced the publication of a magazine; and, to this undertaking, he was indebted for the affluence which attended the last twenty years of his life, and the large fortune he left behind him.

four or five postmasters in all the colonies. It was not until after the expiration of fifteen years, that another publication of the kind issued from any press in this part of the world.

On the 21st day of December, 1719, the second Anglo-American newspaper was published in Boston; and, on the following day, December 22, the third paper appeared, which was printed in the city of Philadelphia.

In 1725, a newspaper was first printed in New York; and after that time, gazettes were gradually introduced into the other colonies on the continent, and into the West Indies.

There are now [1810] more newspapers published in the United States, than in the United Kingdom of Great Britain and Ireland.*

In 1754,† four newspapers only were printed in New England, these were all published in Boston, and, usually, on a small sheet; they were published weekly, and the average number of copies did not exceed six hundred from each press. No paper had then been issued in Connecticut, or New Hampshire. Some years before, one was printed for a short time in Rhode Island, but had been discontinued for want of encouragement. Vermont as a state did not exist, and the country which now composes it was then a wilderness. In 1775, a period of only twenty-one years, more copies of a newspaper were issued weekly from the village press at Worcester, Massachusetts, than were printed in all New England, in 1754; and one paper now published contains as much matter as did all the four published in Boston, in the year last mentioned.

* See further on, a calculation of the newspapers printed in the United States.
† In 1748, five newspapers were printed in Boston, but one of them was discontinued in 1750; a provisional stamp act closed the publication of two more in 1755; but they were afterwards replaced by others.

At the beginning of 1775, there were five newspapers published in Boston, one at Salem, and one at Newburyport, making seven in Massachusetts. There was, at that time, one published at Portsmouth; and no other in New Hampshire. One was printed at Newport, and one at Providence, making two in Rhode Island. At New London there was one, at New Haven one, one at Hartford and one in Norwich; in all four in Connecticut; and fourteen in New England. In the province of New York, four papers were then published; three in the city, and one in Albany.[7] In Pennsylvania there were, on the first of January, 1775, six; three in English and one in German, in Philadelphia, one in German, at Germantown; and one in English and German, at Lancaster. Before the end of January, 1775, three newspapers, in English, were added to the number from the presses in Philadelphia, making nine in Pennsylvania. In Maryland, two; one at Annapolis, and one at Baltimore. In Virginia, there were but two, and both of these at Williamsburg. One was printed at Wilmington, and one in Newbern, in North Carolina; three at Charleston, South Carolina; and one at Savannah, in Georgia. Making thirty-seven newspapers in all the British colonies, which are now comprised in the United States. To these may be added one at Halifax, in Nova Scotia; and one in Canada, at Quebec.

In 1800,* there were at least one hundred and fifty publica-

* In 1796, a small paper, half a sheet medium, 4to, entitled *The New World*, was published at Philadelphia every morning and evening, Sunday excepted, by the ingenious Samuel H. Smith, afterwards the able editor of *The National Intelligencer*, published at Washington. The novelty of two papers a day, from the same press, soon ceased; it continued but a few months. This paper was printed from two forms, on the same sheet, each form having a title; one for the morning, and the other for the evening; the sheet was then divided, and one half of it given to the customers in the forenoon, and the other in the afternoon.

tions of this kind printed in the United States of America, and since that time, the number has increased to three hundred and sixty.[8] Those published before 1775 were weekly papers. Soon after the close of the Revolutionary war, daily papers were printed at Philadelphia, New York, &c., and there are now, 1810, more than twenty published, daily, in the United States.

It was common for printers of newspapers to subjoin to their titles '*Containing the freshest Advices both Foreign and Domestic;*' but gazettes and journals are now chiefly filled with political essays. News do not appear to be always the first object of editors, and, of course, 'containing the freshest advices,' &c., is too often out of the question.

For many years after the establishment of newspapers on this continent, very few advertisements appeared in them. This was the case with those that were early printed in Europe. In the first newspapers, advertisements were not separated by lines from the news, &c., and were not even begun with a two line letter; when two line letters were introduced, it was some time before one advertisement was separated from another by a line, or rule as it is termed by printers. After it became usual to separate advertisements, some printers used lines of metal rules; others lines of flowers irregularly placed. I have seen in some New York papers, great primer flowers between advertisements. At length, it became customary to 'set off advertisements,' and from using types not larger than those with which the news were printed, types of the size of French canon have often been used for names, especially of those who advertised English goods.

In the troublesome times, occasioned by the stamp act in 1765, some of the more opulent and cautious printers, when the act was to take place, put their papers in mourning, and, for a few weeks, omitted to publish them; others not so timid, but doubtful of the consequences of publishing newspapers without stamps, omitted the titles, or altered them, as an evasion; for instance the *Pennsylvania Gazette*, and some other papers, were headed 'Remarkable Occurrences, &c.'—other printers, particularly those in Boston, continued their papers without any alteration in title or imprint.

From the foregoing it appears that, from the time when the first public journal was published in the country, viz. in April, 1704, to April 1775, comprising a period of seventy-one years, seventy-eight different newspapers were printed in the British American continental colonies; that during this period, thirty-nine, exactly one-half of that number, had been, occasionally, discontinued; and that thirty-nine continued to be issued from the several establishments at the commencement of the revolution. The papers published in the West Indies are not included in this computation.

In the course of thirty-five years, newspaper establishments were, as previously remarked, multiplied in a surprising degree; insomuch, that the number of those printed in the United States in June, 1810, amounted to upwards of three hundred and sixty.

A large proportion of the public papers at that date were established, and supported, by the two great contending political parties, into which the people of these states are usually divided; and whose numbers produce an equipollence; consequently, a great augmentation of vehicles for carrying on the political warfare have been found necessary.

I cannot conclude what I have written on the subject of public journals, better than by extracting the following pertinent observations on newspapers, from the Rev. Dr. Miller's *Retrospect of the Eighteenth Century*.[9]

'It is worthy of remark that newspapers have almost entirely changed their form and character within the period under review.* For a long time after they were first adopted as a medium of communication to the public, they were confined, in general, to the mere statement of *facts*. But they have gradually assumed an office more extensive, and risen to a more important station in society. They have become the vehicles of discussion, in which the principles of government, the interests of nations, the spirit and tendency of public measures, and the public and private characters of individuals, are all arraigned, tried, and decided. Instead, therefore, of being considered now, as they once were, of small moment in society, they have become immense moral and political engines, closely connected with the welfare of the state, and deeply involving both its peace and prosperity.

'Newspapers have also become important in a literary view. There are few of them, within the last twenty years, which have not added to their political details some curious and useful information, on the various subjects of literature, science and art. They have thus become the means of conveying, to every class in society, innumerable scraps of knowledge, which have at once increased the public intelligence, and extended the taste for perusing periodical publications. The *advertisements*, moreover, which they daily contain, respecting new books, projects, inventions, discoveries and improvements, are well calculated to enlarge and enlighten the public mind, and are worthy of

* The eighteenth century.

being enumerated among the many methods of awakening and maintaining the popular attention, with which more modern times, beyond all preceding example, abound. . . .

The general circulation of *Gazettes* forms an important era, not only in the moral and literary, but also in the political world. By means of this powerful instrument, impressions on the public mind may be made with a celerity, and to an extent, of which our remote ancestors had no conception, and which cannot but give rise to the most important consequences in society. Never was there given to man a political engine of greater power; and never, assuredly, did this engine before operate upon so large a scale as in the eighteenth century. . . .

Never, it may be safely asserted, was the number of political journals so great in proportion to the population of a country as at present in ours. Never were they, all things considered, so cheap, so universally diffused, and so easy of access. And never were they actually perused by so large a majority of all classes since the art of printing was discovered.*

'The general effect of this unprecedented multiplication and diffusion of public prints, forms a subject of most interesting and complex calculation. On the one hand, when well conducted, they have a tendency to disseminate useful information; to keep the public mind awake and active; to confirm and extend the love of freedom; to correct the mistakes of the ignorant, and the impositions of the crafty; to tear off the mask from corrupt and designing politicians; and, finally, to promote

---

* 'The extreme cheapness with which newspapers are conveyed by the mail, in the United States, added to the circumstance of their being altogether unincumbered with a stamp duty, or any other public restriction, renders their circulation more convenient and general than in any other country.'

union of spirit and of action among the most distant members of
an extended community. But to pursue a path calculated to
product these effects, the conductors of public prints ought to
be men of talents, learning, and virtue. . . .

'In the former part of the eighteenth century, talents and
learning, at least, if not virtue, were thought necessary in the
conductors of political journals.* Few ventured to intrude into
this arduous office, but those who had some claims to literature.
Towards the close of the century, however, persons of less
character, and of humbler qualifications, began, without scru-
ple, to undertake the high task of enlightening the public mind.
This remark applies, in some degree, to Europe; but it applies
with particular force to our own country, where every judicious observer must perceive, that too many of our gazettes are
in the hands of persons destitute at once of the urbanity of
gentlemen, the information of scholars, and the principles of
virtue. To this source, rather than to any peculiar depravity of

* 'This has not been, generally, so much the case in America as in Europe.
From the earliest period too many of our Gazettes have been in the hands of
persons who were destitute both of talents and literature. But in later times, the
number of editors who fall under this description has become even greater
than formerly.'

OBSERVATION.

There are few instances in which I would presume to differ with the ingenious author of these remarks, in opinion; but, on this occasion, I must be
allowed to observe, that I conceive there are among the men who conduct the
public journals of America, many, whose literary acquirements are not inferior
to those of their predecessors. The great difficulty proceeds from the rage of
party spirit, which is kept alive by the frequency of elections, in which the
conductors of newspapers engage as partizans; and some of them, it is true, as
is also the case in Great Britain, display a greater degree of asperity and op-
probriousness than can be justified, which must be a subject of regret to those
who are truly interested in the welfare of the country.

national character, we may ascribe the faults of American news-papers, which have been pronounced by travellers the most profligate and scurrilous public prints in the civilized world.'*

IN an account of Pennsylvania by Gabriel Thomas, published in 1698, he mentions 'all sorts of very good paper are made in the German Town.' The mill at which this paper was made, was the first paper mill erected in the British colonies. What was then called the German Town,[10] was afterwards, and is now, known by the name of Germantown, five miles distant from Philadelphia.† The mill was constructed with logs. The build-ing covered a water wheel set over a small branch of the Wissa-hickon. For this mill there was neither dam nor race. It was

---

* 'These considerations, it is conceived, are abundantly sufficient to account for the disagreeable character of American newspapers. In every country the selfish principle prompts men to defame their personal and political enemies; and where the supposed provocations to this are numerous, and no restraints are imposed on the indulgence of the disposition, an inundation of filth and calumny must be expected. In the United States, the frequency of elections leads to a corresponding frequency of struggle between political parties; these struggles naturally engender mischievous passions, and every species of coarse invective; and, unhappily, too many of the conductors of our public prints have neither the discernment, the firmness, nor the virtue to reject from their pages the foul ebullitions of prejudice and malice. Had they more diligence, or greater talents, they might render their gazettes interesting, by filling them with materials of a more instructive and dignified kind; but wanting these qualifications, they must give such materials, accompanied with such a season-ing, as circumstances furnish. Of what kind these are no one is ignorant.'

† The first settlement of Germans is stated to have been in 1692. This mill, from many circumstances, must have been erected prior to that period, and in 1688, with the log mill and log house of Rittenhouse. Nicholas Rittenhouse, the first paper-maker, died in May, 1734, aged 68, and was succeeded by his son William, who was born in 1691, and died in 1774.

built by Nicholas (or as he was then called Claus) Rittenhouse,[11] about the year 1689, with the assistance of William
Bradford, then the only printer in the colonies southward or
westward of New England, who procured the tract of land,
then considered of little, if any value, on which the log mill and
a log house for Claus were placed. Bradford also procured
molds and other furniture for the mill. Claus was from Holland,[12] and a paper-maker by trade. He was only twenty-one
years of age when he arrived in America. He was something of
a carpenter, and did the chief of the work of these buildings
himself. This small mill was carried away by a freshet.[13] Another mill built of stone was erected near to the spot where the
first mill stood. At length this mill was found to be too small for
the increased business of its owner. He built another of stone,
which was larger than the one already erected. This mill spot
was occupied, and the paper-making business carried on, by the
first Claus, or Nicholas, and his descendants, from 1689 to
1798,[14] one hundred and nine years, who from time to time
made many valuable improvements in the mills, and in the art
of paper-making.

Jacob Rittenhouse, now, in 1818, eighty-six years of age, a
grandson of Nicholas Rittenhouse the first papermaker in British America, is living. He has been many years blind, but posses-
ses an excellent memory, which seems to be unimpaired. He
received from his father and grandfather many interesting narratives of the settlement of Philadelphia and Germantown, and
of the first printers and papermakers in those places.

He says that William Bradford, the first printer in Philadelphia, after he left this city, and settled in New York, often
visited Philadelphia, and that he would sometimes ride from

one of these places to the other in a day. [The connected distance then was one hundred miles.] That when his grandfather and a few others settled in Germantown, there was no gristmill nearer than Chester, fifteen miles southeast of Philadelphia. There was no horse in the settlement for some time afterwards, when an old horse was procured from New York, and this horse was continually employed in carrying sacks of grain to the mill at Chester, to be ground, and bringing it back when ground. This was, at the time, continued Mr. Rittenhouse, the only horse for common use either in the Germantown settlement, or in Philadelphia. The grain for those living in Philadelphia, etc., continued to be ground in Chester, until William Penn built a gristmill in Philadelphia, afterwards called the Globe mill, from a tavern being erected near to it, the site of which is in Third street. This mill was used as a gristmill until a short time before the revolution.

He mentions, among other things, the following, which shows the estimation in which land was held in the early settlement of Philadelphia, and the difference between its value then and at the present day. Claus, the grandfather, was something of a carpenter, as well as a papermaker. He constructed a kind of batteau on the papermill stream, and occasionally descended with it to the Schuylkill, for the purpose of fishing in its stream. A person from Philadelphia who owned a large tract of land on the borders of this river, was one time viewing and examining his possessions, when he espied Claus in his fishing boat. The owner of the ground was so much pleased with the unexpected sight of a boat, the first belonging to a white man which had been seen in that stream, that he became desirous of possessing it, and offered Claus, in exchange, a piece of land bordering on the Schuylkill, of which he described the limits, and which, it is said, contained about two thousand acres. Claus refused the proffer.

Jacob Rittenhouse also mentions that his progenitors, when they first arrived at Philadelphia, dwelt in caves dug in the banks of the Delaware, during part of the winter 1687–8. Robert Proud, in his *History of Pennsylvania* (Philadelphia: Poulson, 1797–1798) 2 vols., mentions these caves, and observes that they were for many years reserved for the habitations of new comers, who had not the means of obtaining other lodgings.

From Claus, or Nicholas Rittenhouse,[15] and his brother, (Garrett) who came with him from Holland to America in 1687, or 1688, are descended all of that name now in Pennsylvania or New Jersey. The late David Rittenhouse, the philosopher of Pennsylvania, was the grandson of Claus, the first manufacturer of paper in British America.

The second establishment of a paper mill erected in Pennsylvania, or in British America, was built with brick on the west branch of Chester creek, Delaware county, twenty miles distant from Philadelphia, by Thomas Wilcox, who was born in England, and there brought up to papermaking.[16] Wilcox came to America about the year 1712, and applied to Rittenhouse for employment, but could not obtain it, as but little business was then done at the mill. For fourteen years Wilcox followed other business, and by his industry and economy he acquired and laid up a small sum of money, when in 1726, he erected a small paper mill, and began to make fuller's boards. He continued this business fourteen years without manufacturing either writing or printing paper. He gave up his mill to his son Mark

in 1767. Wilcox the father died November 11, 1779, aged
ninety.*

The paper-making business was carried on in 1815, by the
sons of Mark, who was then living aged seventy. He made the
paper for the bills issued by congress during the revolutionary
war; for the bills of the first bank established in Philadelphia;
for many other banks and public offices. He was undoubtedly
the first who made good paper in the United States. In 1770 he
was appointed associate judge for Delaware county.

The third paper mill established in Pennsylvania was erected
by William De Wees and John Gorgas, who had been the
apprentices of Rittenhouse. Their mill was on the Wissahickon
creek, eleven miles from Philadelphia, and built in 1728. They
manufactured an imitation of asses skin paper for memorandum
books, which was well executed.†

The fourth mill was also on the Wissahickon, nine miles from
Philadelphia, built by William De Wees, Jr., about 1736.

The fifth was erected by Christopher Sower, the first of the

---

* The first purchase of land that Thomas Wilcox made for his mill seat was
from the proprietors of Pennsylvania. The additional piece for his dam he
agreed for at one shilling sterling a year forever. This seems, at the present
time, to have been a small compensation; but lands were then plenty, and
money scarce. Lands were leased out at one penny an acre; but this price was
thought high. Quantities of land were afterwards taken up at one shilling
sterling for every hundred acres. The state, about the commencement of the
revolution, bought out the quit rents from the proprietors for £30,000, but the
proprietors still retain the manors.

† John Brighter, an aged paper-maker, who conducted a mill for more than
half a century in Pennsylvania, and who gave this account, observed that this
kind of paper was made out of rotten stone, which is found in several places
near and to the northward of Pennsylvania, and that the method of cleansing
this paper was to throw it in the fire for a short time, when it was taken out
perfectly fair.

name, about the year 1744, on a branch of Frankford creek. This was on the lower end of his land.

The improvements in paper-making at Wilcox's and other mills in Pennsylvania, were principally owing to an Englishman by the name of John Readen. He was a man of great professional ingenuity, and a first rate workman. He had indented himself to the master of the vessel who brought him from Europe. Wilcox redeemed him, and employed him several years. He died in 1806, aged sixty.

Engines were not used in the American paper mills before 1756; until then, rags for making paper were pounded.

There were several paper mills in New England, and two or three in New York, before the revolution.

About the year 1730, an enterprising bookseller in Boston, having petitioned for, and received some aid from the legislature of Massachusetts,* erected a paper mill, which was the first set up in that colony. After 1775, paper mills increased rapidly, in all parts of the Union.

PAPER MILLS

M Y endeavors to obtain an accurate account of the paper mills in the United States, have not succeeded agreeably to my wishes, as I am not enabled to procure a complete list of the mills, and the quantity of paper manufactured in all the states. I have not received any particulars that can be relied on from some of the states; but I believe the following statement will come near the truth. From the information I have collected

---

* Daniel Henchman. He produced in 1731, to the General court, a sample of paper made at his mill [which was established in 1728 in Milton on the Neponset River].

it appears that the mills for manufacturing paper, are in number about one hundred and eighty-five, viz: in New Hampshire, 7; Massachusetts, 40; Rhode Island, 4; Connecticut, 17; Vermont, 9; New York, 12; Delaware, 10; Maryland, 3; Virginia, 4; South Carolina, 1; Kentucky, 6; Tennessee, 4; Pennsylvania, about 60; in all the other states and territories, say 18. Total 195, in the year 1810.

At these mills it may be estimated that there are manufactured annually 50,000 reams of paper which is consumed in the publication of 22,500,000 newspapers. This kind of paper is at various prices according to the quality and size, and will average three dollars per ream; at which, this quantity will amount to 150,000 dollars. The weight of the paper will be about 500 tons.

The paper manufactured, and used, for book printing, may be calculated at about 70,000 reams per annum, a considerable part of which is used for spelling, and other small school books. This paper is also of various qualities and prices, of which the average may be three dollars and a half per ream, and at that price it will amount to 245,000 dollars, and may weigh about 630 tons.

Of writing paper, supposing each mill should make 600 reams per annum, it will amount to 111,000 reams; which at the average price of three dollars per ream, will be equal in value to 333,000 dollars, and the weight of it will be about 650 tons.*

Of wrapping paper the quantity made may be computed at

---

* Some of the mills are known to make upwards of 3,000 reams of writing paper per annum; a few do not make any; but there are not many that make less than 500 reams. The quantity of rags, old sails, ropes, junk, and other substances of which various kinds of paper and pasteboards are made, may be computed to amount to not less than three thousand five hundred tons yearly.

least at 100,000 reams, which will amount to about 83,000 dollars.

Beside the preceding articles, of paper for hangings, for clothiers, for cards, bonnets, cartridge paper, pasteboards, &c., a sufficient quantity is made for home consumption.

Most of the mills in New England have two vats each. Some in New York, Pennsylvania, Delaware and Maryland, have three or more—those with two vats can make, of various descriptions of paper, from 2,000 to 3,000 reams per annum. A mill with two vats requires a capital of about 10,000 dollars, and employs twelve or more persons, consisting of men, boys and girls. Collecting rags, making paper, &c., may be said to give employment to not less than 2,500 persons in the United States.

TYPE FOUNDERIES

A N attempt was made to establish a foundery for casting types in Boston about 1768, by a Mr. Mitchelson from Scotland, but he did not succeed.

In 1769, Abel Buel of Killingworth in Connecticut, who was a skillful jeweller and goldsmith, began a type foundery, without any other aid than his own ingenuity, and perhaps some assistance he derived from books. In the course of a few years he completed several fonts of long primer, which were tolerably well executed, and some persons in the trade made use of them.

The first regular foundery was established at Germantown, Pennsylvania, in 1772, by Christopher Sower, the second of that name. All the implements for this foundery were imported from Germany, and intended solely for casting German types. It is somewhat remarkable that the first establishments for paper making and type founding in the English colonies, should be in this place. The interval between the two establishments was eighty-four years. Sower's first object in setting up the foundery was to cast pica types for a quarto edition of the German Bible. His father had, many years before, printed an edition on long primer, and the son had printed another on pica. This was for a third edition, and it was his intention to cast a sufficiency of types to keep the whole work standing.

When the materials for this foundery arrived from Germany, they were placed by Sower in a house opposite to his printing house, and committed to the care and management of one of his workmen, who, although not a type founder, was very ingenious. This workman was named Justus Fox, born in 1736, at Manheim, Germany, where he received a good education. After his arrival in America he served as an apprentice with Sower, and was by him employed in various occupations. Fox is said to have been a farrier, an apothecary, a bleeder and cupper, a dentist, an engraver, a cutler, a tanner, a lamp-black maker, a physician, a maker of printing ink, and a type founder. At most of these pursuits he was a proficient.

The molds of this foundery, and some other implements, were found to be very imperfect; but Fox set himself at work, cut a number of new punches, supplied all deficiencies, and put the whole in order for casting. The first font that was cast was a German pica for the Bible. Afterwards Fox cut the punches for roman and italics of several sizes, for English works. Fox acquired the art of mixing metal. His types were very durable.

As the materials which composed this foundery remained in the possession of Fox they were thought to be his property, and therefore escaped seizure when all the other property of Sower was confiscated. Afterwards, in 1784, Fox purchased them, and continued the business somewhat extensively in partnership with his son for nine years; after which Fox conducted the business till he died, which was on the twenty-sixth of January, 1805, aged seventy years.

Fox was a man of pleasing manners, and his character was in conformity with his name, Justus. He was of the sect of Tunkers; humorous, also very pious, exemplary, humane and charitable. He acquired a handsome property. He had but one child whom he named Emanuel.

The year after Fox died, his son sold the foundery to Samuel Sower, a son of the unfortunate Christopher, junior (or second), the first owner. Samuel Sower had previously begun a foundery in Baltimore, and in 1815, continued the business in that city.

The second type foundery was also established in Germantown, by Jacob Bay, a man of great ingenuity, born near Basil, in Switzerland. He was brought up to silk weaving. He came to Philadelphia in 1771. In this place he worked for a short time at calico printing, and then was engaged by Sower to work in his foundery in Germantown as an assistant to Fox. After being two years in this foundery, he began business for himself in a small house not far from Sower. He made all the apparatus for his foundery himself. The punches which he cut were for roman and italic types of the sizes of pica, long primer, and bourgeois. He cast for Sower a font of German faced bourgeois for the whole of the German Hymn Book of four hundred octavo pages, which Sower kept standing.

He bought a house and removed to it, and continued the business of type-making in Germantown, till 1789. During the time he removed his foundery to other parts of the town. At length he sold all his material to Francis Bailey, a printer, who made use of it chiefly for a supply of types for himself. Bay then commenced diaper weaving, removed to Frankford, and then to Philadelphia. Bay's ingenuity has been exceeded by very few. He was at any time able, without a model before him, to construct, by the aid of his memory, any machine he had ever seen, however complicated. Among his weaving machines was a loom with six shackles. A patent for one of the same kind has since been obtained as a new invention, and the right to use it sold in several places, at a high price. But he was poor, the fate of many ingenious men. He engaged at the mint as an engraver, and about six months after fell a victim to the yellow fever which prevailed in Philadelphia in 1793, aged 54.

Dr. Franklin was desirous of establishing in Philadelphia a more extensive type foundery than either of those just mentioned. For this purpose, he purchased in Paris, of P. S. Fournier, the materials of an old foundery. Fournier was a type founder, and B. F. Bache, Franklin's grandson, resided sometimes with him for instruction in this art, and that he might otherwise be qualified for managing the foundery in Philadelphia. Franklin and his grandson arrived in Philadelphia in 1775, soon after the revolutionary war commenced, and Bache set up his foundery in Franklin court, Market street, where his grandfather resided. Although the materials of this foundery enabled the proprietor to make Greek, Hebrew, Roman, and all other kinds of types in use in Europe or America, the foundery was but little employed. The implements for making roman and italic types, especially, would not produce handsome specimens. This difficulty was in some sort removed by means of a German artist, named Frederick Geiger. This person was a mathematical instrument maker. He came from Germany to Philadelphia, like thousands of others who were called *Redemptioners*. Franklin paid for his passage, and placed him in his foundery. He cut a number of punches, and made great proficiency as a type maker, and in the improvement of the foundery. Geiger, after serving the time stipulated for his redemption, was, in 1794, employed in the mint; but quitting the mint, he plodded a long time on perpetual motion. He appeared confident of success, and anticipated receiving the promised reward for his discovery. Disappointed in this, he next applied himself to finding out the longitude by lunar observations. He was allured to this study by the great bounty which he who should be successful was to receive from the British government. But, unfortunately, perpetual motion caused an irregular motion of his brains, and his observations of the moon caused lunacy. He was eventually confined in the cells of the Philadelphia almshouse.

The foundery was neglected, and Bache turned his attention to printing.

The fourth establishment of this kind was that belonging to the Messrs. Baine, the grandfather and grandson, from Scotland. They settled in Philadelphia by advice of Young & McCullock, printers in that city, about the year 1785. Baine, the senior, possessed a great mechanical genius. His knowledge in type founding was the effect of his own industry, for he was self-taught. He, it is said, communicated to the celebrated Wilson of Glasgow the first insight into the business, and they together set up a foundery in Glasgow. They soon after separated, and Baine went to Dublin, where he established a foundery. He removed thence to Edinburgh, and commenced a type foundery in that city. Thence with his grandson he came with all his materials to America. They were good workmen, and had full employment. The types for the Encyclopedia, which was completed some years ago from the press of Dobson in Philadelphia, were made by them. The elder Baine died in August, 1790, aged seventy-seven. He was seventy-two years of age when he arrived in America. His grandson relinquished the business soon after the death of his grandfather. He removed from Philadelphia, and died at Augusta in Georgia, about the year 1799.

At the commencement of the troubles occasioned by the Prussians, under the Duke of Brunswick, entering Holland for the purpose of reforming the stadtholdership, an ingenious type founder, Adam G. Mappa, left that country, and took with him the whole apparatus of his foundery, and came to New York, where he began business.* His foundery was designed principally for making Dutch and German types, the casts of which were handsome. Those for roman were but ordinary. He soon left type making for other employment, and was concerned in the Holland Land Company.

There were, in 1830, eight or more type founderies in the United States. One was established in Philadelphia, by Binney & Ronaldson, in 1796. They were from Scotland. They had to encounter many difficulties before they could succeed in obtaining a permanency to their establishment, but by perseverance and industry overcame them, and made valuable improvements in their art. Their foundery produced types equal in beauty to those of any foundery in Europe, and was said to excel them all in the economy of operation.

* He was a Dutch patriot, lost most of his property, and was obliged for safety, to leave his country.

Samuel Sower and Co., of Baltimore, had a somewhat extensive foundery. Sower cut the punches, and cast both roman and italics for a font of diamond types, on which has been printed, in that city, an edition of the Bible. An italic to this smallest of types has not been, until very recently, attempted in Europe.

STEREOTYPE
PRINTING

ABOUT the year 1775, an attempt at stereotype printing was made by Benjamin Mecom, printer, nephew of Dr. Franklin.[17] He cast the plates for a number of pages of the New Testament; but never completed them. I shall have occasion to mention Mecom, in the course of this work, several times. He was skillful, but not successful. Stereotyping is now very common in the United States, and is well executed.

The ingenious Jacob Perkins, of Newburyport, Massachusetts, invented a new kind of stereotype, for impressing copper and other plates. From plates so impressed most of the bank bills of Massachusetts and New Hampshire were printed at rolling presses, and were called stereotyped bills.

ENGRAVING

MAN in his primeval state discovered a propensity to represent, by figures, on various substances, the animated works of his Creator. From sketching, painting, or engraving these images, or representations, on the surface of those substances, he proceeded to the business of the sculptor or statuary, and produced all the features and proportions of men, and the other various descriptions of the animal creation, in wood and stone.

The United States contain several vestiges of engraving, by the rude hands of the aborigines. Thus we find that there is hardly any inhabited part of the world, which did not, before it became civilized, produce some specimens of engraving.

The modern European art of engraving was not greatly encouraged in America before the revolution, and the artists did not appear to possess first rate abilities.[18]

THE printing presses made use of in the English colonies, before the revolution, were, generally, imported from England, but some were manufactured in the country. Christopher Sower, Jr., had his printing presses made under his own inspection, in Germantown, as early as 1750.

After 1775, good presses were made in many of the capital towns in the United States, particularly in Philadelphia, and in Hartford, Connecticut. Some of these presses underwent several partial alterations in their machinery, but no essential change in the construction was made from the common English printing press.[19] A few were contrived to perform the operation of printing in a different manner from that press, but these were not found to be useful.

Some years since, Dr. Kinsley, of Connecticut, who possessed great mechanical ingenuity, produced, among other inventions, a model of a cylindrical letter press. It was a subject of much conversation among printers, but was never brought into use. The invention, however, did not originate with Kinsley.* Cylindrical letter presses were invented in 1789, by William Nicholson, of London, who obtained a patent for them in 1790. Kinsley's model was from Nicholson's plan, with some variation. Nicholson placed his forms of type horizontally; Kinsley placed his perpendicularly; his method was not calculated for neat printing. Nicholson's presses were used, and, it is said, made excellent work.[20]

ROLLING PRESSES

THE rolling press, as it is called, by copperplate printers, was not used in England till the reign of King James I. It was carried from Antwerp to England, by one Speed. I cannot determine when it was first brought into English America, but I believe about the beginning of the eighteenth century.

* Dr. Apollos Kinsley was a native of Massachusetts, but settled in Connecticut. He invented a machine for making pins, and another for preparing clay and moulding bricks, etc.

NOTES TO CHAPTER I

INTRODUCTION
OF THE ART

Of recently published works which supplement Thomas's volume, see especially Lawrence C. Wroth, *The Colonial Printer* [2nd edn.] (Portland, Me.: Southworth-Anthoensen Press, 1938); Rollo G. Silver, *The American Printer, 1787–1825* (University Press of Virginia for the Bibliographical Society of the University of Virginia, ᶜ1967); Douglas C. McMurtrie, *A History of Printing in the United States* (New York: Bowker, 1936) only vol. 2, dealing with the Middle & South Atlantic states; Hellmut Lehmann-Haupt, *The Book in America*, 2nd edn. (New York: Bowker, 1952) and *Bookbinding in America* (New York: Bowker, 1941); J. C. Oswald, *Printing in the Americas* (New York: Gregg, ᶜ1937).

The reader is also referred to the bibliographical work of Charles Evans and his successors, Clifford K. Shipton and Roger Bristol, published in *American Bibliography* (Chicago, Worcester and Charlottesville, 1903–1970), 18 vols.

1. The Cape Anne fishermen selected and occupied the position of Salem before the arrival of the colonists of 1628. H

2. See Leonard W. Levy, *Legacy of Suppression; freedom of speech and press in early American history* (Cambridge: Harvard University Press, 1960).

For the modern account, see Clarence S. Brigham, *History and Bibliography of American Newspapers, 1690–1820* (Worcester: American Antiquarian Society, 1947) 2 vols; Frank L. Mott, *A History of American Magazines, 1741–1850* (Cambridge: Harvard University Press, 1957).

3. Newspapers were foreshadowed among the ancients by the *Acta Diurna* of the Romans—daily official reports of public occurrences. H

4. Mr. Thomas Watt, the distinguished bibliographer, ascertained that the copies of this alleged newspaper, in the British Museum, were forgeries, executed about the year 1766.—*Letter to Antonio Panizzi.* H

5. After all that has been written about early newspapers, it is not usual to find perfect accuracy in any one account. The paper which our author refers to as the *The Weekly Courant*, anno 1622, was *The Courant or Weekly Newes from Foreign Parts*, established by Nathaniel Butter. Alexander Andrews, author of *History of British Journalism*, in a communication to *Notes and Queries*, 1st series, XI, 285, expresses the opinion that it appeared first in 1621. He says also that Butter published Sept. 9, 1622, a paper entitled *News from most Parts of Christendom*. It was probably the same paper as the first named, as may have been that entitled *The Weekly News from Italy, Germanie, &c.* Butter is regarded as the father of the regular newspapers press. It is stated in Appleton's *New American Cyclopedia*, that the first attempt at parliamentary reporting was in 1641. But we have before us a facsimile of the 1st No. of | *Perfect Occurrences* | *of* | *Every Daies iournall* | *In* | *Parliament* | *Of England.* | *And other Moderate Intelligence* | *From Tuesday Novemb. 3, to Friday Decemb. 4, 1640.* | *Collected by Hon. Walkar Cleric.* H

6. It was called the Gazette de France. H

7. With all deference to Mr. Thomas's knowledge of what was done in his own time, it still seems hardly probable that the paper begun in Albany in 1771, could have been continued longer than 1773. No copies of it have been discovered here later than the early part of 1772. M

8. It may be remarked that this number of newspapers, which seemed to be worthy of notice at the time Mr. Thomas wrote, in 1810, is only about one-third as great as that which *ceased to exist* in the year 1872; so rapidly do newspapers now come forth, and soon after disappear from want of adequate support. M

9. Samuel Miller, *A Brief Retrospect of the Eighteenth Century* (New York: T. & J. Swords, 1803) II, 251–255.

PAPERMAKING For adequate, recent accounts, see Lyman Horace Weeks, *A History of Paper-Manufacturing in the United States, 1690–1916* (New York: Lockwood Trade Journal Co., 1916) and Dard Hunter, *Papermaking in Pioneer America* (Philadelphia: University of Pennsylvania Press, 1952) which is based on his privately printed *Papermaking by Hand in America* (Chillicothe, 1950).

10. This name of the German Town was not confined merely to what is now known as Germantown, but included also Roxborough township at present forming the Twenty-first ward of Philadelphia. HGJ

11. Mr. Thomas has fallen into error. The first paper-maker was not Nicholas Rittenhouse, but *William* Rittenhouse, a native of the Principality of Broich in Holland. The mill was built in the year 1690, by a company composed of such prominent men as Robert Turner, Thomas Tresse, William Bradford, Samuel Carpenter, William Rittenhouse and others. The mill was erected on a stream of water which empties into Wissahickon creek about a mile above its confluence with the river Schuylkill, in the township of Roxborough. This stream still bears the name of *Papermill run*. The deed for the land on part of which the mill was erected, comprising about twenty acres, is dated 'the Ninth day of the Twelfth month called ffebruary, in the ffourth year of the Reign of Queen Ann 170⅚,' and the grantee was William Rittenhouse. This deed recites that in the year 1690, it was agreed between the said parties 'and others *that undertook to build a paper mill upon the land*,' above referred to, that said Carpenter should demise to them the said land, and then proceeds as follows: 'And whereas the *said paper mill was afterwards built*, but no Lease actually signed or executed according to the said Agreement.' HGJ

12. Claus, or Nicolas, Rittenhouse was born in Holland, June 15, 1666, came to America with his father, William Rittenhouse, who settled in Germantown and afterwards removed to Roxborough, where he had erected his paper mill. Nicholas was a member of the Mennonist meeting at Germantown, and officiated as a minister in that society. HGJ

13. This terrible calamity occurred in the year 1700 or 1701, during the second visit of William Penn to his colony. William Barton, in his *Memoirs of the Life of David Rittenhouse* (Philadelphia: Edward Parker, 1813), pp. 83–84, says: 'There is now before the writer a paper in the hand writing of the celebrated William Penn, and subscribed with his name, certifying that William Rittinghausen and Claus his son, then

part owners of the paper mill near Germantown, had recently sustained a very great loss by a violent and sudden flood, which carried away the said mill, with a considerable quantity of paper, materials and tools, with other things therein, whereby they were reduced to great distress; and therefore recommending to such persons as should be disposed to lend them aid, to give the sufferers "relief and encouragement, in their needful and commendable employment," as they were "desirous to set up the paper mill again." '

The Rittenhouses rebuilt the mill in 1702, and on the 30th of June, 1704, William Rittenhouse became the sole owner of the mill, and in 1705, secured the land from Samuel Carpenter on a lease for 975 years. HGJ

14. William Rittenhouse, the first paper maker in America, died in the year 1708, aged about 64 years. Shortly before his death he gave his share in the paper mill to his son Nicholas, who carried on the business until May, 1734, when he died. He deeded the paper mill to his oldest son William Rittenhouse, and when he died the mill property fell to his son Jacob Rittenhouse, also a paper-maker, who carried on the business, and died in 1811. The mill was erected by a family named Markle, who continued to manufacture paper there for many years. So that the paper-making business was carried on by the same family for a period of *one hundred and twenty-one years* at the same place. HGJ

15. It was not Nicholas but William Rittenhouse who was the progenitor of the family in America. He arrived here about 1688, and settled in Germantown. He had only two sons, Nicholas or Claus, and Garrett or Gerhard, and a daughter Elizabeth who married Heiver Papen. Nicholas married Wilhelmina De Wees, a sister of William De Wees of Germantown. Garrett resided at Cresheim, a part of Germantown, and was a miller. HGJ

16. The second paper mill in America was not that of Thomas Wilcox. Dr. George Smith, in his *History of Delaware County, Pennsylvania* (Philadelphia: Ashmead, 1862), says, that 'the old Ivy Mill of Wilcox was not erected until the year 1729, or very shortly afterwards.' He claims that it was the second place at which paper was manufactured in Pennsylvania. But this is an error. The second paper mill in America was erected by another settler of Germantown named William De Wees, who was a brother-in-law of Nicholas Rittenhouse, and, as Mr. Thomas says, had been an apprentice at the Rittenhouse mill. This second mill was built in the year 1710, on the west side of the Wissahickon creek in that part of Germantown known in early times as *Crefeld*, near the line of the present Montgomery county. I have seen papers which show that this mill was in full and active operation in that year and in 1713. HGJ

TYPE FOUNDERIES   For modern accounts, see Lawrence C. Wroth, *Abel Buell of Connecticut* [2nd edn.] (Middletown: Wesleyan University Press, 1958) and Rollo G. Silver, *Typefounding in America, 1787–1825* (University Press of Virginia, ᶜ1965).

STEREOTYPE PRINTING   17. In 1743, Dr. Cadwallader Colden explained to Franklin a process of stereotyping, which was published in the *American Medical and Philosophical Register*, I, 439–450 (April 1811). The *Larger Catechism of the Westminster Assembly*, stereotyped and printed by J. Watt & Co., of New York, in June, 1813, claims upon its title page to have been the first work stereotyped in America. M

ENGRAVING   18. See David McN. Stauffer, *American Engravers upon Copper and Steel* (New York: Grolier Club, 1907), 2 vols; Mantle Fielding, *American Engravers upon Copper and Steel* (Philadelphia, 1917); Sinclair Hamilton, *Early American Book Illustrators and Wood Engravers, 1670–1870* (Princeton: Princeton University Press, 1958, 1968), 2 vols.

PRINTING PRESSES   19. This remark seems hardly just in respect to the presses of Adam Ramage, unless intended to apply to presses made previous to the revolution. It is true that from Moxon's time in 1683, the English had made no change in the screw of the common book press, which was uniformly two and a quarter inches in diameter, with a descent of two and a half inches in a revolution. The diameter was even smaller in job presses, but the same fall was always maintained, by which the platen was made to rise and fall five-eighths of an inch in a quarter of a revolution; a space deemed necessary for the free passage of the form and frisket under the platen. Mr. Ramage enlarged the diameter of the screw to three inches, and where much power was required to three and a half inches, and at the same time reduced the fall in a revolution to two inches, which very nearly doubled the impressing power, but decreased the rapidity of the action. It was an improvement made necessary by the finer hair lines the type founders introduced, requiring increased power in the press, and the reduction in the descent of the screw to one-half an inch was met by a more careful finish of the frisket and its hinges, which were made to slide freely under the platen in a space of half an inch. Mr. Ramage came from Scotland and settled in Philadelphia. He made his presses of Honduras mahogany, with ample substance and a good finish, which gave them a better appearance than foreign made presses, and they were less liable to warp. Importation had in consequence almost entirely ceased as early as 1800. His great improvement on the screw and working parts connected therewith were made seven years later. He died in 1850, at a great age. See further, *Printers' Circular*, III, 108 (1868). M. See also, Milton W. Hamilton, *Adam Ramage and His Presses* (Portland: South-worth-Anthoensen Press, 1942).

20. For an account of the introduction of cylinder presses into this country, see T. H. Senior's *Mirror of Typography*, III, 2–3 (Spring, 1871). M

II

MASSACHUSETTS

SO far as relates to the introduction of the art of printing, and establishing the press in this section of the continent, Massachusetts claims precedence over all the other colonies. The press was erected here nearly at the end of the year 1638; and it was more than forty years later when printing commenced in any other part of what, before the revolution, was called British America.

Hitherto justice has not been done to the man by whose agency the art was first introduced into the English colonies. Although he was one of the best and firmest friends to New England, his name has not been handed down to us with so much publicity as were those of other distinguished characters, who were his contemporaries and fellow laborers in the great work of settling a dreary country and civilizing the children of the wilderness. The principal cause of this seeming neglect in our historians and biographers may, perhaps, arise from the circumstance, that his destiny was similar to that of Moses, who, although zealously engaged in conducting the children of Israel from Egypt to Canaan, yet never reached the land of promise himself.

As the founder of the Anglo-American press died on his passage from Europe to this country, he, of course, did not become so well known as he would have been had he arrived and resided here. This circumstance, probably, prevented his acquiring that celebrity to which his merits justly entitled him.

Although his name is barely mentioned by two or three jour-
nalists, yet, after a diligent research, I have been enabled to
obtain the following particulars respecting this venerable Father
of the American Press.

THE REV. JOSEPH GLOVER was a worthy and wealthy dis-
senting clergyman in England, who engaged in the business of
the settlement of Massachusetts, and had been attentively pursuing such measures for its interest and prosperity as he judged
would best tend to promote them. Among other things for the
benefit of the infant colony, he was very desirous of establishing
a press to accommodate the business of both church and state;*
he contributed liberally towards a sum sufficient to purchase
printing materials, and for this purpose solicited, in England
and Holland, the aid of others. †

The ancient records of Harvard College mention, that 'Mr.
Joss. Glover gave to the college a font of printing letters, and

---

* 'Wonder-Working Providence of Sion's Saviour in New England' (London, 1654) p. 129. It is *A History of New England. From the English planting in the
yeere 1628, until the yeere 1652.* It was written by Major Edward Johnson, who
was one of the first settlers of Woburn, a very judicious and active man in the
settlement of the colony; he was a member of the general court, and employed
in several important concerns of the government. He was father of the Hon.
William Johnson, who was chosen assistant in 1684. Johnson bears testimony to
the worth of Mr. Glover, and speaks of his exertions to promote the interests of
the infant colony. He mentions him as 'being able in person and estate for the
work in which he was engaged;' and 'for further compleating the colonies in
church and common-wealth-work, he provided [in 1638] a printer, which
hath been very usefull in many respects.'

† Governor Winthrop mentions that 'a printing house was begun at Cambridge, at the charge of Mr. Glover.' See John Winthrop, *A Journal of the
Transactions and Occurrences in the Settlement of Massachusetts* (Hartford, 1790),
p. 171.

some gentlemen of Amsterdam gave towards furnishing of a printing press with letters forty-nine pounds, and something more.'* The same records give us, also, the following names as 'benefactors to the first fonts of letters for printing in Cambridge, in New England, Major Thomas Clark, Capt. James Oliver, Capt. Allen, Mr. Stoddard, Mr. Freake, and Mr. Hues.'

In the year 1638, Mr. Glover, having obtained the means, procured a good printing apparatus, and engaged a printer to accompany it in a ship bound to New England. Mr. Glover, with his family, embarked in the same vessel; but unfortunately he did not live to reach the shores of this new world. His widow and children, it is supposed, arrived in the autumn of that year, and settled at Cambridge; she afterwards became the wife of Mr. Henry Dunster, who was elected the first president of Harvard College.

It is not known whether Mr. Glover had been in New England previous to his embarking for this country in 1638; but I find by the records of the county of Middlesex, that he possessed a valuable real and personal estate in Massachusetts; that he had two sons and three daughters; that John Glover, one of the sons, was educated at Harvard College, and graduated in 1650, and was appointed a magistrate in 1652; that one of the daughters was married to Mr. Adam Winthrop, and another to Mr. Appleton.

Mr. Glover had doubtless been written to and requested by his friends, among whom were the leading men in the new settlement of Massachusetts, who were then establishing an academy, which soon acquired the appellation of college—to

* *Ancient Records of Harvard College*, vol. I, and III, in manuscript.

provide a press, etc., not only for the advantage of the church and state, but particularly for the benefit of the academy; the records of which prove that the types and press were procured for, and, types particularly, were the property of, that institution. The press, as appears by the records of the county court of Middlesex, 1656, was the property of Mr. Glover's heirs. Mr. Glover, it should seem, intended to have carried on both printing and book selling; for, besides the printing materials, he had provided a stock of printing paper, and a quantity of books for sale.

John Glover, one of the sons of Mr. Glover, after the death of his mother brought an action, in the court above mentioned, against his father-in-law Dunster, for the recovery of the estate which had belonged to his father and mother, and which was detained by Dunster. An inventory of the estate was filed in court; among the items were the printing press, printing paper, and a quantity of books. The inventory proves that the press, then the only one in the country, was the property of the plaintiff in the action; and it is shown by the said inventory, and by the records of the general court, that Dunster had had the management of the press, in right of his wife, and as president of the college; and that he had received the 'profits of it.'[1] As it may amuse those who feel an interest in whatever concerns the first press, and the person by whose agency the art of printing was introduced into the colonies, and as others may be gratified by the perusal of the proceedings in, and decision of, one of the courts of justice holden in the primitive state of the country, I have extracted them, *verbatim et literatim*, from the records, and added them with the inventory before mentioned in a note.

At a County Court held at Cambridge, April 1, 1656.

Jno. Glover* Gent. Plant. against Mr. Henry Dunster Defft. in an actōn of the case for an acct. of an estate of houses, lands, goods, and chattels, debts, legacies, and gifts, or other estate, together with the deeds, leases, and other manuscripts, and evidences thereof, wch by any manner of wayes or means, eyther have been (or at present bee) in the possession of the said Henry, or under his rule, costody or dispose. And of right due and belonging unto the said Jno. Glover, by the last will and testament of his father Mr. Josse Glover deceased, or Elizabeth his wife, or their, or eyther of their gifts, or by the last will of Wm. Harris deceased or otherwise to him the said Jno. Glover appteyning and of right due and belonging by any manner of wayes or means whatsoever, and, also for debteyning and with-holding the same, vizt. both the account and estate, with the effects and profits thereof and damages to the said Jno. Glover thereby susteyned.

The Plaintiffe appeared by his attorneyes Edw. Goffe, and Thomas Danforth, the defft. appeared personally and pleaded to the case, The Court having heard the Pl't's demands and the proffe thereof, and Mr. Dunster's acknowledgmts and Answrs wch are upon file with the Records of this Court, the Jury findes for the plaintiffe, as appeareth by their verdict given into Court in writeing (wch is also upon ye file) theis following p'ticrs.

Imps. The Inventory as it is brought in	140 00 00
It. The Presse and the p'fitt of it	040 00 00
It. The prise of Mr. Dayes house	030 00 00
[Three additional items	238 00 00]
	448 00 00

[Three items]	
It. acknowledged by Mr. Dunster 12 Rheam of refuse paper. [And eleven additional items	722 16 00]
	1170 16 00

It. the farme that Robert Wilson now occupieth to be Mr. Glover's.

It. all the Bookes of Mr. Glover's that came to Mr. Dunster, whereof he promised to give in a Cattologue.

* He studied medicine, became a practitioner, married, and settled in Boston.

It. that Mr. Dunster shall give to the Court, an account according to the attachmt when the Honoured Court shall require it.

Charles Chadwicke in the name of the rest.

Execution granted June 17, 1656.

The Court orders that Mr. Dunster shall bring in his full account to the Court the 9th of May next.

[Middlesex County Court Records, vol. 1, p. 77, &c.]

At a second Sessions of the County Court held at Cambridge, 9th (3) mo. 1656.

In the case between Jno. Glover Plant. against Mr. Henry Dunster Defft. entered at the last sessions of this Court, Mr. Henry Dunster presented his answr to the Juries verdict in writeing, containing his account under his hand, also a Cattologue of the bookes. with some other testimonies in refference to the case, all wch are upon file with the Reccords of the last Court, whereupon the Plaintiffe not being sattisfied with the accounts presented, The Court advised both parties to endeavour a peaceable composure of the whole buissines, eyther between themselves or by able men Indifferently chosen between them.

[Middlesex County Court Records, vol. 1, p. 83.]

At a County Court held at Charles-Towne June 19, 1656.

Mr. Henry Dunster Pl. against Mr. Jno. Glover Defft. in an action of Review of the suite upon attachmt. to the value of two thousand pounds comenced and prosecuted in the last County Court holden at Cambridge, by the said Jno. or his attorneys for accounts and estate pretended to be with-held by the said Henry from the said Jno. As also for the auditing the accounts, according to the advice of the Honoured Magistrates, and for the ballancing, setling and sattisfying what upon the said Accounts is right and just to be done, according to attachmt dated 12th 4th mo. 1656.

The Jury found a non liquet.

[Middlesex County Court Records, vol. 1, p. 83.]

At a County Court held at Cambridge, by adjournment, June 24th, 1656.

Mr. Henry Dunster [sometimes husband to Elizabeth the relict widow of Josse Glover deceased] Plant. agt. Jno. Glover Gent. Defft. In an action of the case for debt upon accounts, and for rights and interests in any wise appertayneing to the said Henry from the estate now claimed by the said Jno. Glover by vertue of the last will of his father Josse Glover deceased.

The Plaintive and Defft. appearing in Court legally, They mutually agreed to referre this case to the Hearing and determination of the honoured Bench of Magistrates. The Courts determination and judgmt in the said case is as followeth.

Whereas there hath been some actions and suites of debt, account, and review, in this Court, between Jno. Glover Gent. And Henry Dunster his father in Law and Guardian, concerning the estate, under the managemt. belonging to the said John Glover by the will of his father Josse Glover deceased, The premises considered, and the parties consenting to issue the whole case, included in the former actions, and judgmts to the determination of this Court. The Court having taken paynes to examine all matters explicitly in refference to the whole case, doe find the estate of Josse Glover is Creditor, One thousand foure hundred forty and seaven pounds, nine shillings and nine pence, and a silver tankard in kinde, also Mr. Glover's bookes according to Cattologue given in to the Court, to be delivered in kinde, also the price of a house at Hingham that was received of Payntree at fifteen pounds.

And the estate, is also justly debtor, one thousand thre hundred and thirty pounds, one shilling and seven pence, the particulars whereof are expressed in an account hereunto annexed.

The Court therefore do find for John Glover, one hundred and seventeen pounds, eight shillings and two pence, due from Henry Dunster, according to the account, leaving some debts explicitly expressed in the account to the vallue of fifty seaven pounds eleven shillings foure pence to be further cleared by the said Henry before any credit be given for him it.

Also we find for Mr. Henry Dunster the lands in Sudbury bounds, purchased by the said Henry called the farme now in the occupation of Wilson.

1656. June 25. The account in refference to the aforenamed case, being drawn up and examined by the Honoured Court is as followeth.

Mr. Henry Dunster is debitor	£.	s.	d.
[Sixteen items	690	06	07]

To sale of Bookes	026 10 00
[Six items	361 15 06]
To printing presse and paper	050 00 00
To Mr. Dayes house sold for	030 00 00
[Four items	251 01 08]
To paper—16 Rheams.	002 00 11
[Two items	035 00 00]
	1447 09 09

To a silver tankard in kind.
To all Mr. Glover's bookes unsold, to be delivered
  according to Cattologue. . . .

   Mr. Henry Dunster creditor.

	£. s. d.
[Two items]	086 06 08

By disbursemts for the maintenance of Mrs. Glover for
  diet and apparrell in sicknes and health two yeares
  and two months, after her marriage with Mr. Dunster, until her death, with a mayd to attend her at
  £30 pr. annum   065 00 00

[Family expenses   167 10 00]

By Jno. Glover's liberall education for diet, apparell and
  schooleing mostly at the Colledge for seven years
  and two months at £20 per. anm.   143 03 04

By diet, apparrell of Mrs. Sarah Glover five years at
  sixteen pounds pr. annum   080 00 00

[Other family expenses   788 01 07]
                                                          _____

                                                          1330 01 07

By account of some debts contracted by Mrs. Glover in
  her widowhood, wch Mr. Dunster alleadgeth he
  hath payd; not allowed at present for want of cleare
  proof . . .   57 11 04

   Mr. Bellingham declared his dissent from this account and departed
out of Court before the Court's determination and judgmt. was
drawne up.   [*Middlesex County Court Records.* vol. 1. p. 87, &c.]

THE printing apparatus, as has been related, was, in the year 1638,[2] brought to Cambridge, then as much settled as Boston, both places being founded in a situation which eight years before this event, was, in scriptural language, a howling wilderness. At Cambridge the building of an academy was begun; and, it was at that place the rulers both of church and state then held their assemblies. These circumstances, probably, induced those who had the management of public affairs to fix the press there; and there it remained for sixty years, altogether under their control, as were other presses afterwards established in the colony; but for upwards of thirty years, printing was exclusively carried on in that town.

STEPHEN DAYE was the first who printed in this part of America. He was the person whom Mr. Glover engaged to come to New England, and conduct the press. He was supposed to be a descendant of John Daye, a very eminent printer, in London, from 1560 till 1583, but this cannot be accurately ascertained. He was, however, born in London, and there served his apprenticeship to a printer.

Daye having, by the direction of the magistrates and elders, previously erected the press and prepared the other parts of the apparatus, began business in the first month of 1639.*

The first work which issued from the press was the *Freeman's Oath*—to which succeeded, *an almanack.*

However eminent Daye's predecessors, as printers, might have been, it does not appear that he was well skilled in the art. It is probable he was bred to the press; his work discovers but

---

* Gov. Winthrop's *Journal*, p. 171.

little of that knowledge which is requisite for a compositor. In the ancient manuscript records of the colony, are several particulars respecting Daye; the first is as follows:

'Att a General Court held at Boston, on the eighth day of the eighth moneth [October] 1641. Steeven Daye being the first that sett vpon printing, is graunted three hundred acres of land, where it may be convenient without prejudice to any town.'

In 1642, he owned several lots of land 'in the bounds of Cambridge.' He mortgaged one of those lots as security for the payment of a cow, calf, and a heifer; whence, we may conclude, he was not in very affluent circumstances.*

In 1643, Daye, for some offence, was by order of the general court taken into custody; his crime does not appear on record; the court 'ordered, that Steeven Day shall be released, giving 100 l. Bond for appearance when called for.'

Daye continued to print till about the close of the year 1648, or the beginning of 1649; at which time the printing house was put under the management of Samuel Green. Whether the resignation of the office of manager of the printing house was or

---

* A simple memorandum of the fact, made in the book of records, was then judged sufficient, without recording a formal mortgage; this appears by the first book of records kept in the colony, now in the registry of deeds of the county of Suffolk, Massachusetts, from which the following are extracted, viz: 'Steeven Day of Cambridge graunted vnto John Whyte twenty-Seaven Acres of Land lying in the Bounds of Cambridg for the payment of a cowe and a calf and a two yeares old heiffer.' Dated the 25th of the 5th month, 1642.

'Steeven Day of Cambridg graunted vnto Nicholaus Davidson of Meadford, all his lands on the south side of Charles River, being aboute one hundred Acres in Cambridg bounds, for surety of payment of sixty pounds, with sundry provisions.' Dated the 25th of the 5th month, 1642.

'Steeven Day of Cambridg bound over to Thomas Crosby, five lots of land in the new field beyond the water in Cambridg, number 24, 25, 26, 27, and 29th, in all sixety Acres, for the payment of fiftey seaven pounds, with liberty to take off all wood and timber.' &c. Dated 16th of 2d month, 1643.

was not voluntary in Daye, cannot be ascertained. Neither the press nor the types belonged to him; he had been employed only as the master workman; his wages were undoubtedly low; and it evidently appears he was embarrassed with debts. His industry and economy might not be suited to the state of his finances. Circumstances like these might cause Mr. Dunster, who it seems then conducted the printing business, to be dissatisfied, and induce him to place the printing house in other hands; or, it was possible that Daye, finding himself and the press under a control he was unwilling to be subjected to, resigned his station.[3]

Daye remained in Cambridge; and, some years after he had ceased to be master workman in the printing house, brought an action against President Dunster, to recover one hundred pounds for former services. The record of the decision of the County court in that case, is as follows: 'Att a County Court held at Cambridge, April, 1656, Steeven Day, Plant. against Mr. Henry Dunster, Defft. in an action of the case for Labour and Expenses about the Printing Presse and the utensils and appurtenances thereof and the manageing the said worke to the vallue of one hundred pounds. The jury finds for the Defft. costs of court.'

In 1655, he had not obtained the land granted to him in 1641. This appears by the following extracts from the public records, viz:

'At a General Court of Elections holden at Boston 29th of May 1655, In answer to the Peticōn of Steeven Day of Cambridge craving that the Graunt within the year 1641 of this Court of three hundred Acres of Land to him for Recompence of his Care and Charg in furthering the worke of Printing, might be recorded, the Record whereof appears not,* the Court Graunt his Request and doeth hereby confirme the former graunt thereof to him.'

'At a General Court of Elections holden at Boston, 6th of May 1657, Steeven Day of Cambridg having often complayned that he hath suffered much dammage by Erecting the Printing Presse at Cambridge, at the Request of the Magistrates and Elders, for which he never had yett any Considerable Sattisfaction. This Court doe Graunt him three hundred Acres of Land in any place not formerly Graunted by this Court.'

In the records of 1667, is the following order of the General Court relative to another petition from Daye, viz: 'In answer to the Peticōn of Steeven Daye, It is ordered that the Peticōner hath liberty to procure of the Sagamore of Nashoway [now Lancaster] by sale, or otherwise, to the quantity of one hundred and fifty acres of Vpland, and this Court doeth also graunt the peticōner twenty Acres of meadow where he can find it free of former Graunts.'

Daye died in Cambridge, December 22, 1668, aged about 58 years. Rebecca Daye, probably his wife, died October 17, of the same year.

I have found but few books printed by Daye. I have never seen his name in an imprint, and, I believe, it never appeared in one. Several books printed at Cambridge, by his successor, are without the name of the printer; but some of them do not give even the year in which they were printed.

I have no doubt that the *first book* printed in this country [was] *The Psalms in Metre, Faithfully translated for the Use, Edifi-*

---

* The record appears to have been regularly made in 1641. I extracted it from the original record book of the colony for that year.

cation, and Comfort of the Saints in Publick and Private, especially in New England. 1640. Crown 8vo. 300 pages. The type is Roman, of the size of small bodied English, entirely new, and may be called a very good letter. In this edition there are no Hymns or Spiritual Songs; it contains only the Psalms, the original long preface, and 'An admonition to the Reader' of half a page, at the end of the Psalms after Finis.—This 'admonition' respects the tunes suited to the psalms. The second edition in 1647, contained a few Spiritual Songs. The third edition, revised and amended by President Dunster, &c., had a large addition of Scripture Songs and Hymns, written by Mr. Lyon. The first edition abounds with typographical errors, many of which were corrected in the second edition. This specimen of Daye's printing does not exhibit the appearance of good workmanship. The compositor must have been wholly unacquainted with punctuation. 'The Preface,' is the running title to that part of the work. 'The' with a period, is on the left hand page, and 'Preface,' on the right. Periods are often omitted where they should be placed, and not seldom used where a comma only was necessary. Words of one syllable, at the end of lines, are sometimes divided by a hyphen; at other times those of two or more syllables are divided without one; the spelling is bad and irregular. One thing is very singular—at the head of every left hand page throughout the book, the word 'PSALM' is spelled as it should be; at the head of every right hand page, it has an E final thus, 'PSALME.'[4]

SAMUEL GREEN, was the son of Bartholomew and Elizabeth Green, who, with their children and other relations, were among the early settlers of Cambridge. Samuel Green, then only sixteen years of age, arrived with Governor Winthrop. He was in Cambridge eight years before Daye came from England; but was unknown as a printer until about 1649, nearly eleven years after Daye's arrival. Some writers, since the year 1733, erroneously mention Green as 'the first who printed in New England, or in North America.'*

All the records I have examined are silent respecting the cause of Daye's relinquishing the management of the press; nor do they give any reason why his place in the printing house was supplied by the appointment of Green. The similarity of Green's first printing to that of Daye's, induces me to believe that Green was unacquainted with the art when he undertook the management of the press, and that he was assisted by Daye, who continued to reside in Cambridge; and whose poverty, probably, induced him to become, not only an instructor, but a journeyman to Green.

By the records of the colony, it appears, that the president of the college still had the direction of the concerns of the printing house, and made contracts for printing; and that he was responsible for the productions of the press, until licensers were

* 'December 28th, deceased here Mr. Bartholomew Green, one of the deacons of the South Church; who has been the principal printer of this town and country near forty years, in the 67th year of his age.

'His father was Capt. Samuel Green the famous printer of Cambridge, who arrived with Gov. Winthrop in 1630. He used to tell his children that, upon their first coming ashore, he and several others were for some time glad to lodge in empty casks, to shelter them from the weather. This Capt. Green was a commission officer of the military company at Cambridge for above 60 years together. He died there Jan. 1, 1701–2, aged 87, highly esteemed and beloved both for piety and a martial genius. He had nineteen children, eight by the first wife, and eleven by his second, who was a daughter of Elder Clark of Cambridge.'—*Boston News Letter*, Jan. 4, 1733.

appointed. I have extracted the following from the records of 1650 and 1654:

'At a third meeting of the General Court of Elections at Boston, the 15th of October, 1650, It is ordered that Richard Bellingham, Esquir, the Secretary, and Mr. Hills, or aney Two of them, are appointed a Comittee to take order for the printing of Lawes Agreed vppon to be printed, to determine of all Things in reference thereunto. Agreeing with the President ffor the printing of them with all Expedition and to Alter the title if there be Cawse.

'At a General Court of Elections, held at Boston, the third of May, 1654. It is ordered by this Court that henceforth the Secretary shall, within tenn dayes after this present sessions, and so from time to time, deliver a copie of all Lawes that are to be published unto the President or printer, who shall forthwith make an Impression thereof to the noumber of five, Six, or Seven hundred as the Court shall order, all which Coppies the Treasurer shall take of and pay for in wheate, or otherwise to Content, for the Noumber of five hundred, after the rate of one penny a Sheete, or eight shillings a hundred for five hundred sheetes of a Sorte, for so many sheetes as the bookes shall contajne, and the Treasurer shall disterbute the bookes, to every magistrate one, to every Court one, to the Secretary one, to each towne where no magistrate dwells one, and the rest amongst the Townes that beare publick charge with this jurisdiction, according to the noumber of freemen in each Towne. And the order that Ingageth the Secretary to transcribe coppies for the Townes and others, is in that respect repealed.*

* I have quoted ancient records in many instances, as they not only give facts correctly, but convey to us the language, etc., of the periods in which they were made.

'At a General Court held at Boston 9th of June, 1654, Upon Conference with Mr. Dunster, [president of the college] and the printer in reference to the imprinting of the Acts of the General Court, whereby we understand some inconveniencies may accrue to the Printer by printing that Law which recites the agreement for printing. It is therefore ordered, that the said law be not put forth in print, but kept amongst the written records of this Court.'

Whether Green was, or was not acquainted with printing, he certainly, some time after he began that business, prosecuted it in such a way as, generally, met approbation.* He might, by

* [The Cambridge Platform, 1649] appears to be printed by one who was but little acquainted with the typographic art; it is a proof that Green was not bred to it, and that this was one of the first books from the press after he began printing. The type is new pica, or one but little worn; the press work is very bad, and that of the case no better. The punctuation in the title is exactly copied; the compositor did not seem to know the use of points; there are spaces before commas, periods, parentheses, &c. The head of The Preface is in two lines of large capitals, but has no point after it—nor is there any after FINIS, which word is in two line capitals at the end of the book. The pages of the Preface have a running title; with the folio, or number of the pages, in brackets immediately following in the centre of a line, thus,

The Preface [2]

The printer did not appear to have any acquaintance with signatures. The book is printed and folded in whole sheets, without inserts; in the first sheet, at the bottom of the second page, is Aa, third page Aaa, fifth page Aaa, seventh page Aaaa. The second sheet has the signature A at the bottom of the first page of that sheet; A a, third page, A a a, fifth page, and A a a a, seventh page. The third sheet begins with B, which the following sheets, have as many signatures to each as the first and second; but all, excepting those on the first and third pages of a sheet, were uncommon, and have not any apparent meaning. Every part of the work shows the want of common skill in the compositor. Facs, and ornamented large capitals cut on wood are used at the beginning of the preface, and at the first chapter of the work. A head piece of flowers is placed at the beginning of the text, and a line of flowers between each chapter. In the book are many references to scripture, in marginal notes, on brevier. Letters of abbreviation are frequently used—such as cōmend, allowāce, compāy, acquaīt, frō, offēce, offēded, partakīg, cōfession, &c. The spelling is very ancient, as els, forme, vpon, owne, wildernes, powr, eyther, wee, acknowledg, minde, doc-

frequenting the printing house, when it was under the care of Daye, have obtained that knowledge of the art, which enabled him, with good workmen, to carry it on; be this as it may, it is certain that as he proceeded with the execution of the business, he seems to have acquired more consequence as a printer; his work, however, did not discover that skill of the compositor, or the pressman, that was afterwards shown when Johnson, who was sent over to assist in printing the *Indian Bible*, arrived.

In 1658, Green petitioned the general court for a grant of land. The court took his petition into consideration, and determined as follows, viz.

'At the Second Sessions of the General Court held at Boston the 19th of October, 1658, in answer to the Peticōn of Samuel Green, of Cambridge, printer. The Court judgeth it meete for his Encouragement to graunt him three hundred acres of Land where it is to be found.'

In 1659, the records of the colony contain the following order of the General court. 'It is ordered by this Court that the Treasurer shall be and hereby is empowered to disburse out of the Treasury what shall be necessary tending towards the printing of the Lawes, to Samuel Greene, referring to his Pajnes therein or otherwise.' This edition of the Laws was ordered to be printed December 1658, and was finished at the press, October 16th, 1660.

From the Manuscript records of the commissioners of the United Colonies, who were agents for the corporation in England for propagating the gospel among the Indians in New

---

trin, therin, wherin, himselfe, patrone, choyce, soveraigne, sinne, satisfie, griefe, &c. As I believe this book to be one of the first printed by Green, I have been thus particular in describing it; soon, after this period his printing was much improved.

England, we find that in 1656 there were two presses in Cambridge, both under the care of Green. One belonged to the college, which undoubtedly was the press that Mr. Glover purchased in England, and Daye brought over to America; the other was the property of the corporation in England. There were types appropriated to each.

The corporation, for a time, had their printing executed in London; but when the Indian youth had been taught to read, &c., at the school at Cambridge, established for the purpose, and Mr. Eliot and Mr. Pierson had translated Primers and Catechisms into the Indian language for the common use of the Indians, and eventually translated the Bible, it became necessary that these works should be printed in America, under the inspection of the translators. For this reason the corporation sent over a press and types, furnished every printing material for their work, and even paid for mending of the press when out of repair. In September, 1654, the commissioners in the United Colonies found that a sufficient quantity of paper and types for the purpose of executing the works which were projected had not been received, they therefore, wrote to the corporation in England for an augmentation to the value of £20.* The articles arrived in 1655.

Green judging it necessary to have more types for the Indian work, in 1658, petitioned the General Court to that purpose. The court decided thereon as follows, viz.

'At a General Court holden at Boston 19th of May, 1658. In answer to the Peticōn of Samuel Green, printer, at Cambridge, The Court Judgeth it meete to Comend the consideration therof to the Comissioners of the United Colonjes at their next

* All the sums are in sterling money.

meeting that so if they see meete they may write to the Corporation in England for the procuring of twenty pounds worth more of letters for the vse of the Indian Colledg.'

When the press and types, &c., sent by the corporation in England, for printing the Bible and other books in the Indian Language, arrived they were added to the printing materials belonging to the college, and altogether made a well furnished printing house.* The types were very good, and the faces of them as handsome as any that were made at that time; they consisted of small founts of nonpareil, brevier, long primer, small pica, pica, english, great primer, and double pica; also, small casts of long primer and pica Hebrew, Greek, and blacks. The building occupied for a printing house, was well suited to the business. It had been designed for a college for the Indian youth.

Green now began printing the Bible in the Indian language, which even at this day would be thought a work of labor, and must, at that early period of the settlement of the country, have been considered a business difficult to accomplish, and of great magnitude. It was a work of so much consequence as to arrest the attention of the nobility and gentry of England, as well as that of King Charles, to whom it was dedicated. The press of

---

* General Daniel Gookin, who lived in Cambridge, and who, in 1662, was appointed one of the two first licensers of the press, mentions in his work, entitled *Historical Collections of the Indians of New England* dedicated to King Charles II, that 'the houses erected for the Indian college, built strong and substantial of brick, at the expense of the Corporation in England for propagating the Gospel in New England, and cost between 300*l.* and 400*l.* not being improved for the ends intended, by reason of the death and failing of Indian scholars, was taken to accommodate English scholars, and for placing and using the Printing Press belonging to the college,' &c. This building was taken down many years since. It stood not far from the other buildings of the college.

Harvard college, in Cambridge, Massachusetts, was for a time, as celebrated as the presses of the universities of Oxford and Cambridge, in England. Having obtained many particulars relating to the printing of this edition of the Bible, I will follow Green through that arduous undertaking.

In 1659, Hezekiah Usher, merchant, and bookseller, of Boston, agent for the corporation, charges that body £40 paid Green for printing 'the Psalms and Mr. Pierson's Cattechisme,' &c., and credits 80 £ in printing types; he also gives credit for one hundred and four reams of paper sent by the corporation toward printing the New Testament 'in the Indian language.' The corporation in a letter dated London, April 28, 1660, and directed to the commissioners, observes: 'Conserning youer Printing the New Testament in the Indian Language, a sheet whereof you haue transmitted to vs, wee concurr with youerselues therin, and doe approue of that prouision you have made for printing the same conceiueing and offering as our judgments that it is better to print fifteen hundred than but a thousand; hopeing that by incurragement from Sion Collidge, with whom we haue late conference, you may bee enabled to print fifteen hundred of the Ould Testament likewise.'

Usher, in his account rendered to the corporation in 1660, debits the stock of the corporation with two hundred reams of printing paper, 'bought since he rendered his last account,' and with printing ink and types, and 'setting them in the presse,' the gross sum of £120 1 8; and, to 'cash paid Mr. Green for distributing the ffont of letters and printing six sheets of the New Testament in Indian att four pounds per sheet, £24.'

In September 1661, the commissioners, who that year met at Plymouth, wrote to Mr. Usher; and among other things, thanked him for his 'care in prouiding Matterials and furthering the printing of the Bible, and desire the continuance of the same vntill it bee Issved;' and to 'pay Mr. Green for printing the same as formerly;' also to 'demaund and receiue of Mr. Green the whole Impression of the New Testament in Indian, now finished; and take care for the binding of two hundred of them strongly and as speedily as may bee with leather or as may bee most serviceable for the Indians; and deliuer them forth as you shall haue direction from any of the commissioners for the time being of which keep an exact account that soe it may bee seen how they are Improved and disposed of; alsoe, wee pray you take order for the printing of a thousand coppyes of Mr. Eliotts Catichismes which we vnderstand are much wanting amongst the Indians, which being finished, Receiue from the Presse and dispose of them according to order abouesaid.'

The agent, in his account current with the corporation in 1662, has, among other charges, one for 'Disbursements for printing the Bible as per bill of particulars £234 11 8.'* This bill was only for one year ending September, 1662. At that time Green, by direction, gave to the commissioners:

* The following is the bill of particulars, as charged by Green, viz:

	£		
To mending of the windowes of the printing house	1	0	5
To pack thrid and uellum		5	6
To 2 barrells of Inke and leather for balls	20	0	0
To hide for the presse being broken	1	0	0
To 160 Reams of Paper Att 6s. per ream	48	0	0
To printing the Title sheet to the New Testament	1	0	0
To printing 1500 Cattechismes	15	0	0
To printing 21 sheets of the Old Testament, att 3lb. 10s. per sheet Mr. Iohnson being absent	73	10	0
To printing 25 sheets with his healp att 50 shill. per sheet	62	10	0
To binding 200 Testaments att 6 d. a peece	5	0	0
To Mr. Johnson's board	7	5	9
	£234	11	8

An account of the Vtensils for printing belonging to the Corporation in the custody of Samuell Green of Cambridge Printer and giuen in vnder his hand, viz:

The presse with what belongs to it with one tinn pann and two frisketts.

Item two table of Cases of letters [types] with one ode [odd] Case.

Item the ffontt of letters together with Imperfections that came since.

Item one brasse bed, one Imposing stone.

Item two barrells of Inke, 3 Chases, 2 composing stickes one ley brush 2 candlestickes one for the Case the other for the Presse.

Item the frame and box for the sesteren [water trough.]

Item the Riglet brasse rules and scabbard the Sponge 1 galley 1 mallett 1 sheeting [shooting] sticke and furniture for the chases.

Item the letters [types] that came before that were mingled with the colledges.

At the meeting of the commissioners in September, 1663, the agent charges the corporation with the balance due for printing the Bible, which he paid that month to Green, in full for his services, £140 12 6. Green, at this meeting, gave in an account of all the printing paper he had received at different times, from the corporation and their agent, amounting to 469 reams; 368 reams of which he had used in printing the Bible, 30 reams in printing two Catechisms, and there remained in his hands 71 reams.

At the meeting of the commissioners in September, 1664, among the articles charged in the agent's account with the corporation, was the following bill of sundries paid to Green, viz:

To expences about the presse for mending it; makeing new Chases, and to twenty seauen skins for balls &c.   £ 4 4 4

To two smale Chests to put the Bibles in [20 Copies] that were sent to England.   5 0

To printing the Indian Psalmes to go with the Bible, 13 sheets att 2 lb per sheet,   26 0 0

To printing the Epistle dedicatory to the Bible,	1 0 0
To printing Baxter's Call in Indian, eight sheets at 50s. per sheet,	20 0 0
To printing the Psalter in Indian, 9 sheets, at 20s.	9 0 0
To one yeares board of Johnson,	15 0 0

The agent, in his account for 1669, charges, 'Cash paid Green for binding and clasping 200 Indian Bibles at 2 s. 6 d. £25.—For binding 200 Practice of Piety at 6d. £5.—For do. 400 Baxter's Call at 3s. per 100, 12s.' &c.

I have made a calculation from the documents I have seen, and find the whole expense attending the carrying through the press, 1000 copies of the Bible, 500 additional copies of the New Testament, an edition of Baxter's Call to the Unconverted, an edition of the Psalter, and two editions of Eliot's Catechism, all in the Indian language, including the cost of the types for printing the Bible, and the binding a part of them, and also the binding of a part of Baxter's Call, and the Psalters, amounted to a fraction more than £1200, sterling. The Bible was printed on a fine paper of pot size, and in quarto. After the first edition of the Bible, and some other books in the Indian language, had been completed at the press belonging to the corporation for propagating the gospel, &c., the corporation made a present of their printing materials to the college. On this occasion the government of the college ordered as follows:

'Harvard Colledge Sept. 20, 1670. The honorable Corporation for the Indians having ordered their Printing Presse, letters, and Vtensils to be delivered to the Colledge, the Treasurer is ordered forthwith to take order for the receiveing thereof, and to dispose of the same for the Colledge use and improvement.'*

* *College Records* vol. 1.

Green, by direction, gave to the president a schedule of the articles, and valued them at £80. That sum must have been very low. With these types he began another edition of the Indian Bible.*

Some small religious treatises having been published in 1662, which the general court, or some of the ruling clergy, judged rather too liberal, and tending to open the door of heresy,

* The New Testament, of which five hundred octavo copies were printed, was first put to the press, and finished, in 1681, and the whole Bible completed in 1686.

The Psalms, Hymns, and Spiritual Songs of the Old and New Testament, Faithfully Translated into English Metre. For the Use, Edification and Comfort of the Saints in publick and private, especially in New England. Small 12mo. 100 pages, two columns to each, in nonpareil. 'Cambridge. Printed for Hezekiah Usher of Boston.' This was, I believe, the third edition of the New England Version of the Psalms after it had been revised and improved by President Dunster, &c., and the fifth, including all the former editions. I have a complete copy of this edition, but the name of the printer, and the year in which it was printed, are not mentioned. It is calculated by being printed in a small page, with a very small type, to bind up with English editions of the pocket Bible; and, as the printing is executed by a good workman, and is the best that I have seen from the Cambridge press, I conclude, therefore, it could not be printed by Green before the arrival of Marmaduke Johnson in 1660; I have no doubt it was printed under Johnson's care; and, probably, soon after the Indian Bible came from the press in 1663. Johnson was a good printer, and so called by the corporation in England, who engaged, and sent him over, to assist Green in printing that work. Although in this edition the typography far exceeds in neatness any work then printed in the country, it is very incorrect; but this might have been more the fault of the corrector of the press, than of the printer. My belief that it was published about the year 1664, or 1665, is confirmed by its being printed for Hezekiah Usher, the only bookseller that I can find an account of at that time, in New England. He dealt largely in merchandise, and was then agent to the corporation in England, for propagating the Gospel in New England. It is a curious fact, that nonpareil types were used so early in this country; I have not seen them in any other book printed either at Cambridge, or Boston, before the revolution; even brevier types had been but seldom used in the printing houses in Boston, earlier than 1760. The nonpareil used for the Psalms was new, and a very handsome faced letter.

licensers of the press were appointed;* but on the 27th of May, 1663, the general court 'Ordered that the Printing Presse be at liberty as formerly, till this Court shall take further order, and the late order is hereby repealed.'† After this order was passed, a more free use of the press seems to have been made; this immediately arrested the attention of government, and soon awakened their fears; and the following rigid edict was in consequence passed, viz.

'At a General Court called by order from the Governour, Deputy Governour, and other Magistrates, held at Boston 19th of October 1664. For the preventing of Irregularyties and abuse to the authority of this Country, by the Printing Presse, it is ordered by this Court and the authority thereof, that theeir shall no Printing Presse be allowed in any Towne within this Jurisdiction, but in Cambridge, ‡ nor shall any person or persons presume to print any Copie but by the allowance first had and obtayned under the hands of such as this court shall from tjme to tjme Impower; the President of the Colledge, Mr. John Shearman, Mr. Jonathan Mitchell and Mr. Thomas Shepheard, or any two of them to survey such Copie or Coppies and to prohibit or allow the same according to this order; and in case of non observance of this order, to forfeit the Presse to the Country and be disabled from Vsing any such profession within

---

* Major Daniel Gookin and the Rev. Jonathan Mitchell were the first appointed licensers of the press. [Ancient records of the colony.]

† Ancient records of the colony.

‡ By this order it should seem that another press had been set up, or what is most probable, intended to be, in Boston. But I have not found any book printed in Boston, or in any other town in Massachusetts, excepting Cambridge, until the year 1674.

this Jurisdiction for the tjme to Come. Provided this order shall not extend to the obstruction of any Coppies which this Court shall Judge meete to order to be published in Print.'*

Government appears not only to have required a compliance with the above law, but to have exercised a power independent of it. The licensers of the press had permitted the reprinting of a book written by Thomas à Kempis, entitled *Imitation of Christ* &c., a work well known in the Christian world. This treatise was represented to the court by some of its members, in the session in 1667, as being heretical; whereupon the court passed an order as follows: 'This Court being informed that there is now in the Presse reprinting, a book that Imitates of Christ, or to that purpose, written by Thomas Kempis, a popish minister, wherein is contayned some things that are lesse safe to be infused amongst the people of this place, Doe comend to the licensers of the Presse the more full revisale thereof, and that in the meane tjme there be no further progresse in that work.'

In 1671, the general court ordered an edition of the laws, revised, &c., to be printed. Heretofore the laws had been published at the expense of the colony. John Usher, a wealthy bookseller, who was then or soon after treasurer of the province, made interest to have the publishing of this edition on his own account. This circumstance produced the first instance in this country of the security of copyright by law. Usher contracted with Green to print the work, but suspecting that Green might print additional copies for himself, or that Johnson, who was permitted to print at Cambridge, would reprint from his copy, two laws, at the request of Usher, were passed to secure to him

---

* Ancient manuscript records of the colony.

this particular work. These laws are copied from the manuscript records; the first was in May, 1672, and is as follows, viz: 'In answer to the petition of John Vsher, the Court Judgeth it meete to order, and be it by this Court ordered and Enacted, That no Printer shall print any more Coppies than are agreed and paid for by the owner of the Coppie or Coppies, nor shall he nor any other reprint or make Sale of any of the same without the said Owner's consent upon the forfeiture and penalty of treble the whole charge of Printing and paper of the quantity paid for by the owner of the Coppie, to the said owner or his Assigns.'

When the book was published, Usher, not satisfied with the law already made in his favor, petitioned the court to secure him the copyright for seven years. In compliance with the prayer of his petition, the court in May, 1673, decreed as follows: 'John Vsher Having been at the sole Chardge of the Impression of the booke of Lawes, and presented the Governour, Magistrates, Secretary, as also every Deputy, and the Clark of the deputation with one. The Court Judgeth it meete to order that for at least Seven years, Vnless he shall have sold them all before that tjme, there shall be no other or further Impression made by any person thereof in this Jurisdiction, under the penalty this court shall see cause to lay on any that shall adventure in that Kind, besides making ffull sattisfaction to the said Jno Vsher or his Assigns, for his chardge and damage thereon. Voted by the whole court met together.'

A revised edition of the laws of the colony was put to the press in 1685. Respecting this edition the court 'Ordered, for the greater expedition in the present revisal of the Laws they shall be sent to the Presse Sheete by Sheete, and the Treasurer shall make payment to the Printer for the same, Paper and work; and Elisha Cook and Samuel Sewall Esqrs. are desired to oversee the Presse about that work.'

There is among the records of the colony for 1667, one as follows: 'Layd out to Ensign Samuel Green of Cambridge printer three hundred Acres of land in the wilderness on the north of Merrimacht River on the west side of Haverhill, bounded on the north east of two little ponds beginning at a red oak in Haverhill,' &c. 'The court allowed of the returne of this farme as laid out.' By the records of the earliest English proprietors of Cambridge, it appears that Green was the owner of several valuable tracts of land in and about that town.

Green often mentioned to his children, that for some time after his arrival in New England, he, and several others, were obliged to lodge in large empty casks, having no other shelter from the weather; so few were the huts then erected by our hardy and venerable ancestors. He had nineteen children; eight by his first wife, and eleven by a second, who was daughter of Mr. Clarke, an elder in the church in Cambridge, and to whom he was married Feb. 23, 1662.* Nine of the children by the second wife lived to the age of fifty-two years, or upwards.

The Cambridge company of Militia elected Green to be their captain; and, as such, he bore a commission for thirty years. He took great pleasure in military exercises; and when he became through age too infirm to walk to the field, he insisted on being carried there in his chair on days of muster, that he might review and exercise his company.†

---

* Middlesex Records of Marriages and Deaths, vol. III.
† *Boston News Letter*, Jan., 1733.

He was for many years chosen town clerk. And in the Middlesex Records, vol. I, is the following particular, viz: 'At a County Court held at Cambridge the 5th 8th month 1652, Samuel Green is alowed Clearke of the Writts for Cambridge.'

Green continued printing till he became aged. He was a pious and benevolent man, and as such was greatly esteemed. He died at Cambridge, January 1st, 1702, aged eighty-seven years.

Until the commencement of the revolution in 1775, Boston was not without one or more printers by the name of Green. These all descended from Green of Cambridge. Some of his descendants have, for nearly a century past, been printers in Connecticut. One of them, in 1740, removed to Annapolis, and established the *Maryland Gazette*, which was long continued by the family.[5]

No printing was done at Cambridge after Green's death. The press was established in this place sixty years; and, about fifty of them, Green, under government, was the manager of it. He was printer to the college as long as he continued in business.

Soon after his decease, the printing materials were removed from Cambridge and probably sold. It does not appear that the corporation of the college owned any types after this time till about the year 1718, when Mr. Thomas Hollis, of London, a great benefactor to the college, among other gifts, presented to the university a fount, or cast, of Hebrew, and another of Greek types, both of them of the size of long primer. The Greek was not used till 1761, when the government of the college had a work printed entitled, *Pietas et Gratulatio Collegii Cantabrigiensis apud Novanglos*, dedicated to King George III, on his accession to the throne; two of these poetical essays being written in Greek, called these types into use. They were never used but at that time, and were in January, 1764, destroyed by the fire that consumed Harvard hall, one of the college buildings, in which the types and college library were deposited; the cast of Hebrew escaped, having been sent to Boston some time before to print Professor Sewall's Hebrew Grammar.

MARMADUKE JOHNSON was an Englishman, and had been bred to the printing business in London. The corporation in England for propagating the gospel among the Indians engaged and sent him over to America in 1660, to assist in printing the Bible in Indian.[6]

In a letter dated, Cooper's Hall in London, April 28th, 1660, and directed to the commissioners of the United Colonies, who had the whole management of Indian affairs, the corporation writes: 'Wee haue out of our desire to further a worke of soe great consernment, [printing the whole Bible in the Indian language] agreed with an able printer for three yeares vpon the tearmes and conditions enclosed. Wee desire you at the earnest request of Mr. Johnson the printer, and for his incurragement in this undertaking of printing the bible in the Indian language, his name may bee mentioned with others as a printer and person that hath bine instrumentall therin; for whose diet, lodging and washing wee desire you to take care of.'

The commissioners in their answer to the corporation, dated New Haven the 10th of September, 1660, observe: 'Such order is taken by aduice of Mr. Eliott Mr. Vsher Mr. Green and Mr. Johnson that the Impression of the ould and New Testament shalbee carryed on together which they have alredy begun and Resolue to prosecute with all diligence; a sheet of Geneses wee have seen which wee have ordered shalbee Transmitted vnto you; the printers doubte not but to print a sheete euery weeke and compute the whole to amount to a hundred and fifty sheets. Mr. Johnson wilbee gratifyed with the honour of the Impression and acomodated in other respects wee hope to content.' The commissioners this year charged the corporation with £1 4s. paid for 'the expenses of Johnson the printer att his first arrivall before he settled at Cambridge.'

In a letter dated, Boston Sept. 10, 1662, and addressed to the Hon. Robert Boyle, governor of the corporation in England, the commissioners of the United Colonies observe: 'The bible is now about half done; and constant progresse therin is made; the other halfe is like to bee finished in a yeare; the future charge is vncertain; wee have heer with sent twenty coppies of the New Testament [in Indian] to bee disposed of as youer honors shall see meet. The trust youer honors hath seen meet to repose in vs for the manageing of this worke we shall endeauor in all faithfulness to discharge. Wee craue leave att present for the preuenting of an objection that may arise concerning the particulars charged for the printing wherin you will find 2 sheets att three pounds ten shillings a sheet, and the rest butt att 50 shillings a sheet, the reason wherof lyes heer: It pleased the honored corporation to send ouer one Marmeduke Johnson a printer to attend the worke on condition as they will enforme you; whoe hath caryed heer very vnworthyly of which hee hath bine openly Convicted and sencured in some of our Courts although as yett noe execution of sentence against him: peculiare fauer haueing bine showed him with respect to the corporation that sent him ouer; but notwithstanding all patience and lenitie vsed towards him hee hath proued uery idle and nought and absented himselfe from the worke more than halfe a yeare att one time; for want of whose assistance the printer [Green] by his agreement with vs was to haue the allowance of 21 lb. the which is to bee defallcated out of his sallery in England by the honored Corporation there.'

The commissioners, in this letter to the corporation, mentioned some bad conduct of Johnson, of which he was convicted, but they do not particularize his offence. I find in the records of the county court of Middlesex for 1662, that in April of that year, Johnson was indicted for 'alluring the daughter of Samuel Green, printer, and drawing away her affection without the consent of her father.' This was a direct breach of a law of the colony. Johnson was convicted, fined five pounds for that offence; and having a wife in England, was ordered 'to go home to her,' on penalty of twenty pounds for neglecting so to do. At the same court Johnson was fined twenty pounds for threatening the life of any man who should pay his addresses to Green's daughter. In October, 1663, Johnson, not having left the country agreeably to his sentence, was fined twenty pounds and ordered 'to be committed till he gave security that he would depart home to England to his wife the first opportunity.' Samuel Goffe and John Bernard were his sureties that he should depart the country within six weeks, or in a vessel then bound to England. Johnson, however, for some cause that cannot be ascertained, [the records of the next county court being destroyed by fire] was permitted to remain in the country. His wife might have died; he had influential friends; and made his peace with Green, with whom he was afterwards concerned in printing several books.

The commissioners received an answer to the letter last mentioned, from the governor of the corporation, dated London

April 9th, 1663, at the close of which the governor remarks: 'Conserning Marmeduke Johnson the printer wee are sorry hee hath soe miscarryed by which meanes the printing of the bible hath bin retarded we are resolved to default the 21 lb. you mention out of his sallary. Mr. Elliott whose letter beares date three monthes after youers, writes that Johnson is againe Returned into the worke whose brother alsoe hath bine with vs and gives vs great assurance of his brothers Reformation and following his busines diligently for the time to come; and hee being (as Mr. Elliott writes) an able and vsefull man in the presse we haue thought fitt to make tryall of him for one yeare longer and the rather because vpon Mr. Elliotts motion and the goodnes of the worke; wee have thought fitt and ordered that the Psalmes of Dauid in meter shallbee printed in the Indian language, and soe wee hope that the said Johnson performing his promise of amendment for time to come may bee vsefull in the furthering of this worke which we soe much desire the finishing of: We haue no more but comend you to the Lord. Signed in the name and by the appointment of the Corporation for the propagating of the Gospell in America.

Per Robert Boyle Gouernor.'

The commissioners wrote from Boston, Sept. 18th, 1663, to the corporation, as was their annual custom, rendering a particular account of their concerns, and of the expenditures of the money of the corporation. Respecting Johnson they observe: 'Some time after our last letter Marmeduke Johnson Returned to the Presse and hath carried himselfe Indifferently well since soe farr as wee know but the bible being finished and little other worke presenting; wee dismised him att the end of the tearme you had contracted with him for; but vnderstanding

youer honorable Corporation hath agreed with him for another yeare; wee shall Indeavour to Imploy him as wee can by
printing the Psalmes and another little Treatise of Mr. Baxters
which Mr. Elliott is translateing into the Indian language which
is thought may bee vsefull and profitable to the Indians; and
yett there will not bee full Imployment for him; and for after
times our owne printer wilbee sufficiently able to print of any
other worke that wilbee necessary for theire vse soe that att the
yeares end hee may be dismised; or sooner if hee please: and If
there bee occation further to Imploy him It were much better
to contract with him heer to print by the sheete than by allow-
ing him standing wages: Wee were forced vpon his earnest
Request to lett him fiue pounds in parte of his wages to supply
his present nessesitie which must bee defaulted by youer honors
with his brother: his last yeare by agreement with him begineth
the 20th of August last from the end of his former contract till
that time hee was out of this Imployment and followed his own
occacions.'

The corporation in their next letter to the commissioners
write: 'Concerning Marmeduke Johnson the printer whose
Demeanor hath not been suitable to what hee promised wee
shall leave him to youerselues to dismisse him as soone as his
yeare is expired if you soe think fit.'

The next meeting of the Commissioners was at Hartford,
September 1, 1664; they then informed the corporation in
England, that they had 'dismised Marmeduke Johnson the
Printer att the end of his tearme agreed for hauing Improued
him as well as wee could for the yeare past by imploying him
with our owne printer to print such Indian workes as could be
prepared which hee was not able to doe alone with such other

English Treatises which did present; for which allowance hath bine made proportionable to his laboure; some time hath bine lost for want of imployment but for after time wee hope to haue all books for the Indians vse printed vpon ezier tearmes by our owne printer especially if it please youer honers to send ouer a fonte of Pica letters Roman and Italian which are much wanting for printeing the practice of piety and other workes; and soe when the Presses shallbee Improued for the vse of the English wee shalbe carefull that due alowance be made to the Stocke for the same; It seemed Mr. Johnson ordered all his Sallery to be receiued and disposed of in England which hath put him to some straightes heer which forced vs to allow him fiue pounds formerly (as we Intimated in our last) and since hee hath taken vp the sume of four pounds all which is to be accoumpted as parte of his Sallery for the last yeare; the remainder wherof wee doubt not youer honors will satisfy there.'

Before the Bible was finished, Johnson, being in great want of money, applied to the commissioners of the United Colonies to pay him his wages here instead of receiving them, agreeably to contract, in England. Upon which the commissioners 'ordered in Answare to the request of Marmeduke Johnson for payment of his wages heer in New England; notwithstanding his couenant with the Corporation to receiue the same in England which hee sayeth is detained from him; which yett not appearing to the comissioners they could not giue any order for the payment of it heer; but vpon his earnest request that there might bee some Impowered to relieue him in case it could appeer before the next meeting of the Comissioners that noe payment was made to him in England the Comissioners of the Massachusetts Collonie is Impowered to act therein according to theire Discretion.'

The Rev. Mr. Eliot,* who translated the Bible into the Indian
language, appears to have been very friendly to Johnson. After
he was dismissed from employment at the press of the corporation, Mr. Eliot proposed to the commissioners in September,
1667, that Johnson should have 'the font of letters [types] which
the Corporation sent over for their vse by him, when he came
from England,' and which had been but little worn, at the price
they cost in England, which was £31 17s. 8d. sterling; to which
proposal the commissioners assented. These types he received
in part payment of his salary.

In 1670, April 28th, Johnson, being released by death or
divorce from his wife in England, married Ruth Cane of Cambridge, which is recorded in the register of the town for that
year.

In September, 1672, the commissioners ordered their agent,
Hezekiah Usher, to pay Johnson £6 'for printing, stitching and
cutting of a thousand Indian Logick Primers.' This is the last
business I can find performed by Johnson for the corporation.
His name appeared after Green's in the imprint of the first edition of the Indian translation of the Old and New Testament,
and to several other books which were not printed for the
corporation for propagating the gospel among the Indians. It is
not probable that they had any regular partnership, but printed
a book in connexion when convenient. I have seen no book
with his name in the imprint after 1674.

Johnson was constable of Cambridge in 1673, and perhaps
some years preceding. In April, 1674, the county court allowed
him 'his bill of costs, amounting to three shillings; and ten
shillings and six pence for journeys that were by law to be paid

* Mr. Eliot was by some styled 'Apostolus nostrorum Temporum inter
Indos Nov Angliæ.' He died 1690, aged 86.

by the county treasurer.' It appears that he was poor, and rather indolent. He departed this life in 1675, and his wife soon followed him.

The following is an extract from the Middlesex records, vol. III, p. 176. 'At a County Court held at Charlestowne June 19, 1677. Mr. John Hayward Attorney in behalfe of the Commissioners of the United Coloneys pl'ff against Jonathan Cane, Executor to the last will and testament of Ruth Johnson administratrix to the estate of her husband Marmaduke Johnson deceased, in an action of the case for deteyning a font of Letters, bought by the said Johnson with money yt. he received for yt. end and use of ye. Honourable Corporation in London constituted by his Majestie for propagating of the gospell to the Indians in New England, and also for deteyning a Printers chase, and other implements that belong to a Printing Presse, and is apperteyning to the said Indian Stocke according to attachmt. dated 8, 4, 77. Both parties appeared & joyned issue in the case. The Jury having heard their respective pleas & evidences in the case, brought in their verdict, finding for the pl've that the Defdt. shall deliver the wt. of Letters expressed in the attachment, with other materials expressed in the attachment, or the value thereof in money, which wee find to be forty pounds, with costs of court. The Defdt. made his appeale to the next Court of Assistants.'

BARTHOLOMEW GREEN, son of Samuel Green, by his second wife, was in business a few years with his father at Cambridge. In the year 1690 he removed to Boston, and set up his press. The same year his printing house and materials were destroyed by fire; and he, in consequence of his loss, returned to Cambridge, and was again connected with his father. The few books which I have seen that were printed by his father and him in company, are taken notice of with his father's. He resumed business in Boston in 1692.

ABOUT forty-five years from the beginning of the settlement of Boston a printing house was opened, and the first book I have found printed in this town was by

JOHN FOSTER.[7] He was born in Dorchester, near Boston, and educated at Harvard College, where he graduated in 1667. Printers at this time were considered as mere agents to execute the typographic art; the presses were the property of the college, but all their productions were under the control of licensers appointed by the government of the colony; that government had restricted printing, and confined it solely to Cambridge, but it now authorized Foster to set up a press in Boston. It does not appear that he was bred to printing, or that he was acquainted with the art; the probability is, that he was not; but having obtained permission to print, he employed workmen, carried on printing in his own name, and was accountable to government for the productions of his press.

The General court, at the session in May, 1674, passed the order following: 'Whereas there is now granted that there may be a printing Presse elsewhere than at Cambridge; for the better regulation of the Presse it is ordered and Enacted that the Rev. Mr. Thomas Thatcher and Rev. Increase Mather, of Boston, be added unto the former Licensers, and they are hereby impowered to act accordingly.'

If Foster's printing equalled, it could not be said to excel, that of Green or Johnson, either in neatness or correctness. He printed a number of small tracts for himself and others. The earliest book which I have seen from the press under his care was published in 1676, and the latest in 1680. He calculated and published Almanacks. To his Almanack for 1681 he annexed an ingenious dissertation on comets seen at Boston in November and December, 1680.* He died at Dorchester, September 9, 1681, aged thirty-three years. His grave stone bears the following inscription, viz:

> Astra colis vivens, moriens super æthera Foster
> Scande precor, cœlum metiri disce supremum:
> Metior atque meum est, emit mihi dives Jesus,
> Nec tenior quicquam nisi grates solvere.

In English thus?

Thou, O Foster, who on earth didst study the heavenly bodies, now ascend above the firmament and survey the highest heaven. I do survey and inhabit this divine region. To its possession I am admitted through the grace of Jesus; and to pay the debt of gratitude I hold the most sacred obligation.

Two poems on the death of Foster were printed in 1681; one of them was written by Thomas Tilestone, of Dorchester, and the other by Joseph Capen, afterwards minister of Topsfield, Massachusetts. The latter concluded with the following lines:

> Thy body, which no activeness did lack,
> Now's laid aside like an old Almanack;
> But for the present only's out of date,
> 'Twill have at length a far more active state.

* See *Collections of Massachusetts Historical Society*, IX, 147–199 (1804). 'Chronological and Topographical Account of Dorchester,' written by the Rev. T. M. Harris.

Yea, though with dust thy body soiled be,
Yet at the resurrection we shall see
A fair EDITION, and of matchless worth,
Free from ERRATAS, new in Heaven set forth;
'Tis but a word from GOD, the great Creator,
It shall be done when he saith Imprimatur.

Whoever has read the celebrated epitaph, by Franklin, on himself, will have some suspicion that it was taken from this *original*.

SAMUEL SEWALL. When Foster died, Boston was without the benefit of the press; but a continuance of it in this place being thought necessary, Samuel Sewall, not a printer but a magistrate, &c., a man much respected, was selected as a proper person to manage the concerns of it, and as such was recommended to the General court. In consequence of this recommendation, the court in October, 1681, gave him liberty to carry on the business of printing in Boston. The license is thus recorded:* 'Samuel Sewall, at the Instance of some Friends, with respect to the accommodation of the Publick, being prevailed with to undertake the Management of the Printing Presse in Boston, late under the command of Mr. John Foster, deceased, liberty is accordingly granted to him for the same by this court, and none may presume to set up any other Presse without the like Liberty first granted.'

Sewall became a bookseller. Books for himself and others were printed at the press under his management, as were several acts and laws, with other work for government. Samuel Green, jun., was his printer. In 1682 an order passed the General court

---

* *Records of the Colony* for 1681.

for the treasurer to pay Sewall £10 17*s.*, for printing the election sermon delivered that year by the Rev. Mr. Torrey. I have seen several books printed by the assignment of Sewall.

In 1684, Sewall by some means was unable to conduct the press, and requested permission of the General court to be released from his engagement, which was granted. The record of his release is in the words following: 'Samuel Sewall by the providence of God being unable to attend the press &c., requested leave to be freed from his obligations concerning it, which was granted.'

In 1684, and for several subsequent years, the loss of the charter occasioned great confusion and disorder in the political concerns of the colony. Soon after Sewall resigned his office as conductor of the press in Boston, he went to England; whence he returned in 1692. He was, undoubtedly, the same Samuel Sewall who, when a new charter was granted by King William, was for many years one of the council for the province; and who, in 1692, was appointed one of the judges of the superior court; in 1715 judge of probate; and in 1718 chief justice of Massachusetts. He died January 1, 1729–30, aged seventy-eight years.*

JAMES GLEN. Printed for or by the assignment of Samuel Sewall, to whom government had committed the management of the press after the death of Foster. He printed under Sewall less than two years. I have seen only three or four works which bear his name in the imprint, and these were printed for Sewall. One

* See Thomas Prince's *Sermon at the Publick Lecture in Boston Jan. viii. 1729, 30* (Boston, 1730) and *Dictionary of American Biography*, XVI, 610–612.

was entitled *Covenant Keeping, the Way to Blessedness*, by Samuel
Willard. 12mo. 240 pages. 'Boston: Printed by James Glen, for
S. Sewall, 1682.' I do not recollect the titles of the others, which
were pamphlets. All the printing done by Glen was at Sewall's
press.

SAMUEL GREEN, Junior, was the son, by his first wife, of
Samuel Green, who at that time printed at Cambridge. He was
taught the art in the printing house of his father. His books bear
the next earliest dates to Foster's and Glen's. In 1682, he printed
at the press which, by order of the General court, was under the
management of Sewall, and for some time by virtue of an assignment from Sewall. He worked chiefly for booksellers.
Many books printed for them are without the name of the
printer, and some without date.* After Sewall ceased to conduct the press, Green was permitted to continue printing, subject to the control of the licensers.

John Dunton, a London bookseller, who visited Boston
while Green was in business, in 1686, and after his return to
England published the history of his own *Life and Errors*, mentions Green in his publication in the following manner: 'I contracted a great friendship for this man; to name his trade will
convince the world he was a man of good sense and understanding; he was so facetious and obliging in his conversation
that I took a great delight in his company, and made use of his

---

* Printers should insert in their imprints to books, newspapers, &c., not only
their names, but the year, and mention both the state and town where their
presses are established. Many towns in the United States bear the same name.
Some newspapers, and many books, have been published in certain towns; and
the state not being designated in the imprints, in many instances it cannot be
determined, especially by those at a distance, in which of the states they were
printed.

house to while away my melancholy hours.'* Dunton gives biographical sketches of a number of men and women whom he visited in Boston in 1686, and represents Green's wife as a most excellent woman, even as a model from which to draw *'the picture of the best of wives.'* †

Green printed for government, and soon after his death the General court ordered the treasurer to pay his heirs £22 17s. 'due him for his last printing.'

In 1690, Boston was visited with the small pox. Before the practice of inoculation was introduced, this disease, at every visitation, swept off a large number of inhabitants. In July of that year, Green fell a victim to that loathsome disorder; he died after an illness of three days; and his amiable wife, within a few days after her husband, ‡ was carried off by the same epidemic.

RICHARD PIERCE. On an examination of the books printed in Boston before the year 1700, it appears that Richard Pierce was the fifth person who carried on the printing business in that place. Whether he had been bred a printer in England, or had

---

* *Life and Errors of John Dunton* (London, 1705).

† Her maiden name was Elizabeth Sill. She was born in Cambridge.

‡ I am favored by Rosseter Cotton, Esq., of Plymouth, with an original letter, dated at Plymouth, Aug. 5, 1690, to his great grandfather, the Rev. John Cotton, then on a visit to Barnstable, from his son, which mentions among other articles of information from Boston, 'the small pox is as bad as ever; Printer Green died of it in Three days, his wive also is dead with it.' This letter contains much news of the day; it states that, 'on Saturday Evening about fourteen houses, besides warehouses and Bruehouses, were burnt at Boston, from the Mill Bridgh down half way to the Draw Bridgh.' By this it should seem, that at that time, there was a street along side of the Mill creek.

served an apprenticeship with Green at our Cambridge, cannot
be determined. There was a printer in London by the name of
Richard Pierce, in 1679; and it is not improbable that he emigrated to this country, and set up his press in Boston. I have seen
some books printed by him on his own account, and a number
for booksellers; they are mentioned in the catalogue of books
printed in America before the revolution. I have not found any
thing printed by him before 1684, or after 1690.

BARTHOLOMEW GREEN has been mentioned as a printer at
Cambridge, in connection with his father. He began business at
Boston in 1690, immediately after the death of his brother, with
the best printing apparatus then in the country. He was married
the same year; and soon after his printing house was consumed,
and his press and types entirely destroyed by a fire, which began
in his neighborhood. This misfortune obliged him to return to
Cambridge; and he continued there two years, doing business
in company with his father. Being again furnished with a press
and types, he reestablished himself in Boston, and opened a
printing house in Newbury street. The imprint to several of the
first books from his press, is, 'Boston: Printed by B. Green, at
the *South End* of the Town.'

In April, 1704, he began the publication of a newspaper, entitled *The Boston News Letter*. Published by Authority. It was
printed weekly, on Mondays, for John Campbell, postmaster,
who was the proprietor. After the News-Letter had been printed eighteen years for Campbell, Green published it on his own
account. It was the first newspaper printed in the British colonies of North America, and had been published fifteen years
before any other work of the kind made its appearance. It was

continued by Green and his successors until the year 1776, when the British troops evacuated Boston.*

After his father's death Bartholomew Green printed for the college, and he was for nearly forty years printer to the governor and council of Massachusetts; but the acts and laws printed by him were done for a bookseller, Benjamin Elliot, from 1703 to 1729, as appears from the imprints. He was the most distinguished printer of that period in this country, and did more business than any other of the profession; yet he worked chiefly for the booksellers. John Allen was concerned with him in printing many books, in the imprints of which both their names appeared; there was not, however, a regular partnership between them.

Through the whole course of his life, Green was distinguished for piety and benevolence; he was highly respected; and, for many years, held the office of a deacon in the Old South church in Boston. He died December 28, 1732. The following character of him is extracted from *The Boston News-Letter*, of January 4, 1733:

'Bartholomew Green was a person generally known and esteemed among us, as a very humble and exemplary Christian, one who had much of that primitive Christianity in him which has always been the distinguishing glory of New England. We

* Bartholomew Green began the printing of *The Boston News-Letter*, in Newbury street, in a small wooden building, to which another room was annexed some years after, for the accommodation of his son. This building was burnt down in January, 1734; it was previously occupied as a printing house both by young Green and John Draper, who did business independently of each other. Another house of like dimensions was built on the same spot by John Draper, the successor of the elder B. Green. This building was occupied as a printing house until the British troops evacuated Boston, in 1776. At that place began and ended the printing of *The Boston News-Letter*. That house was built and occupied by Richard, the son and successor of John Draper.

may further remember his eminency for a strict observing the
sabbath; his household piety; his keeping close and diligent to
the work of this calling; his meek and peaceable spirit; his caution of publishing any thing offensive, light or hurtful; and his
tender sympathy to the poor and afflicted. He always spoke of
the wonderful spirit of piety that prevailed in the land in his
youth with a singular pleasure.'

JOHN ALLEN. I have not seen any book with his name in the
imprint, published earlier than the year 1690. He printed, sometimes in connection with Bartholomew Green, and sometimes
with Benjamin Harris; but was not in regular partnership with
either. There is no evidence that he had printing materials of his
own until 1707; at this time he opened a printing house in
Pudding lane, near the post office, and did business on his own
account. In November of this year he began printing *The Boston
News-Letter*, for the proprietor, Mr. Campbell, postmaster.
Soon after this event he published the following advertisement,
viz:

'These are to give Notice, that there lately came from London a Printing Press, with all sorts of good new Letter, which
is now set up in Pudding Lane near the Post-Office in Boston
for publick use: Where all persons that have any thing to print
may be served on reasonable terms.'

Allen printed *The News-Letter* four years; when a fire which
consumed most of the buildings in Cornhill, and many in King
street, Queen street, and the contiguous lanes, is supposed to
have burnt his printing house. The fire broke out on the evening
of the 2d of October, 1711. On the preceding day he had printed *The News-Letter*; but on the next week that paper was again

printed by Green; or as the imprint runs, 'Printed in Newbury-Street, for John Campbell, Post-Master.' I have seen a number of books printed after this time by Allen alone, the last of which is Whittemore's Almanack, bearing the date of 1724.

While he was connected with Green, and previous to 1708, the acts, laws, proclamations, &c., of government, were printed by them, and Allen's name appeared with Green's as 'Printers to the Governour and Council.' Allen printed no book that I have seen on his own account; all the business he executed in the line of his profession was for booksellers. He was from England. There is in an ancient library in Boston, a copy of Increase Mather's *Mystery of Israel's Salvation,* printed in London, by John Allen, in 1669. It is supposed that he came to Boston by encouragement from the Mathers.

BENJAMIN HARRIS. His printing house was 'over against the Old Meeting House in Cornhill.'* He removed several times; and once printed 'at the London Coffee-House,' which I believe he kept, in King's street; at another time in Cornhill, 'over against the Blew Anchor.' The last place of his residence I find mentioned, was in Cornhill, 'at the Sign of the Bible.'[8]

He printed, principally, for booksellers; but he did some work on his own account. He kept a shop, and sold books. I have not met with any book of his printing earlier than 1690, nor later than 1694. In 1692 and 1693, he printed *The Acts and Laws of Massachusetts,* containing about one hundred and thirty

---

* This church in Boston was burnt down in the great fire of 1711; but was soon rebuilt, on a new site, a number of rods to the south of the spot where the old building stood, and was, for many years, known by the name of The Old Brick; which, in 1808, was taken down, a new church having been erected for the society in Summer street.

pages, folio, to which the charter was prefixed. The imprint is,
'Boston: Printed by Benjamin Harris, Printer to his Excellency
the Governour and Council.' His commission from Governor
Phips, to print them, is published opposite to the title page of
the volume in the words following:

By his Excellency.—I order Benjamin Harris to print the Acts and
Laws made by the Great and General Court, or Assembly of Their
Majesties Province of Massachusetts Bay in New England, that so the
people may be informed thereof.

WILLIAM PHIPS.

Boston, December 16, 1692.

In the title page of the laws, printed by him in 1693, is a handsome cut of their majesties' arms. This was in the reign of
William and Mary.[9]

Harris was from London; he returned there about the year
1694. Before and after his emigration to America he owned a
considerable bookstore in that city. John Dunton's account of
him is thus:

'He had been a brisk asserter of English Liberties, and once
printed a Book with that very title. He sold a protestant Petition
in King Charles's Reign, for which he was fined five Pounds;
and he was once set in the Pillory, but his wife (like a kind Rib)
stood by him to defend her Husband against the Mob. After
this (having a deal of Mercury in his natural temper) he travelled
to New England, where he followed Bookselling, and then
Coffee-selling, and then Printing, but continued Ben Harris
still, and is now both Bookseller and Printer in Grace Church
Street, as we find by his *London Post*; so that his Conversation is
general (but never impertinent) and his Wit pliable to all inventions. But yet his Vanity, if he has any, gives no *alloy* to his
Wit, and is no more than might justly spring from conscious

virtue; and I do him but justice in this part of his Character, for in once travelling with him from Bury-Fair, I found him to be the most ingenious and innocent Companion, that I had ever met with.'*

TIMOTHY GREEN was the son of Samuel Green, junior, of Boston, and grandson of Samuel Green of Cambridge. The earliest books which I have met with of his printing, bear date in 1700. He had a printing house at the north part of the town, in Middle street, near Cross street. He printed and sold some books on his own account; but, as was customary, printed principally for booksellers. The imprint to some of his books is, 'Boston: Printed by Timothy Green, at the *North Part of the Town.*' I have seen other books printed at the same time by his uncle Bartholomew, with this imprint, 'Boston: Printed by B. Green, at the *South Part of the Town.*' Although several printers had succeeded each other, there had never been more than two printing houses open at the same time in Boston; and, at this period, it does not appear that the number was increased. T. Green continued in business, at Boston, until 1714. He then received encouragement from the general assembly of Connecticut, and removed his press to New London.

JAMES PRINTER, *alias* James the Printer. This man was an Indian native; born at an Indian town called Hassanamesitt, †

---

* Dunton's *Life and Errors*, printed in London, 1705. Dunton was an English bookseller, who had been in Boston; he was bred to this business by Thomas Parkhurst, who published Mather's *Magnalia*, and other books for New England ministers. Dunton had a knowledge of the booksellers in England, Scotland, Ireland, Holland, and New England; and published sketches of their characters.

† Signifying a place of small stones.

now the town of Grafton, in the county of Worcester, Massachusetts. His father was a deacon of the church of Indian Christians established in that place. James had two brothers; the one, named Anaweakin, was their ruler; the other, named Tarkuppawillin, was their teacher; they were all esteemed on account of their piety, and considered as the principal persons of that Indian village.* James, when a child, was taught at the Indian charity school, at Cambridge, to read and write the English language, where, probably, he received the Christian name of James. In 1659, he was put apprentice to Samuel Green, printer, in that place, which gave him the surname of *Printer*. Green instructed him in the art of printing; and employed him whilst his apprentice as a pressman, &c., in printing the first edition of the Indian Bible.

A war taking place between James's countrymen and the white people, James, fired with a spark of the *amor patriæ*, left his master secretly, and joined his brethren in arms. A number of skirmishes were fought, in all which the Indians were repulsed with loss; they, in consequence, became disheartened; and the associated tribes separated, and retired to their respective places of residence; at which time, 1676, the government of Massachusetts issued a proclamation, or, as Hubbard, in his *Narrative of the Indian Wars*, terms it, 'Put forth a *Declaration*, that whatsoever Indians should within fourteen days next ensuing, come in to the English, might hope for *mercy*. Amongst sundry who came in, there was one named *James* the *Printer*, the *superadded Title* distinguishing him from others of that name, who being a *notorious Apostate*, that had learned so much of the

* Maj. Daniel Gookin's *Historical Collections of the Indians in New England* (Boston, 1792).

English, as not only to read and write, but had attained some skill in printing, and might have attained more, had he not like a *false villain* run away from his *Master* before his time was out; he having seen and read the said *Declaration* of the *English*, did venture himself upon the Truth thereof, and came to sue for his life; he affirmed with others that came along with him, that more Indians had died since the *War* began of diseases (such as at other times they used not to be acquainted withal) than by the sword of the English.'* In this war, the Narraganset Indians lost their celebrated chief, king Philip, of Mount Hope; after which the colony enjoyed great tranquillity.

James, it is supposed, remained in and near Boston till 1680; and, doubtless, worked at the printing business, either with his former master, at Cambridge, or with Foster, who had lately set up a press, the first established in Boston, and must have well known James, who lived with Green when Foster was at college. In 1680, he was engaged with Green at Cambridge in printing the second edition of the Indian Bible. The Rev. John Eliot, in a letter to the Hon. Robert Boyle at London, dated March, 1682–3, observes respecting this second edition, 'I desire to see it done before I die, and I am so deep in years, that I cannot expect to live long; besides, we have but one man, viz., the Indian Printer, that is able to compose the Sheets, and correct the Press with understanding.' In another letter, dated 'Roxbury, April 22, 1684,' to the Hon. Mr. Boyle, from the Rev. Mr. Eliot, he mentions, 'We present your honours with one book, so far as we have gone in the work, and humbly beseech that it may be acceptable till the whole Bible is finished; and then the

---

* William Hubbard's *Narrative of the Troubles with the Indians in New-England* (Boston, 1677), p. 96.

whole impression (which is two thousand) is at your honours command. Our slow progress needeth an apology. We have been much hindered by the sickness the last year. Our workmen have been all sick, and we have but few hands (at printing) one Englishman, and a boy, and one *Indian*,* and many interruptions and diversions do befall us, and we could do but little this very hard winter.'

We hear no more of James until the year 1709, when an edition of the Psalter, in the Indian and English languages, made its appearance with the following imprint.—'Boston, N. E. Printed by *B. Green* and *J. Printer*, for the Honourable Company for the Propagation of the Gospel in New England, &c.'—In Indian thus, *Upprinthomunneau* B. Green, *kah* J. Printer, *wutche quhtiantamwe Chapanukkeg wutche onchektouunnat wunnaunchummookaonk ut New England.* 1709. †

Some of James's descendants were long living in Grafton; they bore the Surname of *Printer*.

THOMAS FLEET[10] was born in England and there bred to

* Undoubtedly *J. Printer*. This surname of *Printer* was continued by the descendants of James, who owned and left to his posterity some valuable tracts of land in Grafton, county of Worcester, Mass., the place of his nativity. An action respecting a part of this land, owned by Abigail Printer, was decided in the Court of Common Pleas, in said Worcester in 1810. She was probably, the great-granddaughter of James.

† Bartholomew Green was the son of James's former master; James was well known among all the neighboring tribes; and one motive for employing him, in printing this Psalter, might have been, to excite the greater attention among the Indians, and give it a wider circulation; besides, his knowledge of both languages enabled him to expedite the work with more facility and correctness than any other person.

Several books were, about this time, translated into the Indian language, and printed, which might have afforded employment to James; but I have seen only the Psalter with his name as the printer.

the printing business. When young he took an actve part in opposition to the high church party. On some public procession, probably that of Dr. Henry Sacheverell, when many of the zealous members of the high church decorated their doors and windows with garlands, as the head of their party passed in the streets, Fleet is said to have hung out of his window an ensign of contempt, which inflamed the resentment of his opponents to that degree, that he was obliged to secrete himself from their rage, and to embrace the first opportunity to quit his country.

He arrived at Boston about the year 1712, and soon opened a printing house in Pudding Lane, now Devonshire street. The earliest book I have seen of his printing bears date 1713. He was a good workman; was a book printer, and he and T. Crump were concerned in printing some books together.

But the principal performances of Fleet, until he began the publication of a newspaper, consisted of pamphlets for booksellers, small books for children, and ballads. He made a profit on these, which was sufficient to support his family reputably. He owned several negroes, one of which worked at the printing business, both at the press and at setting types; he was an ingenious man, and cut, on wooden blocks, all the pictures which decorated the ballads and small books of his master. Fleet had also two negro boys born in his house; sons, I believe, to the man just mentioned, whom he brought up to work at press and case; one named Pompey and the other Cesar; they were young when their master died; but they remained in the family, and continued to labor regularly in the printing house with the sons of Mr. Fleet, who succeeded their father, until the constitution of Massachusetts, adopted in 1780, made them freemen.[11]

Fleet continued printing in Pudding Lane, till early in 1731, he then hired a handsome house in Cornhill, on the north corner of Water street, which he afterwards purchased; and occupied it through the residue of his life. He erected a sign of the Heart and Crown, which he never altered; but after his death, when crowns became unpopular, his sons changed the Crown for a Bible, and let the Heart remain. Fleet's new house was spacious, and contained sufficient room for the accommodation of his family and the prosecution of his printing business, besides a convenient shop, and a good chamber for an auction room. He held his vendues in the evening, and sold books, household goods, &c., as appears by the following advertisement which he inserted in the *Boston Weekly News-Letter*, March 7th, 1731.

'This is to give Notice to all Gentlemen, Merchants, Shopkeepers and others, that *Thomas Fleet* of Boston, Printer, (who formerly kept his Printing House in Pudding Lane but is now removed into Cornhill at the sign of the *Heart & Crown*, near the lower end of School Street), is willing to undertake the Sale of Books, Household Goods, Wearing Apparel, or any other Merchandize, by Vendue or Auction. The said Fleet having a large & commodious Front Chamber fit for *this Business*, and a Talent well known and approved, doubts not of giving entire Satisfaction to such as may employ him in it; he hereby engaging to make it appear that this Service may be performed with more Convenience and less Charge at a private House well situated, than at a Tavern. And, for further Encouragement, said Fleet promises to make up Accompts with the Owners of the Goods Sold by him, in a few Days after the sale thereof.'

In September, 1731, a new periodical paper was published in

Boston, entitled, *The Weekly Rehearsal*; intended principally to contain essays, moral, political and commercial.* John Draper was first employed to print the *Rehearsal* for the editor, but soon relinquished it, and Fleet succeeded him as the printer of it; and, in April, 1733, he published the *Rehearsal* on his own account. It was then, and had been in fact, from the beginning, no more than a weekly newspaper; but, while in the management of Fleet, it was the best paper at that time published in New England. In August, 1735, Fleet changed *The Weekly Rehearsal* into *The Boston Evening Post*. The last number of the Rehearsal was 201, and the first number of the *Evening Post*, was 202, which shows that the *Evening Post* was then intended to be a continuation of the *Rehearsal*; but the next *Boston Evening Post* was numbered 2, and it became a new hebdomadal paper, which was published every Monday evening.

Fleet was industrious and economical; free from superstition; and possessed a fund of wit and humor, which were often displayed in his paragraphs and advertisements. The members of Fleet's family, although they were very worthy, good people, were not, all of them, remarkable for the pleasantness of their countenances; on which account he would, sometimes, indulge himself in jokes which were rather coarse, at their expense. He once invited an intimate friend to dine with him on *pouts*; a kind of fish of which the gentleman was remarkably fond. When dinner appeared, the guest remarked that the pouts were wanting. 'O no,' said Fleet, 'only look at my wife and daughters.'

The following is an advertisement of Fleet, for the sale of a

* See *Rehearsal*, pp. 246–249.

negro woman—it is short and pithy, viz: 'To be sold by the
Printer of this paper, the very best Negro Woman in this
Town, who has had the small pox and the measles; is as hearty
as a Horse, as brisk as a Bird, and will work like a Beaver.' *The
Evening Post*, Aug. 23, 1742.

In number 50 of *The Boston Evening Post*, Fleet published the
following paragraph, under the Boston head: 'We have lately
received from an intelligent and worthy Friend in a neighboring Government, to the Southward of us, the following remarkable Piece of News, which we beg our Readers Patience to
hear, viz: That the printer there gets a great deal of Money, has
Twenty Shillings for every Advertisement published in his
News-Paper, calls *Us* Fools for working for nothing, and has
lately purchased an Estate of *Fourteen Hundred Pounds* Value.*
We should be heartily glad (had we Cause for it) to return our
Friend a like surprizing Account of the Printers Prosperity here.
But alas! the reverse of our Brother's Circumstances seems
hereditary to *Us*: It is well known we are the most humble,
self-denying Set of Mortals (we wish we could say Men) breath-
ing; for where there is a Penny to be got, we readily resign it up
to those who are no Ways related to the Business, nor have any
Pretence or Claim to the Advantages of it. † And whoever has
observ'd our Conduct hitherto, has Reason enough to think,

* This friend, it is supposed, was James Franklin, nephew to Dr. Benjamin
Franklin, who was established in Rhode Island; and, at that time, the paper
currency of that colony was greatly depreciated.

† Two or three of the Boston newspapers were then printed for postmasters,
or past postmasters; and printing in general was done for booksellers. Master
printers had but little more profit on their labor than journeymen.

that we hold it a mortal Crime to make any other Use of our Brains and Hands, than barely to help us

> To purchase homely Fare, and fresh small Beer,
> (Hard Fate indeed, we can't have better Cheer!)
> And buy a new Blue Apron once a year.*

But as we propose in a short Time to publish a Dissertation upon the *mean* and *humble* state of the Printers of this Town, we s hall say no more at present upon this important Subject, and humbly Pardon for so large a Digression. Only we would inform, that in this most necessary Work, we are promised the Assistance of a worthy Friend and able Casuist, who says he doubts not but that he shall easily make it appear, even to the Satisfaction of the Printers themselves, that they may be as good Christians,† as useful Neighbors, and as loyal Subjects, altho' they should sometimes feed upon *Beef* and *Pudding*, as they have hitherto approved themselves by their most rigid abstemious way of living.'

In February, 1744, a comet made its appearance and excited much alarm. Fleet on this occasion published the following remarks: 'The Comet now rises about five o'Clock in the Morning, and appears very large and bright, and of late it has been seen (with its lucid Train) in the Day-time, notwithstanding the Luster of the Sun. This uncommon Appearance gives much uneasiness to timorous People, especially *Women*, who will needs have it, that it portends some dreadful Judgments to

---

* It was usual then, and for many years after, for printers, when at work, to wear blue or green cloth aprons; and it would have been well if this practice had not been laid aside.

† Most of the printers in Boston, at that time, were members of the church; to which circumstance Fleet, probably, alluded.

this our Land: And if, from the Apprehension of deserved Judgments, we should be induced to abate of our present Pride and Extravagance, &c., and should become more humble, peaceable and charitable, honest and just, industrious and frugal, there will be Reason to think, that the *Comet* is the most profitable Itinerant Preacher* and friendly *New Light* that has yet appeared among us.'—*Evening Post*, No. 446.

Fleet had often occasion to complain of the delinquency of his customers in making payment for his paper; and in reminding them of their deficiency he sometimes indulged himself in severity of remark, that men of great religious professions and service should neglect to pay him his just demands. One of his dunning advertisements is as follows:

'It will be happy for many People, if Injustice, Extortion and Oppression are found not to be Crimes *at the last*; which seems now by their Practice to be their settled Opinion: And it would be well for the Publisher of this Paper, if a great many of his Customers were not of the same Sentiments. Every one, almost, thinks he has a Right to read News; but few find themselves inclined to pay for it. 'Tis great pity a Soil that will bear *Piety* so well, should not produce a tolerable Crop of Common Honesty.'—*Evening Post*, No. 690, Oct., 1748.

The preceding extracts from the *Evening Post*, are sufficient to enable our readers to form some acquaintance with the publisher of that paper; and, when they consider the time when the extracts were published, they will be the more pleased with his independence of character. Fleet published the *Evening Post* until his death; and his sons continued it till the memorable

---

* Preachers of this class, who with their adherents were vulgarly called *New Lights*, were then frequent in and about Boston.

battle of Lexington, in 1775, the commencement of the revolutionary war, when its publication ceased. He was printer to the house of representatives in 1729, 1730 and 1731. He died in July, 1758, aged seventy-three years; was possessed of a handsome property, and left a widow, three sons, and two daughters. One of the sons, and the two daughters, were never married.

THOMAS CRUMP. The first book I have seen with Crump's name in it, was printed in 1716, by T. Fleet and himself. Fleet and Crump printed several books together, but never, I believe, formed a regular partnership. It seems to have been the custom with master printers in Boston, at that time, when their business was on a very small scale, instead of hiring those who had served a regular apprenticeship at the trade, as journeymen, to admit them as temporary partners in work, and to draw a proportion of the profit. For example, two printers agreed to a joint agency in printing a book, and their names appeared in the imprint; if one of them was destitute of types, he allowed the other for the use of his printing materials, the service of apprentices, &c., and when the book came from the press, the bookseller (most books were then printed for booksellers), paid each of the printers the sum due for his proportion of the work; and the connection ceased until a contract was formed for a new job. This method accounts for a fact of which many have taken notice, viz., books appear to have been printed the same year by T. Fleet and T. Crump, and by T. Fleet separately; and so of others. This was the case with Samuel Green and Marmaduke Johnson, at Cambridge. Their names appear together in the imprint of a book, and in the same year the name of S.

Green appears alone. The same thing took place with Bartholomew Green and John Allen, and with Benjamin Harris and John Allen. Allen's name often appeared with Green's, and sometimes with Harris's; but still oftener the names of Green and Harris appear alone in the books issued from their respective printing houses. I can recollect that, when a lad, I knew several instances of this kind of partnership.

Crump, after his connection with Fleet, printed some books, in which his name only appears in the imprints. He did but little business. I have not seen any thing printed by him after the year 1718.

SAMUEL KNEELAND[12] began business about the year 1718. His printing house was in Prison Lane,* the corner of Dorset's alley. This building was occupied for eighty years as a printing house by Kneeland and those who succeeded him; Kneeland was born in Boston, and served an apprenticeship with Bartholomew Green. He had respectable friends, who, soon after he became of age, furnished him with means to procure printing materials. Kneeland was a good workman, industrious in his business, and punctual to his engagements. Many books issued from his press for himself and for booksellers, before and during his partnership with Timothy Green, the second printer of that name.

William Brooker, being appointed postmaster at Boston, he, on Monday, December 21st, 1719, began the publication of another newspaper in that place. This was the second published in the British colonies, in North America, and was entitled *The Boston Gazette*. James Franklin was originally employed as the printer of this paper; but, in two or three months after the pub-

---

* Now Court street.

lication commenced, Philip Musgrave was appointed post-master, and became the proprietor. He took the printing of it from Franklin, and gave it to Kneeland.

In 1727, a new postmaster became proprietor of the Gazette, and the printer was again changed. Soon after this event, in the same year, Kneeland commenced the publication of a fourth newspaper,* entitled, *The New England Journal*. This was the second newspaper in New England published by a printer on his own account. In four months after the establishment of this paper, Kneeland formed a partnership with Green already mentioned, son of that Timothy Green who, some years before, removed to New London. The firm was KNEELAND & GREEN. When this partnership took place, Kneeland opened a book-shop in King, now State street, on his own account, and Green managed the business of the printing house for their mutual interest. After attending to bookselling, for four or five years, Kneeland gave up his shop, returned to the printing house, and took an active part in all its concerns. They continued the pub-lication of *The New England Journal*, nearly fifteen years; when, on the decease of the proprietor of the *Boston Gazette*, his heirs, for a small consideration, resigned that paper to Kneeland and Green. They united the two papers under the title of *The Boston Gazette*, and *Weekly Journal*.

The partnership of Kneeland and Green was continued for twenty-five years. In 1752, in consequence of the father of Green, in New London, having become aged and infirm, the partnership was dissolved, and Green removed to that place, where he assumed his father's business.[13] The concerns of the

---

* The *New England Courant* had been printed several years before, but at this time was discontinued.

printing house were, after Green went to Connecticut, continued by Kneeland with his accustomed energy. Soon after the dissolution of their partnership, *The Boston Gazette and Weekly Journal* was discontinued; and Kneeland, when a few months had elapsed, began another paper entitled *The Boston Gazette or Weekly Advertiser.*

The booksellers of this time were enterprising. Kneeland and Green printed, principally for Daniel Henchman, an edition of the Bible in small 4to. This was the first Bible printed, in America, in the English language. It was carried through the press as privately as possible, and had the London imprint of the copy from which it was reprinted, viz: 'London: Printed by Mark Baskett, Printer to the King's Most Excellent Majesty,' in order to prevent a prosecution from those in England and Scotland, who published the Bible by a patent from the crown; or, *Cum privilegio*, as did the English universities of Oxford and Cambridge. When I was an apprentice, I often heard those who had assisted at the case and press in printing this Bible, make mention of the fact. The late Governor Hancock was related to Henchman, and knew the particulars of the transaction. He possessed a copy of this impression. As it has a London imprint, at this day it can be distinguished from an English edition, of the same date, only by those who are acquainted with the niceties of typography. This Bible issued from the press about the time that the partnership of Kneeland and Green expired. The edition was not large; I have been informed that it did not exceed seven or eight hundred copies.[14]

An edition of the New Testament, in duodecimo, was printed by Rogers and Fowle, not long before the time when this impression of the Bible came from the press, for those at whose expense it was issued. Both the Bible and the Testament were well executed. These were heavy undertakings for that day, but Henchman was a man of property; and it is said that several other principal booksellers in Boston were concerned with him in this business. The credit of this edition of the Testament was, for the reason I have mentioned, transferred to the king's printer, in London, by the insertion of his imprint.

Kneeland was, for a great length of time, printer to the governor and council, and during several years he printed the acts, laws and journals of the house of representatives. He was diligent, and worked at case when far advanced in years. The books he published were chiefly on religious subjects; he printed some political pamphlets. He was independent in his circumstances; a member of the Old South church; and was a pious, friendly, and benevolent man. He left four sons, all of whom were printers; two of them, Daniel and John, set up a press, in partnership, before their father's death; but the other two never were in business on their own account.

He died December 14, 1769, aged seventy-three years. The following is extracted from the *Evening Post* of December 18, 1769: 'Last Thursday died, after a long indisposition, Mr. Samuel Kneeland, formerly, for many years, an eminent Printer in this Town. He sustained the character of an upright man and a good Christian, and as such was universally esteemed. He continued in business till through age and bodily Infirmities he was obliged to quit it. His Funeral was very respectfully attended on Saturday Evening last.'

JAMES FRANKLIN was the brother of the celebrated Dr. Benjamin Franklin. He was born in Boston, where his father, who

was a respectable man, carried on the business of a tallow
chandler, at the Blue Ball, corner of Union street. With this
brother Dr. Franklin lived several years, as an apprentice, and
learned the art of printing. I have been informed that James
Franklin served an apprenticeship with a printer in England,
where his father was born, and had connections.

In March, $17\frac{16}{17}$,* J. Franklin came from London with a press
and types, and began business in Boston. At first he printed a
few pamphlets for booksellers. In 1719, a postmaster was appointed who established a second newspaper; for until this time
The Boston News-Letter was the only paper which had been
published in British America. The title of the new paper was
The Boston Gazette, and J. Franklin was employed to print it;†

---

* Before the new style took place in 1752, there was much confusion respecting *dates*, particularly in regard to the months of January and February.
Some writers began the year in January, and others in March. The difficulty
was to determine whether January and February closed an old year, or began a
new one. It became necessary to have some mode, by which it might be known
to what year January and February belonged, whenever these months were
mentioned. For this purpose the following method was adopted: During
January, February, and to the 25th of March, the year was thus marked, 1716–
17, or 17 16 /17, meaning that by the ancient mode of calculating, the month
mentioned belonged to the year 1716; but, by the new calculation, to the year
1717. After the 24th of March there was no difficulty; for by both calculations, the suceeding months were included in the new year.

† Dr. Franklin, in writing his life, was incorrect in asserting, that the *Courant*
was the second newspaper published in America. There were three papers
published at that time, viz., first, *The Boston News-Letter*; secondly, *The Boston
Gazette*; and the third was *The American Mercury*, published at Philadelphia; of
course the *Courant* was the fourth. The doctor probably fell into this mistake,
from his knowledge that his brother first printed the *Gazette*, which, in fact,
was the second paper published in Boston. He seems to have mentioned the
events of his youth from recollection only; therefore, we cannot wonder if he
erred in respect to some circumstances of minor importance. In more material
concerns, he was substantially correct.

but, within seven months, Philip Musgrave, being appointed to the post-office, became the proprietor of the *Gazette*, and employed another printer; and Franklin employed his press otherwise until August 6, 1721; when, encouraged by a number of respectable characters, who were desirous of having a paper of a different cast from those then published, he began the publication, at his own risk, of a third newspaper, entitled, *The New England Courant*. Franklin's father and many of his friends were inimical to this undertaking. They supposed that one newspaper was enough for the whole continent; and they apprehended that another must occasion absolute ruin to the printer. Franklin, notwithstanding their remonstrances, continued.

This weekly publication, like the others issued in Boston, contained only a foolscap half sheet, but occasionally was enlarged to a whole sheet. The patrons of the paper formed themselves into a club, and furnished it with short original essays, generally one for each week, in imitation of the *Spectator* and other periodical publications of that class. These essays soon brought the *Courant* into notice; the rigid puritans warmly opposed it; but men of different sentiments supported it. Among others, the Rev. Increase Mather, who was one of Franklin's first subscribers, very soon denounced *The Courant*, by an advertisement in *The Boston Gazette*, No. 114.*

The *Courant* contained very little news, and but few advertisements. It took a decided part against the advocates of inoculation for the small pox, which was then beginning to be introduced: it was hostile to the clergy, and to some of the most influential men in civil government; and, it attacked some of

* For this advertisement, see pp. 235–236.

the religious opinions of the day; in consequence, frequent assaults were made upon its writers; and, in their defence, they abounded more in severe, and not always the most refined, satire, than in argument. While, therefore, the *Courant* gained a currency with one part of the community, it excited the resentment of another, and soon attracted the notice of government.

Franklin had not published *The New England Courant* twelve months, before he was taken into custody, publicly censured, and imprisoned four weeks, by the government, for publishing what were called scandalous libels, &c.*

Being released from his confinement, he continued the publication of the *Courant* until January 14, 1723, when an order of council, in which the house of representatives concurred, directed, 'That James Franklin be strictly forbidden by this Court to Print or Publish the *New England Courant*, or any Pamphlet or Paper of the like Nature, except it be first supervised by the Secretary of this Province.'† This order, this stride of despotism, could, it seems, at that time, be carried into effect; but, at this day, a similar attempt would excite indignation, or a contemptuous smile.

Franklin was not inclined to subject his paper to licensers of the press, and he was unwilling to stop the publication of it; but, he dared not proceed in defiance of the order of the legislature. The club wished for the continuance of the paper; and, a consultation on the subject was held in Franklin's printing house, the result of which was, that to evade the order of the legislature, the

* See resolve of council, July 5th, 1722, p. 237.
† For this act of the legislature, see pp. 238–240.

New England Courant should, in future, be published by Benjamin Franklin, then an apprentice to James. Accordingly, the next *Courant* had the following imprint: 'Boston, printed and sold by Benjamin Franklin, in Queen Street, where advertisements are taken in.' About a year afterward, J. Franklin removed his printing house to Union street. The *Courant* was published in the name of Benjamin Franklin, for more than three years; and, probably, until its publication ceased; but it appears from Dr. Franklin's life, that he did not remain for a long time with his brother after the *Courant* began to be printed in his name.

In the Life of Dr. Franklin, written by himself, little attention seems to have been paid to dates, particularly in narrating events which took place during his minority. He informs us that he was born in Boston, but does not mention the month nor the year; he, however, observes,* that his brother returned from England in 1717, with a press and types; and, that his father determined to make him a printer, and was anxious that he should be fixed with his brother. He also observes, that he himself held back for some time, but suffered himself to be persuaded, and signed his indentures. By the manner in which he mentions these circumstances, we may suppose that they took place within a short period, and as soon as his brother began business, which was within a few weeks after he returned from London. The doctor mentions that when he signed his indentures, he was only *twelve* years of age; this was in 1717. The New-England *Courant* was not published till August, 1721; at this time Benjamin Franklin must have been in his seventeenth year. The first *Courant* published by Benjamin Franklin,

* In *The Private Life of the Late Benjamin Franklin* (London, 1793), p. 29.

after his brother was ordered to print it no longer, is No. 80, dated February 11, 1723; of course Benjamin must then have been advanced in his eighteenth year. I have seen a file of the *Courant* from the time it began to be published in the name of Benjamin Franklin to the middle of the year 1726,* the whole of which was published in the name of Benjamin Franklin. The doctor does not mention how long the paper was published in his name; he only says that it was for 'some months.' From the doctor's manner of relating this part of his history, we may conclude that he did not leave his brother short of one year after the *Courant* was printed in his, Benjamin's name; and, if so, he must have been nearly nineteen years of age; but, if he remained with his brother till the year 1726, he would then have been twenty-one years old. Yet he states, page 53, that after he left his brother, 'he found himself at New York, nearly three hundred miles from his home, at the age only of *seventeen* years.' It is evident from the doctor's account of himself after he left his brother, that he did not remain with him so long as the *Courant* was published in the name of Benjamin Franklin; for he gives an account of his return to Boston, remaining there some time, his going again to Philadelphia, working with Keimer, and afterward making a voyage to London, where he was near two years a journeyman, and returning back to America, and again arriving in Philadelphia in October, 1726. It is difficult to reconcile all these events with the few dates which the doctor has mentioned. But I leave them with those who are inclined to make further investigation.

J. Franklin remained in Boston for several years. He continued to publish the *Courant*, and printed several small works.

---

* This file is in the Massachusetts Historical Society Library at Boston.

He had a brother, by the name of John, who was married and settled at Newport in the business of a tallow chandler. Not satisfied with his situation in Boston, and receiving an invitation from his brother and other persons in Rhode Island, he removed to Newport, and set up the first printing press in that colony; and, in the latter part of September, 1732, he published the first number of *The Rhode Island Gazette*.

James Franklin had learned, in England, the art of calico printing, and did something at the business, both in Boston and Newport. The *Boston Gazette* of April 25, 1720, then printed by him for the postmaster, contains the following advertisement: 'The Printer hereof prints Linens, Calicoes, Silks, &c., in good Figures, very lively and durable colours, and without the offensive smell which commonly attends the Linens printed here.'[15]

BENJAMIN FRANKLIN. Well known and highly celebrated in this country and in Europe, was born in Boston, January 17th, 170$\frac{5}{6}$. His father was an Englishman, and served an apprenticeship with a silk dyer in Northamptonshire.[16] He came to Boston with his wife and three children; and, after his arrival in America, he had four other children by the same wife. She dying, he married a native of New England, by whom he had ten children; two daughters excepted, Benjamin was the youngest child by the second wife.*

Franklin's father settled in Boston; but, finding the business to which he had been bred insufficient to afford him a maintenance, he relinquished it, and assumed that of a soap boiler

---

* Franklin's *Life*, first London edition, 12mo, from which I have taken most of the particulars respecting him.

and tallow chandler, in which occupations Benjamin was employed from the tenth to the twelfth year of his life.

Franklin was dissatisfied with the business of his father, and felt a strong inclination for a seafaring life. His father was extremely averse to that plan, and through fear that Benjamin might, in a clandestine manner, get to sea, he concluded to bind him apprentice to his nephew, who was settled in Boston, as a cutler; but not agreeing with his nephew on conditions, and Benjamin expressing a wish to be a printer, his father consented to gratify this inclination. At this time, 1717, James Franklin returned from England with printing materials, and commenced business in Boston; and Benjamin, at the age of twelve years, signed indentures, and became his apprentice.

Pleased with his new employment, Franklin soon became useful to his brother. He borrowed books, and read them with avidity and profit. At an early age, he wrote stanzas on the capture of Black Beard, a noted pirate, and on other occurrences. These verses, he observes, 'were miserable ditties,' but his brother printed them, and sent Benjamin about the town to sell them. One of these compositions, he remarks, 'had a prodigious run, because the event was recent, and had made a great noise.'

When his brother printed a newspaper, Benjamin felt increased satisfaction with his business; and he soon began, privately, to compose short essays, which he artfully introduced for publication without exciting suspicion of his being the author. These were examined and approved by the club of writers for the *Courant*, to the great gratification of the writer, who eventually made himself known.

It has already been stated, in the account given of James

Franklin, that he was forbidden by the General court to proceed in the publication of the *Courant*, except on certain conditions. With the terms dictated James determined that he would not comply; and, with a view to evade the injunctions of the government, the name of his brother Benjamin was substituted in the place of his own, and the publication was continued. 'To avoid the censure of the General assembly, who might charge James Franklin with still printing the paper under the name of his apprentice, it was resolved that Benjamin's indentures should be given up to him, with a full and entire discharge written on the back, in order to be produced on any emergency; but that to secure to James the service of Benjamin, it was agreed the latter should sign a new contract, which should be kept secret during the remainder of the term.' This, Benjamin observes, in his Life, was a very shallow arrangement, but it was put into immediate execution. Though the paper was still issued in Benjamin's name, he did not remain with his brother long after this arrangement was made. They disagreed, and in the eighteenth year of his age he privately quitted James, and took passage in a vessel for New York. At this time there was but one printer in New York, and from him Franklin could obtain no employment; but he gave our adventurer encouragement, that his son, who printed in Philadelphia, would furnish him with work. In pursuit of this object, he entered a ferry boat on his way to Philadelphia; and, after a very disagreeable passage, reached Amboy. From that place he traveled on foot to Burlington, where he was hospitably entertained, for several days, by an aged woman who sold gingerbread. When an opportunity presented to take passage in a boat, he embraced it, and reached Philadelphia in safety.

As Franklin afterwards obtained the highest offices in civil
government, and was greatly celebrated as a statesman and a
philosopher, the particulars of this apparently inauspicious period of his life are singularly interesting; I will, therefore, give his
own narrative of his entrance into the capital of Pennsylvania,
of which he was destined to become the governor.

'On my arrival at Philadelphia, I was in my working dress,
my best clothes being to come by sea. I was covered with dirt;
my pockets were filled with shirts and stockings; I was unacquainted with a single soul in the place, and knew not where
to seek for a lodging. Fatigued with walking, rowing, and
having past the night without sleep, I was extremely hungry,
and all my money consisted of a Dutch dollar, and about a
shilling's worth of coppers, which I gave to the boatmen for my
passage. As I had assisted them in rowing, they refused it at first;
but I insisted on their taking it. A man is sometimes more generous when he has little, than when he has much money; probably because in the first case he is desirous of concealing his
poverty. I walked towards the top of the street, looking eagerly
on both sides, till I came to Market street, where I met a child
with a loaf of bread. Often had I made my dinner on dry bread.
I enquired where he had bought it, and went straight to the
baker's shop, which he pointed out to me. I asked for some
biscuits, expecting to find such as we had at Boston; but they
made, it seems, none of that sort in Philadelphia. I then asked
for a threepenny loaf. They made no loaves of that price. Finding myself ignorant of the prices, as well as the different kinds
of bread, I desired him to let me have three penny worth of
bread of some kind or other. He gave me three large rolls. I was
surprized at receiving so much; I took them, however, and

having no room in my pockets, I walked on with a roll under each arm, eating the third. In this manner I went through Market street to Fourth street, and passed the house of Mr. Read, the father of my future wife. She was standing at the door, observed me, and thought, with reason, that I made a very singular and grotesque appearance.

'I then turned the corner, and went through Chestnut street, eating my roll all the way; and, having made this round, I found myself again on Market street wharf, near the boat in which I had arrived. I stepped into it to take a draught of the river water; and, finding myself satisfied with my first roll, I gave the other two to a woman and her child, who had come down the river with us in the boat, and was waiting to continue her journey. Thus refreshed, I regained the street, which was now full of well dressed people, all going the same way. I joined them, and was thus led to a large Quaker's meeting-house, near the market place. I sat down with the rest, and after looking round me for some time, hearing nothing said, and being drowsy from my last night's labor and want of rest, I fell into a sound sleep. In this state I continued till the assembly dispersed, when one of the congregation had the goodness to wake me. This was consequently the first house I entered, or in which I slept, at Philadelphia.

'I began again to walk along the street by the river side, and looking attentively in the face of every one I met, I at length perceived a young quaker, whose countenance pleased me. I accosted him, and begged him to inform me where a stranger might find a lodging. We were then near the sign of the Three Mariners. They receive travellers here, said he, but it is not a house that bears a good character; if you will go with me I will

shew you a better one. He conducted me to the Crooked Billet,
in Water street. There I ordered something for dinner, and
during my meal a number of curious questions were put to me;
my youth and appearance exciting the suspicion that I was a
runaway. After dinner my drowsiness returned, and I threw
myself on a bed without taking off my clothes, and slept till
six o'clock in the evening, when I was called to supper. I afterward went to bed at a very early hour, and did not awake till the
next morning.

'As soon as I got up I put myself in as decent a trim as I could,
and went to the house of Andrew Bradford the printer. I found
his father in the shop, whom I had seen at New York. Having
travelled on horseback, he had arrived at Philadelphia before
me. He introduced me to his son, who received me with civility,
and gave me some breakfast; but told me he had no occasion at
present for a journeyman, having lately procured one. He added, that there was another printer newly settled in the town, of
the name of Keimer, who might, perhaps, employ me; and,
that in case of a refusal, I should be welcome to lodge at his
house, and he would give me a little work now and then, till
something better should offer.

'The old man offered to introduce me to the new printer.
When we were at his house, "Neighbor," said he, "I bring you
a young man in the printing business; perhaps you may have
need of his services." Keimer asked me some questions, put a
composing stick in my hand to see how I could work, and then
said, that at present he had nothing for me to do, but that he
should soon be able to employ me. At the same time, taking old
Bradford for an inhabitant of the town well disposed towards
him, he communicated his project to him, and the prospect he

had of success. Bradford was careful not to betray that he was the father of the other printer; and from what Keimer had said, that he hoped shortly to be in possession of the greater part of the business of the town, led him by artful questions, and by starting some difficulties, to disclose all his views, what his hopes were founded upon, and how he intended to proceed. I was present, and heard it all. I instantly saw that one of the two was a cunning old fox, and the other a perfect novice. Bradford left me with Keimer, who was strangely surprized when I informed him who the old man was.'

Keimer encouraged Franklin with the hope of employment in a short time, and he returned to Bradford's. In a few days after he began to work for Keimer, but continued to board with Bradford. This was not agreeable to Keimer, and he procured a lodging for him at Mr. Read's, who has been already mentioned. 'My trunk and effects being now arrived,' says Franklin, 'I thought of making, in the eyes of Miss Read, a more respectable appearance, than when chance exhibited me to her view, eating my rolls and wandering in the streets.'

Franklin remained about seven months in Philadelphia, worked for Keimer, and formed many acquaintances, some of them very respectable. Accident procured him an interview with Governor William Keith, who made him great promises of friendship and patronage; persuaded him to visit his father, which he accordingly did, and was bearer of a letter the governor wrote to him, mentioning the son in the most flattering terms; and recommending his establishment as a printer at Philadelphia, under assurances of success. Franklin was at this time only in the nineteenth year of his age, and his father declined to assist in establishing him in business on account of his

youth and inexperience; but he answered Governor Keith's
letter, thanking him for the attention and patronage he had
exercised toward his son. Franklin determined to return to Philadelphia. At New York, on his way, he received some atten-
tions from the governor of that colony.* On his arrival at Philadelphia he presented his father's letter to Governor Keith. The
governor disapproved of the caution of his father; still urged
the prosecution of the scheme; promised himself to be at all the
expense of procuring printing materials; and advised Franklin
to make a voyage to England, and select the types, under his own
eye, at the foundery. To this plan Franklin agreed, and it was
settled that the design should be kept secret, until an opportunity presented for his taking passage for London. In the
meantime he continued to work for Keimer.

When a vessel was about to sail, the governor promised from
day to day to give Franklin letters of credit upon his correspondent in London; and, when he was called on board ship, the
governor told him that he would send his letters to him on
board. At the moment of sailing, letters were brought from the
governor and put into the ship's letter bag; among which Franklin supposed were those that had been promised him. But when
he reached his port, he found, on investigation, that he had
neither letters of credit nor introduction. The governor had
deceived him, and he landed a stranger in a strange country.

Destitute and friendless, Franklin's only means of support
consisted in his capacity to labor. He immediately applied to a
printer for employment as a journeyman, and obtained it. In
this situation, he continued for eighteen months and gained
much knowledge in the art of printing. He then formed a con-

* William Burnet, who was soon after governor of Massachusetts.

nection with a mercantile friend, whom he assisted as a clerk; and, with him, he returned to Philadelphia. This friend soon died, and Franklin relinquished the plan of mercantile pursuits. He returned to the business of a printer as a journeyman; but, soon after, opened a printing house of his own in Philadelphia.

TIMOTHY GREEN, JUN. He was the son of Timothy Green, who removed from Boston to New London in 1714; and great grandson of Samuel Green, of Cambridge. I have seen no printing with his name before 1726. One or two pamphlets were then printed by S. Kneeland and T. Green. Several small publications appeared afterwards with Kneeland's name only. In 1727, a regular partnership took place between them, under the firm of S. Kneeland & T. Green. This partnership, as has been mentioned, continued till 1752, when he removed to New London, and succeeded his father.

BARTHOLOMEW GREEN, JUN., was the son of Bartholomew Green, printer of *The Boston News-Letter*, grandson to Samuel Green, who printed at Cambridge, and served an apprenticeship with his father. The earliest works I have seen printed by Bartholomew Green, Jun., are, a small book published in 1726, and the *Boston Gazette*, for the postmaster, Henry Marshall, in 1727.

He made use of his press and types in the printing house of his father, till 1734; and was, occasionally, connected with John Draper, his brother-in-law, in printing pamphlets, etc. Draper succeeded to the business of B. Green the elder in 1732, in the same house. On the night of the 30th of January, 1734, this house, with the greatest part of its contents, was destroyed by

fire. After this misfortune, B. Green, Jr., formed a copartnership with John Bushell and Bezoune Allen.[17] The firm of
this company was GREEN, BUSHELL & ALLEN. They printed
a number of small books for the trade, which were very well
executed. They used handsome types, and printed on good
paper. How long this partnership continued, I cannot say; it was
dissolved before 1751.

In September, 1751, Green with his printing materials removed to Halifax, Nova Scotia, intending to establish a press
in that place; but he died in about five weeks after his arrival
there, at the age of fifty-two years. On his decease, his late
partner Bushell went to Halifax, and commenced business with
Green's press.

Green left several children, and two of his sons were printers.
Bartholomew, the eldest of them, never had a press of his own.
The following peculiarity in his character introduced him to a
particular intercourse with the merchants of the town; he made
himself so well acquainted with every vessel which sailed out of
the port of Boston, as to know each at sight. Perpetually on the
watch, as soon as a vessel could be discovered with a spyglass in
the harbor, he knew it, and gave immediate information to the
owner; and, by the small fees for this kind of information, he
principally maintained himself for several years. Afterwards he
had some office in the custom house. John, another son, will be
mentioned hereafter. One of the daughters of Green was the
mother of Mr. Joseph Dennie, formerly editor of *The Farmer's
Museum*, at Walpole, New Hampshire, and also of *The Port
Folio*, published at Philadelphia. Mr. Dennie was reckoned
among the first scholars in the belles-lettres, which our country
has produced.

GAMALIEL ROGERS served his apprenticeship with Bartholomew Green the elder. About the year 1729, he began business in a printing house near the Mill Bridge. He printed for the booksellers. In 1742, he commenced a partnership with Daniel Fowle, under the firm of ROGERS & FOWLE. They opened a printing house in Prison lane, for some time called Queen street, and now named Court street. For those times they entered largely into business, and the books they printed, in magnitude and variety, exceeded the usual works of the country. A number of octavo and duodecimo volumes issued from their house; and their printing was executed with accuracy and neatness. Several of these books were printed on their own account.

In 1743, they issued *The American Magazine*. It was published in numbers, monthly, printed in a handsome manner, and in its execution was deemed equal to any work of the kind then published in London. Several respectable booksellers were interested in this magazine. It was continued for three years.

In the beginning of the year 1748, they commenced the publication of a newspaper entitled *The Independent Advertiser*. A number of able writers supported and enlivened this publication. Its prominent features were political. In 1750, they closed the business of the firm, and the *Independent Advertiser* was then discontinued.

During the partnership of Rogers and Fowle, they printed an edition of about two thousand copies of the New Testament, 12mo, for D. Henchman and two or three other principal booksellers, as has been already observed. This impression of the Testament, the first in the English language printed in this country, was, as I have been informed, completed at the press before Kneeland and Green began the edition of the Bible

which has been mentioned. Zechariah Fowle, with whom I
served my apprenticeship, as well as several others, repeatedly
mentioned to me this edition of the Testament. He was, at the
time, a journeyman with Rogers and Fowle, and worked at the
press. He informed me that, on account of the weakness of his
constitution, he greatly injured his health by the performance.
Privacy in the business was necessary; and as few hands were
intrusted with the secret, the press work was, as he thought,
very laborious. I mention these minute circumstances in proof
that an edition of the Testament did issue from the office of
Rogers and Fowle, because I have heard that the fact has been
disputed.

Rogers and Fowle were correct printers. They used good
types, paper, and excellent ink of their own manufacture. They
were the only printers, I believe, who at that time could make
good ink. The printing ink used in this country, until later, was
chiefly imported from Europe. In the first stages of printing,
printers made their own ink and types; but the manufacture of
types and ink soon became separate branches of business. Most
of the bad printing in the United States, particularly in New
England, during the revolutionary war, was occasioned by the
wretched ink, and more wretched paper, which printers were
then under the necessity of using.

After the dissolution of the partnership of Rogers and Fowle,
Rogers removed to the west part of the town, then called New
Boston; and there opened a printing house. For two or three
years he did a little business in this place, when his printing house
was, unfortunately, burnt down. By this accident he was deprived of his press, and the principal part of his types. Having
lost most of his property, he did no more business as a printer.

His spirits were broken, and he appeared dejected. At an advanced period of life he opened a small shop opposite to the Old South church, where he supported his family by retailing ardent spirits in small quantities, trifling articles of grocery, and by vending a few pamphlets, the remnant of his stock. I went myself frequently to his shop, when a minor. He knew that I lived with a printer, and for this, or some other reason, was very kind to me; he gave me some books of his printing, and, what was of more value to me, good advice. He admonished me diligently to attend to my business, that I might become a reputable printer. I held him in high veneration, and often recollected his instructions, which, on many occasions, proved beneficial to me.

Rogers was industrious, and an excellent workman; an amiable, sensible man, and a good Christian. In 1775, soon after the battle at Bunker's hill, when Boston was wholly in possession of the British troops, and besieged by the provincials, Rogers was among a number of the infirm and invalid inhabitants of that town who obtained permission from the British general to leave it. He sought an asylum at Ipswich; removed there, and died at that place in the autumn of that year, aged 70. He left several daughters but no sons; two of his daughters married clergymen; one of them was the wife of the Rev. Elijah Parsons of East Haddam, in Connecticut, and the other the second wife of the Reverend Mr. Dana of Ipswich.

JOHN DRAPER,[18] was the son of Richard Draper, a trader in Boston. He served his apprenticeship with Bartholomew Green, Sen., whose daughter he married; and, at the decease of his father-in-law, occupied his printing house in Newbury street.

In September, 1731, Draper commenced the publication of a political paper, entitled *The Weekly Rehearsal*. It was printed, according to the custom of those times, on a half sheet of small paper; and was carried on at the expense of some gentlemen who formed themselves into a political or literary club, and wrote for it. At the head of this club was the late celebrated Jeremy Gridley, Esq.,* who was the real editor of the paper. The receipts for the *Rehearsal* never amounted to more than enough to defray the expense of publication. Draper printed this paper only about a year and a half, and at the expiration of about four years it was discontinued.

On the 28th of December, 1732, Bartholomew Green died, and Draper succeeded him in his business; particularly as publisher of *The Boston Weekly News-Letter*. In 1734, he printed the laws of the province. He was afterward appointed printer to the governor and council, and was honored with that mark of confidence and favor as long as he lived.

Draper not only succeeded Bartholomew Green in his business, but he was heir to his calamities also. On the night of the 30th of January, 1734, the flames were seen to burst from his printing house, but too late for any effectual assistance to be afforded. The fire had kindled in the interior part of the building, which was burnt to the ground, and nearly the whole of the printing materials were destroyed. This loss was in some measure repaired by the friendship of his brethren of the type, who loaned to him a press, and several founts of letters, till he could replace those articles by a new printing apparatus from England.

* Mr. Gridley was afterward attorney general of the province of Massachusetts, grand master of the society of free masons, president of the marine society, and a member of the general court. He died in September, 1767.

He printed a number of books for the trade; but published only a few small pamphlets for his own sales. He annually printed Ames's famous Almanac, for himself and for booksellers; of which about sixty thousand copies were annually sold in the New England colonies.

Draper owned the house in which he resided. It was in Cornhill, the east corner of the short alley leading to the church in Brattle street. He was an industrious and useful member of society, and was held in estimation by his friends and acquaintances. He died November 29th, 1762, and was succeeded in business by his son.

The following character of Draper is extracted from the *Boston Evening Post* of December 6, 1762:

'On Monday Evening last departed this Life after a slow and hectic Disorder, having just entered the 61st Year of his Age, Mr. John Draper, Printer, who for a long Time has been the Publisher of a News-Paper in this Town; and by his Industry, Fidelity and Prudence in his Business, rendered himself very agreeable to the Public. His Charity and Benevolence; his pleasant and sociable Turn of Mind; his tender Affection as a Husband and Parent; his Piety and Devotion to his Maker, has made his Death as sensibly felt by his Friends and Relations, as his Life is worthy Imitation.'*

JOHN BUSHELL was born in Boston, where he served an apprenticeship. He began business about the year 1734; and, as I have been informed, printed *The Boston Weekly Post Boy*, during a short period, for Ellis Huske, postmaster. He was afterward of the firm of Green, Bushell & Allen. They did but little

* See *Historical Magazine*, 2d ser., VII, 219 (1870).

business while together, and the connection was dissolved about 1750. Upon the termination of the partnership, Green, as has been mentioned, removed to Halifax, Nova Scotia; and, as he died a few weeks after his arrival, Bushell went to Halifax, and with Green's apparatus established a press in that place. He was the first who printed in that province.

BEZOUNE ALLEN was, probably, the son of John Allen. He entered on business, according to report, about the year 1734; and was, for several years, of the firm of Green, Bushell and Allen. This copartnership was formed, I believe, in 1736. I have seen books printed by them as late as 1745; but I have not discovered that any thing was printed by Allen separately. They never were in extensive business; and what they did consisted, principally, of small works for the booksellers.

JONAS GREEN was the son of the elder Timothy Green, who removed from Boston and settled at New London in 1714, and great-grandson of Samuel Green, printer at Cambridge. He was born at Boston, and served his apprenticeship with his father in New London. When of age, he came to Boston, and was several years in the printing house of his brother, who was then the partner of S. Kneeland.

I have seen but one book printed by Jonas Green in Boston, viz.: A *Grammar of the Hebrew Tongue*, by Judah Monis, professor of the Hebrew language, at Harvard College, in Cambridge, Massachusetts. Good judges pronounced this work to be correctly printed. I have seen a copy of it in the theological library in Boston, where the original manuscript is preserved. The Hebrew types were a cast belonging to the college, which have since been used in printing Professor Sewall's *Hebrew Grammar*, and I suppose are now in the museum of the University.

Green resided several years in Philadelphia; and during that time was employed in the printing houses of Bradford and Franklin.

In 1739, as there was not a printer in Maryland, the legislature of that province employed an agent to procure one. Green, being well recommended by his employers, made application to the agent, and obtained the place of printer to that government. In consequence of the liberal encouragement he received, he opened a printing house at Annapolis in 1740.

EBENEZER LOVE. I have not been able to obtain much information respecting Love. He was born in, or near Boston, and served his apprenticeship in that town. I have seen nothing of his printing; but he was known in Boston as a printer; indeed, I recollect, myself, that, when a lad, I heard mention made of him; but I cannot ascertain that he was at any time actively engaged in the printing business.

In *The Boston Evening Post* of May 14th, 1770, under the Boston head, is the following paragraph, viz.: 'We hear from New Providence, that on the 23d of January last, died there after a few days illness of a Bilious Cholic, Ebenezer Love, Esq., formerly of this town, Printer. For a number of years past he had resided at that Island, and carried on Merchandize; was well esteemed by the Gentlemen there, and elected a member of their House of Assembly.'

DANIEL FOWLE was born in Charlestown,[19] near Boston, and served his apprenticeship with Samuel Kneeland. He began

printing, on his own account, in 1740, 'north side of King street,
opposite the town house.' In 1742, he, and Gamaliel Rogers,
formed a partnership in business, under the firm of Rogers &
Fowle.* A brother of Fowle, named John, was a silent partner
in this firm. They opened a printing house in Prison lane, the
house next but one to the old stone jail, where the court house
now (in 1815) stands. In the account given of Rogers, I have
mentioned the works done by this company; and particularly,
the New Testament, the American Magazine, and the newspaper, entitled *The Independent Advertiser*. In taking notice of
Fowle, therefore, I shall begin with the period at which the
partnership was dissolved, that is, in 1750. Soon after that event,
Fowle opened a printing house on the south side of Anne street,
not far from the Flat conduit, so called, which at that time stood
in Union street. At the same place he also opened a shop, and
kept a small collection of books for sale. Here he printed a
number of works, chiefly pamphlets, most of which were for
his own sales.

In October, 1754, Fowle, while at dinner, was arrested, by
virtue of an order of the house of representatives, signed by
Thomas Hubbard, their speaker, and taken before that house,
on *suspicion* of having printed a pamphlet which reflected upon
some of the members. It was entitled, *The Monster of Monsters*,
by Tom Thumb, Esq. After an hour's confinement in the lobby,
he was brought before the house. The speaker, holding a copy
of the pamphlet in his hand, asked him, 'Do you know any
thing of the printing of this Book?' Fowle requested to see it;
and it was given him. After examination, he said that it was not
of his printing; and that he had not such types in his printing

* See Rogers and Fowle, pp. 120–121.

house. The speaker then asked, 'Do you know any thing relating to the said Book?' Fowle requested the decision of the house, whether he was bound to answer the question. No vote was taken, but a few members answered, 'Yes!' He then observed, that he had 'bought some copies, and had sold them at his shop.' This observation occasioned the following questions and answers, viz:*

Question. [By the speaker.] Who did you buy them of?

Answer. They were, I believe, sent by a young man, but I cannot tell his name.

Q. Who did he live with?

[Fowle again desired the decision of the house, whether he was obliged to give the required information, and a number of individual members again replied, 'Yes!' Upon which Fowle answered]

The young man, I believe, lives with Royall Tyler.

Q. Did you have any conversation with him [Tyler] about them?

A. I believe I might, in the same manner I had with many others; not that I thought him the author. It was never offered me to print.

Q. Did any of your hands assist in doing it?

A. I believe my negro might, as he sometimes worked for my brother.†

---

* Vide *A Total Eclipse of Liberty* (Boston, 1775), a pamphlet written and published by D. Fowle, containing a full account of this arbitrary procedure.

† This negro was named Primus. He was an African. I well remember him; he worked at press with or without an assistant; he continued to do press work until prevented by age. He went to Portsmouth with his master, and there died, being more than ninety years of age; about fifty of which he was a pressman. There is now [1815] in Philadelphia, a negro pressman named Andrew Cain, but now unable to do hard labor. He is ninety-four years old. It is said that he has been a good workman.

Q. Has your brother any help?

A. No.

Q. Did you see any of it whilst printing?

A. Yes.

Q. Whose house was it in?

A. I think it was my brother's.

Q. Where does he live?

A. Down by Cross street.

Q. What is his name?

A. Zechariah.

One of the members then said to Fowle, *You do not know when you lie!* Fowle replied, 'Begging your pardon, sir, I know when I lie, and what a lie is as well as yourself.'

After this examination, Fowle was again confined for several hours in the lobby; and from thence, about ten o'clock at night, was, by order of the house, taken to the 'common gaol,' and there closely confined 'among thieves and murderers.'* He was denied the sight of his wife, although she, with tears, petitioned to see him; no friend was permitted to speak to him; and he was debarred from the use of pen, ink and paper.

Royall Tyler, Esq., was arrested, and carried before the house. When interrogated, he claimed the right of silence, '*Nemo tenetur seipsum accusare,*' was the only answer he made. He was committed for contempt; but was soon released, on a promise that he would be forthcoming when required.

The house ordered their messenger to take Fowle's brother Zechariah into custody, with some others; but his physician

---

* Fowle was confined in the same room with a thief and a notorious cheat; and, in the next cell, was one Wyer, then under sentence of death for murder, and was soon after executed. [Vide Fowle's *Total Eclipse of Liberty.*]

gave a certificate of his indisposition, and by this means he escaped imprisonment.

After two days close confinement, Fowle was taken to the keeper's house, and told that '*He might go!*' but he refused; observing, that as he was confined at midnight uncondemned by the law, he desired that the authority which confined, should liberate him, and not *thrust him out privily*. He remained with the jailer three days longer; when learning from a respectable physician, that his wife was seriously indisposed, that her life was endangered by her anxiety on account of his confinement, and his friends joining their persuasion to this call upon his tenderness, Fowle was induced to ask for his liberation. He was accordingly dismissed; and here the prosecution ended. He endeavored to obtain some satisfaction for the deprivation of his liberty, but he did not succeed in the attempt.

Disgusted with the government of Massachusetts by this treatment, and being invited by a number of respectable gentlemen in New Hampshire to remove into that colony, he accepted their invitation; and, at the close of the following year, established his press at Portsmouth. He was the first printer who settled in that province; and, in 1756, he began the publication of *The New Hampshire Gazette*.[20]

Fowle was, I believe, the third person whom the legislature of Massachusetts imprisoned for printing what was deemed a libel on that body, or on some of its members, or for publishing heretical opinions, &c.

Living in the family of Daniel Fowle's brother, I early became minutely acquainted with the whole transaction, and deep impressions were then made upon my mind in favor of the liberty of the press. For this liberty I am now an advocate, but I

still, as I ever did, hold the opinion, that a line should be drawn
between the liberty and the licentiousness of the press.

ZECHARIAH FOWLE. He was born at Charlestown, near Boston, of very respectable parents, and served his apprenticeship
with his brother Daniel, who was at that period in partnership
with Gamaliel Rogers. The first book which bears the name of
Z. Fowle as printer, was begun by Rogers and Fowle, viz., John
Pomfret's *Poems on Several Occasions* (1751), on a new small
pica. On the dissolution of that firm, they assigned this book
over to Z. Fowle, who completed it, and sold the greater part of
the copies, in sheets, to booksellers. He soon after opened a
printing house, and a small shop, in Middle street, near Cross
street, where he printed and sold ballads and small pamphlets.

Not being much known as a printer, and living in a street
where but little business was transacted, he was selected by a
number of gentlemen, who were in opposition to the measures
of the general court, and particularly to an excise act, to print a
pamphlet entitled, *The Monster of Monsters* (July 1754), satirizing this act, and bearing with some severity upon individual
members of the court. Daniel was prevailed upon to assist his
brother in carrying this work through the press. Joseph Russell,
his apprentice, then nearly of age, worked at the case, and a
negro man at the press. The pamphlet was small, and appeared
without the name of the printer. It was the custom of that day to
hawk about the streets every new publication. Select hawkers
were engaged to sell this work; and were directed what answers
to give to enquiries into its origin, who printed it, &c. The general court was at the time in session. The hawkers appeared on
the Exchange with the pamphlet, bawling out, '*The Monster of*

Monsters!' Curiosity was roused, and the book sold. The purchasers inquired of the hawkers, where the Monster came from? all the reply was, *'It dropped from the moon!'* Several members of the general court bought the pamphlet. Its contents soon excited the attention of the house. Daniel Fowle, who was suspected to be the printer, was brought before the house of representatives and examined, as has been observed.* Z. Fowle was then ordered into custody, and Russell who assisted him. Russell was brought before the house, examined and released. Z. Fowle hearing that his brother and Russell were arrested, and that the officer was in search of him, was instantly seized with a violent fit of the cholic. His illness was not feigned; he possessed a slender constitution, was often subject to this complaint; and, at this time, it was brought on by the fear of an arrest. When the officer appeared, the attending physician certified that he was dangerously ill. With this certificate the officer departed, and Fowle escaped punishment, the punishment which his brother unjustly experienced.

When Daniel Fowle removed to Portsmouth, Zechariah took the printing house which he had occupied, in Anne street. Until the year 1757, Z. Fowle printed little else than ballads; he then began an edition of the Psalter for the booksellers. In this work he was aided by two young printers just freed from their indentures, and to whom Fowle allowed a proportionate part of the profits of the impression. One of these, Samuel Draper, a very worthy young man, became a partner with Fowle after the Psalter was printed. The firm was FOWLE & DRAPER. They took a house in Marlborough street, opposite the Founder's Arms; here they printed, and opened a shop. They kept a great

* Vide Daniel Fowle, pp. 128–130.

supply of ballads, and small pamphlets for book pedlers, of
whom there were many at that time. They printed several
works of higher consequence, viz.: an edition consisting of
twenty thousand copies of *The Youth's Instructor in the English*
Tongue, commonly called the New England Spelling Book.
This school book was in great repute, and in general use for many
years. Janeway's *Heaven upon Earth* (1750), octavo, Watts's
Hymns and Spiritual Songs (1752), and several smaller duodecimo volumes, all for the trade. They printed, also, many pamphlets of various sizes on their own account; and had full employment for themselves and two lads. Draper was a diligent man,
and gave unremitted attendance in the printing house. Fowle
was bred to the business, but he was an indifferent hand at the
press, and much worse at the case. He was never in the printing
house when he could find a pretence for being absent.

After the death of John Draper, Richard, his son, took his
kinsman Samuel as a partner, and Fowle again printed by
himself. The business in his printing house was then principally
managed by a young lad, his only apprentice. Soon after he
separated from Draper, he removed to Back street, where he
continued printing and vending ballads and small books until
1770; at which time Isaiah Thomas became his partner. This
connection was dissolved in less than three months, and Thomas
purchased his press and types.

Fowle having on hand a considerable stock of the small articles he usually sold, continued his shop till 1775. Boston being
then a garrison town in the possession of the British troops, he
obtained a permit to leave it, and removed to Portsmouth,
New Hampshire. While in this place he resided with his brother, and died in his house in 1776.

Fowle was a singular man, very irritable and effeminate, and better skilled in the domestic work of females, than in the business of a printing house. His first wife dying in 1759, he married a second; but had no children by either. Fowle could not be called an industrious man; yet, in justice to his character, it ought to be mentioned, that he did business enough to give himself and family a decent maintenance. Although he did not acquire property, he took care not to be involved in debt. He was honest in his dealings, and punctual to his engagements.

BENJAMIN EDES was born in Charlestown, Oct. 14, 1732.[21] He began business with John Gill, in the year 1755, under the firm of EDES & GILL. They continued in partnership until the commencement of the revolutionary war. Their printing house, for a time, was in King street, now State street; they afterward occupied the printing house formerly kept by Rogers and Fowle, then the second house west of the Court House in Court street. After the death of Samuel Kneeland, they removed to the printing house which he, for about forty years, occupied, and there they remained until hostilities commenced between the parent state and the colonies.

Two newspapers had been published, entitled *The Boston Gazette*, and were, in succession, discontinued. Edes and Gill began a new paper under the title of *The Boston Gazette, and Country Journal*, which soon gained an establishment, and became distinguished for the spirited political essays which appeared in it. They published many political pamphlets, and for a number of years were appointed printers to the general court. They did some business for booksellers. A small number of octavo and duodecimo volumes were occasionally issued from their press; but their principal business consisted in the publication of the *Gazette*. When the dispute between Great Britain and her colonies assumed a serious aspect, this paper arrested the public attention, from the part its able writers took in the cause of liberty and their country; and it gained a very extensive circulation. Edes was a warm and a firm patriot, and Gill was an honest whig.[22]

Soon after the revolutionary war began, the British troops closed the avenues between Boston and the country; but Edes fortunately made his escape by night, in a boat, with a press and a few types.

He opened a printing house in Watertown, where he continued the *Gazette*, and printed for the provincial congress of Massachusetts. Here he found full employment, and his zeal in the cause of his country animated him to redoubled diligence.

The printing he executed at Watertown, did not, indeed, do much credit to the art; but the work, at this time, done at other presses, was not greatly superior. The war broke out suddenly, and few of any profession were prepared for the event. All kinds of printing materials had usually been imported from England; even ink for printers had not, in any great quantity, been made in America. This resource was, by the war, cut off; and a great scarcity of these articles soon ensued. At that time, there were but three small paper mills in Massachusetts; in New Hampshire there were none; and Rhode Island contained only one, which was out of repair. The paper which these mills could make fell far short of the necessary supply. Paper, of course, was extremely scarce, and what could be procured was badly manufactured, not having more than half the requisite labor bestowed upon it. It was often taken from the mill wet, and unsized. People had not been in the habit of saving rags, and stock for the manufacture of paper was obtained with great difficulty. Every thing like rags was ground up together to make a substitute for paper. This, with wretched ink, and worn out types, produced miserable printing.

In 1776, Edes returned to Boston, on the evacuation of the town by the British army. Gill had remained recluse in Boston during the siege. They now dissolved their connection, and divided their printing materials. Edes continued to print for the state several years. In 1779, he took his two sons Benjamin and Peter into partnership; their firm was BENJAMIN EDES & SONS. About three years after this event Peter began business for himself in Boston, but was not successful. Benjamin continued with his father some time longer, and then set up a press and printed a newspaper in Haverhill, Massachusetts; but he was not more fortunate than his brother. The father continued the business alone, and labored along with *The Boston Gazette*. This paper had had its day, and it now languished for want of that support it derived from the splendid talents of its former writers, some of whom were dead, some were gone abroad, and others were employed in affairs of state. It was further depressed and paralyzed by the establishment of other newspapers, and by the exertions of another class of writers, who enlivened the columns of the new journals with their literary productions.

Edes was a man of great industry. At the beginning of the revolutionary war he had accumulated a very decent property, which was not lessened when he returned to Boston, in 1776. At that time he took a good house in Cornhill, part of which formed the alley leading to Brattle street; it was next to that formerly owned by John Draper; but, some years before his death, he moved into a house which he then owned in Temple street, and hired a chamber over the shop of a tin plate worker in Kilby street, where he erected his press.

The rapid depreciation of paper money proved fatal to the property of Edes, as well as to that of many others. He had a large family to support; and he continued to work, as had been his custom, at case and press, until the infirmities of age compelled him to cease from labor. In the advanced period of his life competence and ease forsook him, and he was oppressed by poverty and sickness. His important services were too soon forgotten by his prosperous, independent countrymen.

He died December 11, 1803, at the age of seventy-one years. His second son, Peter Edes, printed at Augusta, in the district of Maine.[23]

Edes began the *Boston Gazette and Country Journal*, and with him it ended. No publisher of a newspaper felt a greater interest in the establishment of the independence of the United States than Benjamin Edes; and no newspaper was more instrumental in bringing forward this important event than *The Boston Gazette*.

JOHN GILL, the partner of Benjamin Edes, and the junior publisher of *The Boston Gazette and Country Journal*, was born in Charlestown, Massachusetts. He served his apprenticeship with Samuel Kneeland, and married one of his daughters. Gill was a sound whig, but did not possess the political energy of his partner. He was industrious, constantly in the printing house, and there worked at case or press as occasion required. His partnership with Edes continued for twenty years. They separated at the commencement of hostilities by the British, in

1775. Gill remained in Boston during the siege; he did no business, and thought it prudent to confine himself to his own house. He had, fortunately, acquired a competency for the support of his family under that trial.

After the evacuation of Boston, his connection with Edes ended. They divided their stock, and settled their concerns. While Edes continued the publication of the *Gazette*, Gill issued another paper, entitled *The Continental Journal*. Having published this paper several years, he sold the right of it, in 1785, with his printing materials, to James D. Griffith.

Gill was brother to the Hon. Moses Gill, who, subsequently to the revolution, was for several years lieutenant-governor of the commonwealth of Massachusetts. He died August 25, 1785, and left several children. *The Continental Journal*, which announced to the public the death of Gill, contains the following observations respecting him, viz.:

'Capt. John Gill, for disseminating principles destructive of tyranny, suffered during the siege of this town in 1775, what many other printers were threatened with, a cruel imprisonment. He, however, was so fortunate as to survive the conflict; but had the mortification, lately, of seeing the press ready to be shackled by a stamp act fabricated in his native state; he, therefore, resigned his business, not choosing to submit to a measure which Britain artfully adopted as the foundation of her intended tyranny in America. His remains were very respectfully entombed last Monday afternoon.'

JOHN GREEN was the son of Bartholomew Green, Jr., who died at Halifax, and the great grandson of Samuel Green of Cambridge. He was born in Boston, served an apprenticeship with John Draper, whose daughter he married, and in the year 1755 began business with Joseph Russell. The firm was GREEN & RUSSELL. Their press was established in Tremont street, in a house which was taken down to make room for Scollay's Buildings. In August, 1757, they issued from their press a newspaper, entitled *The Boston Weekly Advertiser*. They repeatedly altered the title of this paper, but continued its publication until 1773, when they sold their right in it, to Mills and Hicks.* In 1758 they removed, and opened a printing house in Queen street, in the brick building which made the east corner of Dorset's alley, and nearly opposite to the Court House. They printed for some time the journals of the house of representatives, and the laws of the government. They also did the printing of the custom house, and published a number of pamphlets; but they never engaged largely in book work.

A few years after this partnership was formed, Russell opened an auction office, the profits of which were shared by the firm. Green managed the printing house, and Russell the auction room. They continued together until 1775, and by their attention to business acquired a handsome property.

Green remained in Boston during the siege, and when the British troops left the town he became interested in the *Independent Chronicle*, then published by Powars and Willis, but his name did not appear. He was a man of steady habits, true to his engagements, and well respected. He died November, 1787, aged sixty years. He had no children. He was, I believe, the last of the descendants of Samuel Green of Cambridge who printed in this state.

* See p. 263.

JOSEPH RUSSELL was born in Boston, served an apprenticeship with Daniel Fowle, and in 1755, entered into partnership with John Green.* Russell was a good workman in the printing business; but his talents were more particularly adapted to the duties of an auctioneer. When Green and Russell united auctioneering with printing, Russell took the sole management of the vendue room; he soon arrived at celebrity in this line, and had more employment in it than any other person in Boston. When his partnership with Green was dissolved, he formed a connection with Samuel Clap; and this company, under the firm of Russell & Clap, continued the business of auctioneers till the death of Russell.

Russell was full of life, very facetious, but attentive to his concerns. Few men had more friends, or were more esteemed. In all companies he rendered himself agreeable. He acquired considerable property, but did not hoard up his wealth, for benevolence was one of his virtues. He was a worthy citizen, and a friend to his country. He died at the end of November, 1795, aged sixty-one years.

BENJAMIN MECOM[24] was a native of Boston. His mother was sister of James Franklin and of the celebrated Benjamin Franklin. Mecom served his apprenticeship with his uncle Benjamin Franklin at Philadelphia. When of age, having received some assistance from his uncle, he went to Antigua, and there printed a newspaper; but in 1756, he quitted that island, and returned to Boston. In 1757, he opened a printing house in Cornhill, nearly

---

* Russell lived with Daniel Fowle, at the time Fowle was imprisoned, on suspicion of printing *The Monster of Monsters*. Vid. Zechariah Fowle.

opposite to the old brick church. At the same place he kept a shop and sold books. His first work was a large edition, thirty thousand copies, of *The Psalter*, for the booksellers. He printed these on terms so low, that his profits did not amount to journeymen's wages. This edition was two years worrying through his press. After the *Psalter* Mecom began to print and publish, on his own account, a periodical work, which he intended should appear monthly. It was entitled, *The New England Magazine of Knowledge and Pleasure*. It contained about fifty pages 12mo, but he published only three or four numbers. These were issued in 1758; but no date either of month or year appeared in the title page, or in the imprint. In this magazine were inserted several articles under the head of *Queer Notions*. Each number, when published, was sent about town for sale by hawkers; but few copies were vended, and the work, of course, was discontinued.

His business was not extensive; he printed several pamphlets for his own sale, and a few for that of others. He remained in Boston for a number of years; but when James Parker & Co., who printed at New Haven, removed to New York, Mecom succeeded them. Soon afterwards Dr. Franklin procured Mecom the office of postmaster for New Haven.

He married in New Jersey, before he set up his press in Boston. He possessed good printing materials, but there was something singular in his work, as well as in himself. He was in Boston several months before the arrival of his press and types from Antigua, and had much leisure. During this interval he frequently came to the house where I was an apprentice. He was handsomely dressed, wore a powdered bob wig, ruffles and gloves; gentlemanlike appendages which the printers of that day did not assume, and thus apparelled, would often assist, for an hour, at the press.

An edition of *The New England Primer* being wanted by the booksellers, Z. Fowle consulted with Mecom on the subject, who consented to assist in the impression, on condition that he might print a certain number for himself. To this proposal Fowle consented, and made his contract with the booksellers. Fowle had no help but myself, then a lad in my eighth year. The impression consisted of ten thousand copies. The form was a small sixteens, on foolscap paper. The first form of the Primer being set up, while it was worked at the press I was put to case to set the types for the second. Having completed this, and set up the whole cast of types employed in the work, and the first form being still at press I was employed as a fly; that is, to take off the sheets from the tympan as they were printed, and pile them in a heap; this expedited the work. While I was engaged in this business, I viewed Mecom at the press with admiration. He indeed put on an apron to save his clothes from blacking, and guarded his ruffles; but he wore his coat, his wig, his hat and his gloves, whilst working at press; and at case, laid aside his apron. When he published his magazine with Queer Notions, this singularity, and some addenda, known to the trade, induced them to give him the appellation of *Queer Notions*. Mecom was, however, a gentleman in his appearance and manners, had been well educated to his business, and if *queer*, was honest and sensible, and called a correct and good printer.

THOMAS FLEET, JR., & JOHN FLEET.[25] They were brothers, and having learned from their father the art of printing, succeeded him in business at his house in Cornhill, in 1758. I mention them together, because they commenced printing in partnership, and continued in connection until separated by death. They carried on the publication of *The Boston Evening Post* until the commencement of the revolutionary war; when they suspended the publication of that newspaper, and it was never after resumed. The impartiality with which the paper was conducted, in those most critical times, the authenticity of its news, and the judicious selections of its publishers, gained them great and deserved reputation.

Both brothers were born in Boston. Their father gave them a good school education; they were correct printers, very attentive to their concerns, punctual in their dealings, good citizens, and much respected. They printed several works in octavo, and some volumes in duodecimo, on their own account; and some in connection with other printers. Their shop was always supplied with smaller articles for the benefit of their sisters, who were never married.

They remained in Boston during the siege; and, afterward, revived the publication of the *Massachusetts Register*, which originated with Mein and Fleming some years before, and had been continued by Mills and Hicks. Thomas died a bachelor, March 2, 1797, aged sixty-five years. John was married; he died March 18, 1806, aged seventy-one, and left several children; one of whom, by the name of Thomas, was a printer in Boston at the same house in which his grandfather began the *The Boston Evening Post*.[26]

RICHARD DRAPER. He was the son of John Draper, the successor of Bartholomew Green, proprietor and printer of *The Boston News Letter*. He was brought up a printer by his father, continued with him after he became of age, and, for some years before his father's death, was a silent partner with him. On the death of his father, Richard continued the *News Letter*. He was early appointed to the office of printer to the governor and council, which he retained during life. His paper was devoted to the government; and, in the controversy between Great Britain and the American colonies, strongly supported the royal cause. He added the title of *The Massachusetts Gazette*, to *The Boston News Letter*, and decorated it with the king's arms.* Many able advocates for the government filled the columns of the *News Letter*, but the opposition papers were supported by writers at least equally powerful, and more numerous.

The constitution of Richard Draper was very feeble, and he was often confined by sickness. Soon after his father's death, he took his kinsman, Samuel Draper, who was connected with Z. Fowle, into partnership, under the firm of R. & S. DRAPER. Samuel was not permitted to share in the honor of printing for the governor and council. In all the work done for them, Richard's name alone appeared as printer. Samuel Draper died a few years after this connection was formed.

Richard Draper, having been successful in his business, erected a handsome brick house, on a convenient spot in front of the old printing house in Newbury street, in which he resided. He was attentive to his affairs, and was esteemed the best compiler of news of his day. He died June 6, 1774, aged forty-seven years. He left no children, and was succeeded by his widow.

---

* It was customary, many years before the revolution, among publishers of newspapers, especially those whose titles embraced the word Gazette, to ornament the titles with this ensign of royalty. But the printers in Boston had not followed the fashion.

Draper, alone, did very little book printing; but he was concerned with Edes & Gill, and the Fleets, in publishing several volumes of sermons, etc. One month preceding his death, he commenced a limited copartnership with John Boyle. Boyle's name appeared in the *Gazette* with Draper's, whose ill health rendering him unable to attend closely to business, Boyle undertook the chief care and management of it. The following sketch of the character of Richard Draper is taken from the *Evening Post* of June 13, 1774.

'He was a man remarkable for the amiable delicacy of his mind, and gentleness of his manners. A habit enfeebled and emaciated by remorseless disease, and unremitted distress, could never banish the smile from his countenance. A well founded confidence in the mercies of his God, and the happy consciousness of a life well spent, smoothed the pillow of anguish, and irradiated the gloom of death with the promise of succeeding joy; in every relation he sustained in life, his endearing manners and inflexible integrity rendered him truly exemplary.'

SAMUEL DRAPER was the nephew and apprentice of John Draper. He was born at Martha's Vineyard. In 1758, soon after he became of age, he went into trade with Zechariah Fowle, who stood in much need of a partner like Draper. Their connection was mutually advantageous. Fowle had been in business seven years; but had made no progress in the advancement of his fortune. Draper was more enterprising, but had no capital to establish himself as a printer. He was a young man of correct habits and handsome abilities. He was industrious, and, for those times, a good workman. Draper was an important acquisition to his partner, although Fowle did not appear to be highly sensible of it. The connection continued five years; during which time they printed, as has been remarked, three or four volumes of some magnitude, a large edition of the *Youth's Instructor in the English Tongue*, another of the Psalter; also, a variety of pamphlets, chapmen's small books, and ballads. They so far succeeded in trade as to keep free of debt, to obtain a good livelihood, and increase their stock. Their printing house was in Marlborough street; it was taken down in later years, and a new house built on its site, at the south corner of Franklin street, at the entrance from Marlborough street.

The articles of copartnership contemplated a continuance of the connection of Fowle and Draper for seven years; but, on the death of John Draper, Richard, his son, succeeded to his business. Richard was often confined to his house by ill health, and wanted an assistant; he therefore made liberal proposals to Samuel, which were accepted; and they entered into partnership. In pursuance of this new arrangement, the connection between Fowle and Draper was dissolved; and Draper recommenced business with a more active and enterprising partner. S. Draper continued with his kinsman until his death, which happened March 15, 1767, at the age of thirty years. While he was in partnership with Fowle, he married an agreeable young lady, of a respectable family, by whom he had two daughters. His widow died in 1812. He had two brothers who were printers, the eldest of whom, named Richard, died before 1810; the other whose name was Edward, with a partner, published, for some time during the war, a newspaper in Boston.

DANIEL KNEELAND was the son of Samuel Kneeland, and served his apprenticeship with his father. He began trade as a bookbinder, in plain work, having been bred to binding as well as printing. A dispute had arisen between the printers and booksellers respecting *Ames's Almanack*, the particulars of which I do not fully recollect; but, in substance, it was as follows. John Draper, and his predecessor Bartholomew Green, had always purchased the copy of that Almanac, and printed it on their own account; but they had supplied the booksellers, in sheets, by the hundred, the thousand, or any quantity wanted. About the year 1759, this Almanac was enlarged from sixteen pages on a foolscap sheet to three half sheets. Draper formed a connection with Green & Russel and T. & J. Fleet, in its publication. A half sheet was printed at each of their printing houses; and they were not disposed to supply booksellers as formerly. The booksellers, immediately on the publication of the Almanack, had it reprinted; and soon after a number of the principal of them set up a printing house for themselves and engaged Daniel Kneeland, and John his brother, to conduct it for them, under the firm of D. &. J. KNEELAND. The Kneelands continued to print for these booksellers several years, in part of the building occupied by their father as a printing house; after which some difficulty arising, the booksellers put a stop to their press, and divided among them the printing materials. Daniel Kneeland then dissolved his connection with his brother John; and, being furnished with the press, and a part of the types, which had been owned by the booksellers, he engaged in printing on his own account, but worked chiefly for the trade.

About the year 1772, Daniel took, as a partner, a young man by the name of Nathaniel Davis. The firm was Kneeland & Davis. This company was, in the course of two or three years, dissolved by the death of Davis.

Kneeland's business before the revolutionary war was inconsiderable, and it afterward became still more contracted. He died in May, 1789, aged sixty-eight years.

JOHN KNEELAND was another son of Samuel Kneeland, and he was taught the art by his father. He began printing, in connection with his brother Daniel, for the booksellers; for whom they worked during their partnership, as has been related. When the connection between the brothers was dissolved, John entered into partnership with Seth Adams, under the firm of Kneeland & Adams. They opened a printing house in Milk street, at the corner of the alley leading to Trinity church.

The principal work of Kneeland & Adams was psalters, spelling books, and psalm books, for booksellers. Their partnership continued only a few years. Adams quitted printing, and became a postrider. J. Kneeland did little, if any, business, after the commencement of the revolutionary war. He died in March, 1795, aged sixty-two years.

WILLIAM MACALPINE was a native of Scotland, where he was bred to bookbinding. He came to Boston early in life, and set up the trade of a binder; and, afterward, opened a shop, for the sale of a few common books, in Marlborough street, opposite to the Old South church. His business was soon enlarged by supplies of books from Glasgow. He removed several times to houses in the same street. A disagreement taking place between the booksellers and the printers of *Ames's Almanack*, the principal booksellers, who set up a press for themselves, and reprinted this Almanac,* refused to furnish Macalpine with copies either of their Almanac, or of any books printed at their press. Macalpine, being thus denied a supply of *Ames's Almanack*, both by the original printers of it and by the booksellers who reprinted it, sent to Edinburgh for a press and types, and for a foreman to superintend a printing house. In 1762, he commenced printing; and, annually, furnished himself with *Ames's Almanack*, and other books for his own sales.

John Fleming, previous to his connection with John Mein, was one or two years concerned with Macalpine in printing.

Macalpine continued in business until the commencement of the revolutionary war; he was a royalist, and remained in Boston during the siege; but he quitted the town with the British army. He died at Glasgow, Scotland, in 1788.

JOHN FLEMING[27] was from Scotland, where he was brought up to printing. He came to Boston in 1764; and was, for a short time, connected with his countryman William Macalpine. Mein, a bookseller, from Edinburgh, having opened a very large collection of books for sale, Fleming separated from Macalpine, and formed a partnership with Mein. Fleming made a voyage to Scotland, there purchased printing materials for the firm, hired three or four journeymen printers, and accompanied by them returned to Boston. The company then opened a printing house in Wing's lane, since Elm street, and began printing under the firm of MEIN & FLEMING. Fleming was not concerned with Mein in bookselling. Several books were printed at their house for Mein, it being an object with him to supply

---

* Copyrights were not then secured by law in the colonies.

his own sales; none of them, however, were of great magnitude. Some of these books had a false imprint, and were palmed upon the public for London editions, because Mein apprehended that books printed in London, however executed, sold better than those which were printed in America; and, at that time, many purchasers sanctioned his opinion.

In less than two years after the establishment of this company they removed their printing materials to Newbury street. In December, 1767, they began the publication of a weekly newspaper, entitled, *The Boston Chronicle*. This paper was printed on demy, in quarto, imitating, in its form, *The London Chronicle*.

The Boston Chronicle obtained reputation; but Mein, who edited the paper, soon devoted it zealously to the support of the measures of the British administration against the colonies; and, in consequence, the publishers, and particularly Mein, incurred the displeasure and the resentment of the whigs, who were warm advocates for American liberty. The publishers were threatened with the effects of popular resentment. Mein, according to his deserts, experienced some specimens of it. The *Chronicle* was discontinued in May, 1770, and Mein returned to Europe.

Fleming was less obnoxious. He remained in Boston; and as the *Chronicle* had been discontinued, the popular resentment soon subsided. He married a young lady of a respectable family in Boston; and soon after his late partner went to Europe he opened a printing house in King street, and printed books on his own account. He issued proposals for publishing *Clark's Family Bible* in folio, but did not meet with encouragement.

Fleming continued in Boston until 1773, when he sold his printing materials to Mills and Hicks, and went to England

with his family. He more than once visited this country after
1790, as an agent for a commercial house in Europe; and subsequently resided some time in France, where he died.

JOHN MEIN,[28] of the firm of Mein & Fleming, was born in Scotland, and there bred to the business of a bookseller. He had received a good education, was enterprising, and possessed handsome literary talents. He arrived at Boston, from Glasgow, in November, 1764, in company with Mr. Robert Sandeman,* a kinsman of Mr. Sandeman of the same Christian name who for a short time was the partner of Mein, and a number of other Scotchmen, on a visit to this country with a view of settling here. Mein brought with him a good assortment of books, a quantity of Irish linens and other goods, and opened a shop in Marlborough street in connection with Sandeman.[29] Their shop was an old wooden building at the north corner of the entrance to what is now called Franklin street. Their firm was Mein & Sandeman.

They continued in company only a few months; and, when they separated, Mein took a house in King street, at the corner of the alley leading to the market, and there opened a large bookstore and circulating library. He was connected with a bookseller in Scotland, who was extensively in trade; and, by this means, he was supplied, as he wanted, with both Scotch and English editions of the most saleable books. He soon found that a concern in printing would be convenient and profitable. His countryman, John Fleming, who was a good printer, was then

---

* Mr. Sandeman was the author of the then celebrated letters on the Rev. Mr. Hervey's *Theron and Aspasio*. A type founder by the name of Mitchelson, I believe, arrived in the same vessel with Mein and Sandeman.

in Boston; and with him he formed a connection in a printing establishment. Fleming went to Scotland, and procured printing materials, workmen, etc. On his return they, in 1766, opened a printing house, and printed a number of books for Mein's sales, and published *The Boston Chronicle*, as has been already mentioned.

The *Chronicle* was printed on a larger sheet than other Boston newspapers of that day, but did not exceed them in price. For a time it was well filled with news, entertaining and useful extracts from the best European publications, and some interesting original essays. Mein was doing business to great advantage, but he soon took a decided part in favor of the obnoxious measures of the British administration against the colonies, and the *Chronicle* became a vehicle for the most bitter pieces, calumniating and vilifying some of those characters in whom the people of Massachusetts placed high confidence; and, in consequence, it lost its credit as rapidly as it had gained it. Mein, its editor, became extremely odious, and to avoid the effects of popular resentment, he secreted himself until an opportunity was presented for a passage to England. Mein had unquestionably been encouraged, in Boston, as a partisan and an advocate for the measures of government. In London, he engaged himself under the pay of the ministry, as a writer against the colonies; but after the war commenced he sought other employment.

SETH ADAMS served his apprenticeship with Samuel Kneeland. He began printing in Queen street, with John Kneeland; they afterwards occupied a printing house in Milk street, at the corner of Boarded alley, since known by the name of Hawley street. They were three or four years in business, and printed

chiefly for the booksellers. Adam's father-in-law was the first
postrider between Boston and Hartford. When he died, Adams
quitted printing and continued the occupation of his father-in-
law. He died a few years after.

EZEKIEL RUSSELL was born in Boston, and served an apprenticeship with his brother, Joseph Russell, the partner of
John Green. In 1765, he began printing with Thomas Furber,
at Portsmouth, New Hampshire, under the firm of Furber &
Russell. Not succeeding in business, they dissolved their partnership, and Russell returned to Boston. He worked with various printers until 1769, when he procured a press and a few
types. With these he printed on his own account, in a house
near Concert Hall. He afterward removed to Union street,
where to the business of printing he added that of an auctioneer,
which he soon quitted, and adhered to printing. Excepting an
edition of *Watts's Psalms*, he published nothing of more consequence than pamphlets, most of which were small. In November, 1771, he began a political publication entitled *The Censor*.
This paper was supported, during the short period of its existence, by those who were in the interest of the British government.

Russell afterward removed to Salem, and attempted the publication of a newspaper, but did not succeed. He again removed,
and went to Danvers, and printed in a house known by the
name of the Bell tavern. In a few years he returned once more to
Boston; and, finally, took his stand in Essex street, near the spot
on which grew the great elms, one of which was then standing,
and was called Liberty tree. Here he printed and sold ballads,
and published whole and half sheet pamphlets for peddlers. In

these small articles his trade principally consisted, and afforded him a very decent support.

The wife of Russell was indeed an 'help meet for him.' She was a very industrious, active woman; and assisted her husband in the printing house. A young woman who lived in Russell's family sometimes invoked the muse, and wrote ballads on recent tragical events, which being immediately printed, and set off with wooden cuts of coffins, etc., had frequently 'a considerable run.'

Russell died in September, 1796, aged fifty-two years. His wife continued the business.

ISAIAH THOMAS[30] descended from a respectable family which had settled near Boston not many years after that town was founded. His grandfather carried on mercantile business in that place, in a store which he owned, on the town dock; and died in the year 1746, leaving four sons and two daughters, who were all arrived at the age of maturity. His second son, Moses, lived some time on Long Island, where he married and had two children; the youngest of whom is the subject of this memoir.*

Moses Thomas having expended nearly all his patrimony, went away, and died in North Carolina; leaving his widow in narrow circumstances with five dependent children. Her friends on Long Island took the charge of providing for the two who were born there, and had been left in their care; the others she

---

* He was engaged as clerk to an officer in the expedition against Cuba, in 1740, much against the wishes of his father Peter, from whom he absconded and enlisted as a common soldier. The interest of the father placed him in a better situation than he would have held in the ranks, but did not obtain his discharge. He afterwards sailed on a voyage to the Mediterranean. He owned a farm on Long Island, which he cultivated, while he kept a shop.

supported by the profits of a small shop she kept in Boston. Her
diligence and prudent management ensured success; insomuch
that besides making provision for her family, she was enabled
to purchase a small estate in Cambridge. This place she afterward unfortunately lost; for being fully possessed with the idea
that the continental paper money, issued during the revolutionary war, would ultimately be paid in specie, and having
what she thought a very advantageous offer for her house and
land in that kind of currency, she sold the same, and became one
among the number of unfortunate people who lost nearly the
whole of their property from a misplaced confidence in the
paper currency of the day.

When her son, Isaiah, born at Boston, January 19, 1749, o.s.,
was six years of age, he was apprenticed by his mother to
Zechariah Fowle; who, as has been already stated, principally
made use of his press in printing ballads, and by whom he was
soon employed to set types; for which purpose he was mounted
on a bench eighteen inches high, and the whole length of a
double frame which contained cases of both roman and italic.
His first essay with the composing stick, was on a ballad entitled *The Lawyer's Pedigree* (1755); which was set in types of the
size of double pica.

He remained eleven years with Fowle; after which period
they separated, in consequence of a disagreement. On quitting
Fowle, in 1765, he went to Nova Scotia, with a view to go from
thence to England, in order to acquire a more perfect knowledge of his business. He found typography in a miserable state
in that province; and, so far was he from obtaining the means of
going to England, that he soon discovered that the only printer
in Halifax could hardly procure, by his business, a decent liveli-

hood. However, he remained there seven months; during which time the memorable British stamp act took effect in Nova Scotia, which, in the other colonies, met with a spirited and successful opposition.

The *Halifax Gazette* was printed by a Dutchman, whose name was Henry. He was a good natured, pleasant man, who in common concerns did not want for ingenuity and capacity; but he might, with propriety, be called a very unskilful printer. To his want of knowledge or abilities in his profession, he added indolence; and, as is too often the case, left his business to be transacted by boys or journeymen, instead of attending to it himself. His printing affairs were on a very contracted scale; and he made no efforts to render them more extensive. As he had two apprentices, he was not in want of assistance in his printing house; but Thomas accepted an offer of board for his services; and the sole management of the *Gazette* was immediately left to him. He new modelled the *Gazette* according to the best of his judgment, and as far as the worn out printing materials would admit. It was soon after printed on stamped paper, made for the purpose in England. To the use of this paper, 'the young New Englandman,' as he was called, was opposed; and, to the stamp act he was extremely hostile.

A paragraph appeared in the *Gazette*, purporting that the people of Nova Scotia were, generally, disgusted with the stamp act. This paragraph gave great offence to the officers of government, who called Henry to account for publishing what they termed sedition. Henry had not so much as seen the *Gazette* in which the offensive article had appeared; consequently he pleaded ignorance; and, in answer to their interrogatories, informed them that the paper was, in his absence, conducted by his journeyman. He was reprimanded, and admonished that he would be deprived of the work of government, should he, in future, suffer any thing of the kind to appear in the *Gazette*. It was not long before Henry was again sent for, on account of another offence of a similar nature; however, he escaped the consequences he might have apprehended, by assuring the officers of government that he had been confined by sickness; and he apologized in a satisfactory manner for the appearance of the obnoxious publication. But his journeyman was summoned to appear before the secretary of the province; to whose office he accordingly went. He was, probably, not known to Mr. Secretary, who sternly demanded of him, what he wanted?

A. Nothing, sir.

Q. Why came you here?

A. Because I was sent for.

Q. What is your name?

A. Isaiah Thomas.

Q. Are you the young New Englandman who prints for Henry?

A. Yes, sir.

Q. How dare you publish in the *Gazette* that the people of Nova Scotia are displeased with the stamp act?

A. I thought it was true.

Q. You had no right to think so. If you publish any thing more of such stuff, you shall be punished. You may go; but, remember, you are not in New England.

A. I will, sir.

Not long after this adventure occurred, a vessel arrived at Halifax from Philadelphia, and brought some of the newspapers published in that city.

The *Pennsylvania Journal*, published the day preceding that on which the stamp act was to take effect, was in full mourning. Thick black lines surrounded the pages, and were placed between the columns; a death's head and cross bones were surmounted over the title; and at the bottom of the last page was a large figure of a coffin, beneath which was printed the age of the paper, and an account of its having died of a disorder called the stamp act. A death's head, &c., as a substitute for a stamp, was placed at the end of the last column of the first page. Thomas had a strong desire to decorate *The Halifax Gazette* in the same manner; but he dared not do it, on account of his apprehension of the displeasure of the officers of government. However, an expedient was thought of to obviate that difficulty, which was to insert in the *Gazette* an article of the following import: 'We are desired by a number of our readers, to give a description of the extraordinary appearance of the *Pennsylvania Journal* of the 30th of October last, 1765. We can in no better way comply with this request, than by the exemplification we have given of that journal in this day's *Gazette*.' As near as possible, a representation was made of the several figures, emblems of mortality, and mourning columns; all which, accompanied by the qualifying paragraph, appeared together in *The Halifax Gazette*, and made no trifling bustle in the place.

Soon after this event, the effigy of the stampmaster was hung on the gallows near the citadel; and other tokens of hostility to the stamp act were exhibited. These disloyal actions were done silently and secretly; but they created some alarm; and a captain's guard was continually stationed at the house of the stampmaster, to protect him from those injuries which were expected to befal him. It is supposed the apprehensions entertained on his

account were entirely groundless. The officers of government
had prided themselves on the loyalty of the people of that
province in not having shown any opposition to the stamp act.
'These things were against them;' and a facetious officer was
heard to repeat to some of his friends, the old English proverb:
'We have not saved our bacon.'

An opinion prevailed, that Thomas not only knew the parties
concerned in these transactions but had a hand in them himself;
on which account, a few days after the exhibition of the stampmaster's effigy, a sheriff went to the printing house, and informed Thomas that he had a precept against him, and intended
to take him to prison, unless he would give information respecting the persons concerned in making and exposing the
effigy of the stampmaster. He mentioned, that some circumstances had produced a conviction in his mind that Thomas was
one of those who had been engaged in these seditious proceedings. The sheriff receiving no satisfactory answer to his inquiries,
ordered Thomas to go with him before a magistrate; and he,
having no person to consult, or to give him advice, in the
honest simplicity of his heart was about to obey the orders of
this terrible alguazil; but being suddenly struck with the idea
that this proceeding might be intended merely to alarm him
into an acknowledgment of his privity to the transactions in
question, he told the sheriff he did not know him and demanded
information respecting the authority by which he acted. The
sheriff answered, that he had sufficient authority; but on being
requested to exhibit it, the officer was evidently disconcerted,
and showed some symptoms of his not acting under 'the king's
authority.' However, he answered that he would show his
authority when it was necessary; and again ordered this 'printer

of sedition' to go with him. Thomas answered, he would not obey him unless he produced a precept, or proper authority for taking him prisoner. After further parley the sheriff left him, with an assurance that he would soon return; but Thomas saw him no more; and he afterward learned that this was a plan concerted for the purpose of surprising him into a confession.

A short time before the exhibition of the effigy of the stamp-master, Henry had received from the stamp-office the whole stock of paper that was sent ready stamped from England for the use of the *Gazette*. The quantity did not exceed six or eight reams; but as only three quires were wanted weekly for the newspaper, it would have sufficed for the purpose intended twelve months. It was not many weeks after the sheriff, already mentioned, made his exit from the printing house, when it was discovered that this paper was divested of the stamps; not one remained; they had been cut off and destroyed. On this occasion, an article appeared in the *Gazette*, announcing that 'all the stamped paper for the *Gazette* was used, and as no more could be had, it would in future be published without stamps.'

In March, 1767, Thomas quitted Halifax, and went to New Hampshire; where he worked, for some time, in the printing houses of Daniel Fowle, and Furber & Russell. In July following he returned to Boston. There he remained several months, in the employ of his old master, Z. Fowle.

Receiving an invitation from the captain of a vessel to go to Wilmington, in North Carolina, where he was assured a printer was wanted, he arranged his affairs with Fowle, again left him, by agreement, and went to Newport. There he waited on Martin Howard, Esq., chief justice of North Carolina, who was then at that place, and was about departing for Wilmington. To

this gentleman he made known his intention of going to North
Carolina, and received encouragement from the judge, who
gave him assurances of his influence in procuring business for
him at Cape Fear; for which place they sailed in the same vessel.

A gentleman at Newport also favored him with a letter
of recommendation to Robert Wells, printer, in Charleston,
South Carolina.

When he arrived at Wilmington, he, in pursuance of advice
from Judge Howard, and several other gentlemen, waited on
Governor Tryon, then at that place. The governor encouraged
him to settle there, and flattered him that he would be favored
with a part in the printing for government. But as a printer he
labored under no inconsiderable difficulty, that is, he had neither
press, nor types, nor money to purchase them.

It happened that Andrew Steuart, a printer, was then at
Wilmington, who had a press with two or three very small
founts of letters for sale. He had printed a newspaper, and as
some work was given him by the government, he called himself
king's printer; but at this period he was without business, having given offence to the governor and the principal gentlemen
at Cape Fear. For this reason he was desirous to sell the materials
he had then in that place, and to return to Philadelphia, where
he had another small printing establishment.

Pursuant to the advice of several gentlemen, Thomas applied
to Steuart, to purchase the press, etc.; but Steuart, knowing he
could not easily be accommodated with these articles elsewhere,
took advantage of his situation, and demanded about three
times as much for them as they cost when new. After some
debate, Steuart lowered his price to about double the value.
Several gentlemen of Wilmington offered to advance money,

on a generous credit, to enable Thomas to make the purchase. When Steuart found the money could be raised, he refused to let the types go without an appendage of a negro woman and her child, whom he wished to sell before he quitted the place. An argument ensued; but Steuart persisted in his refusal to part with the printing materials, unless the negroes were included in the sale. Thomas, after advising with friends, agreed to take them, finding he could dispose of them for nearly the price he was to give for them. He then thought the bargain was concluded; but Steuart threw a new difficulty in the way. He had a quantity of common household furniture, not the better for wear, which he also wanted to dispose of; and would not part with the other articles unless the purchaser would take these also. The furniture was entirely out of Thomas's line of business, and he had no use for it. He, therefore, declared himself off the bargain; and afterward, when Steuart retracted respecting the sale of furniture, Thomas began to be discouraged by the prospects the place afforded; he was not pleased with the appearance of the country; his money was all gone; and his inclination to visit England was renewed. For these reasons he renounced all thoughts of settling at Cape Fear at that time; although a merchant there offered to send to England by the first opportunity for a printing apparatus, which he would engage Thomas should have on a long credit.

With a view to go to England, he entered himself as steward on board a ship bound to the West Indies; expecting when he arrived there he should easily find an opportunity to go to London. He did duty on board the vessel ten days; but imbibing a dislike to the captain, who was often intoxicated, and attempted to reduce him into a mere cabin boy, and to employ him about the most servile and menial offices, he revolted at these indignities, and procured his discharge. On this occasion he remembered the recommendation he had received at Newport to a printer at Charleston; and, finding a packet bound there, he quitted a very kind friend he had gained at Wilmington, and after a long passage, in which he met with many adventures, besides that lamentable one of spending his last shilling, he arrived at Charleston.

When he presented the letter of recommendation to Wells, the printer, he had the mortification to learn he was not in want of a journeyman. However, Wells civilly employed him at low wages, and soon put him into full pay. He continued at Charleston two years; and had nearly completed a contract to go and settle in the West Indies; but his health declining, he returned to Boston in 1770, after having visited several of the southern colonies.

He now formed a connection with Zechariah Fowle, and began business by publishing *The Massachusetts Spy*, a small newspaper printed three times in a week.

Thomas's partnership with his former master, Fowle, continued but three months. He then purchased the printing materials which Fowle had in his possession, and gave his security to Fowle's creditor for the payment. Fowle had, during nineteen years, been in possession of his press and types, and had not paid for them. The creditor was a near relation by marriage, and had exacted only the payment of the annual interest of the debt. Thomas continued the *Spy*, but altered the publication of it from three times to twice a week. Each publication contained a half sheet. After having published it three months in the new form, he discontinued it in December, 1770. On the 5th of

March, 1771, he began another paper with the same title, which was published weekly, on a large folio sheet.

It was at first the determination of Thomas that his paper should be free to both parties which then agitated the country, and, impartially, lay before the public their respective communications; but he soon found that this ground could not be maintained. The dispute between Britain and her American colonies became more and more serious, and deeply interested every class of men in the community. The parties in the dispute took the names of Whigs and Tories; the tories were the warm supporters of the measures of the British cabinet, and the whigs the animated advocates for American liberty. The tories soon discontinued their subscriptions for the *Spy*; and the publisher was convinced that to produce an abiding and salutary effect his paper must have a fixed character. He was in principle attached to the party which opposed the measures of the British ministry; and he therefore announced that the *Spy* would be devoted to the support of the whig interest.

Some overtures had been previously made by the friends of the British government to induce him to have the *Spy* conducted wholly on their side of the question; and, these having been rejected, an attempt was made to force a compliance, or to deprive him of his press and types. It was known that he was in debt for these articles, and that his creditor was an officer of government, appointed by the crown. This officer, notwithstanding he was a very worthy man, was pushed on to make a demand of payment, contrary to his verbal agreement, under the apprehension that the money could not be raised. When Thomas assumed the debt of Fowle, he gave his bond, payable in one year, under an assurance that the capital might lay as it had done, if the interest annually due should be punctually paid; and when contrary to stipulation the capital was demanded, he borrowed money, and paid one debt by contracting another.

An essay published in the *Spy*, November, 1771, under the signature of Mucius Scævola, attracted the attention of the executive of the province. Governor Hutchinson assembled his council on the occasion; and, after consultation, the board determined that the printer should be ordered before them. In pursuance of this resolution, their messenger was sent to inform Thomas that his attendance was required in the council chamber. To this message he replied, 'that he was busily employed in his office, and could not wait upon his excellency and their honors.' The messenger returned to the council with this answer, and, in an hour after, again came into Thomas's printing house and informed him that the governor and council waited for his attendance; and, by their direction, inquired, whether he was ready to appear before them. Thomas answered, that he was not. The messenger went to make his report to the council, and Thomas to ask advice of a distinguished law character. He was instructed to persist in his refusal to appear before the council, as they had no legal right to summon him before them; but, should a warrant issue from the proper authority, he must then submit to the sheriff who should serve such a process upon him. This was a critical moment; the affair had taken air, and the public took an interest in the event. The council proceeded with caution, for the principle was at issue, whether they possessed authority arbitrarily to summon whom they pleased before their board, to answer to them for their conduct. The messenger was, however, the third time sent to Thomas, and brought him this verbal order. *Mess.* The governor and council order your immediate attendance before them in the council chamber.

T. I will not go.

Mess. You do not give this answer with an intention that I should report it to the governor and council?

T. Have you any thing written, by which to show the authority under which you act?

Mess. I have delivered to you the order of the governor and council, as it was given to me.

T. If I understand you, the governor and council order my immediate attendance before them?

Mess. They do.

T. Have you the order in writing?

Mess. No.

T. Then, sir, with all due respect to the governor and council, I am engaged in my own concerns, and shall not attend.

Mess. Will you commit your answer to writing?

T. No, sir.

Mess. You had better go; you may repent your refusal to comply with the order of the council.

T. I must abide by the result.*

The messenger carried the refusal to the council. The board for several hours debated the question, whether they should commit Thomas for contempt; but it was suggested by some member that he could not legally be committed unless he had appeared before them; in that case his answers might have been

---

* This conversation with the messenger is taken from a memorandum made at the time.

construed into a contempt of their body, and been made the
ground of commitment. It was also suggested that they had not
authority to compel his appearance before them to answer for
any supposed crime or misdemeanor punishable by law, as particular tribunals had the exclusive cognizance of such offences.
The supposed want of authority was, indeed, the reason why a
compulsory process had not been adopted in the first instance.
There were not now, as formerly, licensers of the press.

The council, being defeated in the design to get the printer
before them, ordered the attorney general to prosecute him at
common law. A prosecution was accordingly soon attempted,
and great effort made to effect his conviction. The chief justice,
at the following term of the supreme court at Boston, in his
charge to the grand jury, dwelt largely on the doctrine of libels;
on the present licentiousness of the press; and on the necessity of
restraining it. The attorney general presented a bill of indictment to the grand inquest against Isaiah Thomas for publishing
an obnoxious libel. The Court House was crowded from day to
day to learn the issue. The grand jury returned this bill, *Ignoramus*. Foiled by the grand jury in this mode of prosecution, the
attorney general was directed to adopt a different process; and
to file an information against Thomas. This direction of the
court was soon known to the writers in the opposition, who
attacked it with so much warmth and animation, and offered
such cogent arguments to prove that it infringed the rights and
liberties of the subject, that the court thought proper to drop the
measure. Unable to convict the printer either by indictment or
information in Suffolk, a proposal was made to prosecute him
in some other county, under the following pretext. The printers of newspapers circulate them through the province, and of

course publish them as extensively as they are circulated. Thomas, for instance, circulates the *Spy* in the county of Essex, and as truly publishes the libel in that county as in Suffolk where the paper is printed. The fallacy of this argument was made apparent; the measure was not adopted, and government for that time gave over the prosecution; but, on a subsequent occasion, some attempts of that kind were renewed.*

It became at length apparent to all reflecting men that hostilities must soon take place between Great Britain and her American colonies. Thomas had rendered himself very obnoxious to the friends of the British administration; and, in consequence, the tories, and some of the British soldiery in the town, openly threatened him with the effects of their resentment. For these and other reasons, he was induced to pack up, privately, a press and types, and to send them in the night over Charles river to Charlestown, whence they were conveyed to Worcester. This was only a few days before the affair at Lexington. The press and types constituted the whole of the property he saved from the proceeds of five years labor. The remainder was destroyed or carried off by the followers and adherents of the royal army when it quitted Boston.

On the night of April 18, 1775, it was discovered that a considerable number of British troops were embarking in boats on the river near the common, with the manifest design to destroy the stores collected by the provincials at Concord, eighteen miles from Boston; and he was concerned, with others, in giving the alarm. At day break, the next morning, he crossed from Boston over to Charlestown in a boat with Dr. Joseph War-

* On account of some essays addressed to the king, published in the *Spy* in September, 1772, and at other periods.

ren,* went to Lexington, and joined the provincial militia in opposing the king's troops. On the 20th, he went to Worcester, opened a printing house, and soon after recommenced the publication of his newspaper.†

The provincial congress, assembled at Watertown, proposed that Thomas's press should be removed to that place; but, as all concerns of a public nature were then in a state of derangement, it was finally determined that his press should remain at Worcester, and that postriders should be established to facilitate an intercourse between that place, Watertown and Cambridge; and at Worcester he continued to print for congress until a press was established at Cambridge and at Watertown.

During the time he had been in business at Boston he had published a number of pamphlets, but not many books of more consequence. Having made an addition to his printing materials, in 1773, he sent a press and types to Newburyport, ‡and committed the management of the same to a young printer whom he soon after took into partnership in his concerns in that place; and in December of the same year, he began the publication of a newspaper in that town. His partner managed their affairs imprudently, and involved the company in debt; in consequence of which Thomas sold out at considerable loss. In January, 1774, he began in Boston the publication of *The Royal*

---

* Dr. Warren was soon after appointed major general of the provincial troops, and was killed in the battle of Breed's, often called Bunker's hill, June 17, 1775.

† The publication of the *Spy* ceased for three weeks. It appeared from the press in Worcester, May 3d, 1775. This was the first printing done in any inland town in New England.

‡ This was the first press set up in Newburyport.

American Magazine; but the general distress and commotion in the town, occasioned by the operation of the act of the British parliament to blockade the port of Boston, obliged him to discontinue it before the expiration of the year, much to the injury of his pecuniary interests.

JOHN BOYLE served an apprenticeship with Green & Russell. He purchased the types of Fletcher of Halifax, and began business as a printer and bookseller in Marlborough street in 1771, and printed a few books on his own account. In May, 1774, Boyle formed a partnership with Richard Draper, publisher of *The Massachusetts Gazette, or Boston News Letter.* Draper died the following month, but his widow continued the newspaper, &c. Boyle was in partnership with the widow until August following; they then dissolved their connection, and Boyle returned to his former stand.

In 1775, Boyle sold his printing materials, but retained his bookstore, which he continued to keep in the same place.[31]

NATHANIEL DAVIS served his apprenticeship with Daniel Kneeland, and during the year 1772 and 1773 was in partnership with him; soon after which he died. They had a small printing house, where Scollay's Building now stands, at the head of Court street.[32] They published a number of pamphlets, and did some work for booksellers.

NATHANIEL MILLS was born within a few miles of Boston, and served his apprenticeship with John Fleming.

Mills had just completed his time of service when Fleming quitted business. John Hicks and Mills were nearly of an age,

and they formed a copartnership under the firm of MILLS &
HICKS.[33] The controversy between Britain and her American
colonies at this period assumed a very serious aspect, and government was disposed to enlist the press in support of the measures of the British ministry. Mills & Hicks were urged by the
partisans of government to purchase Fleming's printing materials, and the right which Green & Russell had in the newspaper entitled *The Massachusetts Gazette, and Boston Post Boy,*
&c. They pursued the advice given them; and being by this
purchase furnished with types and with a newspaper, they
opened a printing house in April, 1773, in School street, nearly
opposite to the small church erected for the use of the French
Protestants.*

The British party handsomely supported the paper of Mills &
Hicks, and afforded pecuniary aid to the printers. Several able
writers defended the British administration from the attack of
their American opponents; and the selection of articles in support of government for this paper as well as its foreign and
domestic intelligence displayed the discernment and assiduity
of the compilers.

Mills was a sensible, genteel young man, and a good printer,
and had the principal management of the printing house. The
newspaper was their chief concern; besides which they printed
during the two years they were in Boston only a few political
pamphlets and the *Massachusetts Register.* The commencement
of hostilities, in April, 1775, put an end to the publication of
their *Gazette.* Soon after the war began, Mills came out of
Boston, and resided a few weeks at Cambridge; but returned to

---

* A number of Separatists afterward purchased this church, and settled as
their minister the Rev. Andrew Croswell.

Boston, where he and his partner remained until the town was evacuated by the British troops. They, with others who had been in opposition to the country went with the British army to Halifax, and from thence to Great Britain. After two years residence in England they came to New York, then in possession of the British troops.

In New York they opened a stationery store, and did some printing for the royal army and navy. They afterwards formed a partnership with Alexander and James Robertson, who published the *Royal American Gazette* in that city. The firm was ROBERTSONS, MILLS & HICKS, and so continued until peace took place in 1783. Mills and Hicks then returned to Halifax, Nova Scotia; but their partnership was soon after dissolved, and Mills went and resided at Shelburne, in that province.

JOHN HICKS was born in Cambridge, near Boston, and served an apprenticeship with Green & Russell. He was the partner of Nathaniel Mills.

Hicks, previous to his entering into partnership with Mills, was supposed to be a zealous young whig. He was reputed to have been one of the young men who had the affray with some British soldiers which led to the memorable massacre in King street, Boston, on the 5th of March, 1770.

Interest too often biasses the human mind. The officers and friends of government at that time, unquestionably gave encouragement to the few printers who enlisted themselves for the support of the British parliament. Draper's *Massachusetts Gazette and Boston Weekly News Letter* was the only paper in Boston, when, and for some time before, Mills & Hicks began printing, which discovered the least appearance of zeal in sup-

porting the measures of the British administration against the
colonies—and Draper was the printer to the governor and
council.

The *Massachusetts Gazette and Post Boy*, &c., printed by Green
& Russell, was a rather dull recorder of common occurrences.
Its publishers, although instigated by printing for the custom
house, and by other profitable work for government, did not
appear to take an active part in its favor. The dispute with the
parent country daily became more and more important; and it
evidently appeared that the administration deemed it necessary
that there should be a greater number of newspapers zealously
devoted to the support of the cause of Great Britain. It was
therefore decided that Green & Russell should resign the printing of their *Gazette* to Mills & Hicks; and these were animated
by extraordinary encouragement to carry it on with spirit and
energy in support of the royal cause. A number of writers, some
of them said to be officers of the British army, were engaged to
give new life and spirit to this *Gazette*. Mills & Hicks managed
the paper to the satisfaction of their employers until the commencement of the revolutionary war, which took place two
years after they began printing.

The father of Hicks was one of the first who fell in this war.
When a detachment of the British troops marched to Concord
to destroy the public stores collected there by order of the
provincial congress, Hicks's father was among the most forward to fly to arms, in order to attack this detachment on its
return to Boston, after it had killed a number of Americans at
Lexington, and partially executed the design of the expedition
to Concord; and in the defence of his country he lost his life.

Notwithstanding this sacrifice of his father on the altar of liberty, Hicks still adhered to the British, and remained with the royal army, supporting, as a printer, their cause, until a peace was concluded by the acknowledgment of the independence of the United States. When the British army quitted New York, Hicks, with many other Americans loyalist, went with them to Halifax. After remaining there a few years, he returned to Boston. Having acquired a very considerable property by his business during the war, he purchased a handsome estate at Newton, on which he resided until his death.

JOSEPH GREENLEAF was a justice of the peace for the county of Plymouth, and lived at Abington, Massachusetts. He possessed some talents as a popular writer, and in consequence was advised, in 1771, to remove into Boston, and write occasionally on the side of the patriots. He furnished a number of pieces for the *Massachusetts Spy*. These displayed an ardent zeal in the cause of American liberty, and in the then state of the popular mind, amidst many pungent, and some elegantly written communications, they produced a salutary effect.

Not long after he came to Boston, a piece under the signature of Mucius Scævola, as has been already mentioned, appeared in the *Massachusetts Spy*, which attracted the attention of the governor and council of Massachusetts. They sent for Thomas, the printer, but he did not appear before them. Greenleaf who was suspected of being concerned in the publication of that paper, was also required to attend in the council chamber; but he did not make his appearance before that board. The council then advised the governor to take from Greenleaf his commission as a justice of the peace, as he 'was generally reputed to be concerned with Isaiah Thomas in printing and publishing a newspaper called the *Massachusetts Spy*.' Greenleaf was accordingly dismissed as a magistrate.

In 1773, Greenleaf purchased a press and types, and opened a printing house in Hanover street, near Concert Hall. He printed several pamphlets, and *An Abridgment of Burn's Justice of the Peace*.

In August, 1774, he continued the publication of *The Royal American Magazine* begun by Thomas. The revolutionary war closed his printing business. Greenleaf was not bred a printer; but having little property, he set up a press at an advanced period of his life, as the means of procuring a livelihood. A son of his, nearly of age, had learned printing of Thomas,* and managed his father's printing house during the short time he carried on business.

MARGARET DRAPER[34] was the widow of Richard Draper. She published the *Massachusetts Gazette and Boston News Letter* after his death. Boyle, who had been connected with her husband a short time before he died, continued the management of her printing house for about four months; and, during that time, his name appeared after Margaret Draper's in the imprint of the *Gazette*. At the expiration of this period their partnership was dissolved. Margaret Draper conducted the concerns of the printing house for several months, and then formed a connection with John Howe, who managed the business of the company, agreeably to the advice of her friends, whilst she remained in Boston. She printed for the governor and council; but the newspaper was the principal work done in her printing house.

A few weeks after the revolutionary war commenced, and

* Thomas Greenleaf, afterward the publisher of a newspaper in New York.

Boston was besieged, all the newspapers, excepting her's, ceased to be published; and but one of them, *The Boston Gazette*, was revived after the British evacuated the town. It is noteworthy that *The News Letter* was the first and the last newspaper which was published in Boston prior to the declaration of independence.

Margaret Draper left Boston with the British army, and went to Halifax: from thence she soon took passage, with a number of her friends, for England. She received a pension from the British government, and remained in England until her death.

JOHN HOWE was born in Boston, and there served a regular apprenticeship at the printing business. His father was a reputable tradesman in Marshall's lane. In the account given of Margaret Draper, mention is made that Howe became connected with her in publishing her *Gazette*, etc. He had recently become of age, and was a sober, discreet young man; Mrs. Draper, therefore, was induced, a short time before the commencement of the war, to take him into partnership; but his name did not appear in the imprint of the *Massachusetts Gazette* till Boston was besieged by the continental army. Howe remained with his partner until they were obliged to leave Boston, in consequence of the evacuation of the town by the British troops in March, 1776. He then went to Halifax, where he published a newspaper, and printed for the government of Nova Scotia.[35]

SALEM Was the third place in the province of Massachusetts in which a press was established.[36] The first printing house was opened in

1768, by SAMUEL HALL. He was born in Medford, Massachusetts, served an apprenticeship with his uncle, Daniel Fowle,
of Portsmouth, and first began business in Newport, in 1763, in
company with Anne Franklin, whose daughter he married.

He left Newport in March, 1768, opened a printing house in
Salem in April following, and began the publication of *The
Essex Gazette* in August of that year. In three or four years after
he settled in this town, he admitted his brother, Ebenezer Hall,
as a partner. Their firm was SAMUEL & EBENEZER HALL.
They remained in Salem until 1775. Soon after the commencement of the war, to accommodate the state convention and the
army, they removed to Cambridge, and printed in Stoughton
Hall, one of the buildings belonging to Harvard University.

In February, 1776, Ebenezer Hall died, aged twenty-seven
years. He was an amiable young man, and a good printer. He
was born in Medford, and was taught the art of printing by his
brother.

In 1776, on the evacuation of Boston by the British troops,
Samuel Hall removed into that town, and remained there until
1781, when he returned to Salem. He continued in Salem until
November, 1785; at which time he again went to Boston, and
opened a printing house, and a book and stationery store, in
Cornhill.

In April, 1789, he began printing, in the French language, a
newspaper, entitled *Courier de Boston*. This was a weekly paper,
printed on a sheet of crown in quarto, for J. Nancrede, a French-
man, who then taught the language of his nation at the university, and was afterward a bookseller in Boston; but his name
did not appear in the imprint of the paper. *Courier de Boston* was
published only six months.

After Hall relinquished the publication of a newspaper, he printed a few octavo and duodecimo volumes, a variety of small books with cuts, for children, and many pamphlets, particularly sermons. He was a correct printer, and judicious editor; industrious, faithful to his engagements, a respectable citizen, and a firm friend to his country. He died October 30, 1807, aged sixty-seven years.

EZEKIEL RUSSELL has been already mentioned. He removed from Boston to Salem in 1774, and opened, in Ruck street, the second printing house established in that place. In the same year he began the publication of a newspaper, but did not meet with success. He printed ballads and small books. Having remained about two years in Salem, he removed to Danvers, and opened a printing house; from thence, about the year 1778, he returned with his press to Boston.

JOHN ROGERS was born in Boston and served an apprenticeship there, with William Macalpine. He began the publication of a newspaper in Salem, at the printing house of Russell, who was interested in the paper; but it was printed only a few weeks. After this failure in the attempt to establish a paper, I do not recollect to have seen Rogers's name to any publication. He did not own either press or types.

MARY CROUCH was the widow of Charles Crouch, of Charleston, South Carolina. She left Charleston in 1780, a short time before that city was surrendered to the British troops, and brought with her the press and types of her late husband. She opened a printing house in Salem, near the east church, where she published a newspaper for a short time. When she sold her press, &c., she removed to Providence, Rhode Island, the place of her nativity, and there resided.

At the request of several gentlemen, particularly the late Rev. Jonathan Parsons, a press was first established in that town, in 1773, by ISAIAH THOMAS. He opened a printing house in King street, Newburyport, opposite to the Presbyterian church. The town was settled at an early period. In point of magnitude it held the third rank, and it was the fourth where the press was established, in the colony. Thomas took as a partner Henry Walter Tinges. The firm was THOMAS & TINGES. Thomas continued his business in Boston, and Tinges had the principal management of the concerns at Newburyport. They there printed a newspaper, and in that work the press was principally employed. Before the close of a year, Thomas sold the printing materials to Ezra Lunt, the proprietor of a stage, who was unacquainted with printing; but he took Tinges as a partner, and the firm of this company was LUNT & TINGES. They continued their connection until the country became involved in the revolutionary war; soon after which Lunt transferred the press and his concern in printing to John Mycall. Tinges now became the partner of Mycall.

The partnership of MYCALL & TINGES ended in six months. The business was then conducted by Mycall, who soon became so well acquainted with it, as to carry it on, and continue it on a respectable footing, for about twenty years; when he quitted printing, and retired to a farm at Harvard, in the county of Worcester, from whence he removed to Cambridgeport.[37]

Tinges was born in Boston, was of Dutch parentage, and served part of his apprenticeship with Fleming, and the residue with Thomas. He went from Newburyport to Baltimore, and from thence to sea, but never returned.

Lunt joined the American army, and finally removed to Marietta. He was a native of Newburyport.

Mycall was not brought up to printing, but he was a man of great ingenuity. He was born at Worcester, in England; and was a schoolmaster at Amesbury at the time he purchased of Lunt. Some years after he began printing his printing house and all his printing materials were consumed by fire. Those materials were soon replaced by a very valuable printing apparatus.

WORCESTER This was the fifth town in Massachusetts in which the press was established.[38] In 1774, a number of gentlemen in the county of Worcester, zealously engaged in the cause of the country, were, from the then appearance of public affairs, desirous to have a press established in Worcester, the shire town of the county. In December of that year, they applied to a printer in Boston, who engaged to open a printing house, and to publish a newspaper there, in the course of the ensuing spring.

ISAIAH THOMAS, in consequence of an agreement with the gentlemen as above related, to send a press, with a suitable person to manage the concerns of it, to this town, in February, 1775, issued a proposal for publishing a newspaper, to be en-

titled *The Worcester Gazette; or, American Oracle of Liberty*. The
war commencing sooner than was expected, he was obliged to
leave Boston, and came himself to Worcester, opened a printing
house, and on the 3d of May, 1775, executed the first printing
done in the town.

Thomas remained at Worcester until 1776, when he let a part
of his printing apparatus, and his newspaper, to two gentlemen
of the bar, William Stearns and Daniel Bigelow, and with the
other part removed to Salem, with an intention to commence
business in that place; but many obstructions to the plan arising
in consequence of the war, he sold the printing materials which
he carried to that town, and, in 1778, returned to Worcester,
took into possession the press which he had left there, and resumed the publication of the *Spy*.

He received his types worn down, and found paper, wretch-
edly as it was then manufactured, difficult to be obtained; but,
in a few months, he was fortunate enough to purchase some
new types which were taken in a vessel from London. After
some time he also procured paper which was superior in quality
to what was generally manufactured at that period; and thus he
was enabled to keep his printing business alive whilst the war
continued.

During two or three years he was concerned with Joseph
Trumbull in a medicinal store. On the establishment of peace,
an intercourse was opened with Europe, and he procured a
liberal supply of new printing materials, engaged in book printing, opened a bookstore, and united the two branches of printing and bookselling.

In September, 1788, he recommenced printing in Boston,
and at the same time opened a bookstore there. At first, the

business was managed by three partners, under the firm of I. THOMAS & CO.; but one of the partners leaving the company, Thomas formed a copartnership with the other, Ebenezer T. Andrews, who had served his apprenticeship with him, and the house took the firm of THOMAS & ANDREWS.

In 1793, he set up a press and opened a bookstore at Walpole, New Hampshire, where he began the publication of a newspaper entitled *The Farmer's Museum*.[39]

In 1794, he opened another printing house and a bookstore at Brookfield, Massachusetts. All these concerns were managed by partners, and distinct from his business in Worcester; where he continued to reside, and to carry on printing and bookselling on his sole account. At Worcester, he also erected a paper mill, and set up a bindery; and was thus enabled to go through the whole process of manufacturing books.

In 1794, he and his partner at Boston extended a branch of their bookselling business to Baltimore. The house there established was known as the firm of THOMAS, ANDREWS & BUTLER; and, in 1796, they established another branch of their business at Albany, under the firm of THOMAS, ANDREWS & PENNIMAN, and there opened a printing house and bookstore.

The books printed by him at Worcester, and by him and his partners in other places, form a very considerable catalogue. At one time they had sixteen presses in use; seven of them at his printing house in Worcester, and five at the company's printing house in Boston. They printed three newspapers in the country, and a magazine in Boston; and they had five bookstores in Massachusetts, one in New Hampshire, one at Albany, and one at Baltimore.

Among the books which issued from Thomas's press at

Worcester, were, in 1791, an edition of the Bible, in folio, with copperplates, and, an edition, in royal quarto, with a concordance; in 1793, a large edition of the Bible in octavo; and, in 1797, the Bible in duodecimo. Of this last size, several editions were printed, as the types, complete for the work, were kept standing. In 1802, he printed a second edition of the octavo Bible.

Among the books printed by the company in Boston, were, *The Massachusetts Magazine*, published monthly, in numbers, for five years, constituting five octavo volumes; five editions of *The Universal Geography*, in two volumes octavo, and several other heavy works; also, the Bible in 12mo, numerous editions; the types for which were removed from Worcester to Boston.

In 1802, Thomas resigned the printing at Worcester to his son Isaiah Thomas, jun., and soon after, transferred to him the management of the *Massachusetts Spy*. His son continued the publication of that paper, and carried on printing and bookselling.

HEZEKIAH USHER, [1652] was the first bookseller in English America of whom I can find any account.[40] Books formed a proportion of his stock in trade; and the first works which were published in this country were printed for him. Of these an edition of the New England version of the Psalms, small 12mo, to bind up with Bibles, claims the precedence. The imprint to that book is, 'Cambridge, Printed for Hezekiah Usher, of Boston.' The date and the name of the printer are omitted; but I have no doubt the book had gone through three or four editions, as early as the year 1652.

Soon after the settlement of some parts of America, a corporation was established in England for propagating the gospel among the Indians in New England; and Usher[41] was agent for managing the pecuniary concerns between the corporation and the commissioners of the United colonies in New England. He procured the types, paper, &c., and managed the transactions relating to printing the Bible in the Indian language, which was in the press from 1660 to 1663. Besides bookselling, he conducted a commercial establishment, and acquired considerable property.

1672. JOHN USHER, the son of Hezekiah. In 1672 an edition of the laws, revised and alphabetically arranged, was printed by S. Green, in Cambridge, for John Usher in Boston. I have seen several books printed for him since that time.

An English bookseller, who was an author, and resided some time in Boston,* wrote thus concerning John Usher. 'This Trader makes the best figure in Boston; he's very Rich, adventures much to Sea; but has got his estate by Book-Selling; he proposed to me the buying of my whole Venture, † but would not agree to my Terms; and so we parted with a great deal of seeming respect.'

John Usher was treasurer of the province when Sir Edmund Andros was governor. He was employed by the government of Massachusetts, when he was in England, to purchase the province of Maine from the heirs of Sir Ferdinando Gorges. In 1683, he became lieutenant governor of New Hampshire, which office he retained some years; but, during the time he resided

---

* John Dunton.

† A large collection of books bought by Dunton to sell in Boston, anno 1686.

chiefly in Boston, and carried on his business as usual. 'He was a man of unpolished manners, severe in the execution of his office, was but little of a statesman, and less of a courtier,* and became so odious to the poeple, that they prevailed on the king and council to remove him.' He had a seat at Charlestown at which he resided after he retired from business, anno 1700.

1673. EDMUND RANGER,[42] was a binder; but had some small concern in bookselling.

1679. WILLIAM AVERY, 'Near the Blue-Anchor.' I have found but few books printed for him.

1680. SAMUEL PHILLIPS, 'At the Brick-Shop at the West-End of the Town-House.' Considering the infant state of the settlement, he was a large dealer in books; many of which were consigned to him by Dunton, who was his factor in London. He published several books which were printed in Boston.

Dunton mentions Phillips as his 'old correspondent;' and observes further, 'On visiting him in Boston, he treated me with a noble Dinner, and (if I may trust my Eyes) is blest with a pretty, obliging Wife; I'll say that for *Sam* (after dealing with him for some Hundred Pounds) he's very just, and (as an Effect of that) very Thriving. I shall only add to his Character, that he's Young and Witty, and the *most Beautiful Man in the Town of Boston*.' He died in October 1720, aged 58; and was charac-terized in the Boston Gazette, as 'an exemplary Christian, an indulgent husband, a kind father and a true friend.'

The descendants of Samuel Phillips continued the bookselling business in Cornhill, till after the revolution. They traded in

* Jeremy Belknap, *History of New Hampshire* (Philadelphia, 1784), I, 288–289.

English goods also, as was customary with the booksellers in Boston for a century after the town was first settled.

1682. JOHN RATCLIFFE[43] did but little work as a bookseller; but I have discovered a few pamphlets which were printed for him.

1682. SAMUEL SEWALL, was a bookseller, although not bred to the trade. He was appointed by the government to the office of a magistrate; and, in 1681, was made conductor of the press in Boston, with permission to carry on printing in that town.[44]

1682. JOHN GRIFFIN. I have seen only two books printed for him, and one for him and John Ratcliffe.

1684. RICHARD WILKINS, 'Near the Town-House.' He had been a bookseller at Limerick, in Ireland, but came to New England as an asylum from religious persecution, and settled in Boston.

Dunton gives the following description of him: 'His Person is Tall, his Aspect Sweet and Smiling, and tho' but Fifty Years old [in 1686*] his Hair is as White as Snow. He is a Person of good Sense, keeps up the Practice of Religion in his Family, and (upon a Nice Search into all his Affairs) I found it had a General Influence on all the Actions of his Life: He was deservedly chosen a Member of Mr. Willard's Church, and I think he's a Pious Man, if there's such a Thing in Boston.' He died at Milton, December 10, 1704, aged 81, and was buried in Boston.

Dunton gives the characters of Wilkins's wife and daughter, who were very amiable and accomplished women. During the eight months that Dunton carried on bookselling in Boston, he

* This statement of Dunton is not altogether correct; Wilkins was then sixty-three years old.

boarded with Wilkins, who did considerable business. When Dunton left that place, he empowered Wilkins to collect such debts as were due to him there.

1684. JOSEPH BRUNNING, *alias* BROWNING, 'At the Corner of Prison-Lane,' now Court street, in Cornhill, was from Amsterdam; he wrote his name Brunning, or Browning, at pleasure. He traded largely and published many books, the imprints in which are indifferently spelled Brunning or Browning; one of these being the Dutch, the other the English way of writing his name.

Dunton mentions him in a very handsome manner. In describing his visits to the various booksellers in Boston, after his arrival there in 1686, he thus characterizes Brunning: 'I rambled next to visit *Minheer* Brunning, he's a Dutch bookseller from Holland, scrupulously just, plain in his cloaths, and if we will believe the Printers in Boston (who are notable Criticks in such cases) a most excellent Paymaster. Brunning is vers'd in the Knowledge of all sorts of books, and may well Be stil'd a Complet Bookseller. He never decries a Book because 'tis not of his own printing; there are some Men that will run down the most Elaborate Pieces, only because they had none of their Midwifery to bring 'em into public view, and yet shall give the greatest Encomiums to the most Nauseous Trash, when they had the hap to be concerned in it. But Brunning was none of these; for he'd promote a good Book whoever printed it; and I found him a Man of that great Interest, that I made him my Partner in printing Mr. Mather's Sermon, preached at the Execution of Morgan, who was the only person executed in that Country for near Seven years.'*

* John Dunton's *Life and Errors* (London, 1705).

1684. DUNCAN CAMPBELL, 'At the Dock-Head over against the Conduit,' was from Glasgow, and was, probably, the father of John Campbell who, in 1704, was post master in Boston, and the proprietor of the first newspaper which was published in the English American colonies.*

Dunton mentions Campbell by name, as 'the Scotch Bookseller,' and says, 'he is very industrious, dresses *a la mode*, and I'm told, a Young Lady of Great Fortune, is fal'n in love with him.'

1685. ANDREW THORNCOMB, from London; he was a bookseller in that city. I believe he, like many others for some years after the settlement of Boston, came over with a quantity of books on speculation, and having sold them, perhaps the greater part by wholesale, returned to Europe.

Dunton writes that he was acquainted with Thorncomb in New England, and mentions that 'his Company was Coveted by the best Gentlemen in Boston, nor is he less acceptable to the Fair Sex; for he has something in him so extremely charming as makes 'em very fond of his company. However he's a vertuous Person, and deserves all the respect they shew'd him.'

1686. JAMES COWSE. I have seen only one book printed for him namely 'The Church of Rome, evidently proved Heretick.'

1686. JOHN DUNTON,[45] was born at Graffham, Huntingdonshire, in England; his father was fellow of Trinity College, Cambridge, and rector of Graffham.

Dunton was brought up to the bookselling business in London; where he entered extensively into the trade; and in the course of time became a very considerable publishing book-

* *Ibid.*

seller. He had a general correspondence with the booksellers of England, Scotland, Ireland and Boston. But fortune did not always smile on Dunton. He lost a large sum through becoming surety for his brother-in-law, and was a great sufferer by the troubles of England in 1685; insomuch that his circumstances became embarrassed.

On the death of Charles II, James II, his brother, ascended the throne of England; who being a great enemy to the duke of Monmouth, the natural son of Charles II, caused him to be expelled from Holland, by the prince of Orange; and was the occasion of his being persecuted in Brussels. Being a favorite with the people, Monmouth was stimulated by that consideration, and by a principle of revenge, to make an attempt to dethrone James, and place the crown of England on his own head. He landed in England, raised a small army, which was defeated, and he was beheaded in consequence of this rebellion. His adherents fled; and Dunton, being one of these fugitives, escaped to Boston, where the sum of five hundred pounds sterling—a considerable object in the deranged state of his circumstances—was due to him; and his design in going there was to collect his debts. The management of his affairs in London he intrusted to his wife, who, according to his own account, was a most excellent woman, and he had a great affection for her. He embarked on board a ship then lying at Gravesend, and took with him books suitable for the Boston market to a large amount. He put others to the value of five hundred pounds sterling on board another vessel, destined to the same port. The ships were overtaken by foul weather, before they cleared the British channel. That which bore the consignment was lost, but the other, in which Dunton had embarked, weathered the

storm. After a tedious passage of more than four months duration he arrived in Boston. Dunton had taken the precaution of
procuring letters of recommendation to the most eminent
clergymen in Massachusetts, and to the principal gentlemen in
Boston; in consequence of which he was kindly received and
politely treated on his arrival. He procured a warehouse where
he exposed his books for sale, and found a good market for
them. At the expiration of seven or eight months he had a considerable number of books unsold; but he opened a store in
Salem, where he soon disposed of the same.

During Dunton's residence in Boston, he visited the governor, lieutenant governor, the principal magistrates, &c., and
dined with them in the town hall, on the day of election. He
paid his respects to all the clergy, in and about Boston, Dr.
Increase Mather, the Rev. Cotton Mather, Messrs. Willard,
Allen, Eliot, Higginson, of Salem, and many other ministers.
Dr. Mather he calls the 'metropolitan clergyman of the country.' When he had sold off his books, he took leave of his
friends, and returned to England.

On his arrival there he was apprehensive of a prosecution, for
which reason, after remaining some time incognito, he went to
Holland, Germany and Ireland. A revolution having been effected in England, in 1688, Dunton returned to London, and
recommenced business on the very day the Prince of Orange
arrived in that city. Dunton again launched forth into extensive
business; and published many works, among which were some
that were periodical. *The Athenian Gazette*, which was afterwards denominated *The Athenian Mercury*, was continued several years, and the editors of it, among whom Dunton was the
principal, were highly complimented in poetical and prosaic

essays, by Gildon, Motteux, De Foe, Richardson, and the celebrated poet laureat, N. Tate, who was concerned in a version of the Psalms, which is well known in America. His other periodical works were *The Post-Angell*, and *The Night Walker*.

As a kind of drawback on Dunton's fame, I ought, perhaps, candidly to mention that he had the misfortune to be introduced into Pope's *Dunciad*,* where the present of the goddess Dulness to Curl is represented as

> A shaggy tapestry, worthy to be spread
> On Codrus' old, or DUNTON's modern bed.

The note of the Scriblerus Club, on this passage, runs thus, 'John Dunton was a broken bookseller, and abusive scribler; he writ *Neck or Nothing*, a violent satire on some ministers of state; a libel on the duke of Devonshire, and the bishop of Peterborough, &c.'

In justice to Dunton I must observe, that this severity was, perhaps, wholly unmerited, and produced solely by a difference of opinion; as the works which the club calls libels might be strictly conformable to truth, and probably met the applause of those who thought like Dunton.

During his second run of business Dunton lost his wife; and married another, whose fortune, though considerable, was not payable till a younger brother came of age. After ten years of success in business, the tide again turned, and through losses in trade, and other misfortunes, Dunton again became embarrassed. On this occasion he pressed his wife's mother to enable him to pay his debts, but could not prevail, although he thought to enforce compliance, by abstaining from the usual intercourse

---

* Book II, v. 144, &c.

with his wife. To these means he added entreaty and argument; but they proved equally ineffectual; and Dunton, who formerly wrote for profit and fame, was now obliged to write for his daily subsistence. At this period, anno 1705, he published *The Life and Errors of John Dunton, late Citizen of London; Written by Himself in Solitude*. He gives an account of his voyage to Boston, of his business there, and of his travels in Holland and Germany. He characterizes upwards of a thousand persons then living, among whom were the booksellers of most note in Boston, many of the clergy and other eminent persons he visited, or with whom he was acquainted, together with several of his male and female customers, in and about 'the metropolis of New England;' after which he proceeds to the authors for whom he published, all the printers, binders, engravers on wood and copper, whom he had employed, and the company of stationers in London; and, he concludes with the most conspicuous of his London customers. He was an adept in writing of this kind, and appeared to engage in it with peculiar pleasure and ease. In this work there is a singular mixture of humor, anecdote and religion, and it is, perhaps, a true picture of the mind and disposition of the author. At the conclusion of it he observes, 'could I not compose a few sheets for the press, I might now starve; but it is well known that in the course of a few years I shall be able to pay all I owe to a half farthing.'

Dunton had a patent from king William and queen Mary, for the sole printing and publishing an English translation of *The History of the Edict of Nantz*, in four volumes. During the life of his first wife he made a will, and appointed her sole executrix, and desired her to bury him the *seventh day after his death, and not before*, lest he should come to life, as his mother had done on the day appointed for her funeral. This circumstance, respecting his mother, he relates at the beginning of his *Life*, &c. Having been sick, she, to all appearance, died. 'After lying three days, her friends were about to put her into a Coffin for interment, when to their astonishment she revived from the trance in which she had fallen, and was thus mercifully restored; in a year after she dy'd in earnest.'

Dunton was a man of a singular character. He appears to have been a complete, enterprising bookseller; and was sensible, humorous and religious.

1690. NICHOLAS BUTTOLPH, 'Next to Guttridge's Coffee-House.'

I have discovered many books which were printed for him. He carried on business about fifty years, and was a man of respectability. On the 29th of January, 1737, he died, considerably advanced in years.

1690. BENJAMIN ELLIOTT, 'Under the Exchange, Head of King-Street.' He was largely concerned in publishing books, among which were the laws of the general court; and he was a noted dealer in books which were printed in Boston. He was about fifty years in business; and died November 9, 1741, aged seventy-six years.

1690. BENJAMIN HARRIS, had a bookstore 'at the London Coffee-House,' two or three years; but removed to 'The Sign of the Bible over against the Blew-Anchor, Cornhill.'

He had been a bookseller and printer in London, and he printed and published several books during his residence in Boston;* where he remained five or six years. He returned to England, and followed printing and bookselling in London.

* See pp. 88–90.

1690. OBADIAH GILL, was but little known as a dealer in books. I have seen only two pamphlets which were printed for him.

1690. JAMES WADE. I have found a few pamphlets with the imprint, 'Boston, Printed for James Wade,' which is all the intelligence I can procure concerning him.

1695. MICHAEL PERRY, 'under the West-End of the Town House,'* was a publisher as well as a vender of books, and did considerable business.

1695. VAVASOUR HARRIS, 'opposite the Old Meeting-House, in Cornhill,' was a short time in the business.

1699. ELKANAH PEMBROKE, 'near the Head of the Dock.'

1700. SAMUEL SEWALL, junior, was the son of Samuel Sewall, who was appointed conductor of the press, and was authorized to print in Boston. I do not find that he was largely in trade.

1701. NICHOLAS BOONE, 'at the Bible in Cornhill.' In 1704, when *The Boston News-Letter* made its first appearance, it was printed by B. Green, and published by Boone, for John Campbell, the proprietor of it, who was postmaster.

Boone was an eminent bookseller, and many books, written in America, were published by him.

1711. ELEAZAR PHILLIPS,[46] 'at the Sign of the Eagle in Newbury Street,' afterwards 'at the Lower-End of King Street;' and, in 1715, he removed to Charlestown, near Boston. He was the only bookseller who had settled in that town prior to the revolution; but never embarked largely in trade. One of his sons established the first press in South Carolina; and died there

---

* The present old state house was built on the site of the town house.

in 1732, soon after he began printing. Some time after the death
of his son, Phillips went to Carolina: and after remaining there
a few months he returned to his business in Massachusetts.

In 1750, Phillips published in the Boston Evening-Post, a
short address to the public, in which he recommended the rais-
ing of silk worms in New England. He stated that when he
resided in Carolina, he was informed by a silk weaver that 'only
one crop' could be raised there in a year; that he had made an
experiment with eggs which he brought from Philadelphia,
and found that he could raise two crops, annually, in New
England. The advantage he attributed to the climate, which he
supposed was more favorable to the growth of the mulberry,
than that of South Carolina, which he thought too warm to
produce food so nutricious and congenial to worms as that
raised in more temperate regions. Where vegetation is less rapid, and the leaves longer in coming to maturity, they do not
ripen and decay so speedily as in Carolina. His advice does not
appear to have been regarded.

Phillips lived to the age of upwards of seventy-five years.

1712. JOANNA PERRY, 'King-Street, near the Town-
House.' She was the widow of Michael Perry, and after his
death continued the business several years. Some pamphlets
were printed for her. She died September 19, 1725.

1712. SAMUEL GERRISH, 'at the Sign of the Buck in Marlborough-Street,' but in 1716, 'North Side of the Town-House.'
He published a number of small books, and seems to have carried on considerable trade.

1713. DANIEL HENCHMAN,[47] 'Cornhill, Corner of King-
Street, opposite to the Old Brick-Meeting-House.'

Henchman was the most eminent and enterprising bookseller that appeared in Boston, or, indeed, in all British America, before the year 1775. He furnished much employment for the presses in Boston; and several books were printed for him in London, which were sent over in sheets. He was principally concerned in an edition of the Bible, and another of the New Testament, which were printed privately in Boston.* Henchman built the first paper mill in New England; in doing which he received aid from the legislature of Massachusetts. During his long connexion with the trade he acquired a handsome estate. He was made a justice of the peace; a lieutenant colonel of the Boston regiment of militia; and, finally, was made a deacon of the Old South church. He died February 25, 1761, aged seventy-two years.

1715. GEORGE BROWNELL, lived at 'the North End,' and advertised that he taught 'Writing, Cyphering, Navigation, also Musick and Dancing.' And he sold books also. I have seen an Almanack which was printed for him; but he was very little known as a bookseller. He removed to Philadelphia.

1717. GILLAM PHILLIPS, 'over against the West-End of the Town-House.' He was neither largely nor long in the trade. I have seen only two small works printed for him. A considerable fortune was left to him, and he retired from business. He died October 18, 1770, aged seventy-five years.

1719. BENJAMIN GRAY, at the 'Head of Town-Dock,' published several books, among which was a pamphlet, the publication whereof brought on him a prosecution on the part of the government, as appears by the following record of the proceedings of the council, viz.:

* Vide pp. 103-104.

'At a Council Held at the Council-Chamber, in Boston, on Thursday the 28th day of February, 1720 [i.e. 1721, new style.]

'A pamphlet, entituled, a letter to an Eminent Clergy-Man in the Massachusetts-Bay; being produced at the Board, was Read and considered, and Unanimously Voted, That it contains in it many Vile, Scandalous, and very Abusive Expressions, which greatly reflect on His Majesty's Government and People of this Province, and tend to disturb the Publick Peace.

'At the same time Benj. Gray of Boston, Bookseller, who Sold the said Pamphlet, being Sent for, Acknowledged that he had caused the same to be Printed, And that the Original in manuscript was delivered to him by an unknown Hand, upon Saturday the Eighth Currant, at Nine a Clock at Night.

'*Advised*, That the Attorney-General be directed to Prosecute in the Law, the said Benj. Gray, or any other Person that may have been concerned in the making or Publishing the said Pamphlet.

'Resolved, That the foregoing Votes be printed in the Weekly Papers.

J. Willard, Secr.'

I am not perfectly acquainted with the result of this affair, but I believe it was terminated by a compromise.

Gray, though not a very considerable bookseller, was many years in trade, and worked at bookbinding. He died January 7, 1751.

1719. JOHN EDWARDS, 'King-Street.' I can learn but little respecting him, further than that he published a few books.

1720. ROBERT STARKEY, 'Fleet-Street,' was from London. Whilst in business in that city, he published a book containing reflections on the British government; and fled to Holland to avoid a prosecution. After the prince of Orange ascended the English throne he returned to England, and continued his business in London several years; he also made a voyage to Boston; but did not go largely into trade there. How long he remained in New England I cannot ascertain. It is said he was a man who possessed much information, and was a zealous asserter of English liberty.

1723. JOSEPH EDWARDS, 'Cornhill,' was a very respectable, and a considerable publisher, bookseller and binder. He continued in business more than forty years.

1723. NATHANIEL BELKNAP, 'Head of Scarlet's Wharf, North End.' He bound books, but did not go largely into the sale of them. Some small pamphlets were published by him.

In April, 1730, he published in the Boston papers the following advertisement: 'To be Sold, Choice black Mold for Gardens, &c. at a very reasonable rate, By Mr. Nath. Belknap, Bookseller, at the North-End of Boston.'

1723. SAMUEL ROBINSON, was born in Dorchester, and served his apprenticeship with Boone. He sold some books, but his principal business was that of a binder. He died at the age of eighty-five years, in February, 1771.

1724. JOHN CHECKLEY,[48] was I believe, an Englishman, and of the high church party. He published and sold a pamphlet, containing 132 pages, octavo, entitled *A Short and Easie Method with the Deists. Wherein the certainty of the Christian Religion is demonstrated, by infallible Proof from Four Rules, which are incompatible to any Imposture that ever yet has been, or that can possibly be.* The imprint to the book was, 'Printed in London, by J. Applebee, and sold by John Checkley at the Sign of the *Crown* and *Blue-Gate*, over-against the West-End of the Town-House, in Boston, 1723.' Checkley was prosecuted at the inferior court in Boston, anno 1724, for publishing and selling this pamphlet, which was called 'a false and scandalous libel, tending to draw into dispute his present majesty's title to the crown—scandalizing the ministers of the gospel, established by law in this province—falsifying the Holy Scriptures—representing the church of Rome as the present mother church; and tending to raise divisions, jealousies, and animosities, among his majesty's loving subjects of this province.' Checkley was convicted, and appealed to the superior court, in which the jury gave the following verdict:

'The Jury find Specially, viz. If the Book entituled a Short and Easy Method with the Deists, containing in it a Discourse concerning Episcopacy, (published, and many of them sold by the said Checkley) be false and scandalous libel; Then we find the said Checkley guilty of all and every Part of the Indictment (excepting that supposed to traduce and draw into dispute the undoubted Right and Title of our Sovereign Lord, King George, to the Kingdoms of Great-Britain and Ireland, and the territories thereto belonging.) But if the said Book, containing a discourse concerning Episcopacy, as aforesaid, be not a false and scandalous Libel; Then we find him not guilty.

Att^t. *Samuel Tyley*, Clerk.'

An able plea in arrest of judgment, was made by his counsel; after which Checkley addressed the court, and in the same handsome manner and style in which he had before addressed the court and jury, he maintained that the church of England, as established in England, and no other, was established in all his majesty's plantations—that no minister was lawfully appointed, but he who was ordained by a bishop—and he gave it as his opinion, that presbyterian and congregational ministers, so called, were no ministers, and that they and their congregations were schismatics, and excommunicated by the laws of the land; or rather by the canons of the church of England, which he said were a part of the laws of the land. The sentence of the court was as follows:

'The Court having maturely advised on this Special Verdict, are of Opinion that the said John Checkley is guilty of publishing and selling of a false and scandalous Libel. It's therefore considered by the Court, that the said John Checkley shall pay a Fine of Fifty Pounds to the King, and enter into Recognizance in the sum of One Hundred Pounds, with two Sureties in the Sum of Fifty Pounds each, for his good Behaviour for six Months, and also pay costs of prosecution, standing committed until this Sentence be performed.

Att^t. *Samuel Tyley*, Clerk.'

Checkley paid the fine and costs of court the next day, according to the sentence, and was discharged. Sometime after he went to England, and there received episcopal ordination. He returned to New England; was many years rector of St. John's church in Providence; and was highly esteemed for his learning and many amiable qualifications. Whether he was a regular bookseller or not, I am not prepared to say; I have seen no book printed for him in America.

1725. JOHN PHILLIPS, 'Stationers'-Arms, Corn-Hill,' was the son of Samuel Phillips, and succeeded him in business.

Besides a considerable trade as a publishing bookseller and binder, he was a dealer in English goods, according to the custom of those times.

During several years, Phillips was engaged in the service of the public, as a magistrate, a colonel of the Boston militia, a member of the general court and a deacon of the church in Brattle street. He died April 19, 1763, and was buried with military honors.

1726. BENNET LOVE, 'in Anne-Street, near the Bridge.' His principal business appears to have been binding; but some pamphlets were printed for him.

1727. SAMUEL KNEELAND,[49] 'in King-Street, next door to the Post-Office.' He kept a bookstore four or five years at that place; but during the remainder of his life he attended wholly to printing.

1726 THOMAS HANCOCK,[50] 'Anne-Street, near the Draw-Bridge;' was the son of the Rev. John Hancock of Lexington. After being in trade a few years as a bookseller and binder, he turned his attention to merchandize, in which pursuit he acquired a very handsome fortune, and became one of the principal commercial persons in New England.

In process of time he became a member of the lower house of assembly, and was afterwards a member of the council. His disposition was naturally benevolent, and his religious and political sentiments were liberal.

I believe he served his apprenticeship with Daniel Henchman, whose daughter he married. By his last will he bequeathed 1000l. sterling to Harvard College, for the purpose of founding a professorship of the Hebrew and other oriental languages; also 750l, sterling to an incorporated society for propagating the gospel among the Indians, in North America; and 450l, sterling to the town of Boston, towards building an hospital for the reception of lunatics. As he had no children, he bequeathed the greater part of his estate to his nephew, the late governor John

Hancock. He built the large stone house near the State House where he lived; and after his death it became the residence of his nephew the governor.

On the 1st of August, 1764, as he was entering the council chamber, he was attacked by a fit of apoplexy, and died in two hours, aged 62.

1727. NATHANIEL PROCTOR, 'At the Bible and Dove in Anne-Street,' born in Boston; was a bookseller and binder, and published a few pamphlets.

He married a woman who was supposed to have been a widow; but a short time after his marriage, the former husband of his wife returned after an absence of ten or twelve years, and claimed her. This event occasioned much embarrassment; but the parties having left the solution of the difficulty to the wife, she decided in favor of Proctor.

He died suddenly, December 8, 1766.

1728. JOHN ELIOT, 'At the Great Elms,* South-End,' was said to be a descendant of the Rev. John Eliot, of Roxbury, who translated the Bible into the Indian language.

He published a few books, and was, many years, a bookseller and binder, but his concerns were not extensive. However, he acquired some property; and being a respectable man, was made deacon of the church in Hollis street. He died, November, 1771, aged 81.

1729. ALFORD BUTLER, 'Lower-End of King-Street, near

---

* One of these elms stood in the yard, fronting Eliot's house, and was afterwards called The Tree of Liberty, occasioned by the effigy of the person appointed distributor of the stamps in Boston, and that of lord Bute, being hung thereon in 1765. This strong method adopted by the people, of expressing their dislike of the obnoxious stamp act, must have had an influence in producing that state of the public mind which brought about the revolution.

the Crown Coffee-House, at the head of the Long-Wharf.' He was born in Boston, and served his apprenticeship with Henchman. His principal business was binding, but he published and sold a few books. He died in 1742, aged 46.

1730.   HOPESTILL FOSTER, did some business as a bookseller, but it was very inconsiderable.

1730.   FRANCIS SKINNER,[51] 'At his shop in Fish-Street near Halsey's Wharf,' afterwards 'at Pope's Head, Corner of Prince-Street,' was not long in business nor much known as a bookseller.

1731.   JOHN PEMBERTON, 'School Street,' was born in Boston. He was the son of the Rev. Mr. Pemberton the elder; and brother of the Rev. Ebenezer Pemberton, of the new brick church, formerly so called, in Middle street. He was an apprentice to Robinson; but was chiefly employed in binding. He died about 1759.

1732.   RICHARD FRY, an Englishman, resided a few years in Boston; and was probably concerned in the paper mill then lately erected at Milton, which was the only one in Massachusetts. I cannot ascertain whether Fry ever had a shop of his own in Boston, or made use of that belonging to Fleet altogether. The principal discoveries I have made concerning him are comprised in the following advertisement, which was published in *The Rehearsal*, May 1732.

'Richard Fry, Stationer, Bookseller, Paper Maker and Rag Merchant from the city of London, keeps at Mr. Tho. Fleet's Printer, at the Heart and Crown in Cornhill, Boston; where said Fry is ready to accommodate all Gentlemen, Merchants and Tradesmen, with Setts of Accompt Books after the neatest Manner. And whereas it has been the common Method of the most curious Merchants in Boston, to procure their Books from London. This is to acquaint those Gentlemen, that I the said Fry will sell all Sorts of Accompt Books done after the most acute Manner, for Twenty per Cent cheaper than they can have them from London. I return the Public Thanks for following the Directions of my former Advertisement for gathering Rags, and hope they will Continue the like Method, having received upwards of Seven Thousand Weight already.

'For the pleasing Entertainment of the Polite part of Mankind, I have Printed the most beautiful Poems of Mr. Stephen Duck, the famous Wiltshire Poet. It is a full Demonstration to me, that the people of New England have a fine Taste for good Sense and polite Learning, having already Sold 1200 of those Poems.

Rich. Fry.'

1733. T. Cox, 'At the Lamb, on the South-Side of the Town-House,' was a bookseller from England, who kept a good supply of English editions, principally of such books as were valuable, and suitable for the market. He generally resided in London, and his business was transacted by an agent. He discontinued his bookstore in Boston, anno 1744; and the remains of his stock in trade were sold by auction.

1733. JOHN BOYDELL, 'In King-Street.' He came from England in 1716, with Governor Shute, to whom he was Secretary; and being afterwards appointed postmaster, he was for many years proprietor and publisher of *The Boston Gazette*. Boydell was greatly esteemed. He died in December, 1739.

1735. JOHN PARKER, 'Head of the Town-Dock,' sold cutlery, groceries, and some books. He died in 1738.

1736. WILLIAM GRAY, 'Milk Street.'

1736. MICHAEL DENNIS, 'Head of Scarlet's Wharf [afterwards Hancock's], North-End,' was, during several years, a respectable dealer in books and stationery; he published some works, and was concerned in the binding business. He died July 12, 1763.

1739. CHARLES HARRISON, 'Over against the Brazen-Head in Cornhill,' was born, and brought up a bookbinder, in England. He settled in Boston as a bookseller and binder; and published Erskine's *Gospel Sonnets*, with other works of a similar description. He joined the expedition which went from Boston against Louisburg, in 1745, and died soon after he returned.

1740. BENJAMIN ELIOT, 'South End.'

1740. SAMUEL ELIOT, 'Corn-Hill,' published a number of pamphlets, which were written in New England; he was a considerable bookseller, and was also a binder and stationer. He died May 9, 1745, aged 32. His widow carried on the business; and his son Samuel Eliot, became an eminent merchant.

1743. JOHN ELIOT, 'At the Great Elms,' was the son of John Eliot who for many years did business at the same place. Some books printed for John Eliot the younger have this imprint: 'for J. Eliot, near the South-Market.'* He lived to an advanced age.

1743. WALTER MACALPINE, 'Near the Mill-Bridge,' afterwards 'in Union-Street near the Town-Dock.' He was from Scotland, and was a bookseller and binder. He removed to Connecticut and died there.

1743. NATHANIEL GOOKIN, 'Cornhill.'

* At that time there were three market houses in Boston; one near the Great elms; one in Dock square, and another in Old North square.

1743. JOSHUA BLANCHARD, 'Sign of the Bible and Crown in Dock-Square,' was an enterprising but not a successful bookseller.

Blanchard was one of the original proprietors and publishers of *The American Magazine*, which was first published in 1743; and was concerned in other publications. He was a dealer in English editions, in stationery, &c., but finally he confined his trade solely to English goods.

1743. ALEXANDER CARLISLE, A Scotchman; served his apprenticeship in Glasgow; he came from that place with a collection of books; sold them chiefly at auction, and returned to Scotland.

1745. DANIEL GOOKIN, 'Over against the Old-South.' He was a descendant of Gen. Daniel Gookin, one of the first appointed licensers of the press, anno, 1662.

Gookin was not largely in trade; he died January 3, 1752, after an illness of only two days. I am of opinion he had a son who was named after him, and succeeded him in the same shop, which was next door north of the house built for the residence of the royal governors, and now belonging to the state.

1745. THOMAS RAND, 'Cornhill, near the sign of the Three Nuns,' afterwards 'in Anne-Street.' He was by trade a binder, but sold stationery and some books.

1745. JOSHUA WINTER, 'Union-Street,' acquired some property as a bookseller, stationer and binder. Winter was a very pious, upright man. He died in December, 1761.

1749. JOHN AMORY, 'Union Street,' followed bookselling and binding a few years; and was afterwards an eminent merchant in company with his brother, under the firm of Jonathan and John Amory.

1753.   THOMAS LEVERETT, 'Cornhill,' was a very respect-able bookseller, binder, stationer, and dealer in English goods. He died June 28, 1778, aged 46.

1753.   WILLIAM MACALPINE, 'Marlborough-Street,' brother to Walter MacAlpine, was bred to binding, &c., by his brother; and became a considerable bookseller. In 1762, he set up a press, and entered into the printing business.

As MacAlpine was a royalist, he left Boston with the British troops in 1776; soon after which he returned to Scotland, and died at Glasgow, anno 1788.

1754.   CALEB BLANCHARD, 'Dock-Square,' was a brother to Joshua. He was originally a dealer in books, but became an importer of English goods.

1755.   TIMOTHY WHITE, 'Marshall's-Lane,' and other sit-uations in Boston; sold small books; but was chiefly employed about plain binding. He did very little business of any kind. During the siege, he remained in the town; and afterwards removed into the country, where he died.

1757.   SAMUEL WEBB, 'Anne-Street,' was born in Boston, where he served his apprenticeship with Henchman. He carried on bookselling and binding a number of years, but not to a very considerable extent. He died January 29, 1792.

1758.   JEREMY CONDY,[52] 'Near Concert-Hall', after-wards in Union-Street, opposite the Sign of the Cornfield,' kept a supply of valuable books, chiefly English editions, and stationery.

He received his education at Harvard College, and was a man of learning and respectability; and minister of the First Baptist Church in Boston. He died in August, 1768, aged 60.

1760.   WILLIAM LANG, 'at the Gilt Bible, Marlboro'-

Street.' He came from Scotland, and was brought up to binding, which business he followed in Boston, and accompanied it with bookselling. His sales were chiefly confined to Scotch editions of school and religious books. He died in Boston before the year 1775.

1761. JOHN WHARTON, 'Cornhill, Corner of King-Street,' opposite the Old Brick Church. He and Nicholas Bowes began business in company under the firm of Wharton & Bowes. They succeeded Daniel Henchman, whose stand, which had been occupied many years as a book and stationery store, with his stock, they took possession of. Their business was not so extensive as that of their predecessor, particularly in the publishing line; very few books were printed for them, as they confined themselves, principally, to trading in English editions.

Wharton died in January 1768, aged 34.

Bowes continued the business till he died, in April 1790.

1762. JOHN HODGSON, 'Marlborough-Street,' was bred to bookbinding in Scotland, and became a good workman. He was chiefly employed in this business, but sold a few books. By permission of the court, he took, in short hand, the trial of the soldiers who were concerned in the massacre at Boston, on the evening of the 5th of March, 1770. He gave up his shop in 1768, and was employed by John Mein. Afterwards he sold small books from a stall in the market place. He died about the year 1781.

1762. PHILIP FREEMAN, 'Union Street.' He was an Englishman, who had been brought up a glover and breeches maker, which trade or trades, he followed in Boston, and was a dealer in what is called soft leather. In the course of time he began to keep a small collection of books for sale, and had several pamphlets printed; these were on religious subjects. He was punctual in his dealings, well respected, and was made a deacon of the First Baptist Church. He died in April 1779, aged 77.

1762.   JAMES RIVINGTON,[53] 'At the London Book-Store, head of King-Street.' He was an Englishman, and a considerable bookseller in London. He never resided in Boston; but employed an agent, who opened a valuable collection of books printed in England, for sale. After Rivington failed in London, he went with a large quantity of books to Philadelphia; and afterwards settled at New York.

1762.   JOHN PERKINS, 'Union-Street,' served his apprenticeship with Joshua Winter, and after his death took his stand and business.

1763.   WILLIAM MILLER, was born in Scotland, and there brought up to bookselling. He went to London, whence he was sent by James Rivington, in 1762, to Boston, with a valuable collection of books. Miller acted as agent to Rivington one year; when he became his partner; and the firm was, 'Rivington & Miller, at the London Book-Store, head of King-Street, North Side of the Court House.' At this period Rivington lived in New York. Miller was a young man of amiable manners, and was well acquainted with the trade. He died in November 1765, and the business was discontinued.

1763.   WILLIAM PHILLIPS, 'Cornhill,' was the son of John Phillips, and succeeded him in business. Being bred a merchant, he turned his attention to the sale of English goods. He died January 6, 1772.

1764.   ALFORD BUTLER, 'Cornhill,' was the son of Alford Butler who has already been mentioned. He was born in Boston, where he served his apprenticeship with William Mac-Alpine, and became a binder and sold a few books. In 1774 he removed to Portsmouth, New Hampshire, and there kept a school near twenty years, after which he returned, and again carried on business as formerly.

1764. ANDREW BARCLAY,[54] 'at the Bible in Cornhill,' from Scotland, was bred to binding, and followed that business several years after he arrived in Boston. He sold a few books.

1764. JOHN MEIN, was from Scotland, and began business as a bookseller, in partnership with his countryman Sandeman, 'in Marlborough Street.' Their sales were wholly confined to Scotch and English editions; and their partnership closed at the expiration of one year.

In 1766, Mein kept the 'London Book-Store North Side of King-Street,' where he opened a large and valuable collection of European books, and a handsome assortment of stationery. As he sold for a reasonable profit, his trade became extensive. He commenced printing in partnership with John Fleming; reprinted several books, and published *The Boston Chronicle*, of which he was the editor.

Mein was a staunch royalist; the publications in the Chronicle rendered him very obnoxious; in consequence of which he returned to Europe in November 1769; his bookstore was then closed; and the Chronicle discontinued in 1770.

1764. SANDEMAN, 'Marlborough-Street,' came from Scotland in 1764, in company with his uncle, the celebrated preacher and founder of the sect called Sandemanians. Mein, the partner of Sandeman, came in the same ship.

1766. COX AND BERRY, first opened a shop 'opposite Brattle-Street Church,' whence they removed to 'two doors above the British Coffee-House,' and, afterwards to 'Cornhill.' Edward Cox and Edward Berry, copartners, were from London; they were dealers in English books, and traded very largely in jewelery. After the commencement of the war, they removed to New York.

1767. JOSEPH SNELLING, 'Fish-Street, Corner of Boarded-Alley.' He was a binder, and sold school books and stationery.

1767. JOHN EDWARDS, 'Cornhill,' was the son of Joseph Edwards, and had a concern in the business with his father a few years. He died March 9, 1778, aged 25.

1768. JAMES FOSTER CONDY, 'Union-Street,' was the son of Jeremy Condy, whom he succeeded, and kept a good supply of English editions, &c. for sale. During the war he removed to Haverhill, where he kept school; and died in June, 1809.

1770. JOHN LANGDON, 'Cornhill,' served his apprenticeship with Wharton and Bowes; he began business with a good assortment of books; sold stationery, and carried on binding. He relinquished business after the beginning of the war.

1771. HENRY KNOX,[55] 'Cornhill,' served his apprenticeship with Wharton and Bowes, binders and booksellers. He opened a large store with a valuable collection of books, &c. The war changed him from a bookseller to a soldier. He joined the army, and continued in it during the war; and, on account of his good conduct, and superior military talents, was promoted by Congress to the rank of major general. He was also made secretary at war before and after the adoption of the present constitution. He died at Thomastown, in the district of Maine, October 25, 1806.

1771. A. ELLISON,[56] 'Newbury-Street,' was born in England, and brought up to binding; which business he followed in Boston, and sold a few books in common use. After living in Boston three or four years, he removed to Newport.

Mr. Brinley, of Hartford, Conn., whose unequalled collection of early American publications, and critical knowledge of them, are well known, kindly furnishes the following memoranda, made by him in his copy of Mr. Thomas's work:

JOB HOWE, was a Bookseller, not mentioned by Thomas. Example—*Neglect of Supporting and Maintaining the Pure Worship of God*, by James Allen. Boston Printed for Job How and John Allen, and are to be sold at Mr. Samuel Green's, by the South Meeting House, 1687.

How is not mentioned, and the earliest seen of *John Allen* is in 1690.

The above sermon seems to be rare, as it is not in the library of the Antiquarian Society, that of the Massachusetts Historical Society, or the Prince Library. It was 'preached on a Solemn Fast Day occasioned by the afflictive Providence of God in sending Worms and Catapillars, which in some places, as God's great army, marched in numerous Companies, and devoured all before them, both Corn and Grass,' &c., &c. *Preface*.

HEZEKIAH USHER, Bookseller. Thomas 1652. Was in business as early as 1650. Example. *The Mystery of God Incarnate*, by Samuel Eaton. Printed for H. Usher at Boston in New England 1650.

JOHN USHER, Bookseller. Thomas 1672. Should be 1669. Example—*God's Call to His People to Turn to Him, in 11 Sermons at two Publick Fasting Dayes* by John Davenport. Cambridge printed by S. G. and M. J. for John Usher of Boston MDCLXIX.

JOHN RATCLIFFE, Bookseller. A good example of his publications is a very rare book of which I do not trace any copy: *A Poem, Dedicated to the Memory of the Reverend and Excellent Urian Oakes*, Boston in New England. Printed for John Ratcliff, 1682. (By Cotton Mather,) a juvenile production, and not in any list of his publications.

BENJAMIN HARRIS, *Bookseller*. Thomas 1690. He printed in 1689 *Massachusetts Charter*. N. B.: This is the first document in Hutchinson's volume of 'Original Papers,' and of which he says in a foot note that it never had been printed.

OBADIAH GILL, Bookseller. Thomas 1690. Should be 1685. Example—*An Elegy on the Much-to-be-deplored Death of that Never-to-be-forgotten Person, the Reverend Mr. Nathaniel Collins*, Boston in New England. Printed by Richard Pierce for Obadiah Gill—Anno Christi 1685. (By Cotton Mather) another juvenile production, not in any list of his publications.

We add from the *Boston Evening Post* of Aug. 14, 1749, the name of OBADIAH COOKSON, who, in 1749, was 'at the Cross Pistols, in Fish Street, Boston.' He sold a few books, and many other articles. H

The chief of the printing done in Cambridge and Boston, previously to the year 1750, was for booksellers; printers did but little on their own account. Even the laws, acts, &c., of the government were printed for booksellers. The books printed during a century, in New England, were nearly all on religion, politics, or for the use of schools.

The booksellers of Boston, in 1742, had a meeting for the purpose of augmenting the prices of sundry books; an addition to the prices was agreed on; but, I believe not generally adopted.

CAMBRIDGE 1641. HENRY DUNSTER,[57] the first president of Harvard college, sold such books as were sent from England by Joseph Glover.

214 1650. SAMUEL GREEN, the second printer at Cambridge, sold school books, versions of the Psalms, and some other religious works, principally such as were printed at his press.

CHARLESTOWN 1715. ELEAZAR PHILLIPS, removed from Boston to that place. He was a dealer in books, which were printed in New England.

NEWBURYPORT 1760. BULKELEY EMERSON, was a binder, and sold a few books. He was the only one of the trade who did business in that place before 1775. The office of post master was held by him many years.

SALEM 1686. JOHN DUNTON, opened a store, and sold a quantity of books which he brought from London. He returned to England.

1761. MASCOL WILLIAMS, was a binder, and traded principally in school books, and stationery. He was postmaster.

These are all the booksellers who lived in Massachusetts previous to the war, or at least they are all concerning whom I have been able to make any discoveries.

THERE was not a newspaper published in the English colonies, throughout extensive continent of North America, until the 24th of April, 1704.

John Campbell, a Scotchman, who was a bookseller and postmaster in Boston, was the first[58] who began and established a publication of this kind. It was entitled,

THE BOSTON NEWS-LETTER (Published by Authority*) is printed on half a sheet of pot paper, with a small pica type, folio. The first page is filled with an extract from *The London Flying Post*, respecting the pretender, who styled himself James VIII of Scotland, sending popish missionaries from France into Scotland, &c., by which the kingdoms of England and Scotland were endangered. The queen's speech to both houses of parliament on that occasion, a few articles under the Boston head, four short paragraphs of marine intelligence from New York, Philadelphia, and New London, and *one* advertisement, form its whole contents. The advertisement is from Campbell, the proprietor of the paper, and is as follows:

'This News Letter is to be continued Weekly; and all Persons who have any Houses, Lands, Tenements, Farmes, Ships, Vessels, Goods, Wares or Merchandizes, &c., to be Sold or Lett; or Servants Runaway; or Goods Stoll or Lost, may have the same Inserted at a Reasonable Rate; from Twelve Pence to Five Shillings, and not to exceed: Who may agree with *Nicholas*

---

* At the time this paper was first published, and for many years afterwards, there were licensers of the press. 'Published by Authority,' I presume means nothing more than this; what appeared in the publication was not disapproved by the licensers.

Boone for the same at his Shop next door to Major Davis's, Apothecary in *Boston* near the Old Meeting House.

'All Persons in Town and Country may have said News-Letter Weekly upon reasonable terms, agreeing with John Campbell Post Master for the same.' The imprint is 'Boston: Printed by *B. Green*. Sold by *Nicholas Boone* at his Shop near the Old Meeting-House.' Green was Campbell's printer, and Boone was for some weeks his publisher.

No. 2, is a whole sheet of pot, folio, three pages of which are printed, and one is blank. Campbell's advertisement is again inserted, and a *single* new one is added.

In No. 4, Campbell desires those who wish to have advertisements inserted in the News-Letter, to apply to him.

Boone's name is left out of the imprint of No. 5, and 'Sold at the Post Office' is inserted.

From No. 2, to No. 6, the News-Letter is contained on half of a pot sheet; and very few advertisements appear, some weeks not any. From No. 6 to No. 192, it is printed on a half sheet of foolscap. No. 192 contains only two short advertisements; and for years after it was but seldom supplied with more than two, and, often, with not one new advertisement in the week.

In No. 71, Campbell inserted the following notice.

'At the Desire of several Gentlemen, Merchants and others, who are willing to Contribute towards supporting this Publick Print of Intelligence, the Undertaker has begun where it was left off, in hopes of others following their good Example, whereby it may be carryed on at least another year: And therefore all Persons in Town and Country, who have a mind to encourage the same, may have said News Letters every week by the year upon reasonable Terms, agreeing with John Campbell Postmaster of Boston for the same.'

It does not appear that Campbell had discontinued the paper, and his real meaning where he says he 'has begun where he left off,' cannot now be well understood. No. 71, is dated August 24, 1705. It is evident from his advertisements in the course of this publication, that he 'labored hard to get it along,' that he had but few subscribers, and that he did not receive much encouragement from advertising customers.

Bartholomew Green printed the News-Letter for Campbell until November 3, 1707. No. 176, November 10, 1707, is 'printed by John Allen, in Pudding Lane near the Post-Office, and there to be Sold.'

In No. 190, Campbell informs 'all who have a mind to encourage this Letter of Intelligence,' to agree with him, 'Post Master of New England, at Boston.'

In No. 210, four years after the first publication, Campbell inserted the following advertisement. 'This being the last day of the fourth Quarter of this Letter of Intelligence: All persons in Town and Country, who have not already paid for this fourth Year are hereby desired now to pay or send it in; with their resolution if they would have it continued and proceeded on for a fifth year (Life permitted); which is only to be known by the number that take it weekly throughout the year; though there has not as yet a competent number appeared to take it annually so as to enable the Undertaker to carry it on effectually; yet he is still willing to proceed with it, if those Gentlemen that have this last year lent their helping hand to support it, continue still of the same mind another year, in hopes that those who have hitherto been backward to promote such a Publick Good will at last set in with it.'

No. 390, completed four years printing of the News-Letter by John Allen in Pudding lane. On the evening following the day on which No. 390 was published, namely, October 2, 1711, happened what, from that time until 1760, was called the great fire in Boston. The postoffice and Allen's printing house were consumed in that conflagration. The following week the News-Letter was again printed at Green's printing house in Newbury street, with this imprint, 'Boston: Printed in Newbury Street, for *John Campbell* Post Master,' which remained unaltered until October 1715. No. 391 contains an account of the fire.

In October, 1715, B. Green added his name to the imprint, as the printer.

No. 664 begins the year 1717 with January—the News-Letter had previously begun the year with March. Although this paper had at that time been published thirteen years it still languished for the want of due support, as appears by an address from Campbell to the public.

It was the design of Campbell that the News-Letter should give a selected, regular succession of foreign events; but the smallness of his paper rendered it impossible for him to publish occurrences seasonably; and at the close of the year he found himself greatly in arrears with his foreign intelligence. In Nos. 769 and 799, he proposes a remedy for this difficulty, which will, perhaps, be best understood in his own words, and may give a correct idea of the state of the News-Letter at that period.

'After near upon Fourteen Years experience, The Undertaker knows that it's Impossible with half a Sheet in the Week to carry on all the Publick News of Europe, (tho' hitherto all those of Great Britain, Ireland, our own and our Neighbour Provinces has been Yearly Inserted). He now intends to make up that Deficiency by Printing a Sheet every other Week for Tryal, by which in a little time, all will become new that us'd formerly to be Old. Jan'y. 12, 1719.

'The Undertaker of this News-Letter, the 12th January last being the Second Week of this Currant Years Intelligence, gave then Intimation that after 14 (now upwards of 15) years experience, it was impossible with half a Sheet a Week to carry on all the Public Occurrences of Europe, with those of this, our Neighbouring Provinces, and the West Indies. To make up which Deficiency, and the News Newer and more acceptable, he has since Printed every other Week a Sheet, whereby that which seem'd Old in the former half Sheets, becomes New now by the Sheet, which is easy to be seen by any one who will be at the pains to trace back former years; and even this time 12 Months, we were then 13 Months behind with the Foreign News beyond Great Britain, and now less than Five Months, so that by the Sheet we have retrieved about 8 months since January last, and any One that has the News Letter since that time, to January next (life permitted) will be accommodated with all the News of Europe &c., contained in the Publick Prints of London that are needful for to be known in these parts. And in regard the Undertaker had not suitable encouragement, even to Print half a Sheet Weekly, seeing that he cannot vend 300 at an Impression, tho' some ignorantly concludes he Sells upwards of a Thousand: far less is he able to Print a Sheet every other week, without an Addition of 4, 6 or 8 Shillings a Year, as every one thinks fit to give payable Quarterly, which will only help to pay for Press and Paper, giving his Labour for nothing. And considering the great Charge he is at for several Setts of Public Prints, by sundry Vessels from London, with the price of Press, Paper, Labour, carrying out the News Papers, and his own Trouble, in collecting and composing, &c. It is afforded by the Year, or by the Piece or Paper, including the difference of Money far cheaper than in England, where they sell several

Hundreds nay Thousands of Copies to a very small number vended here. Such therefore as have not already paid for the half Year past the last Monday of June, are hereby desired to send or pay in the same to John Campbell at his House in Cornhill, Boston. August 10, 1719.'

Campbell's difficulties increased. A new postmaster had just been appointed, and in the December following the publication of the foregoing advertisements, that postmaster began publishing another newspaper. Campbell appeared to be displeased; a 'paper war' of short duration ensued. Both papers were continued; and advertising customers began to increase.

In No. 821, January 11, 1721, Campbell again addressed his customers, and informed them. 'This Publick Letter of Intelligence was begun here at Boston by John Campbell the 24th of April 1704, near upon Sixteen Years ago, and ever since continued Weekly with Universal Approbation and General Satisfaction, giving a true Account of all the Publick Affairs of Europe, with those of this and the Neighbouring Provinces, for the Interest and Advantage of the Post Office, Gentlemen, Merchants and others, both in Town and Country; and preventing a great many false Reports. And the Author being still desired and encouraged to carry on the same by the Gentlemen, Merchants and others, his usual Customers, he intends (Life Permitted) to answer their expectation, and to forward still as regular Account of Affairs as our part of the World will admit of; If he does not Print a Sheet every other Week this Winter Time, he designs to make it up in the Spring, when Ships do arrive from Great Britain. Such Others as have a mind to promote and encourage the said Intelligence may agree with John Campbell in Cornhill, Boston, and have it on reasonable Terms left at any House in the Town, Seal'd or Unsealed; and for the advantage of the Post Office an Intire Sheet of Paper, one half with the News, and the other half good writing Paper to write their Letter on, may also be had there for any one that pleases to have it every Monday.'

By the latter part of this advertisement we are to understand, that some copies of the News Letter would every Monday be printed on a whole sheet of writing paper, one half of which would be blank, on which letters might be written and sent abroad through the medium of the post office; the accommodation was the saving of postage, as a letter and a newspaper might be forwarded in the same sheet; and newspapers thus printed, were sold by Campbell at his house in Cornhill.

In No. 876, December 26, 1720, Campbell, in an address to the public, mentioned, that he had published the News-Letter 'near upon Seventeen Years,' and that it was 'the first and only intelligence on the Continent of America, till about a Year past, one was set up at Philadelphia and another here, and how well either the one or the other has answered the said Design, and People's great Expectation, is left with every one to Determine.' He informs his readers that, 'he designs (God willing) to carry it on another year,' with the usual proviso, that 'he is encouraged by a competant Numbers taking it by the Year, to enable him to defray the necessary charges of Press, Paper, the Publick Prints, and Writing of the same.'

On the 7th of August, 1721, a third newspaper in Boston was published, entitled *The New England Courant.** The publisher of that paper, in an address to the public, hinted that the News

* Printed by James Franklin.

Letter was 'a dull vehicle of intelligence,' &c. This appears to have nettled Campbell, who in his next News-Letter of Monday, August 14, made the following defence.

'☞ N. B. On Monday last, the 7th Currant, came forth a Third Newspaper in this Town, Entituled, The New England Courant, by *Homo non unius Negotii*,* Or, Jack of all Trades, and it would seem, Good at none, giving some very, very frothy fulsome Account of himself; but lest the continuance of that stile offend his readers, wherein with submission, (I speak for the Publisher of this Intelligence, whose endeavours has always been to give no offence, not meddling with things out of his Province) the said Jack promises in pretence of Friendship to the other News-Publishers to amend, like soure Ale in Summer, Reflecting too too much, that my performances are now and then very, very Dull, Misrepresenting my candid endeavours (according to the Talent of my Capacity and Education, not soaring above my Sphere) in giving a true and genuine account of all Matters of Fact, both Foreign and Domestick, as comes any way well Attested, for these Seventeen Years & an half past. It is often observed, a bright Morning is succeeded by a dark Rainy Day, and so much Mercury in the beginning may end in *Album Græcum*. And seeing our New Gentleman seems to be a Scholer of Accademical Learning, (which I pretend not to, the more my unhappiness, and too late to say, *O mihi præteritos referat si Jupiter Annos*) and better qualified to perform a work of this Nature, for want whereof out of a design for publick good made me at first at the Sollicitation of several Gentlemen, Merchants and Others, come into it, according to the Proverb, thinking that half a Loafe was better than no Bread; often wish-

---

* The motto of Franklin's address to the public.

ing and desiring in Print that such a one would undertake it, and
then no one should sooner come into it and pay more Yearly to
carry it on than this Publisher, and none appearing then, nor
since, (others being judges) to excell him in their performances,
made him to continue. And our New Publisher being a Scholler
and Master, he should (me thinks) have given us (whom he
terms low, flat and dull) Admonition and told one and the other
wherein our Dulness lay, (that we might be better Proficients
for the future, Whither in reading, hearing, or pains taking, to
write, gather, collect and insert the Publick Occurrences) before publick Censure, and a good example to copy and write
after, and not tell us and the World at his first setting out, that
he'l be like us in doing as we have done, *Turpe est Doctori cum
culpa redarguit ipsum.* And now all my Latin being spent excepting what I design always to remember, *Nemo sine crimine vivit,* I
promise for my part so soon as he or any Scholler will Undertake my hitherto Task, and Endeavours, giving proof that he
will not be very, very Dull, I shall not only desist for his advantage, but also so far as capable Assist such a good Scribe.'

I have a file of the *New England Courant* for the first two years
of its publication, with the exception of the first sixteen numbers, which are wanting. I cannot, therefore, give Franklin's
reply to Campbell; but the spirit of it is to be discovered from
Campbell's rejoinder, published in the News Letter, August
28, 1721, viz.:

'☞ J. C. *to* Jack Dullman* *sendeth,* Greeting.

'Sir, What you call a Satyrical Advertisement was a just
Vindication of my News Letter, from some unfair Reflections,

---

* This nickname appears to have been given to Franklin by Campbell, as a
retort for calling the *News-Letter* 'dull, very dull.'

in your introduction to your first Courant. Your reply in hobling Verse, had they more Reason and less Railing might possibly have inclined me to think you was some Man of great Learning, or as you please to Word it, a *Meikle Man*; but Railery is the talent of a mean Spirit, and not to be returned by me. In honour to the Muses I dare not acknowledge your Poem to be from Parnassus; but as a little before the Composure you had been Rakeing in the Dunghill, its more probable the corrupt Steams got into your Brains, and your Dullcold Skul precipitate them into Ribaldry. I observe you are not always the same, your History of Inoculation intends the Publick Good,* but Letter to Mr. Compton and Rhyme to me smell more of the Ale Tub than the Lamp. I do not envy your skill in Anatomy, and your accurate discovery of the Gall Bladder, nor your Geography of the Dunghill (*natale solum.*) You say your Ale grows better, but have a care you do not Bottle it too New, lest the Bottles fly and wet your Toyes. You say you are the Wiseman, and his Advice is, Prov. xxvi. Ver. 4. *Answer not a fool according to his folly, lest thou be like unto him.* And not very disagreeable to what I learned when a School Boy.

'*Contra verbosos, noli contendere verbis.*

'Against a man of wind spend not thy Breath. Therefore I conclude with *Verbum Sapienti*,

'*Tutius est, igitur fictis contendere verbis,*

'*Quam pugnare manu.*   Vale.

'Since like the Indian Natives, you Delight,
to murder in the dark, eshun and fly the light,

                                        Farewel.'

---

* *The Courant* strongly opposed inoculating for the small pox, which at that time began to be introduced.

This rivalship produced a whole sheet weekly from Campbell for about two months, after which the News-Letter, like the Gazette and Courant, was reduced to a half sheet weekly.

In January, 1722, Campbell announced in his usual manner his intention to continue the News-Letter another year; but before the close of it, he resigned his right to his printer, Bartholomew Green. Campbell had published this paper eighteen years; and, during that period, had met with many difficulties, and received but little encouragement. The undertaking could not have been attended with profit; for the expense of paper, printing, and European publications from which he selected information, must have swallowed up the proceeds from his small number of subscribers.

'Published by Authority,' had been omitted in the title of the News-Letter for two years before Campbell resigned it, but was resumed when Green began to print it on his own account; and the day of its publication was changed from Monday to Thursday.

When Green became the proprietor of the News-Letter, great difference of opinion existed in the colony respecting the concerns of church and state, as well as concerning matters of a more local nature, and the spirit of party ran high. A writer of that day observes, 'The press has long groaned in bringing forth an hateful but numerous brood of party pamphlets, malicious scribbles, and Billingsgate ribaldry, which have produced rancor and bitterness, and unhappily soured and leavened the tempers of persons formerly esteemed some of the most sweet and amiable.'*

Green appeared to possess a disposition to publish an impar-

* *Courant.* No. 30, February 11, 1723.

tial and chaste paper, and in conformity to this inclination, he inserted in the News-Letter March 7, 1723, the following address to the public.

'☞ The Design of this Paper is not merely to amuse the Reader; much less to Gratify any Ill Tempers by Reproach or Redicule, to Promote Contention, or Espouse any Party among us. The Publisher on the contrary, laments our Dangerous and unhappy Divisions; and he would always approve himself as a Peaceable Friend and Servant to all, and unkind to none; nor would he ever render Evil for Evil, either by action, speaking or writing. He longs for the Blissful Times when Wars shall cease to the Ends of the Earth. He would rather Endeavour his utmost to advance an universal Concord and Harmony; were it not for fear of adding Oyl to the Flames, and he Remembers the Fable which shows him the Danger of Interceding between Fierce and Contending Enemies. The Publisher would therefore strive to oblige all his Readers by Publishing those Transactions only, that have no Relation to any of our Quarrels, and may be equally entertaining to the greatest Adversaries. For this end, he Proposes to extend his Paper to the History of Nature among us, as well as of Political and Foreign Affairs. And agreeable to this Design, he Desires of all Ingenious Gentlemen, in every part of the Country, to communicate the Remarkable Things they observe; and he Desires them to send their Accounts Post-Free, and nothing but what they assuredly know; and they shall be very gratefully Receiv'd and Publish'd: That so this Paper may, in some Degree, serve for the *Philosophical Transactions of New England*, as well as for a Political History; and the Things worthy of Recording in this as well as in other Parts of the World, may not proceed to sink into eternal Oblivion as they have done in all the past Ages of the Aboriginal and Ancient Inhabitants.'

In 1725, 'Published by Authority,' again disappeared from the title of the News-Letter. Green continued its publication without any thing particular attending it, until the last week of December 1726, No. 1196. The week following he altered its title to *The Weekly News-Letter*, and began this alteration of title with No. 1, and discontinued 'the method of carrying on a Thread of occurrences of an Old Date;' intending to publish weekly the latest intelligence he could procure. The paper, with the alteration of title, progressed to No. 200, October 29, 1730; Green then added the No. 200 of the *Weekly* News-Letter, to the former number 1196 of the *Boston* News-Letter, and the following week began with No. 1397, and combined the former and the latter title, calling it *The Boston Weekly News-Letter*.* On this occasion he published the following advertisement, viz.:

'The Publisher of this Boston News-Letter, having in concert with the late Mr. Campbell, began to Print the same with Numb. 1, on April 24, 1704, and it being carried on with the History of Publick Affairs to No. 1196, which was on December 29, 1726, and then with January 5th, 1726–7, began with a new Number which amounted on the last Thursday to 200. It is now tho't adviseable to add the said Number 200, to the former 1196, which makes 1396, the whole of our Number from the said 24th of April, 1704, and now go on with Numb. 1397,' &c.

No other alteration in the News-Letter took place during its

---

* Green did not publish two papers at the same time, as mentioned in *Collections of the Massachusetts Historical Society*, 1st ser., VI, 67 (1796).

publication by Green. He dying, John Draper succeeded him, and began the publication of the News-Letter January 4, 1733. He announced it as follows.

'☞ Mr. Bartholomew Green, who has for some Years past been the Publisher of this *Boston Weekly News-Letter*, being dead, this is to Inform the Publick in general, and those who are the Customers for it in particular, that it will be yet carried on, and sent out every Week on Thursday Morning at the usual Price by John Draper, (Son-in-Law to the said Mr. Green) who has been an Assistant with him in the said News-Letter: And, that Care will be yet constantly taken to insert therein all the most remarkable Occurrences, both Foreign and Domestick, that come to hand well attested. And all the Rev. Ministers, or other Gentlemen, both of Town and Country, who may at any time receive any thing worthy of publishing, are desired to send it to the said John Draper, at the Printing-House in New-bury-Street, that lately belong'd to the said Mr. Green deceas'd, and it will be thankfully received, and communicated to the Publick: And it will yet be endeavoured to render *This* Weekly Paper as informing and entertaining as possibly can be, to the Satisfaction of all who do or may encourage it.'

Draper printed the News Letter thirty years. He died in November, 1762, and his son Richard Draper continued its publication. At that time, the title was enlarged as follows: *The Boston Weekly News Letter and New England Chronicle*. In about a year the title was again altered to *The Massachusetts Gazette; and Boston Newes Letter*, and was decorated with the king's arms.* Richard Draper, about this time, took his kinsman

* The king's arms were first introduced into the title page of the Laws of Massachusetts, 1692.

Samuel as a partner, and the imprint ran thus: 'Published by Richard Draper, Printer to the Governor and Council, and by Samuel Draper, at the Printing Office in Newbury Street.' After the death of Samuel Draper, Richard remained several years without a partner.

In May, 1768, a singular disposition was made of the paper. The dispute between Great Britain and the colonies induced the government particularly to patronize *The Massachusetts Gazette*, and another paper, the *Boston Post Boy and Advertiser*, printed by Green and Russell. To give them the features and the consequence of governmental papers, the publishers of them were directed to insert in the title of each paper, *'Published by Authority.'* The News Letter was published on Thursdays, and the Post Boy on Mondays. Each paper was divided into two equal parts. Half of each paper was entitled, 'The Massachusetts Gazette, Published by Authority;' and the other half bore their former respective titles. For instance, the old title of Boston News Letter was reassumed, and under this title, news and advertisements filled one half of a whole sheet; the other half of this sheet was entitled, 'The Massachusetts Gazette, Published by Authority;' the contents of this half, like the other, being news, advertisements, and, occasionally, the proceedings of government and public bodies. The same method was taken by Green and Russell. One half of the sheet bore the title of Post Boy and Advertiser, and the other half that of 'The Massachusetts Gazette, Published by Authority.' Two hundred and seventy-six weeks previously to this new mode of publication, Draper had added *Massachusetts Gazette* to the title of the News Letter. Green and Russell began publishing in the mode described, on Monday, and Draper on Thursday of the week.

Green and Russell therefore numbered that part of their sheet which was to bear the title of Massachusetts Gazette, 277. Draper on the Thursday following numbered his 278, and as long as this mode of publishing the Gazette by authority continued, the number for one press was reckoned from that of the other. It was in fact publishing a half sheet Gazette 'By Authority' twice in a week, once by Draper and once by Green and Russell. Each press furnished the royal arms for the head of the Gazette.

The first time Draper published this 'Adam and Eve paper,' joined together 'by authority,' the following advertisement was inserted after the title of the News-Letter.

'The Thursday's paper* (the first ever printed in America) *returns* to its primitive title, the Gazette being directed by Authority to be published in another manner. The customers will be served with Care and Fidelity; and those who advertise herein may depend on having their Notifications well circulated.

'N. B. A Gazette will accompany the News Letter every Thursday (tho' not always in a separate paper) Articles of Intelligence and of publick Utility will be thankfully received, and due notice taken of them by directing to Richard Draper.'

This method of publishing the Gazette was discontinued at the close of September 1769, and Draper reestablished the title as it stood at the beginning of May, 1768, viz. *The Massachusetts Gazette and Boston Weekly News Letter*. 'Published by Authority,' was omitted; but it continued to be a government paper.

In May, 1774, Draper took John Boyle as a partner in pub-

---

* There was at this time no other newspaper printed on Thursdays in Boston.

lishing the News Letter; the next month Draper died. His widow, Margaret Draper, succeeded him as proprietor of the paper, and Boyle was for a short time her partner; but they separated before the commencement of the revolutionary war. After the war began, John Howe became her partner, and remained in business with her until the British troops left Boston in 1776; when the publication of the News-Letter ceased, and was never revived.

Thus began and ended *The Boston News Letter*. It was the first newspaper published in this country, and the only one printed in Boston during the siege. I have taken more particular notice of this first paper, than I shall of those which follow. It was published seventy-two years.

For several years before the revolution, many able writers on the side of government, and some of its first officers, under various signatures, appeared in this paper; and while conducted by Richard Draper, its collection of news was not inferior to that of any public journal in Boston.

John Campbell, the first proprietor, lived about five years after he resigned his right to Green. His death is thus mentioned in the News Letter of March 7, 1728. 'On Monday Evening last, the 4th Currant, about 8 a Clock, died here John Campbell, Esq, Aged 75 Years, formerly Post Master in this Place, Publisher of the Boston News Letter for many Years, and One of his Majesties Justices of the Peace for the County of Suffolk.'

THE BOSTON GAZETTE was first published for William Brooker, who succeeded Campbell as postmaster. It was the second which made its appearance in British America.

No. 1 was issued from the press on Monday, December 21,

1719, on a half sheet of printing foolscap, on a small pica type, folio; and it was continued on a half sheet of that size of paper for several years, excepting occasionally a whole sheet, and then one page was often left blank. It had a cut of a ship on the left, and one of a postman on the right of the title, and was 'Published by Authority.' Its imprint was, 'Boston: Printed by J. Franklin, and may be had at the Post Office, where advertisements are taken in.' This paper also began the year with March the first year, but the following with January.

The appearance of the Gazette* occasioned some altercation between its publisher and the publisher of the News-Letter. In No. 3, we have the following advertisement.

'Post Office, January 4th. The Approbation this Paper has already met with from the better Part of the Town, deserves a suitable Acknowledgment from this office, with repeated assurances, that it shall be carried on in such a manner as to render it both beneficial and entertaining.'

The proprietor, printer and publisher of the Gazette, were soon changed. Philip Musgrave succeeded Brooker as postmaster a few weeks after the Gazette was published. No. 36, is printed by S. Kneeland; and the imprint of No. 41, is, 'Boston Printed by S. Kneeland, for Philip Musgrave, Post Master, at his Office in Corn-Hill, where Advertisements are taken in, and all Gentlemen and others, may be Accommodated with this Paper.'

The Gazette was printed by Kneeland for Musgrave until 1726, and that year it was printed by Kneeland for Thomas Lewis, postmaster.

* There were three Boston Gazettes in succession before the revolution. This was the first of them.

In 1727, *Henry Marshall* was postmaster, and the Gazette had another printer, Bartholomew Green, son of the printer of the News-Letter. It was printed for Marshall till May, 1732, when he died, and the Gazette was after his death published by John Boydell, who succeeded Marshall, and was again printed by Kneeland and his partner. In 1734, Ellis Huske, being appointed postmaster, began the publication of another paper, *The Post-Boy*; but Boydell continued to publish the Gazette till he died in December, 1739;* and, it then was printed for his heirs until October, 1741, when Kneeland & Green became the proprietors of it. Four postmasters in succession had conducted *The Boston Gazette*, before it was owned by Kneeland & Green. When this paper became their property, they incorporated it with *The New England Weekly Journal*, which they had printed on their own account for nearly fifteen years. The title was altered to *The Boston Gazette and Weekly Journal*, to show that the Journal was combined with the Gazette. Kneeland & Green continued to publish the Gazette in this altered form until 1752.

* From the Boston Gazette, of December 17, 1739. 'On Tuesday last died here in the 49th year of his age, John Boydell, Esq.; late Publisher of this Paper, and some time Deputy Post-Master within this and the three neighboring Governments; than whom none ever lived in this Province more generally esteem'd and beloved, as an honest worthy man, by Persons of all Ranks, Perswasions and Parties, or was more lamented as such at his Death. He first came over from England into this Country in the year 1716, Secretary to the late worthy Governor *Shute*, and Register of the Court of Vice Admiralty for this Province, New-Hampshire and Rhode-Island; after which he was appointed Register of the Court of Probate of Wills, &c., for the County of Suffolk, and Naval officer for the Port of Boston; all which offices he discharged with such singular diligence, integrity and goodness, that this community never lost a more useful and valuable member, than he was in his degree and station.'

The *Boston Gazette*, of the same date, contains the following advertisement:

'This is to acquaint the Publick, That this Paper will be carried on as usual for the Benefit of the Family of the late Publisher Mr. John Boydell, deceased.'

This paper then, having been published thirty-three years, was succeeded by another with the same title, which I shall mention in its place.

When Kneeland & Green began to publish the Gazette and Journal conjointly, on their own account, they printed it on a half sheet of paper of the size of foolscap, in quarto, and introduced new devices. 'Published by Authority,' had been omitted in the title many years.

While the Gazette was printed for Boydell, its size was altered to a half sheet crown, in quarto; and, after he quitted the postoffice, the cut of a postman on horseback, on the right of the title, was exchanged for a pine tree. When Kneeland & Green began to publish it for themselves, the cut of a ship was placed on the right of the title; the pine tree was omitted, and the cut of a newscarrier, holding a Gazette in his hand, was introduced on the left. After printing it several years in quarto, they again printed it on a half sheet foolscap, folio; but occasionally in quarto. This paper was discontinued in 1752, on account of the dissolution of the partnership of its publishers.

THE NEW-ENGLAND COURANT[59] was the third newspaper which made its appearance in Boston. It was first printed and published Monday, August 17, 1721, by James Franklin, on a half sheet of crown size printing paper, on a small pica type, occasionally on long primer, but after two years generally on pica. It was printed on Saturdays during the latter years of its publication. Imprint—'Boston: Printed by James Franklin, in Queen Street, where Advertisements are taken in.'

Among the reasons which induced Franklin to publish the Courant, probably one, which was not the least considerable,

was grounded on the circumstance of the publisher of the Gazette having taken the printing of it from him, and given it to
another printer. He warmly attacked Musgrave, the publisher
of the Gazette, in some of the first numbers of the Courant, and
endeavored to have him turned out of office.

The Courant contained very little news, and very few advertisements. More than half of the paper was, with few exceptions,
filled weekly with essays, in which men in office, the clergy, and
the prevailing religious opinions of the day, were attacked.
Inoculation for the small pox, then newly introduced, was
warmly, if not rudely, opposed. A society of gentlemen furnished these essays. By moderate people this society was called
a set of 'Free Thinkers;' by others, it was denominated the
'Hell Fire Club.' The essays of this society were at times opposed
in the Gazette, and in the News Letter; and these papers in turn
were warmly attacked in the Courant, but rather by satire than
argument. Some of the essays in the Courant were evidently
written by men of talent.

A periodical paper with these animating features was a novelty in Boston; and of course attracted general notice, and soon
had warm advocates and zealous opposers. It roused the attention of the government, and excited clerical resentment. The
reverend Doctor Increase Mather was one of the first who
openly denounced the Courant, by an address to the public,
inserted in the *Boston Gazette*, January 29, 172$\frac{1}{2}$. This address
may afford entertainment to many who are acquainted with the
present management of the press. It is as follows:

'*Advice to the Publick from Dr. Increase Mather.* Whereas a
wicked Libel called the *New England Courant*, has represented
me as one among the Supporters of it; I do hereby declare, that

altho' I had paid for two or three of them, I then, (before the last Courant was published) sent him word I was *extremely offended* with it! In special, because in one of his *Vile Courants* he insinuates, that if *the Ministers of God approve of a thing, it is a Sign it is of the Devil*; which is a horrid thing to be related! And altho' in one of the *Courants* it is declared, that the *London Mercury* Sept. 16, 1721, affirms that Great Numbers of Persons in the City and Suburbs are under the Inoculation of the Small Pox; In his next Courant he asserts, that it was some *Busy Inoculator, that imposed on the Publick in saying so*; Whereas I myself saw and read those words in the London Mercury: And he doth frequently abuse the Ministers of Religion, and many other worthy Persons in a manner, which is intolerable. For these and such like Reasons I signified to the Printer, that I would have no more of their *Wicked Courants*. I that have known what New England was from the Beginning, cannot but be troubled to see the Degeneracy of this Place. I can well remember when the Civil Government would have taken an effectual Course to suppress such a *Cursed Libel!* which if it be not done I am afraid that some *Awful Judgment* will come upon this Land, and that the *Wrath of God will arise, and there will be no Remedy*. I cannot but pity poor *Franklin*, who, tho' but a *Young Man*, it may be *Speedily* he must appear before the Judgment Seat of God, and what answer will he give for printing things so vile and abominable? And I cannot but Advise the Supporters of this Courant to consider the Consequences of being *Partakers in other Mens Sins*, and no more Countenance such a Wicked *Paper*. January 24th, 1721.'*

* Old style, beginning the year with March, which places January in 1721, instead of 1722, agreeably to the new style.

This address was attacked in the next Courant with considerable ability; and its writers went on as usual.

The New-England Courant had not been published twelve months before Franklin was apprehended by an order from government, and imprisoned four weeks in the common jail. Besides this punishment of the publisher, the council further manifested their disapprobation of the Courant by the following resolve.

'In Council, July 5th, 1722.

'Whereas in the Paper called the *New England Courant*, printed Weekly by James Franklin, many passages have been published boldly reflecting on His Majesty's Government and on the Administration of it in this Province, the Ministry, Churches and College; and it very often contains Paragraphs that tend to fill the Readers minds with vanity to the Dishonor of God, and disservice of Good Men.

'Resolved, that no such Weekly Paper be hereafter Printed or Published without the same be first perused and allowed by the Secretary, as has been usual. And that the said Franklin give Security before the Justices of the Superior Court in the Sum of 100*l*. to be of the good Behaviour to the End of the next Fall Sessions of this Court. Sent down for Concurrence.

'Read and Non-concurred.'

The failure of the council to restrain the freedom of the press in respect to the Courant, and the release of its printer from imprisonment, encouraged the club to proceed with increased boldness. An essay published the week following is thus headed:

'*And then, after they had anathematized and curs'd a Man to the Devil, and the Devil did not, or would not take him, then to make the Sheriff and the Jaylor to take the Devil's Leavings.* Postscript to

Hickeringill's Sermons on the horrid Sin of Man Catching, page 39.'

The club also published the twenty-ninth chapter of *Magna Charta*, with comments;* and then applied the *Lash*, † as it was termed, with the greater energy, especially to the governor and some of the clergy. The governor soon after went to England. ‡

On the 14th January, 1723, the council again took *The New-England Courant* into consideration, and passed an order thereon, which was sent down to the house of representatives. In consequence of which the following act was passed, and ordered to be published three weeks successively in *The Boston News Letter*, and in the *Boston Gazette*.

'At a great & General Court of Assembly of His Majesty's Province of the Massachusetts-Bay, held at Boston the fifteenth Day of November, 1722.

'In Council, Jan. 14, 1722.§

'Whereas the Paper called The New England Courant, of this Day's date, contains many Passages in which the Holy Scriptures are perverted, and the Civil government, Ministers and People of this Province highly reflected on, Ordered, *That*

---

* Dr. Franklin mentions this club. See his *Autobiography* (New Haven: Yale University Press, 1964), pp. 67–70.

† No. 52 has this advertisement: 'This paper (No. 52), begins the fifth quarter, and those that have not paid for THE LASH are desired to send in their money, or pay it to the Bearer.' [See J. T. Buckingham, *Specimens of Newspaper Literature* (Boston, 1850), I, 66, correcting this note. M]

‡ Shute.

§ At this time, in all legal proceedings, the year began with March, of course the Month of January, 1722, was attached to the latter part of that year, but generally the year beginning with January, would carry this month into 1723, as has been already stated.

William Tailer, Saml. Sewal, and Penn Townsend, Esqrs. with such as the Honourable House of Representatives shall join, be a Committee to consider and Report what is proper for this Court to do thereon.

'Sent down for Concurrence. J. WILLARD, Secretary.

'In the House of Representatives, Jan. 14th 1722. Read and Concurred, and Mr. Fulham, Mr. Remington, Mr. Stone, and Mr. Knolton be joined with them.

JOHN CLARK, Speaker.'

'The Committee appointed to consider of the Paper called The New England Courant, published Monday the Fourteenth, Currant, are *humbly of Opinion* that the Tendency of the said Paper is to mock Religion, and bring it into Contempt, that the Holy Scriptures are therein profanely abused, that the Reverend and Faithful Ministers of the Gospel are injuriously reflected on, His Majesty's Government affronted, and the Peace and good Order of His Majesty's Subjects of this Province disturbed, by the said Courant; And for prevention of the like Offence for the Future, the Committee *humbly propose*, That *James Franklin*, the Printer and Publisher thereof, be strictly forbidden by this Court, to Print or Publish the New England Courant, or any Pamphlet or Paper of the like Nature, except it be first supervised by the Secretary of this Province; And the Justices of his Majesty's Sessions of the Peace for the County of Suffolk, at their next Adjournment, be directed to take sufficient Bonds of the said *Franklin*, for his good Behaviour for Twelve Months Time.

'Per Order of the Committee.

WILLIAM TAILER.'

'In Council Jan. 15th, 1722. Read and Accepted.

Sent down for Concurrence.　　　J. WILLARD, Secretary'
'In the House of Representatives, Jan. 16, 1722. Read and
Concurr'd.　　　　　　　　JOHN CLARK, Speaker.'
'Consented to. W. DUMMER. A true Copy. Examined per
J. WILLARD, Secretary.'

Notwithstanding this act of government, Franklin published
the Courant on the Monday following without submitting its
contents to the Secretary. For this neglect, a 'Bill of Indictment
was some months after preferred to the grand jury against him
for contempt of an order of the general court.' The jury returned *Ignoramus* on the bill, but Franklin was bound to the
good behavior pursuant to the order of the General court.

The act of government was voluntarily published in the
Courant; and it also appeared in *The American Weekly Mercury*
of February 26th, 172$\frac{2}{3}$, published in Philadelphia, with the
following severe remarks, which were unquestionably furnished by the Courant club in Boston, viz.

'My Lord *Coke* observes, That to *punish first and then enquire*,
the Law abhors, but here Mr. *Franklin* has a severe sentence
pass'd upon him even to the taking away Part of his Livelihood,
without being called to make Answer. An Indifferent Person
would judge by this vote against *Couranto*, That the Assembly
of the Province of the *Massachusetts Bay* are made up of Oppres-
sors and Bigots who make Religion only the Engine of Destruction to the People; and the rather, because the first Letter in the
Courant of the 14th of *January* (which the Assembly Censures)
so naturally represents and exposes the *Hypocritical Pretenders to
Religion*. Indeed, the most famous Politicians in that Government (as the infamous Gov. D— and his Family) have ever been
remarkable for Hypocrisy; and it is the general Opinion that

some of their Rulers are rais'd up and continued as a Scourge in the Hands of the Almighty for the Sins of the People. Thus much we could not forbear saying, out of Compassion to the distressed People of the Province, who must now resign all Pretences to Sense and Reason, and submit to the Tyranny of Priestcraft, and Hypocrisy. P. S. By private Letters from Boston we are informed, That the Bakers there are under great Apprehensions of being forbid baking any more Bread, unless they will submit to the Secretary as Supervisor General and Weigher of the Dough, before it is baked into Bread, and offered to Sale.'

Franklin and the Courant Club did not choose to submit the contents of that paper, before publishing it, to the secretary of the government for his approbation. After deliberating what was best to be done to evade the act, it was determined to alter the imprint by leaving out the name of *James*, and inserting that of *Benjamin* Franklin.* This determination was carried into im-

---

* The Courant, No. 80, was thus introduced to the public. 'The late Publisher of this Paper finding so many inconveniences would arise by his carrying the Manuscripts and publick News to be supervis'd by the Secretary, as to render his carrying it on unprofitable, has intirely dropt the Undertaking: The present Publisher of this Paper, having receiv'd the following Piece, desires the Readers to accept of it as a Preface to what they may hereafter meet with in this Paper.'

Then follows an address to the public in which the club are mentioned as the writers in the Courant, and that one of them designated by the name of '*Old Janus, is Couranteer.*' The following is an extract from this address. 'The main Design of this Weekly Paper will be to entertain the Town with the most comical and diverting Incidents of Human Life, which in so large a place as *Boston*, will not fail of a universal Exemplification: Nor shall we be wanting to fill up these Papers with a grateful interspersion of more serious Morals, which may be drawn from the most ludicrous and odd Parts of Life.' [A reprint in fac simile of this Courant, No. 80, was issued in 1856, in which it was claimed that it had been printed on a press once used by Benjamin Franklin. It corresponds with the description given above, and is dated February 11, 1723. At the end is this notice:

'*‡* This paper having met with so general an Acceptance in Town and

mediate effect. The Courant now purported to be 'printed and sold by Benjamin Franklin in Queen Street,' although he was a minor. The club proceeded without any apparent mitigation of 'the Lash.' The Courant was published in the name of Benjamin Franklin for some time after he left his brother; and, for anything that appears, until its publication ceased in the beginning of the year 1727. Before this paper was discontinued, the writers for it became languid, and for months in succession no original essay appeared.

James Franklin, at a subsequent period, removed to Newport, and established the first press in Rhode Island. The Courant was published about six years.

THE NEW-ENGLAND WEEKLY JOURNAL was first published March 20th, 1727, on a half sheet of foolscap size, folio. At first it was published on Mondays; but, after several years, Tuesday was substituted. Imprint—'Boston, Printed by S. Kneeland, at the Printing-House in Queen-Street, where Advertisements are taken in.'

During the first year of the Journal, several literary gentlemen furnished it with short essays on miscellaneous subjects, more however of a moral than a political nature, and which, although well written, did not occasion the excitement in the public mind which was produced by the writers for the Courant.

Country, as to require a far greater Number of them to be printed, than there is of the other publick Papers; and it being besides more generally read by a vast Number of Borrowers, who do not take it in, the Publisher thinks proper to give this publick Notice for the Incouragement of those who would have *Advertisements* inserted in the public Prints, which they may have printed in this Paper at a moderate Price.' M]

The first year, the editor of the Journal assumed the name of 'Proteus Echo, Esq.' In No. 3, he requests those who will do him the honor to contribute to the embellishment of *his* Journal, to direct to him at Mr. Samuel Kneeland's in Queen-Street; and he gives a humorous account of himself. In No. 4, he describes, in the same manner, his associates, among whom he mentions 'two divines who sometimes did themselves the honor of half an hour's setting,' &c., and observes, that the gentlemen, whom he had described, 'will have no inconsiderable hand in these weekly entertainments.' At the close of the first year, the editor presents his 'gratitude to those generous hands which have made such considerable presents to the authors of these Essays.' He mentions a piece of Spanish gold from a gentleman, and a silver pen from a lady; and he then informs his readers that, a year being completed since the first publication of the Journal, the essay then published 'is the last piece which will be published by the gentlemen who begun and have till now supplied this paper.' He concludes by observing that the writers were three in number, one of whom supplied the poetry, and signed his pieces with one of the letters composing the word *Musæ*.

The second year, the Journal was not supplied with original essays;[60] the third year, it contained eighteen numbers, moral and entertaining, supposed by some to have been principally composed by governor Burnet; they began the January after his arrival at Boston, and ceased a few weeks before his death. I have seen a file of the Journal, containing these numbers, with an Index written by a former proprietor of the volume, whom I suppose to have been one of those who wrote for the Journal during the first year of its publication. In this index the eighteen numbers are noticed thus, 'Speculation-Govr No. 1.' 2, &c.

The collection of foreign and domestic intelligence for the Journal, even for that day, was but indifferent, though not much inferior to the other Boston papers. In the head, preceding the title, a *signature* was inserted weekly, the signification of which I have not ascertained—it was a letter of the alphabet; first, A, with a figure after it, was used for several months, changing the figure weekly; then B took the place of A, and so on; but the same letter did not appear to be continued for any definite period. After two or three years, the signature consisted of a letter without a figure.

When S. Kneeland had published the Journal four months, to his name in the imprint was added that of T. Green. For the first year of the partnership there was a singularity of this kind. The imprint of the Journal was, 'Printed by S. Kneeland and T. Green,' etc., yet Green alone, it seems, was responsible for the correctness of the paper, and appears to have been the sole conductor of it. In such advertisements, published in the Journal, as required explanation, the public were requested to 'enquire of the Printer.'

In the Journal of February 3, 1729, the following notice appeared: 'The *Printer* of this paper would have emitted herewith his Desire, that some errors of the last Journal might be laid to his Charge; he not having then any Person by Him to correct the Press as *usual*, and being since convinced that they are his own; such as "fresh passage, Imation, Piquanry—distin'd—Spectable —Dictors—executed—Vengance—Destracted": with a few other slips which if the Reader pardons, he will oblige *The Printer*.' Immediately after this notice, the imprint, 'S. Kneeland & T. Green' stands as usual. This may be explained by observing, that Kneeland committed the printing of the Journal to

Green, and for four or five years after their partnership commenced, himself kept a bookshop in King's street. The shop occupied the attention of Kneeland; and although the Journal was printed in the name of Kneeland & Green, yet the former was considered as the proprietor, and the latter as the printer, and the profits were shared between them. Judge Danforth, and the Rev. Mather Byles, the elder, it is said were the principal editors of the Journal, and often corrected the press. Mr. Byles, it is also said, wrote many of the poetical and other essays in that paper.

Kneeland gave up his bookshop about the year 1742; and afterwards attended wholly to printing. Essays, etc., were subsequently addressed to the publishers, and people were directed to inquire of the printers, etc.

The *New England Weekly Journal* was published nearly fifteen years by the same printers, and without any alteration of the title or the imprint. At the close of the year 1741, this paper was incorporated with the *Boston Gazette* by Kneeland & Green, who then became proprietors of that paper, and the title of the paper so consolidated was *The Boston Gazette and Weekly Journal*. The imprint was as before, with the addition of 'Price 16s. a year, and 20s. seal'd,' paid quarterly.

The printers of this paper were great advocates of the reverend George Whitefield, the reverend Mr. Edwards, &c. The reverend Thomas Prince was supposed to have taken an active part in the publication of this paper, and for a time to have assisted in correcting the press. The first publication that issued was a general prospectus, without any number. The second publication was numbered 1.

The Journal was incorporated with the Gazette in 1741; and,

in 1752, the Gazette was discontinued, twenty-five years after the first publication of the Journal.

246   THE WEEKLY REHEARSAL was published on a half sheet of printing foolscap, folio, on a small pica type; and was established by a young gentleman of great literary talents, who afterwards became a celebrated law character;* and Monday was the day of its publication. It was not numbered the first forty-six weeks.

The first paper was printed September 27, 1731. The imprint —'Boston: Printed by *J. Draper*, for the Author, by whom Advertisements are taken in.' Afterwards, 'Printed by *J. Draper*, for the Author. Advertisements are taken in by Mr. Hancock, at the Bible and Three Crowns in Ann-Street, 1732.' For the first six weeks, mottos in Latin from the classics were inserted after the title. The motto was different in each week; and, for the first six months, with very few exceptions, a moral or entertaining essay was weekly published in the Rehearsal, which usually filled more than half the paper. These essays were sometimes selected, but generally original. Before the termination of one year, its original essays were discontinued, and it had become a mere vehicle of intelligence.

Thomas Fleet began to print it with No. 47, and it appears, by an advertisement in that number, that he was interested in the publication. It became a good paper for foreign and domestic news, but was no longer a literary journal.

On April 2, 1733, Fleet became the sole proprietor of the Rehearsal, and thus announced it to the public:

---

* Jeremiah Gridley, afterwards attorney general of the province of Massachusetts Bay.

'The Gentleman who first set up and has hitherto been interested in this Paper, having now resigned all his Right and Interest therein into the hands of the Subscriber, the Subscriber thinks himself obliged to give publick Notice thereof, and informs all such as have taken, or may hereafter take it, that as he has settled a Correspondence with Gentlemen in London, and most of the principal Towns within this and the neighbouring Governments, and is favoured with the Acquaintance of many intelligent Persons in Boston, he doubts not but he shall be able to make the Rehearsal as Useful and entertaining as any of the Papers now published. And the better to effect it, requests all Gentlemen in Town or Country who may be possessed of any thing new or curious, whether in the Way of News or Speculation, worthy the publick View, to send the same to him, and it will be gratefully received and communicated for the Entertainment of the polite and inquisitive Part of Mankind. The publisher of this paper declares himself of no Party, and invites all Gentlemen of Leisure and Capacity, inclined on either Side, to write any thing of a political Nature, that tends to enlighten and serve the Publick, to communicate their Productions, provided they are not overlong, and confined within Modesty and Good Manners; for all possible Care will be taken that nothing contrary to these shall ever be here published. And whereas the publishing of Advertisements in the Weekly News Papers has been found of great Use (especially in such as are sent thro' all the Governments as this is) this may inform all Persons, who shall have Occasion, that they may have their Advertisements published in this Paper upon very easy Terms, and that any Customer for the Paper shall be served much cheaper than others. And whereas the Price of this Paper was set up at twenty Shillings per Year, and so paid till this time; the present Undertaker being willing to give all possible Encouragement to his Readers has now reduced it to Sixteen Shillings; and offers all Gentlemen who are willing to hold a Correspondence, and shall frequently favour him with any thing that may tend to the Embellishment of the Paper, to supply them with one constantly free from Charge. And considering it is impossible for half a Sheet of Paper to contain all the Remarkable News that may happen to be brought in upon the Arrival of Ships from England or other extraordinary Occurrences; the Publisher therefore proposes in all such Cases, to Print a Sheet of what he judges most Material, and shall continue to send the Paper to all such as have hitherto taken it, until he is advised to the contrary by those determined to drop it, which he hopes will not be many. *Thomas Fleet.*'

The imprint from No. 79 to 202, August 11, 1735, when the Rehearsal was discontinued, was, 'Boston Printed by T. Fleet, at the Heart and Crown in Cornhill, where Advertisements are taken in. Advertisements are also taken in by Mr. N. Belknap, Bookseller, near Clark's Wharf, at the North End. Price 16s. per year.'

It was Fleet's intention to alter the time of publication from Monday morning to Monday evening, as appears from an advertisement published in the last number of the Rehearsal, viz:

'☞ The Publisher of this Paper hereby gives Notice, that he intends for the Future to print it every Monday Evening (having the Approbation and Advice of several Gentlemen in Town, who are his customers) and will take Care to collect and publish not only the most fresh and authentic Advices from abroad, but also what occurs among Ourselves or Neighbours, worthy the publick View; And all the Readers in Town may depend upon having it left at their Houses some Time before Dark, (unless upon extraordinary Occasions) which may be a Diversion after the Business of the Day, now the Evenings are grown pretty long.' But Fleet, the next week, instead of continuing the Rehearsal, published a paper with the title of *The Boston Evening Post*; he, however, numbered it 203, as a continuation of the Rehearsal; but on the following Monday, the *Evening Post* was numbered 2. The Rehearsal was discontinued after being published nearly four years. See Evening Post.

THE BOSTON WEEKLY POST-BOY. Postmasters established the first two newspapers published in Boston; and succeeding postmasters seemed to claim a right to such publications, or at least to think that a newspaper was an appendage to their office. Ellis Huske* being appointed postmaster of Boston, and Boydell not choosing to resign the Boston Gazette, Huske began in October, 1734, the publication of another paper, entitled *The Boston Weekly Post-Boy*. It was at first printed on a half sheet of small demy, in quarto, but soon after on a half sheet of crown, in quarto, on a small pica type. Huske retained the device of the postman, and the ship, on the right and left of the title, which

---

* He was afterward appointed deputy postmaster general for the colonies. He was brother to General Huske, who distinguished himself at the battles of Dettingen and Culloden. He had a son, bred a merchant in Boston, who was afterward a member of the British parliament. Huske was superseded in the department of the post office by Franklin and Hunter. [The son (John) is supposed to be the same who published a work, entitled *The Present State of North America*, London, 1755; and also the same who, as a member of parliament in 1764, proposed to lay a tax on the colonies, which would amount to £500,000 per annum, which he said they were well able to pay. S. G. Drake, *The History and Antiquities of Boston* (Boston, 1856), pp. 598, 679, 708. H]

had hitherto appeared in the Boston Gazette published by his predecessors. The Post-Boy was published on Mondays; no printer's name appeared.* The imprint was, 'Boston; Printed for *Ellis Huske*, Post-Master: Advertisements taken in at the Post-Office in King's-Street, over against the North-Door of the Town-House, where all Persons in Town or Country may be supplied with this Paper.' This imprint was continued, without the name of the printer, during the twenty years of its publication, which began and ended with Huske. I have never seen any number of this paper after December, 1754; but, I believe, it was continued until within a few weeks of the time when the provincial stamp act took place, in 1755.

Nothing extraordinary attended this publication. Its features were much like those of the News-Letter and the Gazette. Towards its close it was reduced to half a sheet foolscap, folio. It was not uncommon for the publishers of the New England Journal, and those of the Gazette, to vary the size of their papers, and to print them on half a sheet folio or quarto, of different sizes, as they found it convenient. Most of the paper then used in America was imported from Europe, and paper of a particular size could not, at all times, be obtained.

The devices in the title were twice engraved anew during its publication. Those last engraved were, afterwards, made use of by Green and Russell, when they began to publish *The Boston Weekly Advertiser*.

THE BOSTON EVENING-POST. Fleet having discontinued the Rehearsal on Monday, August 11, 1735, began the publication of *The Boston Evening Post* on the evening of the following

* It was, I believe, some time printed by John Bushell.

Monday. It was printed on a half sheet of large foolscap printing paper. He commonly made use of paper of this description, excepting when he printed a whole sheet; then he generally used the smaller size of foolscap or pot. The imprint—'Boston: Printed by T. Fleet, at the Heart and Crown, in Cornhill, where advertisements are taken in at a moderate Price.' Excepting in the title, the Evening Post did not differ from the Rehearsal. It was the best newspaper then published in Boston. The selection of entertaining and amusing pieces from London publications, and some of Fleet's own humorous paragraphs gave it animation, and its news were well selected and seasonably published. It interfered very little with political controversy, and not greatly with religious disputes. Fleet was a wit, and no bigot; he did not appear to be a great friend to itinerant preachers; and he was not, like the brethren of the type of that day, afraid to attack the highly popular, and greatly distinguished itinerant preacher Whitefield.

A paragraph was published in the Evening Post of March 8, 1741, which was next day taken notice of by the governor and council, who ordered an information to be filed against Fleet, that he might be prosecuted at the next superior court. How the affair ended I never knew, but probably a prosecution did not take place, as Fleet procured five respectable persons to testify to the truth of the contents of the paragraph.

The following is a copy of the proceedings of the Governor and Council of Massachusetts. It shows the difference between what was then, and what is now, judged to be the 'liberty of the press.'

'At a Council held at the Council Chamber in Boston, upon Tuesday the 9th day of March, 1741.

'Whereas there is published in the Weekly Paper called the Boston Evening-Post of yesterday's Date, a Paragraph in the following Words:

'Last Saturday Capt. *Gibbs* arrived here from *Madeira*, who informs, that before he left that Island, Capt. *Dandridge*, in one of his Majesty's ships of forty Guns, came in there from *England*, and gave an Account, that the Parliament had called for all the Papers relating to the War, and 'twas expected the Right Hon. Sir *Robert Walpole* would be taken into Custody in a very few Days.—Capt. *Dandridge* was going upon the *Virginia* Station to relieve the valiant and vigilant Knight there, almost wore out in the Service of his Country, and for which he has a Chance to be rewarded with a *Flag*. Which Paragraph contains a scandalous and libellous Reflection upon his Majesty's Administration, and may tend very much to inflame the Minds of his Majesty's Subjects here and disaffect them to his Government;'

'Therefore, *Ordered*, That the Attorney General do, as soon as may be, file an information against *Thomas Fleet*, the Publisher of the said Paper, in his Majesty's Superior Court of Judicature, Court of Assize and General Gaol Delivery, in order to his being prosecuted for his said Offence as Law and Justice requires.

'*W. Shirley.*

'Copy Examin'd, per *J. Willard*, Sec.'

Fleet had a peculiar faculty in wording his advertisements. The following advertisements of negroes appeared in the Evening Post, in April 1758. 'To be sold by the Printer of this Paper, a Negro Man, about thirty years old, who can do both Town and Country Business very well, but will suit the Country best, where they have not so many Dram Shops as we have in Boston. He has worked at the Printing Business fifteen or sixteen years; can handle an ax, Saw, Spade, Hoe, or other Instrument of Husbandry as well as most Men, and values himself, and is valued by others, for his skill in Cookery and making of Soap.' 'Also, a very valuable Negro Woman, about thirty years old, (sold only for her frequent pregnancy), with a fine healthy Boy two years old.'

In June of the same year, in a dunning advertisement to his customers, he adds, 'In the days of Mr. Campbell, who published a newspaper here, which is forty years ago, Paper was bought for *eight* or *nine* shillings a Ream,* and now tis Five Pounds; his Paper was never more than half a sheet, and that he had *Two Dollars* a year for, and had also the Art of getting his Pay for it; and that Size has continued till within a little more than one year, since which we are expected to publish a whole Sheet, so that the Paper now stands us in near as much as all the other charges.'

In the Evening-Post of November 7, 1748, Fleet inserted this advertisement viz: 'Choice *Pennsylvania* Tobacco Paper, to be Sold by the Publisher of this Paper, at the Heart & Crown; where may also be had the BULLS or Indulgencies of the present Pope *Urban* VIII, either by the single Bull, Quire or Ream, at a much cheaper Rate than they can be purchased of the *French* or *Spanish* Priests, and yet will be warranted to be of the same Advantage to the Possessors.'

These *Bulls*, or Indulgences, of his holiness, were printed on the face of a small sheet; several bales of them were taken in a

---

* He did not inform his readers that the paper currency had depreciated.

Spanish ship, captured by an English Cruiser, and sent into Boston during the war between England and France and Spain, in 1748. I have one of them now in my possession. Fleet purchased a very large quantity at a low price, and printed various editions of ballads on the backs of them. One side of the sheet was blank, and the paper very good; one bull answered for two half sheet ballads, or songs such as 'Black Eyed Susan'—'Handsome Harry'—'Teague's Ramble to the Camp,' &c. I have seen large quantities of them which were thus worked up by Fleet.

Fleet continued to publish the Evening Post until he died, in 1758. His sons, Thomas and John, in copartnership, continued it with much approbation, till April 1775, when the revolutionary war occasioned its immediate termination. It was published forty years.[61]

When T. and J. Fleet succeeded their father, they introduced a cut of their sign, the Heart and Crown, into the centre of the title of the Evening Post, and published it every Monday morning instead of Monday evening.

THE INDEPENDENT ADVERTISER was of a political cast. It was first published Tuesday, January 4, 1748, by Rogers & Fowle, printers and copartners. It was printed on a half sheet of good paper, of crown size, folio, with a new long primer type. The device in the centre of its title was a large cut of Britannia liberating a bird confined by a cord to the arms of France. Britannia is represented sitting, the arms of France lying on the ground before her; the bird is on the wing, but being impeded by the cord, one end of which is fastened to the arms of France, and the other to the bird, Britannia is in the act of cutting the cord with a pair of shears, that the bird may escape.

This paper was published weekly on Tuesday, but the day of the week was not mentioned in the title. The imprint: 'Boston: Printed and Sold by Rogers & Fowle in Queen-Street, next to the Prison, where Advertisements are taken in at a reasonable Price. And all Gentlemen and others may be supplied with this paper.' This, like all the English American newspapers then published, had two columns to a page.

The following is an extract from a pertinent and well written address of the publishers to the public: 'As our present political state affords Matter for a variety of Thoughts, of peculiar Importance to the good People of *New-England*, we purpose to insert every thing of that Nature that may be pertinently and decently wrote. For ourselves, we declare we are of no Party, neither shall we promote the narrow and private Designs of any such. We are ourselves free, and our Paper shall be free—free as the Constitution we enjoy—free to Truth, good Manners, and good Sense, and at the same time free from all licentious Reflections, Insolence and Abuse. Whatsoever may be adapted to State and Defend the Rights and Liberties of Mankind, to advance useful Knowledge and the Cause of Virtue, to improve the Trade, the Manufactures, and Husbandry of the Country, whatever may tend to inspire this People with a just and proper Sense of their own Condition, to point out to them their true Interests, and rouse them to pursue it, as also any Piece of Wit and Humor, shall at all Times find (free of Charge,) a most welcome reception. And although we do not altogether depend upon the casual Benevolence of the Publick to supply this Paper, yet we will thankfully receive every Thing from every quarter conducing to the Good of the Publick and our general Design.'

The Advertiser was supplied with well written essays, chiefly political. A number of gentlemen associated for this purpose, among whom, we are told, was the late governor Samuel Adams. This association consisted of whigs, who advocated the rights of the people against those measures of the government which were supposed to infringe upon the privileges of the province secured by charter.

The Advertiser was handsomely printed. It contained but little foreign intelligence, and not much domestic news. Its principal object was political discussion, as the means to rouse the people of the colony to maintain their rights. The continuance of this paper was short. Rogers & Fowle dissolved their copartnership in April, 1750; and, their *Independent Advertiser* ceased with their connection, after being published two years.

THE BOSTON GAZETTE, OR WEEKLY ADVERTISER was published by Samuel Kneeland after the dissolution of his partnership with Timothy Green. It superseded the old *Boston Gazette and Weekly Journal*, and was created upon its foundation. For the want of a more appropriate device, a very singular cut was used in its title which had been designed and engraved for the lxxvth fable of Croxall's Esop; representing the boy viewing himself in the glass, his little sister, who was offended with his vanity, and their father who moralized on the subject of their difference.*

This Boston Gazette made its first appearance on Wednesday, January 3, 1753. It was printed on a half sheet of crown, quarto,

---

* Several of the cuts for Esop's Fables were engraved by a remarkably good workman, whose name was Turner, of Boston. He was the best engraver which appeared in the colonies before the revolution, especially on type metal. D. Fowle having a part of this set of cuts, used them from time to time to decorate the title of *The New Hampshire Gazette*.

on a new long primer type, with the following rather singular introduction after the title. 'As the Types generally us'd in the Printing of the late *Boston Gazette* or *Weekly Journal*,* are worn out, it has been tho't proper, on the Return of the Year, to alter the Form and Title of this Paper, as it now appears. 'Tis proposed to publish the same, as usual, every Tuesday; and hope Care will be taken to furnish it from Time to Time with the most remarkable Occurrences, both of a foreign and domestick Nature.'

After the first number it was regularly published every Tuesday, and continued to be printed in quarto, on paper of the same size. No printer or publisher's name appeared in the imprint, which was, 'Boston: Printed opposite the prison in Queen street, where Advertisements are taken in.' This imprint remained unaltered the first year; the second year Kneeland added his name to it, and exchanged the cut before mentioned, in the title, for a well executed one of the arms of the province.†

Kneeland published this Gazette two years, when it was discontinued on account of the provincial stamp act, and never revived. This paper was better printed than the old Boston Gazette, and had, for those days, a considerable number of advertising customers.

THE BOSTON GAZETTE, OR COUNTRY JOURNAL was the third newspaper bearing the title of The Boston Gazette. No. 1 was published April 7, 1755, on a crown half sheet, from a long

---

* It had been discontinued several months.

† An Indian with a bow in one hand, an arrow in the other, and a quiver at his back.

primer type. The title had two cuts, which had before been used, the one for the last Boston Gazette, and the other for the Independent Advertiser. The province arms, or the Indian, was placed on the left, and Britannia liberating a bird on the right of the title; but the disproportion in the width of the cuts, Britannia being twice the width of the Indian, pressed the title from the centre of the page, and destroyed the uniformity which would have been preserved had the parts been properly arranged. The imprint, 'Boston: Printed by Benjamin Edes and John Gill, at their Printing-Office near the East End of the Town-House, in King Street; where all persons may be supplied with this paper, and where Advertisements are taken in. Also printing done at a moderate Rate with Care and Dispatch.' Edes and Gill removed soon after to the printing house which had been occupied by Rogers and Fowle, in Prison lane; the imprint was altered and shortened, and the Gazette was occasionally printed on a whole sheet crown. About the year 1760, it became a common custom in Boston to print all newspapers on a whole sheet.

Several of the gentlemen who had associated to write for the Independent Advertiser, joined by some others, encouraged the establishment of this paper; they were the editors of its literary department, and the purveyors of its political information. During the long controversy between Great Britain and her American colonies, no paper on the continent took a more active part in defence of the country, or more ably supported its rights, than the Boston Gazette; its patrons were alert and ever at their posts, and they had a primary agency in events which led to our national independence.*

* The most distinguished revolutionary patriots in Boston, several years preceding 1775, frequently convened at this celebrated *Gazette* office, and also

A provincial stamp act, or, as it was called, 'An act for grant-
ing to his Majesty several Duties on Vellum, Parchment and
Paper, for two years, towards the defraying the Charge of this
Government,' was passed by the legislature of the province a
few months before Edes & Gill began the publication of the
Boston Gazette, and it took effect the first of May following.
The act embraced newspapers, which were to pay *one-half
penny* for each paper. Of the several newspapers which had
been established in Boston previously to this period, only three
were now in being, viz: the News-Letter, the Evening Post,
and this *new* Boston Gazette. These were all printed from May
1st, 1755, to April 30, 1757, on paper stamped by the colonial
government. The figure of the stamp was round, of the size of
half a dollar, and the words 'HALF PENNY–HALF PENNY,'
were inclosed between two circular lines, and formed the border; in the centre was a bird, probably meant for an eagle on the
wing; this device was stamped with red ink on a corner of the
sheet.*

---

at that of the *Massachusetts Spy*. Amongst them were Samuel Adams, John
Hancock, Thomas Cushing, Joseph Warren, William Cooper, William Young,
etc., etc. It may be truly said, that in those meetings were concocted many of
the measures of opposition to the British acts of parliament for taxing the
colonies—measures which led to, and terminated in the independence of our
country.

* Fleet, printer of *The Evening Post*, the first week he used this stamped paper,
published the following, which may serve as a specimen of his talent at rhym-
ing, viz:

On the Pretty Bird in the margin.

The little, pretty Picture here
O' th' Side looks well enough,
Though nothing to the Purpose is
'Twill serve to set it off.

Again,

Although this Emblem has but little in't,
You must e'en take it, or you'l have no print.

In 1768, after the death of Samuel Kneeland, Edes & Gill occupied his printing house, where the two former Boston Gazettes, and the New England Weekly Journal had been printed. There they continued to publish the Gazette, of which they were proprietors, until April, 1775, when the revolutionary war commenced. Before this event took place, the device in the title underwent a change. The figure of Britannia was exchanged for that of Minerva, seated; before her was a pedestal on which was placed a cage; Minerva with her left hand supported a spear, on which was placed the cap of Liberty, and with her right opened the door of the cage, and liberated a bird which appeared in the act of flying towards a tree that stood at a distance from a city. This cut was coarsely executed.

The publication of the Gazette was suspended from April, 1775, to the 5th of June following, when Edes, having set up a press at Watertown, renewed the printing of the paper, and continued it until November, 1776, when he returned to Boston, and again published the Gazette in Queen street. Gill had no concern in printing the Gazette after April, 1775; but in 1776 he began another paper, entitled *The Continental Journal*.

Edes's sons, Benjamin and Peter,[62] were, sometime after his return to Boston, concerned with him in printing the Gazette. In 1784, Edes and his eldest son Benjamin,[63] only, were together, and published this paper in Cornhill, No. 42,* under the firm of Edes & Son; and they introduced a new cut—the goddess of liberty was represented standing instead of sitting; this was the only alteration in the device; but the following motto was added and engraved underneath the figures, '*Libertas et*

---

* The houses in Boston were numbered about 1784.

natale solum.' The Gazette was printed afterwards in Marlborough street, and then again in King street, now State street.

Some time after, Edes printed and published it on his own account in Kilby street. But the Gazette no more 'thundered in the capitol.' Its former writers were silent, and age and infirmity overtook its publisher. The paper however, lingered along, unnoticed by its rivals, and almost by the public, to whom it had been a faithful and useful servant, until 1798. Forty-five years having completed their revolutions since its first publication, Edes at this time took his farewell of the public, and the Gazette expired![64]

THE BOSTON WEEKLY ADVERTISER was first published August 22, 1757, by John Green and Joseph Russell, in Queen street, printers and copartners. It was printed weekly, on Mondays, with a new long primer type, on paper of crown size, folio, two columns in a page, and generally on a whole sheet. The imprint—'Boston: Printed by Green and Russell, opposite to the Probate-Office in Queen-Street, where all Persons may be supplied with this Paper at Five Shillings and Four Pence Lawful Money per Annum, and where Advertisements are taken in, and all sorts of Printing Work done at a moderate rate, with Care and Dispatch.'

After it had been published about two years, the title was altered to *Green & Russell's Post-Boy and Advertiser*, &c. It was changed a second time, to *The Boston Post-Boy and Advertiser*; and again to *The Massachusetts Gazette and Boston Post-Boy and Advertiser*.

When its title was *The Boston Weekly Advertiser*, it had for the first year the cut of the postboy in the centre of the title; the second year the ship was added. The cuts were placed like those in the former Boston Post-Boy, published for Huske, and were identically the same which had been used for that paper; the ship on the left, and the postman on horseback on the right of the title. When the paper was called *The Massachusetts Gazette*, &c., the old devices were thrown aside, and the king's arms were substituted. Its circulation was not extensive, and it was not distinguished for original essays of any kind, nor as the channel of important intelligence; but it was well printed, and always on good types. All the printers in Boston were on friendly terms respecting business; their papers were all of one size, and the columns and pages of one measure. Draper printed the News-Letter on Thursdays. Columns of news, advertisements, &c., in types, were weekly interchanged by Green & Russell with Draper. They followed this practice as long as the Post-Boy was published by Green & Russell, and found it very convenient. Their readers did not complain, although whole columns, which had been published in the News-Letter on Thursday, appeared again from the same types, on the following Monday, in the Post-Boy.

Green and Russell were appointed printers to the British commissioners, and supplied the blanks and other work for the custom house. This induced them, apparently, to become advocates for the measures which the British administration adopted toward the American colonies, and accordingly *The Boston Post-Boy*, on the 23d of May, 1768, appeared with the insignia of government. It had for several years been printed on a whole sheet, as other newspapers in Bosten then were. One-half of this sheet now bore the title of, 'The Massachusetts Gazette, Published by Authority;' and the other half, its usual title of Boston

Post-Boy, &c., as has been already described.* The royal arms were substituted, in the title, for the postman and the ship.

This mode of publication continued till September, 1769, when printing the Gazette by *Authority* was discontinued, and the Post-Boy and Gazette were united under the title of *The Massachusetts Gazette and Boston Post-Boy and Advertiser*, and the cut of the king's arms was retained.

In April, 1773, Green & Russell resigned the printing and publishing of this paper to Mills & Hicks, two young printers, who, having received patronage and encouragement from the officers of the crown, &c., continued it with renewed spirit; and several good writers in favor of government became its supporters, the animation and weight of whose communications attracted more notice from the public for the Post-Boy than it had before received. In this manner the paper was printed until a short time after the commencement of the war in 1775, when it was discontinued. The *Weekly Advertiser* was published about eighteen years.

THE BOSTON CHRONICLE. From the first publication of *The Boston Weekly Advertiser*, more than ten years passed before an attempt was made to establish another newspaper in that town. During this period four journals, viz: The News-Letter, The Evening Post, The Gazette, and The Advertiser, or Post-Boy, were regularly published.

December 21, 1767, *The Boston Chronicle* was added to the number. It was printed on a whole sheet demy, in quarto, on a broad faced long primer, from an Edinburgh foundery. It was

* See account of the *Boston News-Letter*, published in like manner, at the same time, by Draper.

published weekly, on Mondays, for the first year, and intended to imitate in its appearance the London Chronicle. The price per annum, being six shillings and eight pence, was but a very small consideration for a newspaper on a large sheet, and well executed. It was 'Printed by Mein and Fleming, in Newbury Street, opposite the White Horse Tavern.' Mein and Fleming were Scotchmen. John Mein was a bookseller, and John Fleming a printer. The Chronicle was published by Mein. For the first year, this paper was well supplied with essays on various subjects judiciously selected from British authors, and it contained the celebrated letters of the Pennsylvania Farmer.* It grew daily into reputation, and had a handsome list of subscribers.

With the beginning of the second year, the size of the paper was altered to a crown folio, and published every Monday and Thursday, without any addition to the price. This was the first newspaper published twice a week in New England. Before the close of the second year of publication, its publisher, Mein, engaged in a political warfare with those who were in opposition to the measures of the British administration. In the Chronicle he abused numbers of the most respectable whigs in Boston; and he was charged with insulting the populace. To avoid the effects of popular resentment, it became necessary for him to leave the country. Fleming continued the Chronicle during the absence of Mein, in the name of the firm; but it had fallen into disrepute, and its subscribers in rapid succession withdrew their names. Many supposed that Mein was privately assisted by the agents of government, and several circumstances rendered this opinion probable. But when the paper lost its subscribers it

* John Dickinson, Esq.

could neither be profitable to its publishers, nor answer the design of its supporters. Its publication, therefore, ceased on the 25th of June, 1770. On this occasion its remaining subscribers were thus addressed.

' *** The Printers of the Boston Chronicle return thanks to the Gentlemen who have so long favoured them with their subscriptions, and now inform them that, as the Chronicle in the present state of affairs cannot be carried on, either for their entertainment or the emolument of the Printers, it will be discontinued for some time.'

It was never revived.

THE MASSACHUSETTS SPY. Although *The Boston Chronicle* had become unpopular, and the times were deemed unfavorable for publishing a new paper; yet, under inauspicious circumstances, an attempt was made to establish one on a new plan. The Massachusetts Spy was calculated to obtain subscriptions from mechanics, and other classes of people who had not much time to spare from business. It was to be published three times a week, viz: on Tuesday, Thursday and Saturday. Twice in the week it was to be printed on a quarter of a sheet, and once on a half sheet. When published in this way, news were conveyed fresh to subscribers, and the contents of a Spy might with convenience be read at a leisure moment.

This plan was detailed in the first number, which appeared in July, 1770, and was sent gratis to the inhabitants in all parts of the town. In a short time such a subscription was obtained as to warrant a prosecution of the design, and the publication of the Spy commenced with No. 2, August 7, 1770, and was printed in this form for three months by Z. Fowle and I. Thomas; the partnership was then dissolved; and the Spy was continued by Thomas, but published only on Mondays and Thursdays, each number containing half a sheet of large crown, in quarto. In this manner the Spy was issued three months longer. At the expiration of that time, the object of publishing it in this introductory form being obtained, it was set aside to make way for the appearance of a weekly newspaper on a larger sheet than any that had at that time been published in Boston.

THE MASSACHUSETTS SPY. Number 1, of this newspaper, was published March 7, 1771, on a whole sheet, royal size, folio, four columns in a page. Massachusetts Spy, was in large German text, engraved on type metal between two cuts; the device of the cut on the left was the Goddess of Liberty sitting near a pedestal, on which was placed a scroll, a part of which, with the word SPY on it, lay over on one side of the pedestal, on which the right arm of Liberty rested. The device on the right was, two infants making selections from a basket filled with flowers and bearing this motto: 'THEY CULL THE CHOICEST.' The imprint, 'Boston: Printed and Published by Isaiah Thomas, in Union Street, near the Market, where Advertisements are taken in.' The day of publication was Thursday. The majority of the customers for the former Spy preferred the way in which it had been published, and withdrew their subscriptions. On the appearance of this the subscribers did not amount to two hundred, but after the first week they increased daily, and in the course of two years the subscription list was larger than that of any other newspaper printed in New England.

A number of gentlemen supplied this paper with political essays, which for the time were more particularly calculated for that class of citizen who had composed the great majority of its readers. For a few weeks some communications were furnished by those who were in favor of the royal prerogative, but they were exceeded by the writers on the other side; and the authors and subscribers among the tories denounced and quitted the Spy. The publisher then devoted it to the cause of his country, supported by the whigs, under whose banners he had enlisted.

Writers of various classes, in the whig interest, furnished essays, which in a very considerable degree aided in preparing the public mind for the events which followed.

Common sense in common language is necessary to influence one class of citizens, as much as learning and elegance of composition are to produce an effect upon another. The cause of America was just, and it was only necessary to state this cause in a clear and impressive manner, to unite the American people in its support.

Several attempts were made by the government of the province to prosecute the printer, but without effect, as demonstrated by the following paragraphs respecting the piece over the signature of *Mucius Scævola*, published in the *Massachusetts Spy*, No. 37, November 14, 1771, extracted from the *Evening Post* and the *Gazette*, of the Monday following.

'We hear that at a council held at the Council Chamber last Saturday, a piece signed *Mucius Scævola*, published in the *Massachusetts Spy* of November 14th, printed by Isaiah Thomas, was taken into consideration, when it was unanimously ordered, that the Attorney General be directed to prosecute the publisher thereof.—It is said the piece referred to above (from its nature, and tendency), is the most daring production ever published in America.'—*Boston Evening Post.*

'On Friday last, in the afternoon, his Excellency the Governor laid before the Council for their advice thereon, a paper in the Massachusetts Spy of Thursday, signed by Mucius Scævola, said to contain divers seditious expressions, &c. The council after debating till sundown adjourned till the next day, when they met again and sent for the printer, who in answer to the summons, told the messenger he was *busy in his office, and should not attend*: Upon which it is said a motion was made for his commitment to prison for contempt—but did not obtain. Whether the *abundant lenity* of the honourable Board, or from their having no *legal authority* in the case, has not yet transpired to us. —The final result was, their *unanimous* advice to the Governour to order the King's Attorney to prosecute the Printer at Common-Law.'—*Boston Gazette.*

Joseph Greenleaf, a justice of the peace for the county of Plymouth, being suspected of having some concern, either as a writer, or otherwise, in The Massachusetts Spy, received a summons of the purport following, which he laid before the public in the Spy of November 22, 1771.

'Province of Massachusetts Bay—*To Joseph Greenleaf, of Boston, in said province, Esq.—*

'You are required to appear before the Governor and Council, at the Council-chamber in Boston, on Tuesday the tenth day of December next, at ten of the clock in the forenoon, then and there to be examined touching a certain paper called the Massachusetts Spy, published the fourteenth day of November, 1771; whereof you are not to fail at your peril. Dated at Boston, the 16th day of November, 1771.

'By order of the Governor, with the advice of Council.
                                        Thomas Flucker, Secretary.'

Greenleaf did not obey the summons, and on the 12th of December following, the Boston News-Letter, [Court Gazette] contained the proceedings of the Governor and Council of the 10th of that month in consequence thereof, viz.

'*At a Council held at the Council Chamber in Boston, Tuesday, December 10th, 1771.*

His Excellency having acquainted the Board at their last meeting, that Joseph Greenleaf, Esq; a Justice of the Peace for the county of Plymouth, was generally reputed to be concerned with Isaiah Thomas, in printing and publishing a News-Paper, called the Massachusetts Spy, and the said Joseph Greenleaf having thereupon been summoned to attend the board on this day, in order to his examination touching the same, and not attending according to summons, it was thereupon unanimously advised, that the said Joseph Greenleaf be dismissed from the office of a Justice of the Peace, which advice was approved of and consented to by his Excellency; and the said Joseph Greenleaf is dismissed from the said office accordingly.

'A true copy from the minutes of Council.

Thomas Flucker, Secretary.'

The following fact I relate, principally with a view to show that one of the most eminent patriots, who was concerned in achieving our revolution, and of whose love for his country many instances are recorded, although he was so unfortunate as to become mentally deranged, yet he still retained his political integrity, and his *amor patriæ* was not extinguished.

The Hon. James Otis was a lawyer of great note and distinction. Under him the late president of the United States, Mr. Adams, studied law, and became qualified for the bar. Mr. Otis's great misfortune originated in a dispute with Mr. Robinson, one of the commissioners of the customs in Boston. The unhappy disagreement terminated in an affray, in which Mr. Otis received a blow on his head, which occasioned, through the remainder of his life, lucid intervals excepted, a derangement of his intellects. During those intervals he still paid considerable attention to politics. On account of his disorder he was put under the care of a physician at Andover, and, at that place, in May, 1783, whilst leaning on his cane, at the door of a house, 'he was struck by a flash of lightning, which instantly liberated his spirit from its shattered tenement.'* Mr. Adams was in France when this fatal occurrence took place; but he there heard of the death of the unfortunate Otis; and, on that occasion, wrote to a friend in America, as follows: 'It is with very afflicting sentiments I learned the death of Mr. Otis, my worthy master. Extraordinary in death as in life, he has left a character that will never die whilst the American revolution remains, whose foundation he laid with an energy and with masterly abilities which no other man possessed.'

I have mentioned the consequences which resulted from the publication of Mucius Scævola; but, notwithstanding I, afterward, ventured to republish some very strong addresses to the king, which had appeared in English papers. These addresses were very offensive to the officers of the crown, and produced considerable agitation. A prosecution was expected to take place; and, I was informed by some friends, on whose intelligence I thought I could place full reliance, that Governor Hutchinson had said, that, 'in order to secure a verdict against

* William Allen, *American Biographical Dictionary* (Cambridge, Mass., 1809), p. 463.

me stronger ground would be taken than in the case of Mucius Scævola.' Some weeks before the most obnoxious of these addresses appeared in the Massachusetts Spy, Mr. Otis, who was then under the influence of his disorder, called at my house one evening, and desired to have a private conference with me in what he called 'my *sanctum sanctorum*;' meaning a private apartment,* adjoining the printing rooms, up two pair of stairs. The workmen had retired, and we ascended to the place he mentioned; where being seated in due form, he demanded two sheets of paper and scissors, which I presented to him. He doubled each sheet, and after putting them together, in a formal manner, indented them at the top. On one of the sheets of paper he wrote his private signature, and demanded my countersign on the other, which I gave him. He folded it carefully, deposited it in his pocket, left the other with me and having assured me I should hear from him, he departed.

From this period I had no communication of any kind with Mr. Otis, until the report of a prosecution, on account of publishing the addresses to the king, became very prevalent. On that occasion he again appeared, and was apparently perfectly composed, and in the undisturbed possession of reason. He informed me that, he had heard much of my having published an address to the king; and that in consequence, a prosecution seemed to impend, *in terrorem*, over me. As he had not seen the address in question, I handed him the paper which contained it; and, sitting down, he read it very attentively. After reading it once, he went over the same again, paragraph by paragraph, repeating at the end of each, 'There is no treason in that.' When

---

* Called by the tories, 'The Sedition Foundry.'

he came to the strongest passage, he paused—read it again and again—and, after pondering upon it some time, he exclaimed, 'Touch and go, by G—' Having read the address entirely through the second time, he civilly assured me that, on due consideration, he was convinced the whole of it was defensible, and that in case the prosecution should take place, he would voluntarily come forward in my defence, without fee or reward; or, would point out to my counsel the ground of defence, which, in his opinion, ought to be taken.

He appeared to be animated by the subject to such a degree as produced some agitation; but on taking leave he said, 'James Otis still retains some knowledge of law.' The projected prosecution fell to the ground, and I saw Mr. Otis no more.

The printer had the further honor of being exhibited and burnt in effigy by the royalists of North Carolina, and he was threatened with having a coat of tar and feathers by a regiment of British soldiers, which paraded before his house.*

In October, 1772, the addition of *Thomas's Boston Journal* was

* A soldier in one of the British regiments stationed in Boston, instigated by his officers, inveigled a countryman, one Thomas Ditson, jun., of Billerica, to purchase a musket. When the purchase was made, the officers appeared, and the countryman was taken into custody, under pretence of enticing the soldier to steal and sell the property of the king, &c. The countryman was kept under guard during the night. Before daylight the next morning, after a sham trial in the barracks, he was stripped of his clothes, and coated from head to foot with tar and feathers; the soldiers then bound him in a chair to a truck, and before sunrise he was paraded by a regiment through the streets. The regiment, with the colonel at its head, halted before the Spy office, the music playing the Rogue's March; some of the soldiers vociferating 'the printer of the Spy shall be the next to receive this punishment.' This riot took place on the 10th of March, 1775. It occasioned great commotion among the citizens, and produced a well written and spirited remonstrance from the town of Billerica to the governor, Gage.

made to the title of the Spy; a political motto from Addison's Cato had been previously added.*

On the 7th of July, 1774, during the operation of the Boston port bill† so called, and just after the landing of four additional regiments of troops, with a train of royal artillery, a new political device appeared in the title of this paper—a snake and a dragon. The dragon represented Great Britain, and the snake the colonies. The snake was divided into nine parts, the head was one part, and under it N. E. as representing New England; the second part N. Y. for New York; the third N. J. for New Jersey; the fourth P. for Pennsylvania; the fifth M. for Maryland; the sixth V. for Virginia; the seventh N. C. for North Carolina; the eighth S. C. for South Carolina; and the ninth part, or tail, for Georgia. The head and tail of the snake were supplied with stings, for defence against the dragon, which appeared furious, and as bent on attacking the snake. Over the several parts of the snake was this motto, in large capitals, 'JOIN OR DIE!' This device, which was extended under the whole width of the title of the Spy, appeared in every succeeding paper whilst it was printed in Boston. Its publication ceased in that town on the 6th of April, 1775, and on the 19th of that month hostilities between Great Britain and America commenced. A few days before this event took place, its publisher sent, pri-

---

* Do thou, great Liberty, inspire our souls,
And make out Lives in thy possession happy,
Or our Deaths glorious in thy just defense.

† This act of the British government hastened the revolution. It was designed to punish Boston for destroying the tea sent over by the East India company, &c. See the various histories of those times for an account of the pretexts which led the British ministry to lay the port of Boston under an interdict, &c.

vately, a press and types to Worcester; and, on the 3d of the following May, the publication of the Spy was resumed, and was the first printing done in that town. The title of the paper, of course, was again altered; it was now *The Massachusetts Spy; or, American Oracle of Liberty*; headed with 'Americans! Liberty or Death! Join or Die!' The day of publication at Worcester was Wednesday.

SALEM THE ESSEX GAZETTE was the first newspaper printed in Salem. No. 1 was published August 2, 1768; and it was continued weekly, on Tuesday, crown size, folio, from small pica and brevier types. In the centre of the title was a cut, of which the design was taken from the official seal of the county. The principal figure a bird with its wings extended, and holding a sprig in its bill; perhaps intended to represent Noah's dove; and this device was far from being ill adapted to the state of our forefathers, who having been inhabitants of Europe, an old world, were become residents in America, to them a new one. Above the bird a fish, which seems to have been intended as a crest, emblematical of the codfishery, formerly the principal dependence of the county of Essex, of which Salem is a shire town. The whole supported by two aborigines, each holding a tomahawk, or battle axe. Imprint, 'Salem: Printed by Samuel Hall, near the Town-House, Price 6s. 8d. per annum.'

It was afterwards 'printed by Samuel and Ebenezer Hall.' The Gazette was well conducted, and ably supported the cause of the country.

In 1775, soon after the commencement of the war, the printers of this paper removed with their press to Cambridge, and there published the Gazette, or, as it was then entitled, *The New England Chronicle: Or, the Essex Gazette*. The junior partner died in 1775, and S. Hall became again the sole proprietor. When the British army left Boston Hall removed to the capital, and there printed *The New England Chronicle*, the words Essex Gazette being omitted. After publishing the paper a few years with this title, he sold his right to it, and the new proprietor entitled it *The Independent Chronicle*,[65] and began the alteration with No. 1.

THE SALEM GAZETTE AND NEWBURY AND MARBLE-HEAD ADVERTISER, the second paper published in the town, made its first appearance in June, 1774, printed on a crown sheet, folio, on an old long primer type, published weekly on Friday. Imprint, 'Salem: Printed by E. Russell, at his New Printing-Office, in Ruck-street, near the State-House.'*

This Gazette was of short continuance; its circulation was confined to a few customers in Salem and the neighboring towns, which were inadequate to its support.

THE AMERICAN GAZETTE: OR, THE CONSTITUTIONAL JOURNAL was first published June 18, 1776. It was published on Tuesday, printed on a crown sheet, folio. Imprint, 'Salem: Printed by J. Rogers, at E. Russell's Printing-Office, Upper End of Main-Street,' &c. Russell was the conductor of this paper, Rogers being only his agent; it was published only a few weeks. In the head was a large cut, a coarse copy of that which then appeared in the title of the Pennsylvania Journal; the de-

---

* Meaning court house.

vice, a ship and a book, or journal, &c., as has already been described.

It was several years after this newspaper was discontinued before the printing of another commenced in Salem. In January, 1781, Mary Crouch and company issued from their press *The Salem Gazette and General Advertiser*. This Gazette was printed only nine months, when Samuel Hall, who first published *The Essex Gazette*, returned to Salem, and, on the 18th of October, 1781, established *The Salem Gazette*, afterwards printed by T. Cushing.[66]

THE ESSEX JOURNAL, AND MERIMACK PACKET: OR, THE MASSACHUSETTS AND NEW-HAMPSHIRE GENERAL ADVERTISER, the first newspaper in Newburyport, was issued from the press, December 4, 1773, by Isaiah Thomas, printed on a crown sheet, folio, equal in size to most of the papers then published in Boston. At first its day of publication was Saturday; afterwards, Wednesday. Two cuts were in the title; one, the left, representing the arms of the province, that on the right, a ship under sail. Imprint, 'Newbury-Port: Printed by Isaiah Thomas & Henry Walter-Tinges, in King-Street, opposite to the Rev. Mr. Parsons's Meeting-House,' &c. Thomas was the proprietor of the Journal; he lived in Boston, and there published the *Massachusetts Spy*. Tinges, as a partner in the Journal, managed the concerns of it. Before the full expiration of a year Thomas sold his right in this paper to Ezra Lunt, and, about two years after, Lunt sold to John Mycall. Tinges was a partner to both; but to the latter only for about six months, when the partnership was dissolved, and Mycall became the proprietor and sole publisher of *The Essex Journal*, the publication of which he continued many years.

THE MASSACHUSETTS SPY: OR, AMERICAN ORACLE OF LIBERTY. The printer of the *Massachusetts Spy, or Boston Journal*, was obliged to leave Boston, as has been mentioned, on account of the commencement of hostilities between the colonies and the parent country. He settled in this place, and on the 3d of May, 1775, recommenced the publication of that paper, which he continued until the British troops evacuated Boston, when he leased it for one year to William Stearns and Daniel Bigelow. They adopted another motto: 'Undaunted by Tyrants, we will die, or be free.' After the first lease expired, the paper was leased for another year to Anthony Haswell, printer. Owing to unskillful workmen, bad ink, wretched paper, and worn down types, the Spy appeared in a miserable dèshabillè during the two years for which it had been leased, and for two years after. At the end of that term, the proprietor returned to Worcester, and resumed its publication, with a new motto: 'Unanimity at Home, and Bravery and Perseverance in the Field, will secure the Independence of America.'

Good materials of the kinds just mentioned could not be immediately procured, and the Spy from necessity was continued under numerous disadvantages until 1781, when it was printed from a good type, on better paper, with new devices and an engraved title. The device on the left was a figure representing America, an Indian holding the cap of Liberty on a staff with the left hand, and in the right a spear, aimed at the

British lion, which appeared in the act of attacking her from an opposite shore. Round the device was 'LIBERTY DEFENDED FROM TYRANNY.' That on the right was a chain of thirteen links, with a star in each link, representing the union of the thirteen states. This chain was placed in a circular form, leaving an opening for the arms of France, to which the ends of the chain were attached, and which perfected the circle. Above the arms were two hands clasped, and directly over them a sword, with its hilt resting on the clasped hands; the motto, 'UNION.' The title was thus new modelled, *Thomas's Massachusetts Spy; or the Worcester Gazette*. Motto: 'The noble Efforts of a Virtuous, Free and United People, shall extirpate Tyranny, and establish Liberty and Peace.'

At the conclusion of the war the Spy was enlarged, and each page contained five columns. It was printed from new types; and the motto was changed to '*Noscere res humanas est Hominis*. Knowledge of the world is necessary for every man.'

About that time, its editor began to publish, in the paper, as room would permit, Robertson's *History of America*, and completed the whole in about one year.* This was followed by a history of the revolutionary war. Besides these, the Spy contained valuable, useful, and entertaining extracts, on various subjects, from European and American publications, as well as original essays.†

---

* The English edition of Robertson's History, in three volumes, 8vo, then sold for six dollars. The price of the Spy was only nine shillings per annum.

† The Worcester Speculator, inserted in the Spy, in numbers, weekly, was furnished by a society of gentlemen in the county of Worcester. A selection from these numbers, all the composition of the late Reverend Doctor Fiske of Brookfield, together with some other pieces by that gentleman, was afterwards printed in two duodecimo volumes, entitled *The Moral Monitor*.

This paper was printed with continued improvements until March, 1786, when the publication was, on the following account, suspended. The legislature of Massachusetts had in March, 1785, passed an 'act, imposing duties on licensed vellum, parchment and paper.' This act laid a duty of two-thirds of a penny on newspapers, and a penny on almanacs, which were to be stamped. The British stamp act of 1765, violently opposed in the colonies, rendered this act so unpopular from its very name, that the legislature was induced to repeal it before it went into operation. But, in the July following, another act was passed, which imposed a duty on all advertisements inserted in the newspapers printed in this commonwealth. This act was thought by the publisher of the Spy, and by many others, to lay an improper restraint on the press. He therefore discontinued the Spy during the period that this act was in force, which was two years. But he published as a substitute a periodical work, entitled *The Worcester Weekly Magazine*, in octavo.

The restoration of the Spy took place in April, 1788, and a motto was at that time introduced from the constitution of Massachusetts, viz.: 'The Liberty of the Press is essential to the security of freedom.'

In 1801, Thomas resigned the printing and publishing of the Spy to his son Isaiah Thomas, Jr. The Spy is the oldest newspaper in Massachusetts.[67]

In 1785, a neat, small paper, was published semi-weekly in Charlestown, Massachusetts, entitled *The American Recorder and Charlestown Advertiser*. It was printed about three years by Allen & Cushing, and then discontinued. I mention this, because it was the only newspaper issued from a press in the county of Middlesex.

THE BOSTON WEEKLY MAGAZINE made its first appearance March 2, 1743, on a half sheet, octavo. No. 1 contained some extracts from the magazines published in London: a Poem to a political lady, an Ode by Mr. Addison, two short domestic articles of intelligence from the Boston newspapers, and the entries at the custom house for the week. The day of publication was Wednesday. It was continued only four weeks, and was printed by Rogers & Fowle.

THE CHRISTIAN HISTORY. No. 1 of this periodical work was published on Saturday, March 5th, 1743, on a large half sheet of fine medium in octavo, printed on a new small pica type. After the contents is a quotation from the Psalms: 'That I may publish with the voice of thanksgiving, and tell of all thy wondrous works.'—Psal. xxvi, 7. The imprint: 'Boston, N. E. Printed by Kneeland & Green, 1743, for Thomas Prince, Jun. A.B.' The price was *two shillings* new tenor per quarter, and *six pence* more new tenor per Quarter covered, sealed, and directed.' The editor and publisher was the son of the Reverend Thomas Prince, of Boston, author of *The New England Chronology*.

The Christian History was regularly published, in numbers of eight pages each, every Saturday, for two years; each year making a volume, to which was prefixed a title page, and an index. The title page to the first volume reads thus: 'The Christian History, containing Accounts of the Revival and propagation of Religion in Great Britain and America. For the year 1743.'

The editor gave the general contents as follows: '1. Authentic Accounts from Ministers, and other creditable Persons, of the

Revival of Religion in the several Parts of New England. 2. Extracts of the most remarkable Pieces in the Weekly Histories of religion, and other accounts, printed both in England and Scotland. 3. Extracts of written Letters, both from England, Scotland, New-York, New-Jersey, Pennsylvania, South Carolina, and Georgia, of a Religious Nature, as they have been sent hither from creditable Persons and communicated to us. 4. Remarkable Passages, Historical and Doctrinal, out of the most famous old writers both of the Church of England and Scotland from the Reformation, as also the first Settlers of New-England and their Children; that we may see how far their pious Principles and Spirit are at this Day revived; and may guard against all Extreams.'

THE AMERICAN MAGAZINE AND HISTORICAL CHRONICLE. The first number of this Magazine, for September, 1743,[68] was published on the 20th of the following October. It was printed on a fine medium paper in 8vo. Each number contained fifty pages; and was published, monthly, by 'Samuel Eliot, in Cornhill, and Joshua Blanchard in Dock-Square,' booksellers; and printed by Rogers & Fowle, 'in Prison Lane,' who were also concerned in the publication, and, after the first year, were sole proprietors of it. Jeremy Gridley, Esq., who had edited the Rehearsal, it has been said, was also the editor of this magazine.

The following is an extract from the prospectus, viz: It will contain '1. A summary Rehearsal of the proceedings and debates in the British Parliament. 2. A View of the weekly and monthly Dissertations, Essays, &c., selected from the publick Papers and Pamphlets published in London and the Plantations, viz: Political State, Transactions of the Royal Society, &c., with Extracts from new Books. 3. Dissertations, Letters and Essays, moral, civil, political, humorous and polemical. 4. Select Pieces, relating to the Arts and Sciences. 5. Governour's Speeches, with the Proceedings of the Assembly, and an Abridgment of the Laws enacted in the respective Provinces and Colonies. 6. Poetical Essays on various Subjects. 7. Monthly Chronologer, containing an Account of the most remarkable Events, Foreign and Domestick. 8. Price Current. 9. Births and Deaths. 10. A Catalogue of New Books. The Magazine will be continued of the same Size, that so the Twelve Months may be bound in the same Volume at the Year's end with a compleat Index, which shall be added to the Month of December.'

This Magazine imitated *The London Magazine* in its appearance; a large cut of the town of Boston, in the title page, answered to a similar cut of the city of London in the title page of the London Magazine. Its pages were like those of that publication in size, two columns in a page, divided by the capital letters, A B C D E and F, at a distance from each other, and not by a line, or as printers term it, by rules. The imprint, 'Boston: Printed by *Rogers & Fowle*, and Sold by *S. Eliot & J. Blanchard*, in *Boston*; *B. Franklin*, in *Philadelphia*; *J. Parker*, in *New York*; *J. Pomroy*, in *New Haven*; *C. Campbell*, Post-Master, *New Port*. Price *Three Shillings*, New Tenor, a Quarter,' equal to half a dollar. It was well printed, on a long primer type, and was not inferior to the London and other magazines, then published in that city; but the extensive plan marked out in its prospectus could not be brought within the number of pages allowed to the work. In the general title page for the year, the before-mentioned view of the town of Boston, was impressed from a copperplate engraving; both the cut and the plate were as well executed as things of the kind generally were for the English magazines.

This work was issued three years and four months, and then discontinued. It has no cuts or plates excepting those for the title pages.

THE NEW-ENGLAND MAGAZINE is without date, either in the title, in the imprint, or in any of its numbers. No. 1 was published August 31, 1758. The title page is as follows: *The New-England Magazine of Knowledge and Pleasure.* In the centre of the page is a small cut, the device a hand holding a *bouquet,* or bunch of flowers, with the motto, '*Prodesse et Delectare e pluribus unum.*' One-half of this motto is on the left of the cut, and the other half on the right; underneath the device is this couplet:

> 'Alluring *Profit* with *Delight* we blend,
> *One out of many* to the Publick send.

'By various Authors.

'Ye shall know *them* by their fruits. Do men gather Grapes of Thorns, or Figs of Thistles? Every good Tree bringeth forth good Fruit, but a corrupt Tree bringeth forth evil Fruit. A good Tree cannot bring forth evil Fruit, neither can a corrupt Tree bring forth good Fruit.

'Printed by Benjamin Mecom, and sold at his shop under the New-Printing-Office, near the Court-House, *on* Corn-hill in Boston.'

Each number of this Magazine contained sixty pages 12mo. Its publication was intended to have been monthly, but it came from the press irregularly, and was printed from types of various sizes. Some pieces were, both in prose and verse, on pica, and some on long primer; the pages were not in columns. Its contents were a collection of small fugitive pieces from magazines, newspapers, &c. These were not arranged under general heads, excepting poetry, which was headed 'Poetical Entertainment;' and we make one more exception for a head of '*Queer Notions.*' The price was eight pence for each number.

Mecom, the publisher of this Magazine, gave the following poetical description of its contents in an advertisement, viz:

> Containing, and to contain,
> Old fashioned writings and Select Essays,
> Queer Notions, Useful Hints, Extracts from plays;
> Relations Wonderful, and Psalm and Song,
> Good Sense, Wit, Humour, Morals, all *ding dong*;
> Poems and Speeches, Politicks and News
> What *Some* will like, and other *Some* refuse;
> Births, Deaths, and Dreams, and Apparitions too;
> With some *Thing* suited to each different *Geû*,*
> To Humour *Him*, and *Her*, and *Me*, and *You*.

This work found very few purchasers. Three or four numbers were published in the course of six or seven months, and it was then discontinued.

THE CENSOR was altogether a political publication. The first number appeared November 23, 1771. It was printed in a small sheet, foolscap, folio, on an English type, by Ezekiel Russell, in Boston, and published on Saturdays.

It made its appearance without any formal introduction. A dissertation in the *Massachusetts Spy*, under the signature of Mucius Scævola, probably occasioned the attempt to establish this paper. Mucius Scævola had attacked Governor Hutchinson

* Goût.

with a boldness and severity before unknown in the political disputes of this country. The piece excited great warmth among those who supported the measures of the British administration, and they immediately commenced the publication of the Censor; in which the governor and the British administration were defended. Lieutenant Governor Oliver was the reputed author of several numbers of the Censor, under the signature of A Freeman, and these were thought to be better written than any other communication to that paper. Several other politicians were engaged as writers for the Censor,* but they gained no proselytes to their cause; and, although numbers of the first characters on the side of government came forward with literary and pecuniary aid, yet the circulation of the paper was confined to a few of their own party. As the Censor languished, its printer made an effort to convert it into a newspaper; and, with this view, some of its last numbers were accompanied with a separate half sheet, containing a few articles of news and some advertisements. But neither its writers nor its printer could give it a general circulation, and it was discontinued before the revolution of a year from its first publication.

THE ROYAL AMERICAN MAGAZINE. A Prospectus of this work appeared many months before the magazine; but the disordered state of public affairs, and the difficulties which indi-

---

* Dr. Benjamin Church, a reputed whig, who when the Revolutionary war commenced was appointed surgeon general of the American army, but was soon after arrested and confined, being detected in a traitorous correspondence with the British army in Boston, I have been informed by a very respectable person, whom I have long known, was a writer for the Censor. This person, then an apprentice to Russell, was employed to convey, in a secret manner, the doctor's manuscripts to the press, and proof sheets from the press to the doctor.

viduals experienced from them, prevented it from being sooner put to press; and after a few numbers had been published, the distress occasioned to the inhabitants of Boston by shutting up and blockading their port, obliged its editor to suspend the publication.

The first number for January, 1774, was published at the close of that month. It was printed on a large medium paper in octavo, on a new handsome type. Each number contained three sheets of letter press, and two copperplate engravings. The title was, *The Royal American Magazine, or Universal Repository of Instruction and Amusement.* The type metal cut in the title page, represented, by an aboriginal, America seated on the ground; at her feet lay a quiver, and near her a bow on which her right hand rested; in her left hand she held the calumet of peace, which she appeared to offer to the Genius of Knowledge standing before her dispensing instruction. Imprint, 'Boston: Printed by and for Isaiah Thomas, near the Market.' Then follow the names of several printers on the continent who sold the work.

The editor, after having been at considerable trouble and expense in bringing the work before the public, published it six months, and then was obliged, first to suspend, and afterwards to relinquish it; but Joseph Greenleaf continued the publication until April following, when the war put a period to the magazine.

This was the last periodical work established in Boston before the revolution. It had a considerable list of subscribers.

NOTES TO CHAPTER II

Useful general works from a considerable body of literature relating to the early Massachusetts press are: George Parker Winship, *The Cambridge Press, 1638–1692* (University of Pennsylvania Press, 1945); George E. Littlefield, *The Early Massachusetts Press, 1638–1711* (Club of Odd Volumes, 1907), 2 vols.; Rollo G. Silver, 'Government Printing in Massachusetts, 1700–1750,' in *Proceedings of the American Antiquarian Society*, n.s. LXVIII, 135–162 (April 1958); and 'Government Printing in Massachusetts, 1751–1801,' in *Studies in Bibliography*, XVI, 161–200 (1963).

1. We gather some additional facts respecting Mr. Glover from the *Glover Memorials and Genealogies* by Anna Glover (Boston, 1867).

The Rev. Joseph Glover was rector of Sutton, in Surrey, England, from 1628 to 1636, when he tendered his resignation for the purpose of coming to New England. He preached in London, and traveled through parts of England endeavoring to obtain funds for the college already commenced at Cambridge. He embarked in the summer of 1638, with his family, consisting of wife and five children, in the John of London, bound for New England, and died on the passage. He had with him a printing press, and a printer (Stephen Daye) who was to superintend the printing; and also three men servants to work the press.

His name, which has been variously stated by different writers, was *Joseph*. It is so written by Gov. Winthrop in his journal, vol. I, p. 242, and in the Records of Sutton in Surrey, and wherever it occurs in English documents.

Mr. Glover was twice married. His first wife was Sarah Owfield, daughter of Roger Owfield of London. They had three children, (viz).:

1 Roger, died in Scotland.

2 Elizabeth, married Adam Winthrop, Esq.

3 Sarah, married Deane Winthrop, Esq.

The second wife to whom he was married about 1630, was Elizabeth Harris of England. By her he had two children, (viz.):

1 Priscilla, married John Appleton, Esq., of Ipswich.

2 John, died in London in 1668, unmarried. Mrs. Elizabeth Glover, soon after her arrival at Cambridge, married Rev. Henry Dunster, and died in 1643. See also *New England Historical & Genealogical Register*, XXIII, 135–137 (April 1869).   H

2. The press was set up in the house of the president of Harvard College, the Rev. Henry Dunster, in 1639. M

3. In some legal papers after 1650, Daye is styled locksmith. L. R. Paige, *History of Cambridge, Mass.* (Boston, 1877), p. 44; *Dictionary of American Biography*, V, 163. H

4. *Memorandum* by Mr. Thomas—[Inquire of John Farmer the date of an Almanack printed at Cambridge by Matthew Daye. Matthew Daye, I presume, was a brother or son of Stephen Daye. He is not noticed as a printer in any record. I have discovered nothing printed by him but this almanac. It was undoubtedly done in Stephen Daye's office by his permission.]

The Almanac referred to as in the possession of Mr. Farmer, the well known antiquary, is now in the rich collection of George Brinley, Esq., of Hartford, Conn. The date is 1647. The imprint 'Cambridge printed by Mathew Daye; and to be sold by Hezekiah Usher, at Boston.' For notice of Mathew Daye, see *Proceedings of the Massachusetts Historical Society*, V, 154–156 (Feb. 1861). H

5. Thomas's genealogy of the Green family is vey confused. See William C. Kiessel, 'The Green Family, a Dynasty of Printers,' in *New England Historical & Genealogical Register*, CIV, 81–93 (April 1950).

6. *Dictionary of American Biography*, X, 110.

7. Samuel A. Green, *John Foster* (Massachusetts Historical Society, 1909).

8. W. C. Ford, 'Benjamin Harris, Printer and Bookseller,' in *Proceedings of the Massachusetts Historical Society*, LVII, 34–68 (1924).

9. The following is a more accurate description of this rare volume from the copy in the library of the Antiquarian Society: It contains 1. *The Charter of William and Mary*. Printed at *London*, and Re-Printed at *Boston*, in *New England*. By *Benjamin Harris*, over against the *Old Meeting House*, 1692, 13 pp. 2. *Several Acts and Laws*, &c. BOSTON. Printed by Benjamin Harris, Printer to His Excellency the Governour and Council, 1692. 16 pp. These are the Acts, &c., of the first Session, begun June 8, 1692. 3. *Acts and Laws, &c.*, with the Imprint and the order of Gov. Phips as stated by Mr. Thomas. These are the Acts, &c., of what is called in the title page the *Second Session*, 'Begun the eighth day of June, 1692, and continued by adjournment unto Wednesday the twelfth day of October following.' Besides the title and table of contents there are ninety pages to this part. 4. Another title page, with the Acts and Laws of the *Third Session*, terminating on the succeeding eighth of February.

6 pp. The date is 1693.   5. Another title page, with the Acts and Laws of the *Fourth Session*, ending on the second day of March. 2 pp. This has upon the title page the arms of the English crown. Subsequent Acts and Laws of 1693, bear the imprint of Bartholomew Green.   H

10. *Dictionary of American Biography*, VI, 457–458.

11. See discussion of this question in *Collections of the Massachusetts Historical Society*, 4th ser., IV, 333–346 (1858) and in G. H. Moore, *Notes on the History of Slavery in Massachusetts* (New York, 1866), p. 200.   H

12. *Dictionary of American Biography*, X, 458.

13. In the *Historical Magazine*, n.s. IX, 39, and *Boston Traveller*, Sept. 5, 1866, the *Christian History*, printed weekly for Thomas Prince, Jr., by Kneeland and Green in 1743–4, is claimed to have been the first religious newspaper in the world.   M

14. The authenticity of this statement has been questioned by Bancroft, the historian, and an account of some fruitless investigations concerning the edition is given in E. B. O'Callaghan's *List of Editions of the Scriptures printed in America* (Albany, 1861), p. xiii.   M

15. James Franklin died in 1735, leaving his printing office to his wife and family, who continued it successfully for several years after his death.   M

16. More probably a wool dyer in Oxfordshire. See Benjamin Franklin's *Autobiography* (Yale University Press, 1964), p. 53.   H

17. Bezoune, Bozoun, Bozoune or Bozoon Allen was an ancient and respectable name in Boston. In 1647, an order of the court was signed by John Winthrop, Governor, and Bozoun Allen, on the part of the house. In 1691, Capt. Bezoone Allen was one of the selectmen. In 1693, Bozoun Allen held the same office. In 1694, Capt. Bozoone Allen was assessor. In 1700, Bozoon Allen was chosen representative. S. G. Drake, *The History and Antiquities of Boston* (Boston, 1856), pp. 327, 492, 503, 506, 522.   H

18. See T. W.-M. Draper, *The Drapers in America* (New York, 1892), pp. 193–197.

19. *Dictionary of American Biography*, VI, 560–561.

20. This paper is still [1874] printed, and is the oldest paper extant in the United States.   M [It went out of existence in 1942.]

21. *Dictionary of American Biography*, VI, 17–18.

22. In September, 1775, Gill underwent an imprisonment by the British of twenty-nine days for printing treason, sedition and rebellion. Peter Force, comp., *American Archives* (Washington, 1840), 4th ser., III, 712.   M

23. In September, 1775, Peter Edes was a prisoner of the British in

Boston under the sentence of seventy-five days for having fire-arms concealed in his house. *Ibid.* See also *Historical Magazine*, 2d ser., VII, 219–220. He was one of the Boston tea party, so called. He died at Bangor, Me., March 30, 1840. Benjamin Edes, Jr., died at Boston, May 15, 1801, aged 46. M S. L. Boardman, *Peter Edes, Pioneer Printer in Maine* (Bangor, 1901).

24. *Dictionary of American Biography*, XII, 488–489.

25. J. T. Buckingham, *Specimens of Newspaper Literature* (Boston, 1850), I, 145–153. M

26. Ann Fleet, the daughter of John, and the last of the name, died in Boston, July, 1860, aged 89. The estate of Thomas Fleet, Sen., at the northerly corner of Washington and Water streets, which he purchased in 1744, and from which the *Evening Post* was issued for upwards of thirty years, still remained in the hands of his descendants in 1860, although they had discontinued the business of printing in 1808.—*Boston Transcript.* Thomas Fleet, Sen., was the putative compiler of *Mother Goose's Melodies*, which he first published in 1719. Among the entries of marriages in the City Registry, under date of June 8, 1715, is that of Thomas Fleet to Elizabeth Goose, and the idea of the collection is said to have arisen from hearing his mother-in-law repeat nursery rhymes to his children. It was characteristic of the man to make such a collection; and the first book of the kind known to have been printed in this country bears his imprint, and the title of *Songs for the Nursery, or Mother Goose's Melodies for Children.* The name of Goose is now extinct in Boston, but monuments remaining in the Granary burial ground in that city mark the family resting place. M [*Mother Goose's Melody* was first printed in this country by Isaiah Thomas in 1786.]

27. Also spelled FLEEMING. *Dictionary of American Biography*, VI, 459–460.

28. John Alden, 'John Mein: Scourge of Patriots,' in *Transactions of the Colonial Society of Massachusetts*, XXXIV, 580–591; and 'John Mein, Publisher,' in *Papers of the Bibliographical Society of America*, 1942, 3rd Quarter, pp. 202–214.

29. The first Robert Sandeman, above mentioned, was brought up a linen manufacturer. He became a preacher, and adopting the peculiar views of Rev. John Glass, of Dundee, his father-in-law, he established in Great Britain and in this country the sect called after him *Sandemanian.* He was settled in Danbury, Conn., where he died in 1771. H

30. C. K. Shipton, *Isaiah Thomas* (Rochester, N.Y., 1948); Charles L. Nichols, *Isaiah Thomas* (Club of Odd Volumes, 1912); Isaiah Thomas, *Three Autobiographical Fragments* (American Antiquarian Society, 1962).

31. Boyle died in 1819. See Buckingham's *Specimens*, I, 42, for further particulars of him. M Also, see 'Boyle's Journal of Occurrences in Boston, 1759–1778,' in *New England Historical & Genealogical Register*, LXXXIV, 142 ff., LXXXV, 5 ff. (1930, 1931).

32. Scollay's Buildings have recently been removed and the land made part of the street [1874]. H [And in 1970, Scollay Square has been transformed from the haunt of sailors into the Government Center.]

33. R. E. Moody, 'The Letter-Book of Mills & Hicks,' in *North Carolina Historical Review*, XIV, 39–83 (Jan. 1937).

34. Ellen M. Oldham, 'Early Women Printers of America,' in *Boston Public Library Quarterly*, X, 6–26, 78–92, 141–153 (1958).

35. A letter from Mr. E. M. MacDonald of Halifax, states that John Howe died in that city in 1835, aged 82. For some years previous to his death he held the office of postmaster at Halifax, and also that of king's printer for the province, the latter office securing to him all the government printing, including the publishing of the official gazette. He also for some years had an interest as partner with John Munro in the *Halifax Journal*, although his name did not appear in it. M

36. Harriet S. Tapley, *Salem Imprints, 1768–1825; a History of the First Fifty Years of Printing in Salem, Mass.* (Essex Institute, 1927).   SALEM

37. John Mycall died in 1833 in Newburyport. These three printers   NEWBURYPORT
are noticed by Buckingham in his *Specimens*, I, 289–303. M

38. Charles L. Nichols, *Bibliography of Worcester*, 2nd edn. (Worcester,   WORCESTER
1918).

39. It was finally abandoned, after several suspensions and revivals, in October, 1810. See Buckingham's *Specimens*, II, 174, for an account of its career. M

40. George E. Littlefield, *Early Boston Booksellers, 1642–1711* (Club   BOOKSELLERS
of Odd Volumes, 1900). This work contains considerable information   IN BOSTON
on all of the earlier men considered by Thomas.

41. In 1692, a respectable man whose name was Hezekiah Usher, was accused of witchcraft, in consequence of which accusation he was ordered to be confined in the common prison; but on account of the goodness of his character, he was, by connivance, allowed to secrete himself in the house of a friend; and, afterwards to escape out of the hands of his persecutors, until the delusion or madness of the times, in part, subsided,

and reason restored the balm of tranquility to the public mind. The person so accused was, probably, the bookseller, or one of his sons.　H

42. Thomas J. Holmes, 'The Bookbindings of John Ratcliff and Edmund Ranger,' in *Proceedings of the American Antiquarian Society*, XXXVIII, 31–50; 291–306 (April 1928, Oct. 1929).

43. *Ibid.*

44. This was the celebrated Chief Justice. See pp. 81–82.　H

45. *Dictionary of National Biography*, XVI, 236–238. *Collections of the Massachusetts Historical Society*, 2nd ser., II, 97–124 (1814).

46. D. C. McMurtrie, *The First Decade of Printing in … South Carolina* (London, 1933), pp. 425–431.

47. R. G. Silver, 'Publishing in Boston, 1726–1757: the Accounts of Daniel Henchman,' in *Proceedings of the American Antiquarian Society*, LXVI, 19–36 (April 1956).

48. Wilkins Updike, *A History of the Episcopal Church in Narragansett, R.I.* (Boston, 1907), I, 234–241.

49. *Dictionary of American Biography*, X, 458.

50. *Dictionary of American Biography*, VIII, 220–221.

51. Perhaps this is the man dealt with by William Spawn in 'Francis Skinner, Bookbinder of Newport,' in *Winterthur Portfolio*, II, 47–61 (1965).

52. C. K. Shipton, *Biographical Sketches of those who attended Harvard College* (Massachusetts Historical Society, 1951), VIII, 20–30.

53. *Dictionary of American Biography*, XV, 637–638.

54. H. D. French, 'The Amazing Career of Andrew Barclay,' in *Studies in Bibliography*, XIV, 145–162 (1961).

55. W. C. Ford, 'Henry Knox and the London Book-Store in Boston, 1771–1774,' in *Proceedings of the Massachusetts Historical Society*, 2nd ser., LXI, 227–304 (June 1928). *Dictionary of American Biography*, X, 475–477.

56. ABRAHAM Ellison.

BOOKSELLERS
IN CAMBRIDGE

57. *Dictionary of American Biography*, V, 524.

NEWSPAPERS
IN BOSTON

Joseph T. Buckingham's *Specimens of Newspaper Literature* (Boston, 1850), 2 vols., contains a good deal of material on the newspapers and printers to which Thomas refers.

58. The first attempt to set up a newspaper in North America, so far as can be ascertained, was made at Boston in 1690. Only one copy of

this sheet is known to be in existence, that being in the state paper office in London. See an entire copy of this, by Samuel A. Green, M.D., in the *Historical Magazine* for August, 1857. The authorities objected to it. They called it a *pamphlet*. Felt's *Annals of Salem* (1849), II, 14. If this can be claimed as a newspaper, may also the sheet printed by Samuel Green in 1689, the placard mentioned in the *New Hampshire Historical Society Collections*, I, 252? This was issued at the time Dr. Increase Mather was in England, endeavoring to procure a new charter for the colony of Massachusetts. It was entitled *The Present State of the New English Affairs*, and was published to prevent false reports. Among the notes to a reprint of the first number of the *Boston News Letter*, we are informed that Campbell was accustomed to *write* news letters. Nine of these, dated 1703, have been published by the Massachusetts Historical Society, in *Proceedings*, 1st ser., IX, 485–501 (March 1867). M

59. W. C. Ford, 'Franklin's New England Courant,' in *Proceedings of the Massachusetts Historical Society*, 2nd ser., LVII, 336–355 (April 1924). Benjamin Franklin, *The New-England Courant* (American Academy of Arts and Sciences, 1956).

60. A reprint in facsimile of No. LV of this paper, dated April 8, 1728, bears the imprint of S. Kneeland & T. Green. It is stated that 'There are Measures concerting for rendring this Paper yet more universally esteemed and, useful, in which 'tis hop'd the Publick will be gratified, and by which those Gentlemen who desire to be improved in History, Philosophy, Poetry, &c. will be greatly advantaged.' It is mentioned that the burials in Boston for the past week were five whites and one black. The baptisms in the several churches, nine. A very likely negro woman and a very likely negro girl are advertised to be sold, while Mr. Nathaniel Pigott advertises to open a school for negroes in Mr. Checkley's Meeting House. M

61. For a further account of this paper, and of its publisher, see Buckingham's *Specimens*, I, 129–153. M

62. Peter Edes not only printed the *Boston Gazette*, but he afterwards printed the *Kennebec Journal* at Augusta, Maine, and the *Bangor Gazette* at Bangor; and some time during his life printed at Hallowell, Me., Newburyport, and Haverhill, Mass., and at Newport, R.I. He was born Dec. 17th, 1756; and died at Bangor, Me., March 30th, 1840. (See p. 137.) Benjamin Edes, son of Peter, printed at Baltimore. Maria, a daughter of Peter, still living at the age of 83, was a compositor in her father's office. M

63. Benjamin Edes, Jr., was born in Boston, June 5, 1755, and died there May 15, 1801, aged 46. M

64. See Mr. Buckingham's account of the *Boston Gazette*, and Edes & Gill, in his *Specimens*, I, 165, *et seq*. The following is from a recent newspaper: 'The *Bangor Whig* office was honored on Monday by a visit from the widow of the late Michael Sargent, Esq., and daughter of Peter Edes, who printed the first paper on the Kennebec as well as on the Penobscot. When her father published *The Bangor Gazette*, in 1816, Maria, then at the age of twenty-seven years, worked regularly at the case, and is, probably, the oldest living female compositor in the United States. She has a lively recollection of events of the past, and relates, with much spirit, incidents and anecdotes of people long since passed away, and known to the public only by history and tradition.' H

65. This being the only allusion by Mr. Thomas to that paper, a portion of a letter from the late Mr. Nathaniel Willis referring to it, dated Boston, March 20, 1861, is quoted: 'When I was an apprentice in the office of the *Independent Chronicle*, about 1796, I found in the garret enough of these papers to make a volume, which I arranged, had them bound, and have recently presented the volume to the Boston Public Library. From this it appears in their notices to the public, that Samuel Hall transferred the paper to Nathaniel Willis and Edward E. Powars, June 13, 1776; in December, 1779, N. Willis appears as sole publisher until 1784; it was then transferred to Adams & Nourse, afterwards Adams & Rhoades; and then my father went to Virginia. I was an apprentice in the *Chronicle* office from 1796 to 1803. Samuel Hall was a bookseller in the same store where Gould & Lincoln so long remained, in Washington street.' The *Chronicle* was united with the *Boston Patriot* in 1819, when its title ceased. For a full account of this paper, see Buckingham's *Specimens*, I, 248–287. M

66. In 1857, the editor of the *Gazette* stated that 49 other papers had been started in Salem since the *Gazette*, of which 46 had broken up in bankruptcy. Samuel Dodge died at Rowley, Mass., June 17, 1860, aged 82, who had taken and paid for the Salem Register sixty years. M

67. In 1843, there were 79 newspapers published in Massachusetts, and the *Spy*, although it had met with some interruptions, was still recognized as the oldest paper in the state. In 1845, it began to be published daily; and now, in 1872, is one of the most flourishing papers in the country. There are now (1872) about 175 newspapers and other periodicals published in Boston alone. M [The *Spy* passed from the scene in 1904.]

68. It will be observed that this was twelve years after the appearance of the *Gentleman's Magazine*, still [1874] published in London. M

★ III ★

CONNECTICUT

THERE was no press in this colony until 1709; and, I believe, not more than four printing houses in it before 1775. The first printing done in Connecticut was in New London; forty-five years before a press was established elsewhere in the colony.[1]

THOMAS SHORT was the first who printed in Connecticut. He set up his press in the town of New London in 1709.[2] He was recommended by Bartholomew Green, who at that time printed in Boston, and from whom he, probably, learned the art of printing.

NEW LONDON

In the year 1710,[3] he printed an original work, well known in New England, by the title of *The Saybrook Platform of Church Discipline*. This is said to be the first book printed in the colony. After the *Platform* he printed a number of sermons, and sundry pamphlets on religious subjects, and was employed by the governor and company to do the work for the colony. He died at New London, three or four years after his settlement there.[4]

TIMOTHY GREEN[5] has already been taken notice of, as the son of Samuel Green junior, of Boston, and grandson of Samuel Green senior, of Cambridge. He conducted a press in Boston thirteen years. Receiving an invitation from the council and assembly of Connecticut colony,[6] in the year 1714 he removed to New London, and was appointed printer to the governor and company, on a salary of fifty pounds per annum.* It was stipulated that for this sum he should print the election sermons, proclamations, and the laws which should be enacted at the several sessions of the assembly.

Besides the work of government, Green printed a number of pamphlets on religious subjects, particularly sermons. It has been said of him, that whenever he heard a sermon which he highly approved, he would solicit a copy from the author, and print it for his own sales. This honest zeal in the cause of religion often proved injurious to his interest. Large quantities of these sermons lay on hand as dead stock; and, after his decease, they were put into baskets, appraised by the bushel, and sold under the value of common waste paper.

He printed a revised edition of the laws, entitled, *Acts and Laws of his Majestie's Colony of Connecticut in New England.* New-London, Reprinted by Timothy Green, Printer to his Honour the Governour and Council, 1715. He published, also, an edition of the laws from 1715 to 1750. As early as 1727, he printed Robert Treat's Almanack; the celestial signs for which were rudely cut on em quadrates, and raised to the height of the letter. Some years before his death he resigned his printing house and business to his son Timothy, who at the time was a printer in Boston, and the partner of Samuel Kneeland.

Green was a deacon of the church in New London; and as a

* Benjamin Trumbull, *A Complete History of Connecticut* (New London, 1898), II, 385.

Christian was held in high estimation. His piety was free from the gloominess and asperity of the bigot, and he was benevolent in his heart, and virtuous in his life. He was of a very facetious disposition, and many of his anecdotes are handed down to the present time.

He died May 5, 1757, aged seventy-eight years. He left six sons, and one daughter who died in East Haddam in 1808. Three of his sons were printers; the eldest, who succeeded him; the second settled at Annapolis, in Maryland; and the third who was connected with his father, but died before him. Another of his sons by the name of Thomas, by trade a pewterer, settled in Boston, where he died leaving several children.

SAMUEL GREEN, third son of Timothy Green, was born in Boston two years before his father left that town. He was taught printing by his father, and was for several years in partnership with him. He died in May, 1752, at forty years of age, leaving a family of nine children, three of them sons, who were printers, and of whom due notice will be taken in course.

TIMOTHY GREEN, JUNIOR, was born in Boston, and came to New London with his father, who instructed him in the art. He began printing in Boston,[7] and was for twenty-five years the partner of Samuel Kneeland, as has been related. On the death of his brother Samuel, his father being aged, and unable to manage the concerns of the printing house, he closed his partnership with Kneeland, and, in compliance with his father's request, removed to New London. The whole business was resigned to him. He succeeded his father as printer of the colony; and, at that time, there was not another printing house in Connecticut.

On the 8th of August, 1758, he published a newspaper. This was the second establishment of the kind in the colony.

After a life of industry, he died October 3,[8] 1763, aged sixty years. He was amiable in his manners, and much esteemed by his friends and acquaintances. [See pp. 233–234.]

TIMOTHY GREEN, 3d, was the son of Samuel Green, and nephew to the last mentioned Timothy. He was born in New London, and was taught the art by his uncle, to whose business he succeeded. The newspaper begun by his uncle was discontinued, and he established another, afterwards published by his son. In 1773, he set up a press in Norwich, in company with his brother-in-law, which was afterwards removed to Vermont.

Green was printer to the colony. In his profession, and as a citizen, he was respectable; a firm and honest whig, he was attached to the federal constitution of the United States. He died on the 10th of March, 1796, aged fifty-nine years. He had eleven children, eight sons and three daughters. Two sons were printers, one of whom, Samuel, succeeded his father, the other settled at Fredericksburg, Virginia, and, in 1787, first printed *The Virginia Herald*. Two of his sons, Thomas and John, were booksellers and binders; another son, named William, was an Episcopal clergyman.

NEW HAVEN THE second printing house, established in Connecticut, was in New Haven.

JAMES PARKER & COMPANY. At the commencement of the war between England and France, in 1754, Benjamin Franklin and William Hunter were joint deputy postmasters general for

America. As the principal seat of the war with France, in this country, was to the northward, the establishment of a post office in New Haven became an object of some consequence. James Parker, in 1754, obtained from Franklin the first appointment of postmaster in that place, associated with John Holt, who had been unfortunate in his commercial business, and was brother-in-law to Hunter.

Having secured the post office, Parker,[9] who was then the principal printer at New York, by the advice of Franklin established a press in New Haven at the close of the year 1754. The first work from his press was the laws of Yale College, in Latin. On the first of January, 1755, he published a newspaper.

Holt directed the concerns of the printing house and post office in behalf of James Parker & Co. Parker remained at New York. Post riders were established for the army, and considerable business was done at the post office and printing house during the war.

Parker had a partner, named Weyman, in New York, who managed their affairs in that city until the year 1759, when the partnership was dissolved. This event made it necessary that a new arrangement should take place. Holt went to New York in 1760, took the direction of Parker's printing house in that city, and conducted its concerns. The press and post office in New Haven were left to the agency of Thomas Green; Parker & Co. still remaining proprietors, and continuing their firm on the *Gazette* till 1764, when they resigned the business to Benjamin Mecom.

BENJAMIN MECOM, who has been mentioned as a printer, first at Antigua, and afterward in Boston, removed to New

Haven in 1764, and succeeded Parker & Co. Franklin appointed him postmaster. He revived the *Gazette* which had been discontinued, but did very little other printing. He remained in that city until 1767, and then removed to Philadelphia. [See p. 394.]

SAMUEL GREEN was the third son of Samuel Green, and grandson of the first Timothy Green, both printers in New London, where he was born. He was taught printing by his uncle Timothy, who succeeded his father and grandfather, in New London; and was the successor of Mecom, at New Haven, in 1767. He was joined by his brother Thomas, from Hartford, and they became partners, under the firm of THOMAS & SAMUEL GREEN. The newspaper, which was begun by Parker & Co., and continued by Mecom, had again been discontinued. These brothers established another. Their partnership remained until dissolved by the death of Samuel, one of the parties, in February, 1799, aged fifty-six years.

After the death of Samuel, the son of Thomas became a partner with his father, under the firm of THOMAS GREEN & SON. This son was also named Thomas. The establishment continued ten years.

In 1809, a nephew of Richard Draper, Thomas Collier, who had been a printer at Litchfield, was connected with Green and his son; but the same year Thomas Green the father retired from business. On this occasion he published a very affectionate and pathetic address to the public. He died May, 1812, aged seventy-seven years.

THOMAS GREEN,[10] who has been just mentioned as the partner of Samuel Green in New Haven, was born at New London. He was the eldest son of Samuel Green, printer, in that place. His father dying, during the early part of his life he was instructed in printing by his uncle. Green first commenced printing in Hartford, in 1764. Until that time New London and New Haven were the only places in the colony in which presses had been established. He began the publication of a newspaper, which was the third printed in Connecticut; he remained there till 1767, when he removed to New Haven, and went into a partnership with his brother. Previous to his leaving Hartford, he formed a connection with Ebenezer Watson, and conducted the press two years under the firm of GREEN & WATSON.

Thomas Green was a great-great-grandson of Samuel Green, who printed at Cambridge, Massachusetts. He died in 1812, aged 73.

Frederick Green, printer of the *Maryland Gazette*, at Annapolis, was from the same stock, and also a great-great-grandson of the same Samuel Green.

Samuel Green, printer of the *Connecticut Gazette* at New London, and Thomas Green junior, one of the publishers of the *Connecticut Journal*, at New Haven, were of the sixth generation of the name of Green, who had been printers in this country, being great-great-great-grandsons of Samuel Green of Cambridge.

EBENEZER WATSON succeeded Thomas Green, in Hartford, from whom he learned printing. He continued the newspaper established by Green. Publishing this paper was his principal employment, and he became its proprietor at the close of the year 1769. It does not appear that Watson was a thoroughly taught printer, though he practised the art ten years. He died September 16, 1777, aged thirty-three years. He was remarkable for his humanity, and anxious for the safety of his country, then contending for its independence, devoted his press to her cause. He was an ensign in the governor's company of cadets. This company attended his funeral, and he was buried with military honors.

Watson's widow continued the *Connecticut Courant* in company with George Goodwin, until she married Barzillai Hudson. Goodwin served his apprenticeship with Watson, and was a correct printer. Hudson was not bred a printer, but came into the business by marrying the widow of Watson. Goodwin became the partner of Hudson, and they were very respectable printers under the firm of HUDSON & GOODWIN.

NORWICH is the fourth town in Connecticut where a press was established before the revolution. Two printing houses were opened in the same year.

GREEN & SPOONER. Timothy Green the third, printed in New London. Judah Paddock Spooner was his brother-in-law, and served his apprenticeship with him.

Green took Spooner into partnership and furnished press and types; and they opened a printing house in Norwich in 1773. Spooner, by agreement, managed the concerns of the firm. Their business not answering their expectations, after the trial of a few years, they removed their press to Westminster in Vermont.[11]

ROBERTSONS & TRUMBULL. Alexander and James Robertson were sons of a respectable printer in Scotland. I have mentioned them as at Albany, where they began printing and remained for several years. John Trumbull was, I believe, born in Charlestown, Massachusetts; he served an apprenticeship with Samuel Kneeland in Boston. Trumbull entered into partnership with the Robertsons, and in 1773 they opened a second printing house in Norwich, and soon after published a newspaper. This connection was not dissolved until after the British troops took possession of the city of New York in 1776. The Robertsons were royalists; and, soon after that event, they left Norwich, and went to New York.

Trumbull remained at Norwich, and continued printing. He differed in his politics with his partners, one of whom, James, had been in the political school of Mein & Fleming of Boston, for whom he worked two or three years as a journeyman; but, politics apart, James was a worthy man and a very good printer. Of Alexander I had no knowledge; but I have been informed that he was, unfortunately, deprived of the use of his limbs, and incapacitated for labor. He was, however, intelligent, well educated, and possessed some abilities as a writer.

Trumbull was an honest, well meaning man, and attached to his country. His printing was chiefly confined to his newspaper, and small articles with which he supplied country chapmen. He died in August, 1802, at the age of fifty-two years.

Alexander and James Robertson remained in New York till 1783, when the royal army and the refugees quitted the city. The Robertsons went to Shelburne, in Nova Scotia, where they published a newspaper. Alexander died in Shelburne, in December, 1784. James returned to Scotland, his native country, and began business as a printer and bookseller in Edinburgh.[12]

1743. J. POMEROY, bookseller, and postmaster.

1749. SAMUEL COOK, imported and sold some English books, but did not continue long in business.

1756. JAMES PARKER & CO., printers, dealt, in a small way, in books and stationery.

1759. JOHN HOTCHKISS, sold merchandise of various kinds; and dealt somewhat largely in books, supplies of which he received from New York.

1763. BENEDICT ARNOLD, well known afterwards as a major general in the American army, and as deserting the cause of his country, combined the bookselling business with that of a druggist, and was in the trade from 1763 to about 1767; he imported books from England.

1768. JAMES LOCKWOOD, dealt largely in books until about the year 1775.

1768. ISAAC BEERS. A respectable bookseller. He died in August, 1813.

1726. SOLOMON SMITH, was a bookseller and druggist from 1763 to about 1775.

NEWSPAPERS were not printed in this colony until 1755, and till this period there had been but one printing house established in Connecticut.

The war with the French at this time, in which the British colonies were deeply interested, increased the demand for public journals, and occasioned the publication of one in Connecti-

cut. Before the commencement of the revolutionary war, four
newspapers were published in this colony.

THE CONNECTICUT GAZETTE made its appearance January
1, 1755. It was printed on a half sheet of foolscap, in quarto; but
occasionally on a whole sheet of pot, folio, by James Parker &
Company; and was published weekly, on Friday. John Holt
was the editor, and the junior partner of the firm; he conducted
the Journal till 1760, when he removed to New York, and
Thomas Green was employed by the company to conduct the
Gazette.

By the establishment of postriders to the seat of the war at the
northward, and to several parts of the colony, the Gazette had,
for that time, a considerable circulation. The publication was
continued by Parker & Company till 1764, when it was for a
short time suspended, but afterwards revived by Benjamin
Mecom.

Mecom continued the Gazette, and added a cut to the title—
one which he had used in the title page of *The New England
Magazine*, published by him three or four months in Boston.
The device was a hand clasping a bunch of flowers. He afterwards exchanged this for another, which represented a globe
placed on the head of a seraph, an eagle with extended wings
lighting with one claw on the globe, holding in the other a book
encircled by a glory; from the book was suspended a pair of
dividers. Motto, 'Honor Virtute Paratur.' Another motto, extending the whole width of the page, was added after the title,
viz: 'Those who would give up *Essential Liberty*, to purchase a
little *Temporary Safety*, deserve neither *Liberty* nor *Safety*.' Imprint, 'Printed by *Benjamin Mecom*, at the Post-Office in New-

Haven.' There were two columns in a page of this paper, which was printed from long primer and pica types.

Holt, and Mecom his successor, appear to have been attentive in making selections for the Gazette, which was sometimes supplied with original essays on various subjects. It was discontinued in 1767.

THE CONNECTICUT JOURNAL and New-Haven Post-Boy was first published in October, 1767, soon after the Gazette was discontinued. It was printed on a pot sheet, folio, three columns in a page; types, long primer and pica. A cut of a postman on horseback, copied from The Boston Post-Boy, but badly engraved, divided the title. It was published weekly, on Friday. Imprint, generally, 'Printed by Thomas and Samuel Green, near the College.' Some years after, the title was Connecticut Journal only, the cut omitted, and the size of the paper enlarged to a crown sheet; but it was occasionally varied.

The Journal gained an establishment, and maintained its ground against several other papers which have from time to time appeared in New Haven. It continued to be published by Thomas and Samuel Green, until February, 1799; Samuel then died, and the Journal was continued till January, 1809, by Thomas Green & Son.[13] It has lately (1810) been enlarged to a sheet of royal, and the title altered to The Connecticut Journal and Advertiser. In January, 1809, it was printed by Thomas Green & Co.* In July of the same year, Thomas Green retiring from

* The company were Thomas Green, jun., and Thomas Collier. Collier served his apprenticeship with his uncle Richard Draper, at Boston, and was the publisher of a newspaper at Litchfield, in 1785, entitled, The Weekly Monitor and American Advertiser.

business, the new firm was dissolved, and the Journal published, on Thursdays, 'by Eli Hudson,[14] successor to T. Green & Co.'

THE NEW-LONDON SUMMARY was the second newspaper established in that colony, and was first published August 8, 1758, by the second Timothy Green. It was printed on a small half sheet, and occasionally on a whole sheet, weekly; at first on Tuesdays, and afterwards on Friday. A small cut of the colony arms was in the title. Green continued the Summary until his death, which happened in October, 1763, and three weeks after his demise it was discontinued.[15]

THE NEW-LONDON GAZETTE was substituted for the Summary, which it immediately succeeded. It had a cut of the king's arms in the title, and was first published November 1, 1763,[16] by Timothy Green, the third printer of this name in New London. This paper was issued weekly, on Friday, on a sheet of foolscap, folio, principally from a long primer type.

On the 17th of December, 1773, the title was altered to *The Connecticut Gazette*. It was enlarged to a sheet of crown, and afterwards to a sheet of larger size.

This paper outlived several which, since 1775, were published in the same place; it uniformly defended the rights of the country before our revolution, and supported federal republican principles after the adoption of the constitution.[17]

Timothy Green, the first printer of the Gazette, in May, 1793, resigned his right in the paper to his son, Samuel Green, who continued its publication.

THE CONNECTICUT COURANT was the third newspaper established in the colony. It was first published in December, 1764,[18] by Thomas Green, on a sheet of pot size, and continued, weekly on Tuesday, until 1767. Green then took as a partner Ebenezer Watson, and removed to New Haven. Watson managed the Courant for two years, under the firm name of Green & Watson, after which Watson became its proprietor. The paper was for a number of years printed with a much worn long primer type, occasionally intermixed with columns and half columns of old pica. About the year 1773, it was enlarged to a crown sheet; a coarse cut of the king's arms was inserted in the title, to which was added, 'Containing the freshest and most important Advices, both Foreign and Domestic.' The Courant was afterwards printed on a new type, when it made a more respectable appearance. The king's arms were discarded, and the arms of Connecticut took their place in the title, which was now altered to *The Connecticut Courant and Hartford Weekly Intelligencer*: Containing, &c. Imprint: 'Printed and published by Ebenezer Watson, near the Great-Bridge.'

After the British troops gained possession of New York, and the newspapers on the side of the country in that place were discontinued, and the printers of them dispersed, the Courant became of much consequence; its circulation rapidly increased; and, for some time, the number of copies printed weekly was equal to, if not greater, than that of any other paper then printed on the continent.

Watson, the publisher, died in September, 1777, and the Courant was continued by his widow and George Goodwin, under the firm of *Watson & Goodwin*, until March, 1779.

Barzillai Hudson[19] married the widow of Watson, and became the partner of Goodwin in March, 1779; and, from that
time to the present [1810], the Courant has been published by
the well established firm of Hudson & Goodwin; the latter of
whom has the management of the press.[20] From the commencement of the war, in 1775, many respectable writers occasionally
furnished this paper with political essays in favor of measures
adopted by the country in the time of the great contest; and in
defence of those since pursued by the federal administration.

THE NORWICH PACKET, *And, the Connecticut, Massachusetts,*
New-Hampshire, and Rhode Island Weekly Advertiser, began publication in October, 1773. It was handsomely printed with a
new long primer type, on a sheet of crown paper, weekly, on
Thursday.[21] 'Norwich Packet' was engraved in large German
text, and the title was divided by a large cut of a ship under
sail. Imprint, 'Norwich: Printed by Alexander Robertson,
James Robertson & John Trumbull, at the Printing-Office near
the Court-House, at Six Shillings and Eight Pence per Annum.
Advertisements, &c., are thankfully received for this Paper, and
all Manner of Printing Work is performed with Care, Fidelity,
and Expedition.'

The Packet was continued by this company until June, 1776;
Trumbull then became the sole publisher, and continued it with
various alterations in the title, size, and appearance, until he
died, in 1802. After his decease, it was printed for his widow,
Lucy Trumbull, but under a new title, viz: *The Connecticut
Centinel.* The Centinel in fact was a new paper, established on
the foundation of the Packet.

CONNECTICUT

310

More recent works pertaining to printing in Connecticut are: J. H. Trumbull, *List of Books Printed in Connecticut, 1709–1800* (Acorn Club, 1904) and A. C. Bates, *Supplementary List of Books Printed in Connecticut, 1709–1800* (Acorn Club, 1938). A. C. Bates, *Some Notes on Early Connecticut Printing* (Meriden, 1934), reprinted from *Papers of the Bibliographical Society of America*, XXVII, 1st quarter.

1. 'The state of the case is thus: Nov. 27th, 1707, Gov. Winthrop died. Dec. 7th, following, the general court was called together, and chose Gov. Saltonstall. He, minding to have the government furnished with a printer, moved to the assembly to have one sent for.' 'Timothy Green was first applied to, but declined the invitation. Afterwards an engagement was made with Mr. Short.'—Green's Memorial, 1745, in Connecticut Archives (Finance, III, 282). T

NEW LONDON

2. In October, 1708, the general court accepted Mr. Short's proposition to print the *Public Acts of the Colony* for four years, commencing May, 1709, and 'to give a copy for every Town or place in the Colony that hath a Clerk or Register,' for £50 a year; and to print all proclamations, etc., with 'all other public business.' It was provided, however, that 'he shall set up a printing press in this Colony.' *The Public Records of the Colony of Connecticut* (Hartford, 1870), V, 69. T See also W. DeL. Love, *Thomas Short, the First Printer of Connecticut* (Acorn Club, 1901).

3. Although the title page has the date 1710, the work was not completed before 1711, and the greater part, if not the whole, of the edition remained in the hands of Mr. Short's widow until 1714. Records of the Council of Connecticut, 1714, p. 36. T

4. Miss Caulkins records that a small headstone in the burial ground at New London bears this inscription: 'Here lyeth the body of Thomas Short, who deceased Sept. 27th, 1712, in the 30th year of his age.' Two children of Thomas and Elizabeth Short are on record in New London —Catharine, born 1709, and Charles, 1711. His widow married Solomon Coit, Aug. 8, 1714. M

5. The Green family was prolific and most of the sons, all named alike, seem to have become printers. For an account of the genealogy, see William C. Kiessel, *op. cit.*

6. He had received a similar invitation before the engagement of Mr. Short in 1708. In a memorial to the general court in 1738, he says: 'Thirty years since, this Government sent to me to come to be their

printer. I then answered the gentlemen that treated with me, that I was not willing to leave a certainty for an uncertainty. Mr. Short then came up, and died here.' Connecticut Archives (Finance, III, 1–2). T

7. Thomas had 'seen no printing with his name before 1726.' In 1724, Cotton Mather's *Memoirs of Remarkables in the Life of Dr. Increase Mather* was printed in Boston, in the name of Bartholomew Green. In an 'Advertisement' of errata, at the end of the volume, Mather says: 'My young printer, *the nephew* of him whose name stands in the title page, tho' this be the *first book that has entirely passed thro' his hand*, has bid pretty fair towards the exactness of that honest and careful Christian' [Wechsel, the 'faultless printer' of Paris]. The 'young printer' was Timothy Jr., the grand-nephew of Bartholomew. T

8. August 3, according to F. M. Caulkins, *History of New London, Conn. ... 1612 to 1860* (New London, 1895), p. 655. M

9. *Dictionary of American Biography*, XIV, 226–227.

10. A. C. Bates, 'The Work of Hartford's First Printer,' in *Bibliographical Essays, a Tribute to Wilberforce Eames* (Harvard University Press, 1925), pp. 345–361. T. R. Harlow, *Early Hartford Printers* (Columbiad Club, 1940).

11. Spooner established himself first at Hanover, in 1778, and removed to Westminster in 1781. See F. M. Caulkins, *History of Norwich, Conn. ... to the Year 1866* (Hartford, 1874), p. 364. M

12. Miss Caulkins, in her *History of Norwich* has additional facts relating to these partners. She says of Trumbull: 'He was remarkable for his genial humor, and always had a merry turn or witty remark at hand.' H

13. Samuel Green died at New Haven, Feb., 1799, aged 46. His brother Thomas died there also, May, 1812, aged 77. Thomas, Jr., died in May, 1825, aged 60. M

14. In 1819 it would seem that Hudson had passed the Journal to other hands, as he was in that year a journeyman in the office of the *Connecticut Herald*. He was inefficient and dissipated. The Journal was published until about 1834, by Newton & Peck, on whose hands it died, or was merged in another concern. M

15. We learn from Miss Caulkins, that it was entitled *The New London Summary, or the Weekly Advertiser, with the Freshest Advices, Foreign and Domestic.* The colophon was, *Printed by Thomas Green.* It was a folio

sheet; the size of the page 8 × 12 inches, in two columns. A cut of the colony seal, surmounted by an escutcheon of the town, a ship under full sail, by way of crest. No. 1 was issued Aug. 8, 1758; the editor died Aug. 3, 1763, and the paper was discontinued. M

16. After the peace of Paris, in 1763, the trade of New London revived, and the *Gazette* was printed on the 3d Nov. The size was considerably increased, the print arranged in three columns, and the price 3*s.* per annum. It changed owners often, the last Green surrendering it in 1841, and in 1844 it was discontinued, after an existence of more than 80 years. See Caulkins, *History of New London*, pp. 478, 654–655. M

17. In 1797, Charles Holt began to publish a paper in New London, called *The Bee.* So fully did the Greens possess the ground, that it was seriously inquired of Mr. Holt if he had obtained permission of them to publish a paper there. Holt removed to Hudson, N.Y., in 1802. M

18. A facsimile of the first *Courant* was published, in 1864, which is dated Monday, October 29, 1764. It appears to have been a prospectus number, unknown to Mr. Thomas. It was issued as Number 00, and is dated 'Hartford: Printed by Thomas Green, at the Heart and Crown, near the North Meeting House.' The following is the editor's address:

Hartford, October 29th, 1764.

Of all the Arts which have been introduc'd amongst Mankind, for the civilizing Human-Nature, and rendering Life agreeable and happy, none appear of greater Advantage than that of Printing: for hereby the greatest Genius's of all Ages, and Nations, live and speak for the Benefit of future Generations.—Was it not for the Press, we should be left almost intirely ignorant of all those noble Sentiments which the Antients were endow'd with. By this Art, Men are brought acquainted with each other, though never so remote, as to Age or Situation; it lays open to View, the Manners, Genius and Policy of all Nations and Countries and faithfully transmits them to Posterity.—But not to insist upon the Usefulness of this Art in general, which must be obvious to every One, whose Thoughts are the least extensive. The Benefit of a Weekly Paper, must in particular have its Advantages, as it is the Channel which conveys the History of the present Times to every Part of the World. The Articles of News from the different Papers (which we shall receive every Saturday, from the neighboring Provinces) that shall appear to us, to be most authentic and interesting shall always be carefully inserted; and great Care will be taken to collect from Time to Time all domestic Occurrences, that are worthy the Notice of the

Publick; for which, we shall always be obliged to any of our Corre-
spondents, within whose Knowledge they may happen. The CON-
NECTICUT COURANT, (a Specimen of which, the Publick are now
presented with) will, on due Encouragement be continued every Monday, beginning on Monday, the 19th of November, next: Which Encouragement we hope to deserve, by a constant Endeavour to render
this Paper, useful and entertaining, not only as a Channel for News, but
assisting to all Those who may have Occasion to make use of it as an
Advertiser.

This paper is still [1872] in successful career, being published daily,
and weekly; the latter issue is stated at 9000 copies. M And in 1970 it
continues. See J. E. Smith, *One Hundred Years of Hartford's Courant*
(New Haven, 1949) and J. B. McNulty, *Older than the Nation, the Story
of The Hartford Courant* (Stonington, Conn., 1964).

19. Mr. Hudson died July 31, 1823, aged 82, at which time he was the
senior proprietor of the *Courant*. M

20. Mr. Goodwin was yet hale and active when I knew him in Hartford in 1829, and for more than twelve years afterwards, was still in the
habit, although no longer a partner in the concern, of walking to the
printing office daily, and setting up paragraphs in type, to gratify long
established habit. He died May 14, 1844, aged 88. In 1842, an old
gentleman called at the office of the *Courant*, who stated that he was in
his 86th year, and that he had been a subscriber to the paper sixty-five
years. M

21. Caulkins, *History of Norwich*, pp. 357–364, gives a facsimile of the
head of this paper, and an extended account of it and its publishers. See
also J. W. Stedman, *The Norwich Jubilee* (Norwich, 1859), p. 292, for a
historical sketch of printers and printing in that place. M

★ IV ★

RHODE ISLAND

PRINTING was introduced into Connecticut about twenty-two years before a press was established in Rhode Island. There were but three printing houses in the colony before 1775, and only two newspapers.

GREGORY DEXTER, a printer in London, was a correspondent of the celebrated Roger Williams the founder of Providence. Dexter[1] printed, in England, in 1643, Williams's *Key into the Language of America*, and the first *Almanack for Rhode Island and Providence Plantations in New England*. Soon after, Dexter quitted printing, left his native country, and joined Williams in Providence, where he became a distinguished character in the colony. He was one of the parties named in the charter, and for a number of years one of the assistants under the authority granted by that charter. He was one of the first town clerks, and wrote an uncommonly good hand. He possessed handsome talents, and had been well educated. From him descended the respectable family of the Dexters in Rhode Island.

It is said that after Samuel Green began printing at Cambridge, Dexter went there, annually, for several years, to assist him in printing an Almanac.*

* Manuscript papers of President Ezra Stiles, of New Haven.

314

THE press was first established in Newport in the year 1732; and was the only one in the colony till 1762.

JAMES FRANKLIN.[2] It has been stated that Franklin was the publisher of *The New-England Courant*. Soon after that paper was discontinued he removed from Boston with his printing materials to Newport, and there set up his press in a room 'under the Town School-House.' He did some printing for government, published a newspaper a few months, and an Almanac annually.

He was the first who printed in Rhode Island; but only published a few pamphlets, and other small articles, beside those mentioned above. He died in February, 1735. [See pp. 104–110.]

ANNE FRANKLIN, the widow of James Franklin, succeeded her husband. She printed for the colony, supplied blanks for the public offices, and published pamphlets, &c. In 1745, she printed for government an edition of the laws, containing three hundred and forty pages folio. She was aided in her printing by her two daughters, and afterward by her son when he attained to a competent age. Her daughters were correct and quick compositors at case; and were instructed by their father whom they assisted. A gentleman who was acquainted with Anne Franklin and her family, informed me that he had often seen her daughters at work in the printing house, and that they were sensible and amiable women.

JAMES FRANKLIN JUNIOR, the son of James and Anne Franklin, was born in Newport: and, as soon as he was of age, became the partner of his mother, and conducted their concerns in his own name. He began printing about the year 1754, published *The Mercury* in 1758, and died August 22, 1762. He possessed integrity and handsome talents, which endeared him to very respectable associates.[3]

After his death, his mother resumed the business; but soon resigned the management of it to Samuel Hall, with whom she formed a partnership under the firm name of FRANKLIN & HALL.* This firm was of short duration, and was dissolved by the death of Anne Franklin, April 19, 1763, at the age of sixty-eight. They printed an edition of the laws in folio, which was completed about the time that Anne Franklin died.

SAMUEL HALL. After the death of his partner, Hall printed in his own name. An account of him has already been given among the printers of Massachusetts. He remained at Newport five years, continued the publication of the *Mercury*, and found considerable employment for his press.

In March, 1768, he resigned the printing house in Newport to Solomon Southwick, and removed to Salem, Massachusetts. [See pp. 176–178.]

SOLOMON SOUTHWICK was born in Newport, but not brought up to the business of printing. He was the son of a fisherman; and, when a lad, assisted his father in selling fish in the market place. The attention he paid to that employment, the comeliness of his person, and the evidences he gave of a sprightly genius, attracted the notice of the worthy Henry

---

* Anne Franklin's brother-in-law, the celebrated Benjamin Franklin, who then printed in Philadelphia, had, at that time, a partner by the name of Hall; and the firm in Philadelphia was likewise Franklin & Hall.

Collins, who at that time was said to be the most wealthy citizen in Newport, one of the first mercantile characters in New England, and greatly distinguished in the colony of Rhode Island for philanthropy and benevolence. Mr. Collins took a number of illiterate boys, whose parents were poor, under his patronage, and gave each an education suited to his capacity; several of whom became men distinguished in the learned professions. Among the objects of his care and liberality was young Southwick, who was placed at the academy in Philadelphia, and there provided for till he had completed his studies. Mr. Collins then established him as a merchant, with a partner by the name of Clarke.

Southwick and Clarke did business on an extensive scale. They built several vessels and were engaged in trade to London and elsewhere; but eventually they became bankrupts, and their partnership was dissolved.

After this misfortune, Southwick married a daughter of Colonel John Gardner, who for several years had been governor of the colony, and by this marriage he became possessed of a handsome estate.

About this time Samuel Hall, who had a desire to leave Newport and remove to Salem, offered his printing establishment for sale. Southwick became the purchaser in March, 1768, and succeeded to the business of Hall. He continued the publication of *The New York Mercury*, and made some attempts at book printing. He published for his own sales several small volumes; but the turbulence of the times checked his progress in this branch of printing.

Southwick discovered a sincere and warm attachment to the interests of the country. He was a firm whig, a sensible and spirited writer, and in other respects was qualified to be the editor of a newspaper, and the conductor of a press in times of revolutionary commotion.

The severity of the British government, to the province of Massachusetts particularly, was manifested by several acts of parliament which were passed in 1774. By one of these acts the people were deprived of many of their chartered rights and privileges. By another the port of Boston was shut, and the transaction of every kind of commercial business on the waters of this harbor was interdicted. These arbitrary edicts aroused the indignation of the people in all the colonies. They loudly expressed their resentment in various ways, and the press became the organ through which their sentiments were energetically announced.

Southwick was among the number of printers who were not backward to *blow the trumpet* in our *Zion*, and to *sound an alarm in the holy mountain* of our liberties. He wrote and printed an address to the people of Rhode Island, which was headed with the motto, 'JOIN OR DIE!' This motto had appeared in several of the newspapers, as will be mentioned hereafter. In this appeal, Boston was represented as in a state of siege; which was actually true; for the harbor was completely blockaded by ships of war, and a large number of troops were quartered in the town. It was also further stated that these measures of the British government were a 'direct hostile invasion of all the colonies.' The address was concluded by observing, that 'the generals of despotism are now drawing the lines of circumvallation around our bulwarks of liberty, and nothing but unity, resolution and perseverance, can save ourselves and posterity from what is worse than death, slavery.'

Southwick, by his publications and exertions in the cause of
the country, became very obnoxious to those who were of the
opposite party; and he, with other zealous whigs, were marked
as objects for punishment. When the British fleet and army
took possession of Newport, in 1776, he barely eluded the
threatened evil. As soon as a part of the army had landed, de-
tachments of both horse and foot were sent into all parts of the
town to arrest the patriots, who were endeavoring to effect an
escape. Southwick, his wife, with a child in her arms, and some
other persons, had got on board an open boat, and were just
putting off from the shore into a very rough sea, occasioned by
a high wind, when a party of soldiers who were in pursuit of
them came in sight. Southwick's wife had a brother who was a
royalist, and as such was known to the British officers; who
however, wished to secure the retreat of his sister and her
husband. Aware of their danger, this brother put himself in the
way of their pursuers, and for a few moments arrested their
attention, by giving them information of the several parts of the
town whence the proscribed whigs would probably attempt to
make their retreat, &c. This friendly interference gave Southwick and his friends time to get a few rods from the shore before
the party arrived at the spot they had just quitted. The boat was
yet within reach of their shot. The soldiers fired at them but
without effect. The passangers fortunately received no injury,
and were soon wafted to a place of safety.[4]

Southwick was, at this time, a member of the general assembly of Rhode Island. He owned two new houses in Newport, that, with other property which he left at that place, were
destroyed. He sought an asylum in Attleborough, on the frontier of Massachusetts, and there erected a press; but being soon

after appointed commissary-general of issues for the state of Rhode Island, he removed to Providence.

As soon as the British troops evacuated Newport he returned to that town and resumed the publication of his newspaper, which he continued till the year 1787, when, by ill health, and embarrassed circumstances, he was obliged to relinquish business, and to place the *Mercury* in other hands.[5]

His pecuniary concerns were greatly impaired by the rapid depreciation of the paper currency, before the establishment of peace. He, like many others, cherished a belief that the nominal sum specified in the bills would eventually be made good in specie. The impracticability of the thing was not considered, even when one hundred dollars in paper would purchase but one of silver. The delusion was not discovered by some till they found themselves involved in ruin. The government of the union were indebted to Southwick both for his services and for money loaned. This debt, like others of the kind, was liquidated by notes known by the name of final settlement. In the course of some months after they were issued, they were sold in the market for one-eighth part of their nominal value. To this depreciated state was national paper reduced before the assumption of the public debt by the new government; and, when it was in that state, Southwick was compelled to sell his final settlement notes for the support of himself and family. He was engaged in the cause of his country in the times of her adversity and danger, but he had no portion of the benefits resulting from her prosperity. Assailed by poverty, and borne down by infirmity, he lived in obscurity from the year 1788 to the time of his death; and, being unable to provide for his children, he left them to make their own way in the world.

He lost his wife, who was an excellent woman, in 1783; and
he died himself December 23, 1797, aged sixty-six years.

His son who bore his name, settled at Albany, and was for
many years the publisher of *The Albany Register*.[6]

FOR many years the principal part of the trade of the colony was carried on at Newport. At length Providence rose
to eminence and became the successful rival of Newport. Printing was introduced there in 1762.[7]

WILLIAM GODDARD, the son of Doctor Giles Goddard, postmaster at New London, in Connecticut, was the first who established a printing press in Providence,[8] and was soon after appointed deputy post-master.

Goddard served his apprenticeship with James Parker, printer
in New York. He opened a printing house in Providence in
1762, and soon after published a newspaper. There was at that
time but one other paper printed in the colony, viz. at Newport;
yet after a trial of several years, Goddard did not meet with such
encouragement as to induce him to continue his *Gazette*. He
left his printing house, &c., in the care of his mother, and sought
for himself a more favorable place of residence.

On leaving Providence he was for a short time concerned
with Holt, in New York, in publishing *Parker's Gazette and
Post Boy*; and as a silent partner drew a share of the profits. After
the repeal of the stamp act, in 1766, he closed his concerns with
his friends Parker and Holt, and went to Philadelphia, and there
printed a newspaper, &c.

I shall have occasion again to mention Goddard, who was in

business several years in Philadelphia; and afterwards at Baltimore, where he finished his professional labors.

As a printer he was ingenious and enterprising. He made several strong efforts to acquire property, as well as reputation; but by some means his plans of business frequently failed of success. He was most fortunate in his concerns for a few years after the termination of the war. At length he supposed that he had become possessed of a competency to carry him through life 'without hard rubbing.' In this apprehension he quitted business, returned to New England, and resided several years on a large farm near Providence, of which he was the proprietor, and died Dec. 23, 1817, aged 77.

Major General Charles Lee, an officer in the American army during the revolutionary war, owned a landed estate in Berkeley county, Virginia, and left by will one-third part of this estate to Goddard and Eleazer Oswald, to whom he professed himself to have been under obligations.

Few could conduct a newspaper better than Goddard. He was a capable editor, and his talents were often drawn into requisition. He, like many others, was a laborious agent in the cause of his country, and in many instances where he had neither honor nor profit for his reward. When the loaves and fishes were to be divided, aspiring, interested, nominal patriots, crowded him into the background, and his services were in a great measure forgotten.

Goddard, however, received from the postmaster general the appointment of surveyor general of post roads; and, in this instance, fared better than many others, whose public services were never rewarded by any office whatever, either of profit or honor. [See pp. 390–393, 534–540.]

SARAH GODDARD, the mother of William Goddard, was the daughter of Lodowick Updike, whose ancestors were among the first settlers of Rhode Island, and her brother was for some years attorney general of the colony. She received a good education, acquired an acquaintance with several branches of useful and polite learning, and married Dr. Giles Goddard, of New London, who left her a widow.

After her son had been a few years in business, she became his partner. He left the management of the printing house and newspaper to her, and she conducted them with much ability for about two years, when John Carter supplied the place of her son; the firm was then SARAH GODDARD & COMPANY. She resigned the business to Carter in 1769, removed to Philadelphia the same year, and died there in January, 1770.

JOHN CARTER[9] was born in Philadelphia, and served his apprenticeship with Franklin & Hall, in that city. He was the partner of Sarah Goddard from 1766 to 1768 inclusive; and, in 1769, he became the successor of William and Sarah Goddard, and proprietor of the *Providence Gazette*.

For more than twenty years his printing house was 'at Shakespear's Head, opposite to the Court House;' after which it was near the bridge, and opposite to the market.

He was postmaster before the revolution, and for many years subsequent to it. He was well acquainted with the art which he practised, and the productions of his press exhibit evidence of a good and correct workman.

He was a staunch supporter of the cause of our country, before its independence; and after that important event took place, he did not lose sight of her best interests. He prosecuted printing in an accurate manner for forty-six years. His character as a man of honor and integrity was well established: he died in August, 1814, aged sixty-nine years.

JOHN WATERMAN was bred a seaman, and became the master of a vessel. Perferring the mechanic arts, he left the pursuits of commerce, and built a paper mill two miles from Providence, which probably was the first erected in the colony. In 1769, he purchased the press and types which were, for many years, owned and used by Samuel Kneeland of Boston; with these he opened a printing house near his paper mill, but made little use of them.

BOOKSELLERS
IN RHODE ISLAND

1760.   C. CAMPBELL, bookseller and postmaster in Newport.

PROVIDENCE

1762.   ANDREW OLIPHANT, a Scotchman of good education. He was an acquaintance of the poet Thomson, author of *The Seasons*. He resided but a few years in Providence and then removed to South Carolina.

NEWSPAPERS
IN RHODE ISLAND

ALTHOUGH the press had been established many years in Connecticut before it was introduced into Rhode Island, yet a newspaper was published in Rhode Island twenty years earlier than in Connecticut.

NEWPORT

THIS town was the fourth in New England where a press was established, and the second from which a newspaper was issued.

THE RHODE-ISLAND GAZETTE was the first paper issued in the colony. No. 1 was published September 27, 1732, printed on a small sheet of pot size, from a pica type much worn. Its contents were generally comprised on half a sheet. The day of publication was Wednesday. Imprint, 'Newport, Rhode-Island: Printed and Sold by James Franklin, at his Printing-House under the Town-School-House, where Advertisements and Letters to the Author are taken in.'

The Gazette was discontinued the 24th of May, 1733, seven months from its first appearance.[10] Some attempts were made to revive this paper by Franklin's widow, but without success.[11]

THE NEWPORT MERCURY, first published about September, 1758,[12] gained a permanent establishment. It was printed on Mondays by James Franklin, son of the printer of *The Rhode Island Gazette*, generally on paper of crown size, folio, but usually consisting of half a sheet only. When the publisher died, in August, 1762, the Mercury was continued by his mother, Anne Franklin, until she went into partnership with Samuel Hall, under the firm of Franklin & Hall, in Thames street. Mrs. Franklin died in April, 1763. Hall then became the proprietor of the Mercury, and published it until 1768.

Under the management of Hall, the Mercury made a more respectable appearance than before. It was printed handsomely and correctly; its columns were filled with well selected intelligence from the papers printed in the neighboring colonies, and due attention was paid to domestic information. Advertising customers increased, and its circulation became more extensive.

In 1768, Hall resigned the Mercury to Solomon Southwick, who conducted it until several years subsequent to the revolution. During the war, while the British troops possessed New-port, Southwick set up a press at Attleborough, Massachusetts, and there published the Mercury. He returned to Newport as soon as that town was evacuated, and reestablished his press.[13]

This paper, when first published, had a large cut of the figure of Mercury in its title. Hall exchanged it for a small king's arms. Southwick enlarged the king's arms, and added to the title: 'Containing the freshest advices,' &c. His printing house was 'in Queen Street, near the Middle of the Parade.'

Southwick continued the Mercury on the respectable ground on which it was placed by Hall; and, during the contest for the independence of our country, he conducted it with firmness and patriotic zeal. Southwick's successors have continued the Mercury to this time [1810]. It is the fourth oldest paper now published in the United States.[14]

NEWSPAPERS
IN PROVIDENCE

THE PROVIDENCE GAZETTE, *and Country Journal* was the only newspaper printed in Providence before 1775. It was first published October 20, 1762, by William Goddard, on a sheet of crown size, folio; a cut of the king's arms decorated the title. It was printed every Saturday, from types of english and long primer. Imprint, 'Providence: Printed by William Goddard, at the Printing-Office near the Great Bridge, where Subscriptions, Advertisements and Letters of Intelligence, &c., are received for this Paper; and where all Manner of printing Work is performed with care and Expedition.'

The Gazette was discontinued from May 11, to August 24, 1765. On that day a paper was published, headed '*Vox Populi, Vox Dei*. A Providence Gazette Extraordinary, Printed by S.

and W. Goddard.' After this it was, till January, 1767, 'Printed by Sarah Goddard and Co.' It then appeared with this imprint: 'Printed (in the Absence of William Goddard) by Sarah Goddard & Co.' In a short time after this, it was published by Sarah Goddard and John Carter.

In 1769, William and Sarah Goddard resigned their right in the Gazette to John Carter, who has published it from that time to the present [1810].

This paper zealously defended the rights of the colonies before the revolution, ably supported the cause of the country during the war, and has weekly diffused federal republican principles since the establishment of independence. The Gazette has, from time to time, been supplied by various writers, with many well composed political, moral and entertaining essays. Its weekly collection of intelligence is judiciously selected, and it was correctly and regularly printed more than forty years by its respectable publisher, John Carter.

NOTES TO CHAPTER IV

See John E. Alden, *Rhode Island Imprints, 1727–1800* (Bibliographical **RHODE ISLAND** Society of America, 1949). H. G. and M. O. Brown, *A Dictionary of Printing, Publishing, Bookselling & Allied Trades in Rhode Island to 1865* (New York, 1958).

1. B. F. Swan, *Gregory Dexter of London and New England, 1610–1700* (Rochester, N.Y., 1949).

2. *Dictionary of American Biography*, VI, 599. **NEWPORT**

3. H. M. Chapin, 'James Franklin, Jr., Newport Printer,' in *The American Collector*, II, 325–329 (1926).

4. Mr. Southwick escaped with his wife and eldest son, Solomon, but a younger child and its nurse were captured. M

5. In a historical sketch of the *Mercury*, published in that paper when it had completed a century of its existence, June 12, 1858, it is asserted that Southwick did not return to resume his paper, but that Henry Barber revived its publication in 1780. As yet no copies of the *Mercury* have been found that were published from 1776 to 1780, when Barber's name appears; but it is mentioned by Mr. Thomas elsewhere in this work, that Southwick resumed its publication at Attleborough, Mass. Copies of the *Mercury* are preserved in the library of the American Antiquarian Society at Worcester, which show that Southwick was associated with Barber in May, 1785; that he was printing it alone in 1787; and that Barber was again printing it in his own name in 1788. Southwick's monument is still seen in the cemetery at Newport. A copy of the inscription has been furnished by Mr. Fred A. Pratt, the present editor of the *Mercury*, as follows:

'In memory of | Solomon Southwick, Esq., | a gentleman of liberal | education and expansive mind, | for many years | editor and proprietor of the | *Newport Mercury* | and commissary general for the | state of Rhode Island | in the Revolutionary war. | He died Dec. 23, 1797, | in the 66th year of his age.

> Just, generous, benevolent and sincere,
> Was he whose hallowed dust reposes here;
> If e'er a partial prayer he breathed to heaven,
> That prayer was for his country's glory given.'

The house which Mr. Southwick occupied on his return to Newport with his printing office, is that in which the Newport Bank is now located. Children of his son, Henry C., reside in Albany, and preserve volumes of the *Mercury* and other mementos of their ancestor, among which is a diploma from the College and Academy of Philadelphia for proficiency in Philosophy and Mathematics, 1757, conferring upon him the degree of B.A. M

6. Mr. Southwick left five children: Solomon, Henry C., Wilmarth, Eliza, and John. Solomon became editor of *The Albany Register*, which was begun in 1788 as a democratic paper, and with which he was connected for a period of nearly thirty years. He was successively clerk of the house of assembly at Albany; clerk of the senate; sheriff of the county; manager of the state literature lottery; state printer; regent of the university; postmaster of the city; and president of the Mechanics and Farmers' bank. For a considerable time he was at the head of the

democratic party, wielding almost unlimited influence upon the political destinies of the state. Besides the *Register*, which he published in his own name from 1808 to 1817, he also published *The Christian Visitant*, in 1815, and *The Plough Boy*, an agricultural paper, in 1819. He edited the *National Democrat*, in 1817; the *National Observer*, in 1826; the *Family Newspaper*, in 1838. He was twice nominated for governor, but his party was at the time in the minority. He was a voluminous writer, and left several published volumes. He died suddenly Nov. 18, 1839, aged 66. His brother Henry C. was a practical printer, and was sometime associated with him in the business. He married Jane, a sister of John Barber who established the *Register*, and whom he succeeded as its proprietor. She survived him several years. Of six sons but one left posterity. The Albany Barbers were of a different family from those of Newport. M

7. L. C. Worth, 'The First Press in Providence,' in *Proceedings of the American Antiquarian Society*, LI, 351–383 (Oct. 1941). *Printers and Printing in Providence, 1762–1907* (Providence, 1907?).

8. W. L. Miner, *William Goddard, Newspaperman* (Durham, N.C., 1962). *Dictionary of American Biography*, VII, 341–342.

9. *Dictionary of American Biography*, III, 540–541.

10. This would be eight months, but it does not seem to have been regularly published; no. 17 is dated Jan. 25; no. 19, Feb. 22; no. 20, March 1. M

11. The press used by the Franklins was preserved in the office of the *Mercury* to a late period, and an effort was made to sell it for $100 by the administrator of the Barbers; but the claim that it was the press on which Benjamin Franklin wrought could not be verified, and it remained unsold in a worm-eaten and disabled condition in 1858. M

12. The first number appeared June 12. M

13. It is stated in *The Historical Magazine*, IV, 37 (Feb. 1860), that the British plundered his office of £200. Another report (*Newport Mercury*, Sept. 12, 1858) states that before leaving the island, Southwick buried his press and types in the garden in the rear of the old Kilburn House, in Broad street; that a tory, having knowledge of the fact, gave the enemy information, and they were dug up, and used by the British during their stay, and that copies of a paper published by them are preserved in the Redwood Library. M

14. Henry Barber, who published the *Mercury* in 1780, learned printing of Southwick. The family emigrated from England, and settled in

Westerly, R.I. He died Sept. 11, 1800, and was succeeded by his sons, William and John H.; they were finally succeeded by William Lee Barber, the son of John H., who died Dec. 27, 1850, aged 25, and the paper, which had been published by them almost uninterruptedly during seventy years, passed out of the family. It is still [1872] continued, and is the oldest paper in the country except the *New Hampshire Gazette*, which is two years its senior. M It ended its separate existence in 1928.

★ V ★

NEW HAMPSHIRE

THE printing for this colony was executed in Boston, Massachusetts, until 1756. Only two printing houses were opened in New Hampshire before the year 1775, and one of these had for several years been shut. The productions of the press were few: the largest work printed was the laws of the province.

ALTHOUGH this place was the capital of the colony, and had been settled a long time, yet no means had been used to introduce printing into it until about the year 1755, when several of the influential inhabitants exerted themselves for this purpose; and, in the year following, the press was established there, at which was executed the first printing done in New Hampshire.

DANIEL FOWLE, who had been arrested and imprisoned in Boston, on a charge of having published a libel against the government of Massachusetts, was, as has been stated, solicited by several gentlemen in Portsmouth, and afterwards encouraged by the government, to set up a press in that town. He accordingly removed from Boston to Portsmouth in July, 1756, and soon after published a newspaper. Fowle did but little at book printing; it being his principal business to publish

331

the newspaper. He was appointed printer to the government; and the laws, &c., were issued from his press.

In September, 1764, he took his nephew Robert Fowle as his partner. The firm of the company was DANIEL & ROBERT FOWLE. They remained together until 1774, when they separated, and Robert soon removed to Exeter.

Daniel Fowle continued in business until his death, but did not acquire much property. He married into a very respectable family in Boston, some years before he removed from that town, but had no children. He received the commission of a magistrate a short time after he settled at Portsmouth. He was a correct printer and industrious. He was mild in his disposition, agreeable in his manners, liberal in his sentiments, and attached to the cause of his country. He died in June, 1787, aged 72 years. [See pp. 126–131.]

THOMAS FURBER was born in Portsmouth, and served his apprenticeship with Daniel Fowle. Some zealous whigs, who thought the Fowles were too timid in the cause of liberty, or their press too much under the influence of the officers of the crown, encouraged Furber to set up a second press in the province. He in consequence opened a printing house in Portsmouth, toward the end of 1764, and soon after published a newspaper. In 1765, he received as a partner Ezekiel Russell. Their firm was FURBER & RUSSELL. Excepting the newspaper, they printed only a few hand-bills and blanks. The company became embarrassed, and in less than a year its concerns terminated, and the partnership was dissolved. Upon the dissolution of the firm, the press and types were purchased by the Fowles. Furber became their journeyman, and Russell went to Boston.

Furber had been taught plain binding, and undertook to con-nect it with printing. Although he was not very skillful, either as a printer or as a binder, he began the world under favorable circumstances; and, had he been attentive to his affairs, he might have been successful. He was good natured and friendly, but naturally indolent; and, like too many others, gave himself up to the enjoyment of a companion, when he should have been attending to his business. He died in Baltimore, at the house of William Goddard, who had employed him for a long time and shown him much friendship. He left a widow and several children.

A DIFFERENCE in the political sentiments of D. and R. Fowle, printers and copartners at Portsmouth, was the cause of their separation in 1774; and probably the reason of the establishment of a press in Exeter.

ROBERT FOWLE was the son of John Fowle, who was several years a silent partner with Rogers & Fowle in Boston, and afterwards an Episcopal clergyman at Norwalk in Connecticut. He served his apprenticeship with his uncle, at Portsmouth; and when of age became his partner, as has been mentioned. This copartnership being ended they divided their printing materials. Robert, who was neither a skillful nor a correct printer, took the press and types which had been used by Furber, and settled at Exeter. He did some work for the old government, and, in 1775, some for the new. He made several attempts to establish a newspaper, and in 1776 began one, which he published more than a year.

The new paper currency of New Hampshire had been printed by Fowle, and it was counterfeited; and suspicion rested on
him as having been concerned in this criminal act. He was a
royalist, and fled within the British lines in New York. By this
step the suspicion, which might not have been well founded,
was confirmed. Thus ended the typographical career of Robert
Fowle. With other refugees from the United States, he was
placed upon the British pension list. Some time after the establishment of peace, he returned to this country, married the
widow of his younger brother, who had succeeded him at
Exeter, and resided in New Hampshire until he died. Robert
Fowle had very respectable connections.

**BOOKSELLERS
IN PORTSMOUTH**

1716. ELEAZAR RUSSELL, sold books, principally such as
were used in schools.

The laws of New Hampshire were printed in Boston, anno
1716, 'for Eleazar Russell at his shop in Portsmouth.' He died in
May, 1764, aged seventy-three years.

1757. DANIEL FOWLE, kept a very small stock of books
for sale, but never paid much attention to bookselling.

Before the revolution there was not a bookstore of any note
in New Hampshire.

1770. WILLIAM APPLETON, served his apprenticeship in
Boston, and sold books in common use. He died a few years
after he settled in Portsmouth.

**NEWSPAPERS
IN PORTSMOUTH**

A PRESS having been established in Portsmouth by
Daniel Fowle from Boston, he in August, 1756,[1] began
the publication of a public journal, entitled

THE NEW-HAMPSHIRE GAZETTE. It was first printed from
a long primer type, on half a sheet foolscap, in quarto; but was

soon enlarged to half a sheet crown, folio; and it sometimes appeared on a whole sheet crown. Imprint, 'Portsmouth, in New Hampshire, Printed by Daniel Fowle, where this Paper may be had at one Dollar per Annum; or Equivalent in Bills of Credit, computing a Dollar this year at Four Pounds Old Tenor.'

Fowle had several type metal cuts, which had been engraved and used for an abridgment of Croxall's Esop; and as he thought that there should be something ornamental in the title of the Gazette, and not finding an artist to engrave any thing appropriate, he introduced one of these cuts, designed for the fable of the crow and the fox. This cut was, in a short time, broken by some accident, and he supplied its place by one engraved for the fable of Jupiter and the peacock. This was used until worn down, when another cut from the fables was substituted. Eventually, the royal arms, badly engraved, appeared; and at the same time, 'Historical Chronicle' was added to the title; a cut of the king's arms well executed, afterwards took the place of the other.

In September, 1764, Robert Fowle became the partner of Daniel in the publication of the Gazette, and in 1774 they separated. In 1775, there was a little irregularity in the publication of the paper, occasioned by the war; but D. Fowle in a short time continued it as usual. The Gazette was not remarkable in its political features; but its general complexion was favorable to the cause of the country.

In May, 1776, Benjamin Dearborne, to whom Fowle taught printing, became the publisher of this paper, and altered its title to, *The Freeman's Journal, or New-Hampshire Gazette*. Dearborne continued the paper a few years, after which it was again published by Fowle, who made several alterations in the title.

In 1785, Fowle relinquished it to Melchor & Osborne, who published it for a number of years; and it is, at the present time (1810), issued from the press of their successors with its original title. The New-Hampshire Gazette is the oldest newspaper printed in New England; and only two of those which preceded it are now published in the United States.[2]

THE PORTSMOUTH MERCURY *and Weekly Advertiser* was the second newspaper published in New Hampshire. Its first appearance was on the 21st of January, 1765. It was introduced with an address to the public, which states that,

'The Publisher proposes to print Nothing that may have the least Tendency to subvert good Order in publick or private Societies, and to steer clear of litigious, ill natured and trifling Disputes in Individuals; yet, neither opposition, arbitrary Power, or publick Injuries may be expected to be screen'd from the Knowledge of the People, whose Liberties are dearer to them than their lives.'

The Mercury was published weekly, on Monday, on a crown sheet, folio, from a new large faced small pica from Cottrell's foundry in London.* Imprint: 'Portsmouth, in New-Hampshire, Printed by Thomas Furber, at the New Printing-Office near the Parade, where this Paper may be had for one dollar or near the Parade, where this Paper may be had for one Dollar or Six Pounds O.T. per year; One Half to be paid at Entrance.'

The Mercury a few weeks after its first appearance was very irregular as to its size. It was most commonly comprised in sheet of pot or foolscap, printed *broadsides*, but occasionally on half a sheet of medium or demy, according as paper could be

* Not celebrated for producing the best types.

purchased at the stores the moment it was wanted. The typography of the Mercury, the new type excepted, did not exceed that of the Gazette. The collection of intelligence was inferior; and this paper was not more supported by any number of respectable writers than the Gazette. Before the first year of the publication of the Mercury ended, Furber took as a partner Ezekiel Russell, and his name appeared after Furber's in the imprint.

They who in the greatest degree encouraged the Mercury, very warmly opposed the stamp act, laid on the colonies at this time by the British parliament; indeed, the spirit of the country rose in opposition to this act; and, although some publishers of newspapers made a faint stand, yet few among those more immediately attached to the British administration, were hardy enough to afford the measure even a feeble support. *The New Hampshire Gazette*, which some thought would not appear in opposition to the stamp act, came forward against it; and, on the day preceding that on which it was designed the act should take place, appeared in full mourning, contained some very spirited observations against this measure of government, and continued to be published as usual without stamps.

The Mercury did not gain that circulation which it might have obtained had its editors taken a more decided part, and either defended government with energy, or made the paper generally interesting to the public by a zealous support of the rights and liberties of the colonies. In consequence of the neglect of the publishers to render the Mercury worthy of public attention, the customers withdrew, and the paper, after having been published about three years, was discontinued. From this time to the commencement of the war, the Gazette was the only newspaper published in the province of New Hampshire.

THE third newspaper which appeared in New Hampshire, was issued from the press in Exeter, near the close of the year 1775, and published, irregularly, by Robert Fowle, under various titles, in 1776 and part of 1777, until discontinued. It was printed on a large type, small paper, and often on half a sheet. It was first entitled, *A New-Hampshire Gazette*, afterwards *The New Hampshire Gazette*; *The New Hampshire Gazette, or Exeter Morning Chronicle*; *The New Hampshire* [State] *Gazette, or, Exeter Circulating Morning Chronicle*; *The State Journal, or The New Hampshire Gazette and Tuesday's Liberty Advertiser*. These and other alterations, with changes of the day of publication, took place within one year. It was published, generally, without an imprint. In the last alteration of the title, a large cut, coarsely engraved, was introduced; it was a copy of that which had for several years been used in *The Pennsylvania Journal*,* and the same which Rogers, some time before, had introduced into the *Salem Gazette and Advertiser*.

Several other newspapers since 1777, have had a beginning and ending in Exeter.

* See account of *The Pennsylvania Journal, Salem Gazette*, &c.

NOTES TO CHAPTER V

NEW HAMPSHIRE No general account of New Hampshire printing has been published, although Miss Caroline Whittemore compiled a checklist of imprints, 1756–1790, which exists in typescript, and Professor Ralph Brown has work in progress. Thus, the reader is referred to appropriate New Hampshire local histories for further information.

1. On the 6th of October, 1856, a centennial anniversary of the first newspaper in New Hampshire was held at Portsmouth, for which occasion a facsimile of the first number of the *Gazette* was printed. It appears by that, that the date was Thursday, October 7. It is possible that a prospectus number was issued in August, as was the case with the *Newport Mercury*. Although the anniversary of the establishment of the *Gazette* was celebrated with great spirit and eclat in 1856, the paper was discontinued in 1861, for about two years, when it was revived and published with eminent success. Abner Greenleaf, who had printed and edited the Gazette, died Sept. 28, 1868, aged 83. An almanac was also printed at this office in 1756 for the ensuing year. M

2. This paper is now, 1872, the weekly issue of the *Portsmouth Chronicle* published daily on a sheet of eight pages. M It died in 1942, except as a subtitle to a Sunday supplement.

★ VI ★

PENNSYLVANIA

THIS was the second English colony in America, where the press was established. The charter of the province was granted to William Penn, in the year 1681; and, about the year 1686, a printing press was established 'near Philadelphia.'

PHILADELPHIA PHILADELPHIA was laid out, and the building of it begun by its proprietor, in 1683. In less than six years after the city was founded printing was practiced here.

WILLIAM BRADFORD was the first printer who settled in this colony. He was the son of William and Anne Bradford, of Leicester, England, at which place he was born in the year 1660.[1] He served his apprenticeship in London, with Andrew Sowle, printer in Grace Church street, and married his daughter Elizabeth. Sowle was intimately acquainted with George Fox, a shoemaker of Nottingham, and the founder of the English sect of quakers. Sowle was one of this sect, and printed for the society. Bradford adopted the principles of the quakers, and was among the first emigrants from England to Pennsylvania in 1682, and landed at the spot where Philadelphia was soon

340

after laid out before a house was built. The next year his wife arrived.*

At what place he first settled is rather uncertain; but it was, as he expresses it, 'near Philadelphia.' The Swedes had begun a colony in Delaware as early as 1626, and made a settlement at Chester, now a part of Pennsylvania. The Dutch conquered the Swedes and attached Delaware to the government of New York. By agreement with the Duke of York, Penn, after his arrival, assumed the government of Delaware, and united it, in matters of legislation, with Pennsylvania. The general assembly was holden at Chester, and this borough became for a time a place of consequence. It is probable that Bradford resided there until Philadelphia assumed the appearance of a city. He might, however, have set up his press at Burlington, which is but eighteen miles distant from Philadelphia, and was then the capital of New Jersey. The first work printed by Bradford, which has reached us with a date, is, *An Almanack for the year of the Christian account 1687. Particularly respecting the Meridian and Latitude of Burlington, but may indifferently serve all places adjacent.* By Daniel Leeds, Student in Agriculture. Printed and sold by William Bradford, near *Philadelphia* in *Pennsilvania* pro Anno 1687. This is a sheet almanac in twelve compartments for the twelve months. The year begins with March and ends with February, as was usual in the seventeenth century. At the bottom of the sheet are an explanation of the almanac, an ac-

---

* Thomas Holme, who was William Penn's surveyor general, drew a plan of the city of Philadelphia, which was engraved and printed in London, in 1683, and has this title and imprint, viz: 'A portraiture of the city of Philadelphia in the Province of Pennsylvania in America, by Thomas Holme, surveyor-general. Sold by Andrew Sowle in Shoreditch, London.' By this it appears that in 1683, Sowle either lived or had a shop in Shoreditch.

count of the eclipses for the year, courts and fairs at Burlington and Philadelphia, and short rules in husbandry.[2]

It appears that at the time Bradford printed this almanac he lived near Philadelphia, and Chester, as I have said, was near this city.*

In 1689, Bradford lived in the city. I possess a quarto pamphlet by George Keith, respecting the New England churches, printed by Bradford in Philadelphia that year.

It is the oldest book I have seen printed in the city. I have another pamphlet, of seventy-four pages, printed by him in 1690, entitled, *A Refutation of Three Opposers of Truth by plain Evidence of the holy Scriptures, viz: Pardon Tillinghast, B. Keech, and Cotton Mather; and a few Words of a Letter to John Cotton.* By George Keith. Philadelphia, Printed and Sold by William Bradford Anno 1690. I have another quarto pamphlet, of seventy-two pages, written by George Keith, entitled: *A Serious Appeal to all the more Sober, Impartial and Judicious People of New England, to whose Hands this may come.* It is a vindication of the quakers from the attack of Cotton Mather, etc., Printed and Sold by William Bradford at Philadelphia in Pennsylvania, in the year 1692.

* It has been suggested that Bradford first settled at Kensington, about two miles to the eastward of Philadelphia, on the banks of the Delaware; at which place there were at that time two or three houses, and where remained the great oak tree, under which William Penn held a treaty with the Indians, until the 3d of March, 1810, when it was overthrown by a tornado. Robert Proud, in his *History of Pennsylvania* (Philadelphia, 1797–1798), 2 vols., observes in a note: 'The quakers had meetings for religious worship, and for the economy of their society, as early as the fore part of the year 1681, at the house of Thomas Fairlamb, at Shakamaxon, near or about the place where Kensington now stands, nigh Philadelphia.' This fact renders it, in a degree, probable, that Bradford did settle at Kensington. The creek at the north end of the city is known to this day by the Indian name Shakamaxon.

In the year 1692, much contention prevailed among the quakers in Philadelphia, and Bradford took an active part in the quarrel. George Keith, by birth a Scotchman, a man of good abilities and well educated, was surveyor general in New Jersey; and the society of Friends in the city employed him in 1689, as the superintendent of their schools. Keith having attended to this duty nearly two years became a public speaker in their religious assemblies; but being, as the quakers asserted, of a turbulent and overbearing spirit, he gave them much trouble. They forbade him speaking as a teacher, or minister, in their meetings. This, and some other irritating circumstances, caused a division among the Friends, and the parties were violently hostile to each other. Bradford was of the party which was attached to Keith, and supported him; their opponents were the majority. Among them were Lieutenant Governor Lloyd, and most of the quaker magistrates. Keith and Thomas Budd wrote against the majority, and Bradford published their writings.

Keith was condemned in the city meetings, but appealed to the general meeting of the Friends; and, in order that his case might be generally known and understood, he wrote an address to that body which he caused to be printed, and copies of it to be dispersed among the Friends previous to their general meeting. This conduct was highly resented by his opponents. The address was denominated seditious, and Bradford was arrested and imprisoned for printing it. The sheriff seized a form containing four quarto pages of the types of the address; and also took into his custody a quantity of paper, and a number of books, which were in Bradford's shop, with all the copies of the address which he could find. The civil authority took up the business; and, as Keith and Bradford state the facts, they who persecuted them in the religious assemblies condemned and imprisoned them by civil process; the judges of the courts being the leading characters in the meetings. Several of Keith's party were apprehended and imprisoned with Bradford; and among them, Thomas Budd, and John MacComb. The offence of the latter consisted in his having two copies of the address which he gave to two friends in compliance with their request.

The following was a warrant for committing Bradford and MacComb:

'Whereas William Bradford, printer, and John MacComb, taylor, being brought before us upon an information of Publishing, Uttering and Spreading a Malitious and Seditious paper, intituled An Appeal from the twenty-eight Judges* to the Spirit of Truth, &c. Tending to the disturbance of the Peace and the Subversion of the present government, and the said Persons being required to give Securitie to answer it at the next Court, but they refused so to do These are therefore by the King and Queens Authoritie and in our Proprietarys Name, to require you to take into your Custody the Bodies of William Bradford and John MacComb, and them safely keep till they shall be discharged by due Course of Law. Whereof fail not at your Peril; and for your so Doing, this shall be your sufficient Warrant. Given under our Hands and Seales this 24th of August, 1692.

'These to John White Sheriff of Philadelphia or his Deputies.'
Signed by Arthur Cook, and four others.

The day after the imprisonment of Bradford and his friends, a 'Private Sessions,' as it was called, of the county court, was

---

* 'Twenty-eight,' meaning those who condemned Keith, in what he called 'their Spiritual Court.'

holden by six justices, all quakers, who, to put a better complexion on their proceedings, requested the attendance of two magistrates who were not quakers.

This court assembled, it seems, for the purpose of convicting
Keith, Budd, and their connections, of seditious conduct, and
of condemning them without a hearing; but the two magistrates who were not quakers, if we credit Keith and Bradford,
reprobated the measure, and refused to have any concern in it,
declaring that the whole transaction was a mere dispute among
the quakers respecting their religion, in which the government
had no concern. They, however, advised that Keith, and others
accused, should be sent for, and allowed to defend themselves,
and affirmed that if any thing like sedition appeared in their
practice, they would join heart and hand in their prosecution.
To this the quaker magistrates would not consent, and the
others in consequence left the court. The court then, as is stated
in a pamphlet,* 'proceeded in their work, and as they judged
George Keith in their spiritual court, without all hearing or
trial, so in like manner, they prosecuted him in their temporal
court without all hearing.' The pamphlet further states that 'one
of the judges declared that the court could judge of matter of
fact without evidence, and therefore without more to do pro-
claimed George Keith, by the common cryer, in the market
place, to be a seditious person, and an enemy to the king and
queen's government.'

---

* This pamphlet is entitled, *New England Spirit of Persecution, transmitted to
Pennsilvania, and the Pretended Quaker found Persecuting the True Christian
Quaker in the Tryal of Peter Boss, George Keith, Thomas Budd and William Brad-
ford, at the Sessyons held at Philadelphia the Ninth, Tenth, and Twelfth Days of
December, 1692. Giving an account of the most Arbitrary Proceedings of that Court.*

Bradford and MacComb, who had been imprisoned, appeared at this court, and requested that they might be brought to trial; pleading that it was very injurious to them and their families to remain in confinement. They claimed, as free born English subjects, the rights secured by Magna Charta, among which was the prompt administration of justice; and Bradford, in particular, desired that his trial might then take place, 'because, not only his person was restrained, but his working tools, and the paper and books from his shop, were taken from him, and without these he could not work and maintain his family.'

At this court the following conversation took place between the judges and the prisoners, all of whom were quakers:

'*Justice Cook*. What bold, impudent and confident men are these to stand thus confidently before the Court?

'*MacComb*. You may cause our hats to be taken off if you please.

'*Bradford*. We are here only to desire that which is the right of every free born English subject, which is speedy justice, and it is strange that that should be accounted impudence, and we impudent fellows therefore, when we have spoke nothing but words of truth and soberness, in requesting that which is our right, and which we want; it being greatly to our prejudice to be detained prisoners.

'*Justice Cook*. If thou hadst been in England, thou would have had thy back lashed before now.

'*Bradford*. I do not know wherein I have broke any law so as to incur any such punishment.

'*Justice Jennings*. Thou art very ignorant in the law. Does not thee know that there's a law that every printer shall put his name to the books he prints, or his press is forfeited?

'*Bradford*. I know that there was such a law, and I know when it expired.

'*Justice Cook*. But it is revived again, and is in force and without any regard to the matter of the book provides that the printer shall put his name to the books he prints, which thou hast not done.'

The prisoners continued to press for a trial.

'*Justice Cook*. A trial thou shall have, and that to your cost, it may be.

'*Justice Jennings*. A trial thou shalt have, but, for some reason known to us, the court defers it to the next sessions, and that is the answer we give, and no other you shall have.'

The trial was, accordingly, put over to the next term. The only offence which appeared against MacComb was his joining with Keith and his party, and disposing of two copies of Keith's printed address to his quaker brethren. For this he was not only imprisoned, but also deprived by Lieutenant Governor Lloyd of a license to keep an ordinary, or house of public entertainment, for which he had, a few months before his confinement, paid the lieutenant governor twelve pieces of eight, or three pounds twelve shillings of the then currency.

At the next session of the court, on the 6th of the following December, Bradford was placed at the bar. 'The presentment was read,' the substance of which was, that the 9th, 10th, 11th and 12th articles of the pamphlet called 'An Appeal,' had a tendency to weaken the hands of the magistrates; and William Bradford was presented as the printer of that seditious paper. The following proceedings of the court are extracted from the pamphlet above mentioned:

'*Clerk*. What say you William Bradford, are you guilty as you stand presented, or not guilty?

'*Bradford.* In the first place, I desire to know whether I am clear of the mittimus, which differs from the presentment?

'The clerk and the attorney for the government read and perused the mittimus and presentment, and finding them to differ, said, that when William Bradford was cleared according to law he was cleared of the mittimus. Bradford insisted on knowing whether, on the issue of the presentment, he was clear of the mittimus. After a long debate on the subject, Bradford was told that he was clear of the mittimus on the issue of the presentment.

'*Bradford.* What law is the presentment founded on?

'*Attorney for the Government.* It is grounded both on statute and common law.

'*Bradford.* Pray let me see that statute and common law, else how shall I make my plea? Justice Cook told us last court, that one reason why ye deferred our trial then, was that we might have time to prepare ourselves to answer it; but ye never let me have a copy of my presentment, nor will ye now let me know what law ye prosecute me upon.

'*Attorney.* It's not usual to insert in indictments against what statute the offence is, when it's against several statutes and laws made.

'*Justice White.* If thou wilt not plead guilty, or not guilty, thou wilt lose thy opportunity of being tried by thy country.

'The court then ordered the clerk to write down that William Bradford refused to plead; which he did; but as he was writing it down, Bradford desired they would not take advantage against him, for he refused not to plead, but only requested that which was greatly necessary in order to his making his own defence. Several in the court requesting on the prisoner's behalf that the court would not take advantage against him, they admitted him to plead, and he pleaded not guilty.

'The jury was then called over, and attested; but before they were attested, Bradford was asked if he had any exceptions to make against any of them that were returned for the jury.

'*Bradford.* Yes, I have, and particularly against two of them, Joseph Kirle and James Fox; for at the time when I was committed to prison, Arthur Cook [one of the judges] told me, that Joseph Kirle had said, that if the proceedings of the magistrates were thus found fault with, that they must not defend themselves against thieves and robbers, merchants would be discouraged of coming here with their vessels, &c.; and I except against James Fox, because the first day after Babbit and his company were taken, I being at Sam Carpenter's, there was Governor Lloyd, James Fox, and several others, and in discourse concerning the taking of the said privateers, James Fox greatly blamed William Walker, because he found fault with some justices that were quakers for commanding men, and as it were pressing them to go against the said privateers; and also James Fox joined with Thomas Lloyd in saying he would mark them as enemies to the government and well being of the province, who were neutral in the case of going against Babbit and his crew; by which instances I think it appears that these two persons have prejudged the cause that is now to come before them.

'Joseph Kirle acknowledged that he had spoken such words, and desired to be discharged; but the court would not allow of the exceptions.

'*Clerk.* These are no exceptions in law.

'*Attorney.* Hast thou at any time heard them say that thou

printed that paper? for that is only what they are to find.

'*Bradford*. That is not only what they are to find, they are to find also, whether this be a seditious paper or not, and whether it does tend to the weakening of the hands of the magistrates.

'*Attorney*. No, that is matter of law, which the jury is not to meddle with, but find whether William Bradford printed it or not, and the bench is to judge whether it be a seditious paper or not, for the law has determined what is a breach of the peace, and the penalty, which the bench only is to give judgment on.

'*Justice Jennings*. You are only to try, whether William Bradford printed it or not.

'*Bradford*. This is wrong, for the jury are judges in law as well as the matter of fact.

'The attorney again denied it; whereupon some of the jury desired to know what they were to try, for they did believe in their consciences, they were obliged to try and find whether that paper was seditious, as well as whether Bradford printed it; and some of them desired to be discharged.

'A great noise and confusion among the people.

'Some on the bench showing their willingness to allow of Bradford's exceptions to the two jurors, Justice Cook said, "I will not allow of it; is there four of us a mind?" Then the attorney read the 9th, 10th, 11th and 12th articles of the said printed appeal, &c., and commented thereupon, and then said, William Bradford is presented for printing and publishing this seditious paper, whereof you of the jury are to find him guilty, if it appears to you that he has printed it.

'*Bradford*. I desire you of the jury, and all men present to take notice, that what is contained in this paper is not seditious, but wholly relating to a religious difference, and asserting the quakers' ancient principles, and it is not laid down positive that they ought not to have proceeded against the privateers, but laid down by the way of query for the people called quakers to consider and resolve at their yearly meeting, whether it was not a transgression of the quakers' principles to hire and commissionate men to fight?

'*Justice Cook*. If it was intended for the yearly meeting at Burlington, why was it published before the meeting?

'*Bradford*. Because it might be perused and considered of by Friends before the meeting, even as the bills that are proposed to be passed into laws, they are promulgated a certain number of days before the assembly meets, that each may have opportunity to consider them.

'Then the attorney read the act* against printing any book without the printer's name to them; and he said, That was one act which they prosecuted William Bradford upon.

'George Keith answered the attorney. "It may be observed the singular and extraordinary severity of those justices, called quakers, who will pick out a statute made in Old England, and prosecute a man upon it here, which might ruin him and his family, though it's not certain whether that act be in force; most of William Penn's and the quakers' books were printed without the name of the printer when that act was in force, and yet we never heard that any printer in England was prosecuted for that; these here because they cannot fix the matter to be any breach of the peace they'll prosecute for not putting his name to what they suppose he printed."

'*Note*. That all the time those persons were on trial, the grand

---

* An act of the British parliament. 14 Car. 2 cap. 33.

jury sat by them, overawing and threatening them, when they spoke boldly in their own defence, and one of the jury wrote down such words as they disliked, signifying that they would present them. Justice Cook bid them take notice of such and such words, thereby overawing the prisoners, that they had not liberty to plead freely. When Thomas Harris, at the request of the prisoners, began to say something to the matter, they stopt him and bid an officer take him away, and Arthur [justice] Cook said that he should plead no more there.

'After a long pleading, D. Lloyd, their attorney, began to *summons* up the matter to the jury, and concluded by saying, it was evident William Bradford printed the seditious paper, he being the printer in this place, and the frame* on which it was printed was found in his house.

'*Bradford.* I desire the jury and all present to take notice, that there ought to be two evidences to prove the matter of fact, but not one evidence has been brought in this case.

'*Justice Jennings.* The frame on which it was printed is evidence enough.

'*Bradford.* But where is the frame? There has no frame been produced here; and if there had, it is no evidence, unless you saw me print on it.

'*Justice Jennings.* The jury shall have the frame with them; it cannot well be brought here; and besides the season is cold, and we are not to sit here to endanger our health. You are minded to put tricks upon us.

'*Bradford.* You of the jury, and all here present, I desire you to take notice, that there has not one evidence been brought to

---

* Called by printers, 'form,' containing the pages in types.

prove that I printed the sheet, called An Appeal; and, whereas they say the frame is evidence which the jury shall have; I say, the jury ought not to hear, or have any evidence whatsoever, but in the presence of the judges and prisoners.

'Yet this was nothing minded, but Sam [justice] Jennings *summoned* up to the jury, what they were to do, viz: to find, first, whether or not that paper, called the Appeal, had not a tendency to the weakening the hands of the magistrates, and the encouragement of wickedness? Secondly, whether it did not tend to the disturbance of the peace? and, thirdly, whether William Bradford did not print it, without putting his name to it as the law requires? The jury had a room provided for them, and the sheriff caused the frame to be carried in to them for an evidence that William Bradford printed the Appeal. The jury continued about forty-eight hours together, and could not agree; then they came into court to ask whether the law did require two evidences to find a man guilty? To answer this question, the attorney read a passage out of a law book, that they were to find it by evidences, or on their own knowledge, or otherwise; now, says the attorney, this *otherwise* is the frame which you have, which is evidence sufficient.

'*Bradford*. The frame which they have is no evidence for I have not seen it; and how do I, or the jury, know that that which was carried in to them is mine?

'Bradford was interrupted; the jury were sent forth again, and an officer commanded to keep them without meat, drink, fire, or tobacco. In the afternoon the jury came into the court again, and told, they were not like to agree; whereupon the court discharged them.

'Bradford then said to the court, that seeing he had been

detained so long a prisoner, and his utensils with which he should work had been so long kept from him, he hoped now to have his utensils returned, and to be discharged from his imprisonment.

'*Justice Jennings.* No! Thou shalt not have thy things again, nor be discharged; but I now let thee know thou stand in the same capacity to answer next court, as before.

'Next court being come, Bradford attended, and desired to know, if the court would let him have his utensils, and he be discharged?

'*Justice Cook.* Thou shalt not have thy goods until released by law.

'*Bradford.* The law will not release them unless executed.

'*Justice Cook.* If thou wilt request a trial, thou may have it.

'Whereupon Bradford queried, whether it be according to law to seize men's goods, and imprison their persons, and to detain them under the terror of a gaol, one six months after another, and not bring them to trial unless requested by the imprisoned? Whether, when a jury is sworn, well and truly to try, and true deliverance make between the proprietor and prisoner, it is not illegal to absolve them from their oaths, dismiss them, and put the cause to trial to another Jury?'[3]

Soon after this session of the court Bradford was by some means released from his confinement. It is said, that in the examination of the frame, the jury, not being acquainted with reading backwards, attempted to raise it from the plank on which it was placed, and to put it in a more favorable situation for inspection; and that one of them assisting with his cane, pushed against the bottom of the types as the form was placed perpendicularly, when, like magic, this evidence against Bradford instantly vanished, the types fell from the frame, or chase as it is termed by printers, formed a confused heap, and prevented further investigation.*

Bradford having incurred the displeasure of the dominant party in Pennsylvania, and receiving encouragement to settle in New York, he, in 1693, removed to that city; but it is supposed he had a concern in the press which was continued in Philadelphia. [See pp. 457-461.]

REINER JANSEN.[4] At this distance of time, it cannot be ascertained how long before or after 1699 Jansen printed in Philadelphia; nor is it certain that he owned a press. It has been supposed by some, that after William Bradford differed and seceded from his quaker brethren who had the principal concern in public affairs, they procured and set up another press; and by others, that Jansen was either an apprentice, or a journeyman to Bradford; that after Bradford had removed to New York, in 1693, he left Jansen to manage a press in Philadelphia;

* Proud, in his *History of Pennsylvania*, mentions, that George Keith had published several virulent pieces, one of which indecently reflected on several of the principal magistrates in their judicial capacity, whereby their authority with the lower classes of the people was lessened. The printer, William Bradford, and John MacComb who had published it, were apprehended by a warrant from five magistrates, and examined, and upon their contemptuous behavior, and refusal to give security, were committed. He adds, 'But they were soon discharged, without being brought to a trial.' This does not altogether agree with the account of the trial printed at the time, and which it is probable had not come to the knowledge of Proud. Respecting Keith and Budd, Proud says, they were also presented by the grand jury of Philadelphia, as authors of another book of the like tendency, entitled, *The Plea of the Innocent*, in which they defamed Samuel Jennings, 'a judge and a magistrate.' This presentment was prosecuted; 'so the matter was brought to a trial, and the parties fined 5l. each; but the fines were never exacted.'

and that, for prudential reasons, Jansen conducted the press in his own name, and had a share in the profits of the business. Some arrangement of this kind, probably, took place, and continued during the minority of Andrew, the son of William Bradford.

Whatever was the nature of this connection, it is certain that there was little business for the press in Philadelphia, excepting the disputes among the quakers; but there was more employment for that in New York; and that the materials of both the printing houses united would not have formed a large apparatus.

I have met with only one book with Jansen's name in the imprint. The title of that one, at large, is, 'God's Protecting Providence Man's surest Help and Defence in the Times of the greatest difficulty and most Imminent danger, Evidenced in the Remarkable Deliverance of Divers Persons from the Devouring Waves of the Sea, amongst which they Suffered Shipwreck. And also from the more cruelly devouring jawes of the inhumane Canibals of Florida. Faithfully related by one of the persons concerned therein. Printed in *Philadelphia* by *Reinier Jansen*, 1699.'

JACOB TAYLOR. I have not met with any thing printed by him, and doubt his having been a printer. As it appears by the journals of the assembly that he was consulted about printing the laws of the province in 1712, some persons have been of opinion that at that time he printed in Philadelphia. I can find no other evidence of this fact than what appears in the following extracts from the journals of the assembly of Pennsylvania, viz:

In 1712, 'on the ninth of the third month,' the assembly determined that it would 'be of great use and benefit to the country to have the laws printed, and thereupon sent for Jacob Taylor, to treat with him about the same. He informed the house, that according to the best of his judgment, the charges thereof would amount to *one hundred pounds* besides paper.'

It was this circumstance, I am led to suppose, that induced Andrew Bradford, who was connected with his father in New York, to leave that city, and commence printing in Philadelphia; for on the 'twenty-fourth of the ninth month,' the assembly chose a committee, 'to treat with Jacob Taylor, *and the other printers in town*, about the charge it will require to print the laws of this province, and report the same to this house *this afternoon*.' The printers *then in town** were doubtless William and Andrew Bradford from New York, as it cannot be discovered that, at that time, there were any other professors of the art nearer than New London and Boston. It is possible that Jansen might have been of the number, but it is believed that he died, or had left Philadelphia, before this time. However this may have been, the committee performed the service which was required of them, and made their report in the after part of that day. Seven persons were then immediately chosen, who 'with the speaker's assistance, were appointed trustees on behalf

---

* I conceive that this expression, to correspond with others in the extracts from the journals which follow, should read thus, 'to treat with Jacob Taylor, and others who are printers in town'—meaning the printers who came to town on this business. This remark is justified, in some measure, by the delay of the assembly, which it seems waited a fortnight after they took up the subject before they proceeded farther with it. This gave time for the printers in New York to get information of what was transacting relative to printing the laws, and to come to Philadelphia; and, it appears that as soon as they arrived, a committee was chosen to consult with them and Taylor, and was directed to make a report the same day.

of the province to employ one or more persons in printing five hundred volumes of the laws thereof, and that 50 pounds of the province stock shall be paid by the treasurer as money comes into his hands, (after paying 500*l*. to the lieutenant governor, &c.), unto the said trustees, towards defraying the charges aforesaid; and, that what it amounts to more by a true account of the whole expense, and due credit given for the sales made of the said books, produced to the assembly for the time being, the same shall be a debt chargeable on this province, to be paid out of the public stock thereof.'

As there would not be sufficient money in the treasurer's hands for the use of printing the laws, after paying the 500*l*. to the lieutenant governor, and the members of the assembly for their services, it was, on the 'seventh of the fourth month, Ordered, That the trustees appointed to get the laws printed may take up money at interest to defray the charges thereof, which shall be allowed a debt upon this province, to be discharged with the first public money that comes to the treasurer's hands, after the aforesaid payments are discharged, and that the note issued for the said fifty pounds be made payable accordingly.'

Notwithstanding all these preparatory measures for printing the laws, the trustees did not proceed with the business. On 'the thirteenth of the eleventh month in $171\frac{2}{3}$,' the subject was again brought forward in the assembly, and a committee of three persons was appointed, 'to treat with any printer, *or other person or persons of this city*, about the charge and method of printing the said laws, and bring their proposals in writing to this house.'

On the 'fifteenth of the eleventh month,' the same year, 'the committee appointed to treat, &c., brought in a proposal in writing from Jacob Taylor, which was read, and ordered to lie on the table.' On the 'third of the twelfth month, a proposal from Andrew Bradford, *printer*, was read and ordered to lie on the table.' And on the tenth of that month, another committee was chosen to contract *'with such printer as they shall think fit* to print the laws;' and were authorized to 'employ such clerks as they shall find necessary, to procure *a correct copy* of the said laws for the press.' The committee had power, 'where they shall observe any two or more laws of the same tenor or effect, (unless they be supplementary to each other) to omit such of them as shall appear to be redundant, only taking care that their *titles* be printed.' Andrew Bradford was employed to print the laws; and, it is probable that it was at this time he established himself in Philadelphia.

Although the following extract from the journals of the assembly relates to Bradford, I will insert it in this place as it is the conclusion of the business respecting this edition of the laws, which made a volume of one hundred and eighty-four pages, folio, viz:

'1714. 6th mo. 4. A petition from Andrew Bradford, setting forth that by order of the governor and assembly he has printed the laws of this province; that the repeal of several laws by her Majesty, has put a stop to the sale of them; and desiring to be relieved by this house; was received, and ordered to lie on the table.'

'1714. 6th mo. 5. Resolved that the speaker issue his warrant unto Richard Hill, to pay unto Andrew Bradford, printer, thirty pounds for fifty bound volumes of the laws of this province.'

If Taylor was not a printer, it is not improbable that he might be desirous to contract for printing the laws, with a view of having the work executed in Boston, and making a profit thereby. There was a Jacob Taylor, who for about thirty years annually calculated an almanac, which was published in Philadelphia, by Andrew Bradford; he was probably the same person; he died in 1746. I can learn nothing farther of him.

ANDREW BRADFORD,[5] was the son of William Bradford, who first printed in Pennsylvania. He was born in Philadelphia, went to New York with his father, and of him learned the art of printing. When his minority ended, he was one year the partner of his father. About the year 1712, he returned to Philadelphia, and from that time to 1723, was the only printer in the colony.

His printing house was 'in Second street, at the sign of the Bible.' He sold pamphlets and school books, and till 1730 frequently advertised other articles for sale, such as whalebone, live geese feathers, pickled sturgeon, chocolate, Spanish snuff, &c., and executed common binding. He printed for the government, and published polemical pamphlets, which, during many years, afforded employment for the press wherever it was established. In 1732, he was postmaster,[6] and, in 1735, became a considerable dealer in books and stationery. December 22, 1719, Bradford published the first newspaper printed in Pennsylvania, *The American Mercury*. John Copson appears to have been a partner in this publication for about two years.* In 1739, his foster son, William, was his partner; this connection lasted about eleven months, and ended in 1740.

---

* Bradford, in 1720, calls Copson a bookseller; but, in 1721, Copson styles himself a merchant.

When Franklin made his first visit to Philadelphia in 1723, a second printing house was opening by Keimer. Franklin, although a journeyman in this rival printing house, boarded some time with Bradford. It is evident from Franklin's statement, that Bradford was not merely civil, he was friendly to this young stranger; and, although he had no employment for him, yet he made him welcome to his house, 'till something better should offer.' When mentioning Bradford, and his rival Keimer, Franklin observes, they were both 'destitute of every qualification necessary to their profession.' The first 'was very illiterate,'[7] and the latter 'ignorant of the world.'

In 1738, Andrew Bradford purchased the house, in South Front street, which was kept in possession of the family, and long after occupied as a printing house by Thomas Bradford, publisher of *The True American*, a daily newspaper. He printed three or four Almanacs annually,[8] viz: Jacob Taylor's, Titan Leeds's, John Jerman's, and William Birkett's; these he published many years.

Bradford increased his property, and became easy in his circumstances. He was postmaster; and retained the office for several years after Franklin opened a third printing house in Philadelphia. However correct Franklin's opinion of him may be, it is certain that Bradford possessed, in a considerable degree, the confidence and esteem of his fellow citizens; as he was chosen one of the common council of the city, and was in this office at the time of his death.

In 1741, he published a periodical work, entitled, *The American Magazine, or Monthly View of the Political State of the British Colonies*. This work was soon discontinued.

His wife died in December, 1739; and, in 1740, he married

Cornelia Smith, a native of New York, who was related to his father's second wife. He died November 23, 1742,[9] aged about fifty-six years; and was buried in Christ church burying ground. On this occasion *The American Mercury* appeared in mourning six weeks. [See pp. 432–433.]

SAMUEL KEIMER[10] was bred to printing in London, where he married; and leaving his wife in England, he came to this country and opened a printing house 'in High street, near the Market-House, at Philadelphia,' in 1723. Until that time Bradford was the only printer in the colony. Keimer's printing materials consisted 'of an old damaged press, and a small cast of worn out English types, contained in one pair of cases.'* He soon made a small addition to his types, which enabled him to print pamphlets, and other small works. He was bred a compositor, and like other European compositors, knew little of the management of the press. When he wanted to use this small printing apparatus, he had neither man nor boy to assist him. His press was found to be deficient in some of its parts, and it had not been put together. At this time Franklin arrived in Philadelphia, and sought employment. Keimer engaged him to put his press in order, and hired him as a journeyman.

The first production of Keimer's press was an elegy of his own on the death of Aquilla Rose, printer, a young man of excellent character, secretary to the general assembly, and the principal workman in Bradford's printing house. Keimer was engaged on this elegy mentally and manually when he first saw Franklin, who observes that Keimer was a poet, but 'could

---

* Franklin's *Autobiography*, p. 78.

not be said to *write* in verse, for his method was to set the lines in
types as they flowed from his muse.'*

Soon after printing this elegy he published a small pamphlet,
which he called *A Parable*. This was said to be the joint work of
himself and Franklin. It gave offence to the quakers, and produced the following advertisement in *The American Mercury*,
viz:

'Whereas one Samuel Keimer, who lately came into this
Province of Pennsylvania, hath Printed and Published divers
Papers, particularly one Entituled *A Parable*, &c., in some Parts
of which he assumes to use such a *Stile* and *Language*, as that
perhaps he may be Deemed, where he is not known, to be one
of the People called *Quakers*. This may therefore Certifie, That
the said Samuel Keimer is not one of the said People, nor
Countenanced by them in the aforesaid Practices. Signed by
Order of the Monthly Meeting of the said People called
Quakers, held at Philadelphia, the 29th Day of the Ninth
Month, 1723.

'SAMUEL PRESTON, *Cl.*'

Keimer kept a small shop and sold blanks, and a few other
articles. Among other things, in July, 1724, bayberry wax
candles, and fine white *Liverpool soap*. He printed pamphlets,
and 'rubbed along' for some time, till Franklin left him. His
business, thus far, had not been very productive of profit; but,
during the absence of Franklin, he took a larger house, procured
new types, opened a shop which was well supplied with stationery, employed four or five hands in his printing house, and
improved his condition in life. Franklin found Keimer in this

* See the article on Barbadoes, for a specimen of Keimer's poetry.

situation when he returned from England; and having been disappointed in his expectations he again became a journeyman to his former employer.

Among other small works printed by Keimer, was a spurious edition of Jacob Taylor's Almanac for 1726, of which all but the calculations were compiled and written by Keimer. Taylor disowned the work in a long poetical essay, not of the most delicate kind, which he published in Bradford's paper, and it was soon after followed by an advertisement of the following purport:

'Whereas there hath been lately Published and Spread abroad in this Province and elsewhere, a lying Pamphlet, called an Almanack, set out and Printed by Samuel Keimer, to reproach, ridicule, and rob an honest Man of his Reputation, and strengthening his Adversaries, and not only so, but he hath Notoriously Branded the Gospel Minister of the Church of England with ignominious Names, for Maintaining a Gospel Truth, and reproacheth all the Professors of Christ and Christianity, as may be seen in his Almanack in the Month of December; now all judicious Readers may fairly see what this Man's Religion Consisteth in, only in his Beard and his sham keeping of the Seventh Day Sabbath, following Christ only for Loaves and Fishes. This may give Notice to the Author of this Mischief, that if he do not readily Condemn what he hath done, and Satisfy the Abused, he may expect to be Prosecuted as the Law shall direct.
'AARON GOFORTH, Senior.'

The following year he printed another Almanac for 1727, which he called Titan Leeds's, and sent a parcel of them to

Boston, New York, &c., for sale, where they met a good market. The publication of this Almanac was the cause of a quarrel between him and Bradford, who pronounced it to be a forgery. Keimer made a contract with the legislature of New Jersey, to print the money bills for that province; and he sent Franklin with a press to Burlington to execute this business; who, having accomplished the job, returned to Philadelphia. He soon after quitted the employment of Keimer, and, with a partner, opened another printing house.

No friendship appeared to exist between Keimer and Franklin, who soon became a powerful rival to Keimer, whose affairs were in an embarrassed state. Franklin intended to publish a newspaper, and kept, as he thought, his intention secret, until he could make the necessary preparation for the undertaking. The design, however, came to the knowledge of Keimer, who immediately published a prospectus of one which would speedily issue from his own press; and, notwithstanding Franklin's endeavors to prevent it, the paper made its appearance December 24, 1728. Franklin, being thus anticipated in the execution of a favorite plan, under a borrowed signature ridiculed Keimer and his paper in Bradford's *Mercury*; and by this and other means, succeeded in counteracting the circulation of the paper. Keimer soon found that he was unable to continue his gazette. Franklin well knew his situation, and offered to pay him a small sum, if he would resign the paper to him. The offer was accepted.

Soon after this transaction, Keimer became inattentive to business; and, in consequence, involved himself in debt and was obliged to sell his stock and his printing materials to satisfy his creditors; which having done, he went to Barbadoes and settled there. Franklin mentions Keimer as 'having been one of the French prophets,' and that 'he knew how to imitate their supernatural agitations.'* He characterizes him as 'a perfect novice, and totally ignorant of the world;' but, afterward observes, that 'he was a great knave at heart, that he possessed no particular religion, but a little of all upon occasion.' It does not appear that he was destitute of all worldly knowledge, but he was unfortunate. He might possibly have been more successful in business, had not his exertions been counteracted by those who in pecuniary concerns possessed more sagacity than he did. [See pp. 604–606.]

BENJAMIN FRANKLIN.[11] A sketch of the early part of the life of Franklin, as one of the printers in Boston, has already been given. We left him, after his return from England, employed for a second time in the printing house of Keimer. Hugh Meredith was then an apprentice in the same house, but his apprenticeship had nearly expired. Dissentions took place between Keimer and Franklin, and they parted. Franklin was about returning to Boston; but Meredith persuaded him to remain in Philadelphia. He represented to him that Keimer was embarrassed in business and must soon fail; and observed that this event would make an opening for Franklin, who said he could not go into business for the want of capital. Meredith proposed a connection, and mentioned that his father, who had a high opinion of Franklin, would advance whatever sum was necessary to establish them in business. Franklin closed with the proposal. Meredith's father approved of the partnership; and

* The visionaries he referred to appeared about the year 1724.

engaged with a merchant in the city to send to England for a
press and types.

Franklin, in consequence of this arrangement, compromised
his difference with Keimer and returned to his employment.
The agreement was kept secret, until the printing apparatus arrived. At this time Meredith's indentures expired; and he and
Franklin immediately completed articles of association. They
took a house near the market, set up their press, and began to
use it under the firm of MEREDITH & FRANKLIN. Their first
work was forty sheets of foolscap, folio, of the *History of the*
Quakers, printed for the use of those of that sect who resided in
or near Philadelphia. Franklin daily completed at case the work
of a sheet and distributed the forms; Meredith did the press
work. The text was on a pica type, and the notes, which were
long, on smaller letter. After they had been in business twelve
months, they became, as has been mentioned, the proprietors
of Keimer's newspaper; and were appointed printers to the
general assembly. These advantages resulted from the management of Franklin, who soon after succeeded in his plan of sup-
planting Bradford in the post office.

Before the complete revolution of two years, this partnership
was dissolved, and Franklin came into possession of the whole
business, which he conducted with skill and reputation. By
means of his industry and economy he soon paid his debts, and
began to accumulate property. He opened a shop well filled
with stationery, and did something at bookbinding and bookselling. He annually published *Poor Richard's Almanack*, which
became celebrated; likewise a neat pocket almanac; and in 1741,
he commenced the publication of a magazine, which was continued six months. In 1741, he printed Cicero's *Cato Major on*

old Age, with numerous notes in octavo and quarto. This work was translated by J. Logan of Philadelphia, and is, probably, the very first translation of a Latin classic, made and published in British America.[12] The Greek words were printed from *Italic* characters. After this he became a considerable bookseller.

Franklin remained fifteen years without another partner, but being much engaged in public life, he, in January 174$\frac{7}{8}$, entered into a connection with David Hall. The firm was FRANKLIN & HALL. At this time the Gazette had an extensive circulation in Pennsylvania and in the neighboring colonies, and the business of the printing house was very lucrative. Hall took the sole management of the concern; and, as I am well informed, Franklin received £1,000. currency per annum, for a number of years, as a relinquishment of his share of the profits of the business. In 1765, Franklin sold out all his interest in the printing house to Hall, and the partnership was dissolved February 1, 1766. Besides his connection with Hall, Franklin had a copartnership with Anthony Armbruster,* the printer of a newspaper in Philadelphia, in the German language. This concern began in 1754 or 1755, and ended in 1758.

In 1730, he married the daughter of Mr. Read.[13] She was the young woman whom he saw standing at the door of her father's house, when he walked the streets of Philadelphia with a roll of bread under each arm, while eating a third.

In 1753, Franklin was appointed a deputy postmaster general for the colonies. In 1755, he received a commission as colonel of a regiment of militia, and after the defeat of General Braddock, he raised, by order of government, a body of troops, and

* See Anthony Armbruster, further on.

marched them to the western frontier, then invaded by the
enemy. He built a fort, and placed a competent garrison in it,
and then returned to Philadelphia. In 1757 he was appointed
agent for the province of Pennsylvania, and in this capacity
went to England, with a petition to the king. He remained in
England until 1762, when he returned to Philadelphia. In 1764
he again went to London as agent for the province. In 1766 he
visited Holland, and the next year went to France. While in
England, he was appointed agent for the province of Massachusetts Bay. Soon after the commencement of the revolutionary war he returned to America, and was employed in her
councils. In 1776 he was appointed to assist in the negotiations
at the court of France, and went to Paris for that purpose; and in
1778 he concluded a treaty of alliance between that cabinet and
the United States of America. In September, 1783, he, with
Mr. Jay and Mr. Adams, signed at Paris the articles of peace on
the part of the United States, with Mr. David Hartley on the
part of Great Britain. He afterward signed articles of amity and
commerce between this country and Sweden, and Prussia. In
1784 he returned to Philadelphia. In 1786 he was elected president of the supreme executive council of Pennsylvania, and was
soon after chosen president of several distinguished societies
formed in Philadelphia, some of which had, by his former
exertions, been greatly aided in their establishment.

Franklin was celebrated as an electrician; but as my principal
object is only to take notice of him as a printer, I must refer
those who wish to be acquainted with him as a philosopher, to
his *Life and Works*.

His son, William, was postmaster in Philadelphia in 1754;
clerk of the assembly of Pennsylvania in 1756; appointed gov-

ernor of New Jersey in 1762, and was in that office when the revolutionary war began.

The following anecdote, which has been published on both sides of the Atlantic, discovers the spirit with which Franklin edited his paper, and marks his pointed dislike of prostituting the press to purposes of defamation and scurrility.

Soon after the establishment of his paper, a person brought him a piece, which he requested him to publish in the *Pennsylvania Gazette*. Franklin desired that the piece might be left for his consideration until next day, when he would give an answer. The person returned at the time appointed, and received from Franklin this communication: 'I have perused your piece, and find it to be scurrilous and defamatory. To determine whether I should publish it or not, I went home in the evening, purchased a two penny loaf at the baker's, and with water from the pump made my supper; I then wrapped myself up in my great coat, and laid down on the floor and slept till morning, when, on another loaf and a mug of water, I made my breakfast. From this regimen I feel no inconvenience whatever. Finding I can live in this manner, I have formed a determination never to prostitute my press to the purposes of corruption, and abuse of this kind, for the sake of gaining a more comfortable subsistence.'*

The following facts will show that Franklin retained a regard for the trade until the close of his life. In 1788, about two years before his death, a number of printers and booksellers met

* Bills of lading formerly began with 'Shipped by the Grace of God,' &c. Some people of Philadelphia objected to this phraseology as making light of serious things. Franklin therefore printed some without these words and inserted in his paper the following advertisement: 'Bills of Lading for sale at this office, with or without the Grace of God.'

together in Philadelphia, to form some regulations for the benefit of the trade. Bache, grandson of Franklin, and myself, were of the number. After the first meeting, I conversed with Dr. Franklin on the subject of our convention. He approved the measures proposed, and requested that the next meeting might be at his house, as he was unable himself to go abroad. The meeting was accordingly holden there; and although he was much afflicted with pain, he voluntarily took minutes of the proceedings, and appeared to be interested in them.* He evidently had much at heart the success of his grandson, who was then printing, at the recommendation of his grandfather, an edition of the minor classics.

Franklin, after the commencement of the war, brought from Europe a very valuable printing apparatus, which he purchased in London. He also imported the materials of a type foundery, which had been used in Paris. These articles for a foundery, though extensive, did not prove very valuable. He put the whole into the possession of his grandson, Benjamin Franklin Bache, who for some time carried on book printing, but eventually published a newspaper well known by the name of *The Aurora*; and made little use of the materials for the foundery.

In 1788, Franklin retired from public business. He had, for several of the preceding years, been troubled with a calculus, which increased to such a degree as, during a few months preceding his death, to confine him to his bed. In April, 1790, he was seized with an inflammation of the breast, attended with a fever, which terminated his earthly existence on the 19th of

---

* Several attempts have been made to establish rules and regulations for the benefit of the trade, but they have generally not proved successful.

that month, at the age of eighty-five years.* He left by will 1,000*l.* to the city of Philadelphia, and the same sum to his native town Boston. These sums were to be loaned annually to young mechanics of a certain description in the manner and on the conditions by him prescribed for one hundred years, a certain part of the proceeds then to be applied to particular public uses, and the other part again loaned for another hundred years, after which the final amount to be appropriated for the benefit of the public in the manner directed in his will. He bequeathed to the Pennsylvania Hospital the old debts due to him as a printer, stationer and postmaster previous to the year 1757. The sums are small, and although numerous, have produced little or nothing.

Long before his death, he wrote the following epitaph upon himself:

The Body of
Benjamin Franklin, Printer,
(Like the cover of an old Book,
Its contents worn out,
And stript of its lettering and gilding)
Lies here, food for worms!
Yet the work itself shall not be lost,
For it will, as he believed, appear once more
In a new
And more beautiful edition,
Corrected and amended
By its Author.

* On the 30th of April, 1800, ten years after his death, 'a fete was celebrated in the Temple of Victory, at Paris [France] in memory of Benjamin Franklin, one of the benefactors of humanity.'—*Publiciste Paris paper.* Franklin's father died in Boston, January 16, 1745. Peter Franklin, brother to the doctor, and postmaster in Philadelphia, died in July, 1766, aged 74.

HUGH MEREDITH was the son of a worthy and respectable
farmer. He was born in Pennsylvania, and bred to husbandry.

Having more taste for books than for agriculture, at the age
of thirty he came to Philadelphia, and bound himself for several
years as a pressman to Keimer. He was with him when Franklin
returned from his first voyage to London. Franklin, being again
employed in Keimer's office, became intimate with Meredith.
Their acquaintance produced the copartnership of which an
account has already been given. Franklin mentions Meredith as
'honest, sensible, having some experience, and fond of reading,
but addicted to drinking.' Meredith, the father, aware of this
propensity in his son, was the more ready to promote his connection with Franklin, and readily helped them, in the hope
that Franklin, whom he knew to be temperate, 'would cure his
son of the too free use of brandy.' Franklin, however, in that
attempt, did not succeed. He soon considered Meredith as a
dead weight, and was desirous to throw him off, which he
effected with ease.

Meredith was frank and ingenuous. He found that his partner
was dissatisfied, and discovered that he himself was not well
qualified to be a printer. His father, owing to some recent disappointments, was not able to make the last payment for the
press and types, now become due to the merchant who imported them. From these considerations, Meredith was induced
to propose a dissolution of the partnership, and offered to relinquish his right in the stock and business, on the moderate
condition that Franklin should take upon himself the debts of
the company, pay Meredith thirty pounds currency, and furnish
him with a new saddle. The offer was gladly embraced; the
necessary writings were immediately executed, and the part-

nership was dissolved. Meredith received the thirty pounds and the saddle, joined a number of his Pennsylvania friends who were farmers, and with them went and settled in North Carolina.

DAVID HARRY was born in Pennsylvania. His parents were respectable, and his connections opulent. He served an apprenticeship with Keimer, and had just completed it when Keimer was obliged to sell his press and types. Harry purchased them, and succeeded his master in business. This took place about July, 1729.

Franklin, who had then separated from Meredith, was fearful that in Harry he should find a powerful rival, and was induced to propose a partnership to him. Harry rejected the proposal with some disdain. Franklin observes, that 'Harry lived extravagantly, pursued amusements, neglected business, and business neglected him.' Before the expiration of the year 1730, he followed his late master, Keimer, to Barbadoes, and took with him his printing materials.

In Barbadoes Harry began printing, and employed Keimer as his journeyman. He had never acquired the habit of industry, and Barbadoes was not a place calculated to cure him of a dissipated course of life. In a few months he became deeply involved in debt, and was induced to sell his press and types to Keimer, who found friends to assist him in the purchase. Harry returned to Pennsylvania, and followed husbandry.

WILLIAM BRADFORD, Third, was the son of William Bradford Junior, and grandson of the first William Bradford who printed in Philadelphia. He was born in New York. When very young, his uncle, Andrew Bradford, who had no children, adopted and educated him as his son and heir, and instructed him in the art of printing. When he was about nineteen years of age, his affectionate foster mother, the wife of Andrew, died, and some time after, his foster father married Cornelia Smith, of New York. She had an adopted niece, whom she was desirous that William Bradford, the adopted nephew of her husband, should marry when he became of age. William's affections being engaged by another object, the plan was frustrated; and, in consequence, she imbibed a settled prejudice against him, and did not attempt to conceal it. She treated him unkindly, and finally he was obliged to leave the house of his foster father. She prevailed on her husband to revoke the will which he had made in favor of William, and to make one in her own favor. It has been said, that her conduct in general was such as rendered her husband very unhappy. William when about twenty years of age became the partner of Andrew; but the wife caused this partnership to be dissolved, after it had continued one year. It began in December, 1739, and ended in December, 1740.*

In 1741 Bradford went to England; visited his relations there; returned in 1742 with printing materials and a collection of books, and began business on the west side of Second street, between Market and Chestnut streets. In the same year he married the daughter of Thomas Budd who was imprisoned with the first William Bradford in 1692. In December, 1742, he commenced the publication of a newspaper, which was continued by him and his successors until after the year 1800. In 1743, he removed to the southeast corner of Blackhorse alley, where, at the sign of the Bible, he printed and sold books.

* These circumstances were related to me by one of the family.

In 1748 he was chosen lieutenant of a militia company, and in 1756 was made captain.

In 1754 Bradford removed to the corner of Market and Front streets, and there opened a house for the convenience of the commercial part of the community, which was called the London Coffee House. In 1762 he opened, in company with a Mr. Kydd, a marine insurance office, where much business was done. In 1766 he took his son Thomas as a partner in the printing business. Their firm was WILLIAM & THOMAS BRADFORD.[14]

Bradford was a warm advocate for, and a staunch defender of the rights of his country. He was among the first in the city to oppose the British stamp act, in 1765; and he was equally hostile to the succeeding offensive measures of the British ministry. He literally compiled with a resolve of the early revolutionists, 'to risk life and fortune for the preservation of the liberty of his country' by taking arms in an early stage of the revolutionary war; and, although he had reached the age at which the law exempts men from military service, he encountered the fatigues of a winter campaign, and did duty as a major of militia in the memorable battle of Trenton. He shared the honors of the day at Princeton, and returned colonel of the regiment of which he went out major. He was at Fort Mifflin when it was attacked by the Hessians; and in several other engagements.*

A few days before the British troops took possession of Philadelphia, Bradford was entrusted by Governor Wharton with the command of the city, and the superintendence of removing

* He was afterwards appointed deputy commissary general. On September 11, 1777, congress resolved: 'That Major General Armstrong be directed, forthwith to cause all the printing presses and types in this city and Germantown, to be removed to secure places in the country, excepting Mr. Bradford's press in this city, with English types.' But it does not appear that this resolve was carried into effect.

the stores. Having performed this duty, he left the city as the enemy was entering it, and repaired to Fort Mifflin, where he remained until that fortress was evacuated. From that time Bradford remained at Trenton until the British army left Philadelphia, when he returned to the city, and reopened his printing house and coffee room; but the customs and manners of the citizens were changed, and he perceived that business had found new channels. He returned from the hazards of public service with a broken constitution and a shattered fortune. He soon lost his affectionate wife. Age advanced upon him with hasty steps, and a paralytic stroke warned him of his approaching dissolution. After a few more feeble attacks, he calmly yielded to the king of terrors.

After peace was established, he had consoled himself under his misfortunes; and, in his most solitary hours, reflected with pleasure, that he had done all in his power to secure for his country a name among independent nations; and he frequently said to his children, 'though I bequeath you no estate, I leave you in the enjoyment of liberty.' He was a very respectable printer.

He died September 25, 1791, aged 72. His body was interred in the Presbyterian graveyard, in Arch street; and his obsequies were attended by a large number of citizens, and particularly by those who were the early and steady friends of the revolution.

Bradford left three sons, and three daughters. His eldest son, Thomas, has been mentioned as the partner of his father. The second son, William, studied law, became attorney general of the United States, and died August 25, 1793; Schuyler, the third son, died in the East Indies.

CORNELIA BRADFORD was the second wife, and eventually the widow of Andrew Bradford. She succeeded her husband in the business of printing and bookselling in 1742. About four months after his death, she took Warner as a partner in the concerns of the printing house. The firm was ISAIAH WARNER & CORNELIA BRADFORD. This partnership lasted only till October, 1744, when the widow resumed the press, and continued printing until 1746, at which time, or soon after, she retired from business. She died in 1755. Her estate was settled by George Smith and Cornelia his wife, who, on the 11th of September of that year, published an advertisement for that purpose in *The Pennsylvania Journal*.

ISAIAH WARNER was born in Philadelphia, and served his apprenticeship either with Bradford or Franklin. In 1742, he opened, in Chestnut street, the fourth printing house in that city; and published Jacob Taylor's Almanack, and several small works, which appear to be well executed. Soon after the death of Andrew Bradford, Warner entered into partnership with his widow. This partnership ended in the autumn of 1744. I have seen none of his printing after that time, and cannot find any further account of him. At the close of this year, three newspapers were printed in Philadelphia, viz.: The *Mercury*, the *Gazette*, and the *Journal*.

GEORGE BRINTAL. I am not sure that Brintal was a printer. All that I can gather respecting him, is, that when Warner's partnership with Cornelia Bradford ceased, Brintal managed the concerns of her printing house; and some time after had an interest in the publication of the *American Mercury*. I have not

found his name in the imprint to that paper, of which I have
files to 1746.

JOSEPH CRELLIUS. In 1743, he lived in Market street, but the
same year removed to Arch street. He was a German, and
printed a newspaper weekly in his native language. He kept an
evening school, and taught the English and German languages
grammatically.

His was the first German newspaper published in Philadelphia. I cannot learn how long it existed; but it was certainly
continued several years.

GODHART ARMBRUSTER. He was from Manheim, Germany,
where he served his apprenticeship to the printing business. He
came to Philadelphia in the year 1743, and soon after began
printing in the German language. In 1746, he advertised several
small books from his press, to be sold by him 'at the German
printing house in Race street.' About this time he began the
publication of a newspaper in German.

His brother, Anthony Armbruster, was for some time connected with him; but the business appears to have been conducted in the name of Godhart till 1752, when it was carried on
by Anthony. A few years after Godhart returned to Europe,
where he died.

DAVID HALL[15] has been mentioned as the partner of Franklin.
He was born in Scotland; and brought up a printer in Edinburgh. From that place he went to London, and worked in a
printing house in which Strahan, afterward a famous law
printer to the king, was at that time a journeyman. After Hall
came to this country he was eighteen years in partnership with

Franklin; and, in May, 1766, when that connection was dissolved, he formed another with William Sellers, under the firm of HALL & SELLERS. Their business was lucrative; they printed for government, and continued the *Pennsylvania Gazette*. Besides printing, Hall, before, during, and after his partnership with Franklin, conducted a book and stationery store on a large scale, on his own account. Had he not been connected with Franklin he might have been a formidable rival to him in the business of printing and bookselling. Hall & Sellers were the printers of the paper money issued by congress during the revolutionary war.

He died December 24, 1772, aged fifty eight years. Hall was well acquainted with the art of printing; and was an industrious workman, of first rate abilities; a prudent and impartial conductor of the Gazette; and a benevolent and worthy man.

JAMES CHATTIN printed in Philadelphia as early as 1752. His printing house was 'in Church-Alley, next door to the Pipe.' He was employed chiefly on pamphlets; and was, I believe, a quaker. In 1755 he advertised his publications at reduced prices, for sale 'at the Newest Printing-Office in Market Street, South Side of the Jersey Market.' In 1771 he informed the public that he had long been out of employment; and that he proposed to do business punctually, and with secresy, as a conveyancer and bookkeeper, and had taken an office for that purpose in Second street. After being several years a master printer, he was reduced to the condition of a journeyman.

ANTHONY ARMBRUSTER was born in Manheim, in Germany and was the brother of Gotthart, alias Godhart, Arm-

bruster, who has been mentioned as a printer of books etc., in
the German language, in Philadelphia. Anthony left Germany
and came to Philadelphia with his brother, or arrived soon
after him, about 1743. Whether he served a part, or the whole
of his apprenticeship in Germany, is not known, but he was
employed in the printing house of his brother many years after
his arrival. Although his name did not at any time appear in
copartnership with his brother, they were thought to be connected together in business from 1748 to 1753.

A society was formed in London for the benevolent purpose
of 'promoting religious knowledge among the German emigrants in Pennsylvania.' I cannot ascertain the exact time when
this society was instituted, but it was, probably, as early as 1740.
A press for printing religious tracts, school books, etc., in the
German language, was, by this society, established in Philadelphia. From the funds of this society it is supposed Joseph Crellius received some aid in printing a newspaper and some small
school books in the German language, in Philadelphia, as early
as 1743. Sower of Germantown, about this time, was assisted in
carrying through his press an edition of the German translation
of the Bible.

Crellius, in his publication of a German newspaper, was followed by Godhart Armbruster, and he was succeeded by his
brother Anthony, all of whom, it is probable, were printers to
the society, and made use of their press. The fact is substantiated
as relates to Anthony Armbruster.*

In 1753 the business was conducted by him, and until 1756, in
Third street. He there printed in German, *The History of the
First Martyrs*, 326 pages, 12mo. Also *The True Christian's Monu-*

* See farther on, an account of German newspapers published in Philadelphia.

ment, with copper plates. Anthony understood copper-plate as well as letter-press printing. The latter he could perform, as was then fashionable, with two colors, black and red. In this way he printed, for several years, his German Almanac. Sower of Germantown, at that time, printed his Almanac in like manner, but both discontinued the practice about 1758.

Anthony Armbruster, in 1754, entered into a copartnership with Benjamin Franklin, which continued till 1758.* Part of the time Franklin was in England. In Anthony's books is kept, from 1754 to 1758, an account current with Benjamin Franklin, which relates to the German office. Before, and for the first two or three years of the partnership between Armbruster and Franklin, they were on very intimate terms. Armbruster named one of his children Benjamin Franklin, and on this occasion Franklin stood its godfather. Armbruster failed in business while Franklin was in England, and a general settlement of his printing concern did not take place until after Franklin's return, in 1762. They then differed, and it seems were no longer friends. Armbruster soon after, to ridicule Franklin, published a caricature print, in which, within a group, Franklin was conspicuously represented in a very ludicrous situation.

Anthony Armbruster's printing materials, in 1760, passed into the hands of Lewis Weiss and Peter Miller, neither of whom were printers. They were conveyancers, and both Germans. They continued the German paper, and Anthony was their printer during the short time they had the press.

---

* This appeared from the account books of Armbruster, in the possession of one of his sons who resided in Philadelphia. In these books Armbruster charges Franklin for translating the Almanac into German, £200 each year; 4 years, £800. The almanacs were charged at 5s. per dozen; demy paper is charged at 12s. per ream; calf skins, 1s. per pair.

In 1762 Anthony again obtained the press and types which had been used by Weiss and Miller, or otherwise procured a printing apparatus, for in July, that year, he opened a printing house 'at the upper end of Moravian Alley.' There he printed German school books, and some small articles in English. Nicholas Hasselbaugh, it is said, was for a short time the silent partner of Anthony. Whether Anthony continued the publication of the German newspaper in 1763, I cannot learn, but he published one in 1764, when the press was removed to Arch street. Miller at the same time advertised that 'he has now set up a new printing office in Moravian Alley, near the Brethren's church.' During the time he was in business, Anthony made several removals, and at one time he resided in Race street.

Armbruster again failed in business, and could not recover his standing as a master printer. Again his press and types went into other hands. He now became a journeyman, and was employed for several years by printers in the city; after which he was a pressman to Isaac Collins, in Trenton, New Jersey. After remaining some considerable time with Collins, he returned to Philadelphia, and from thence went to Germantown, where he was again employed as a journeyman. He was three times married. His first wife was a good worker at press, and often assisted her husband in that employment.

Anthony was naturally very superstitious, and after he became a journeyman, he was, at times, under a species of insanity. Many accounts are given of his extraordinary conduct when he was afflicted with mental derangement. Like many others, he believed that Blanchard and other pirates had, in their time, hid money and other treasures along the sea coast of the northern part of this continent, and on the shores of the Delaware and other rivers. With a number of associates he spent much time in fruitless searches after that which he could not find. He imagined that he could, by a special charm, raise or lay the devil; notwithstanding which he was often in great fear and dread of a visit from his Satanic majesty. He believed in witchcraft, and was in fear of attacks from witches. Like Baron Swedenborg he apprehended that he had intercourse with invisible spirits. Many stories are related of him as evidence of his mental delusion.

He died at Germantown, July, 1796, at the age of seventy-nine years, and was buried in the Dutch church burying ground, in Fifth street, Philadelphia. He left several children.

WEISS & MILLER. Lewis Weiss and Peter Miller were Germans. They were both conveyancers, and unacquainted with printing. They appear to have been friends to Anthony Armbruster, and in 1760, when he failed in business, took his press and types, and employed him to conduct the concerns of the printing house. The *German Gazette* was continued, and the printing of that and other works, done in their names, for about two years, when this connection seems to have dissolved, and Armbruster again began printing on his own account.

Whilst this partnership continued, they published the *German Almanack* that had for many preceding years been printed by Armbruster. The imprint to that for 1762 is, in English, thus: 'Printed and to be sold at the High Dutch Printing-House, in Race street, and also sold by Peter Miller, and by distant merchants.' At the end of this Almanac is an advertisement of 'Peter Miller, in Second street, at the sign of the hand and pen, where he writes deeds, &c., agreeably to the latest forms.' In

1762 'Lewis Weiss and Peter Miller' advertise 'just published and to be sold by them in Philadelphia, the characters and acts,' etc.

The same year William Bradford, David Hand, and Lewis Weiss, advertised to take in subscriptions, at their several places of abode, for an engraved plan of the city and liberties of Philadelphia. In 1764, Armbruster advertises his intention of printing 'a new edition of *Backmeyer's English and Dutch Grammar*,' for which subscriptions were received by himself, and several others whose names are mentioned. Among them is that of Peter Miller, in Second street. This Peter Miller was called a man of wit. He was for many years employed by the city proprietors as a surveyor. He died of the dropsy, in 1794, and was buried in the Quaker's burying ground, between Third and Fourth streets.

Weiss & Miller, August 12, 1762, advertise 'Charters and Acts of Assembly from the first settlement of the province, and collection of Laws that have been in force, etc., in 2 volumes, to be had either in folio or . . . . . . price 40s. bound. Published by Lewis Weiss and Peter Miller.'

ANDREW STEUART was born in Belfast, Ireland, and served his apprenticeship with James Macgee, in that city. He set up a press 'in Lætitia-Court,' Philadelphia, in 1758. His business was confined to pamphlets, ballads, and small jobs. He afterwards lived at the Bible-in-Heart in Second street, between Market and Arch streets.

Steuart was not over nice as it respected the publications of others. In 1762, he reprinted, immediately after its first appearance from the press, *Science, a Poem*, by Francis Hopkinson,

Esq. This poem was published in quarto, price 1s. 6d. by Dunlap, Hall, and others. Steuart's edition was in 12mo. and he advertised it for sale 'at three pence single, one shilling per dozen, or six shillings a hundred,' with this remark, that as his 'object was to promote the circulation of this excellent piece, he hoped that neither the author or any one else would imagine that he intended to "Rob him of his gain," or, that his design was "To reap the labour'd harvest of his brain."'

About the year 1764, Steuart went to Wilmington, North Carolina, with a press, and part of his types; and he left the other part, and his book shop, in the care of Thomas Macgee and his apprentice Joseph Crukshank. He never returned. The business was continued in Philadelphia, in his name, until he died. This event took place in 1769, at Cape Fear.

He owned a lot of land in Spruce street, and had accumulated other property. [See p. 562.]

WILLIAM DUNLAP was a native of the north of Ireland. He served his apprenticeship in Philadelphia, with William Bradford. In 1754, he began printing at Lancaster; but removed from thence to Philadelphia in 1757, and married a relation of Mrs. Franklin, wife of Benjamin Franklin, in consequence of which connection Franklin appointed him postmaster.

He opened a printing house and bookstore in Market street, and did considerable business as a printer, bookseller and stationer, till 1765. His printing was correctly and handsomely executed. He also engaged in the study of divinity. In the year 1766, he sold off the principal part of his stock in trade at auction, resigned the management of his printing house to his nephew John Dunlap, as a partner, and went to England. He

obtained ordination in the church of England, and returned to
America in 1767; and in 1768 became the rector of the parish of
Stratton, in King and Queen's county, Virginia.

He printed *John Jerman's Almanack* in 1757, and began the
publication of *Father Abraham's Almanack*, which he continued
annually. When he settled in Virginia, he resigned his business
and his printing materials to his nephew for an ample consideration, to be paid by installments.

HENRY MILLER.[16] A friend of his, well acquainted with his
history, has informed me his name was John Henry Miller; but
that he styled himself in the imprint to the books he published
in Philadelphia, Henry Miller only. He was born in the principality of Waldeck on the Upper Rhine, March 12, 1702, where
his parents then resided. In 1715, they returned to their native
place, a town near Zurich, in Switzerland, and took with them
their son whom they apprenticed to a printer in Basle. After his
apprenticeship he was at first employed in a printing house at
Zurich, but soon set up a press and published a newspaper.
Quitting business at Zurich, he traveled to Leipsic and Altona;
from thence to London; from London to Amsterdam; then
through France; and again to Germany and Holland. In 1741 he
came to America, and was for sometime in Franklin's printing
house in Philadelphia. In 1742 he returned to Europe; married
there in 1743, and in 1744 opened a printing house in Marienburg, Germany, and there published a newspaper. His residence
at Marienburg was not of long continuance; as he again set out
on his travels, visited England a second, and Holland a third
time, and returned to Germany. In 1751 he came again to

America, and was concerned in a German printing house in Philadelphia or Lancaster; but soon after was employed by William Bradford. In 1754 he once more embarked for Europe, where he remained until 1760, when he returned to Philadelphia with new printing materials and opened a printing house in Second street.

In 1762 he began the publication of a newspaper in the German language, which he continued some years after the revolutionary war ended. He published annually a German almanac.

He printed school and some other books in the German, and a few in the English language; and dealt considerably as a bookseller. In 1771, his printing house was 'in Race Street, opposite Moravian Alley.' In 1776, he completed printing in six volumes, folio, *The Votes*, etc., of the General assembly of Pennsylvania, passed in many of the preceding years.

Miller was a good scholar and an excellent printer. He corresponded with some literary characters in Germany and Holland. In his religion he was a Moravian, and in politics a whig. He was a warm advocate of American liberty. He removed from Philadelphia at the time the royal army took possession of the city in 1777. He left his printing materials in his house. These were used by the British in printing proclamations, etc. They carried off part of them when they left Philadelphia. After they evacuated the city, Miller returned to it, and resumed the publication of his newspaper, etc.

On the 26th of May, 1779, he discontinued his public journal, and at that time published a farewell address to his readers. In that address he observed, that it was nearly fifty years since he first published a newspaper in Switzerland; that he had been obliged to continue business till that time of life; that he was then approaching the age of fourscore; but, that a man, when he arrives to his sixtieth year, should commence his sabbath, or day of rest from the cares and troubles of this life. In 1780, he resigned business altogether; sold his printing materials, and retired to Bethlehem, Pennsylvania. He died there March 31, 1782, aged eighty years. His wife died some years before, at the same place. She was a well-bred woman; spoke the French language fluently, and was an excellent painter in water colors. In this employment she was for some time engaged as a preceptress in Bethlehem. Miller was noted as a pedestrian, and frequently went to Bethlehem, fifty-three miles from Philadelphia, and returned on foot. Having no family, he bequeathed, it is said, a part of his property to Melchior Steiner, who had been his apprentice.

JAMES ADAMS began printing in Philadelphia about the year 1760; and, in 1761, he removed to Wilmington, Delaware. [See pp. 527–528.]

THOMAS BRADFORD was the eldest son of William Bradford, the second printer of that name in Philadelphia, and was born on the 4th of May, 1745.[17] Thomas's mother was daughter of Thomas Budd, who sided with George Keith, etc., in their opposition to Lieutenant Governor Lloyd and his party, in the noted quarrel among the quakers in 1692. Budd, at this time, was arrested and imprisoned with the first William Bradford for writing and publishing against the prevailing party of their quaker brethren. Thomas was named after his father-in-law. He was for several years in the college at Philadelphia; but in 1762, his father took him from that seminary, and placed him in his printing house; and in 1766, received him as a partner in business, as has been before related. Their printing house was then at the corner of Front and Market streets. The father died in 1791; the son continued the business, and published a daily paper in Philadelphia, till 1814.

Thomas Bradford was the great grandson of William Bradford, who first printed in Pennsylvania, and who was one of the first settlers of the colony.

WILLIAM SELLERS, the partner of David Hall, was from England, and served his apprenticeship in London. He began business about 1764, and kept a book and stationery store 'in Arch Street, between Second and Third Street.' On the death of David Hall, his sons, William and David, became the partners of Sellers. The firm of HALL & SELLERS was continued, and printing executed, as usual, at the old stand in Market street.* Sellers was a correct and experienced printer, a good citizen, well known, and as well respected.

He died February, 1804, aged seventy-nine years.

WILLIAM GODDARD has already been mentioned as a printer at Providence. He opened a printing house in Philadelphia, November, 1766. There he entered into partnership with two men of eminence in their line, Joseph Galloway, by profession a lawyer, speaker of the house of assembly, and afterwards a delegate to congress, and Thomas Wharton the elder, a merchant of the sect of quakers; both men of large property and

---

* 'The Newest Printing Office' on the board over the door, remained until 1814. It was placed there by Franklin.

great influence. They were to supply a capital to carry on business extensively, and each of them to own a quarter part of the printing materials, and to draw a proportional part of the profits. Goddard was to pay for and to own half of the materials, to manage the concerns of the printing house in his own name, and to draw one half of the proceeds of trade. The last clause in the contract between the parties, was, from the political character of Galloway and Wharton, thought to be singular; it was as follows, viz.: 'In case Benjamin Franklin, Esq., [then in England] on his return to Philadelphia, should incline to become a partner in the business, he shall be admitted as such; and in that case, the shares, parts and proportions of the expense, charges and profits aforesaid, shall be as follows, viz., two ninths thereof shall belong to Joseph Galloway, two ninths thereof to Thomas Wharton, two ninths to Benjamin Franklin, and three ninths thereof to William Goddard.' Galloway and Wharton were strongly attached to the measures of the British ministry, but cautious of expressing their opinions. The firm printed for the assembly of Pennsylvania, and published a newspaper, *The Pennsylvania Chronicle*, which for some time bore the appearance of impartiality; but at length Mr. Dickinson, author of the celebrated *Farmer's Letters*, and several other reputable characters on the side of the country, were violently attacked and abused. Galloway and others, behind the curtain, wrote, and Goddard,* who was tied to the pursestrings of his partners, was compelled to publish as they directed. Difficulties soon arose, from various causes, between the members of this partnership. Goddard was dissatisfied with the power which Galloway and

* See his account of the partnership.

Wharton arrogated over him, and they were displeased with his management of the paper, and other concerns of the firm. He stated, in a pamphlet entitled *The Partnership*, which he published after their separation, that they threatened to ruin him, if he did not follow their directions, and accede to their proposal to admit another partner into the firm, viz., Benjamin Towne, then a journeyman printer. This intended partner Goddard knew was to be a spy upon his actions, and a check upon his management of the concerns of the company; but he was obliged to submit and receive him in November, 1769. The firm of the company was now GODDARD & TOWNE. In July, 1770, their disagreement grew to a rupture; and after a connection of about nine months with Towne, they separated.

A state of hostility ensued, and newspapers, handbills, and pamphlets were filled with the ebullitions of their animosity. Goddard endeavored to prevent the reelection of Galloway to a seat in the house of assembly, but failed; for although Galloway did not succeed in the county of Philadelphia, he obtained his election in the county of Bucks. His real political character was not then known, and his influence continued to be greater than Goddard could counteract, although he fought like a veteran. Goddard was unable to answer the demands of the creditors of the company, who were urged to press him for payment; and he became embarrassed, but was enabled to leave the city honorably in 1773, and go to Baltimore, where he hoped to obtain business more lucrative, and a residence more tranquil. He succeeded in gaining many valuable friends in Maryland and the states adjacent.

Goddard's partners, Galloway, Wharton, and Towne, after the establishment of independence, were all proscribed as ene-

mies to the country, by the legislature of Pennsylvania.* [See
pp. 321–322, 534–540.]

JOHN DUNLAP[18] was born in the north of Ireland. He was the
nephew of William Dunlap, by whom he was taught printing
in Philadelphia. When William went to England to take orders
for the church, in 1766, he left the management of his printing
house to his nephew, who, in his own name, conducted the
business for their joint benefit. Book printing had been their
object; but, after the uncle was settled in the church at Virginia,
he resigned the printing house and its concerns to John, who
purchased the printing materials and printed on his own account, and established a newspaper. His printing house was 'on
the south side of the Jersey Market.' In 1778 congress appointed
Dunlap to print their journals, and for five years he continued
to be their printer. He retired from business in 1795, with a
handsome fortune and a good reputation. He received from
government, as payment for printing, several lots of land in
Philadelphia. This land when it came into his possession was
valued at only a few hundred pounds, Pennsylvania currency;
but the great increase of buildings soon made it more valuable,
and in 1809 he sold one square, extending from Market to
Chestnut street, and from Eleventh to Twelfth street, for more
than one hundred thousand dollars.

Dunlap executed his printing in a neat and correct manner.
It is said that, whilst he conducted a newspaper, he never inserted a paragraph which wounded the feelings of an individual!

* Galloway fled to England at the commencement of the revolution, and his
large estate was confiscated. Wharton, who had more prudence, remained in
the country. He had many worthy connections, and, politics aside, was not
destitute of those amiable qualities which create respect. His estate was not
confiscated.

After the war commenced, in 1775, he was appointed a captain of a company of horse in the city militia. In 1808 he resigned his commission.

Dunlap died, in Philadelphia, November 27, 1812, of apoplexy, aged sixty-five. His funeral was attended by the field, staff and commissioned officers of the first brigade, first division, of Pennsylvania militia, the troop of horse of which he was formerly commander, and by a large concourse of other citizens.

BENJAMIN MECOM has been mentioned as a printer in Antigua, Boston, and New Haven. He removed from Connecticut, and opened a printing house in Philadelphia, in 1768. He attempted a small periodical work, which will be mentioned with the newspapers and magazines published in that city. Afterwards he was in the printing house of Goddard in Philadelphia, and, in 1774, he left the city, and was employed by Isaac Collins, at Burlington, New Jersey, where he closed his typographical career. He lived some time in Salem county, and finished his earthly pilgrimage soon after the beginning of the revolutionary war.

Mecom, though singular in his manners, and deficient in the art of managing business to profit, was a man of ingenuity and integrity; and as a printer he was correct and skillful. He was the first person in this country, as far as I know, who attempted stereotype printing. He actually cast plates for several pages of the New Testament and made considerable progress towards the completion of them, but he never effected it.

ROBERT BELL was born in Glasgow, Scotland, where he was brought up to book-binding. He then went to Berwick-upon-

Tweed, and worked sometime at that business; after which he removed to Dublin and commenced bookseller, and had an extensive trade; but in a few years failed. He married in Dublin, and was for some time the partner of George Alexander Stevens, of facetious memory.

He came to America about the year 1767, and established himself first as a book auctioneer, and afterwards as a bookseller, in Philadelphia. In 1772, he published Blackstone's *Commentaries* in four volumes octavo; in which undertaking he was supported by a liberal subscription. He had before published Robertson's *Charles Fifth*. These two works may be considered as the first fruits of a spirit of enterprise in book printing in that city. Soon after the publication of Blackstone's *Commentaries*, he opened a printing house in Third street, where the Union library had lately been kept, and printed several other works of less magnitude.

Bell was the publisher of the celebrated pamphlet entitled *Common Sense*, written by Thomas Paine. He employed Paine some time afterwards as a clerk, etc. When *Common Sense* was committed to the press, there was a scarcity of paper; and all the broken quires of paper in Bell's warehouse were collected and culled for the first impression. The work had a very rapid sale, went through several editions in Philadelphia, and was republished in all parts of United America.

After the war took place, Bell became celebrated as a book auctioneer; and as such was known from Virginia to New Hampshire. He disposed, in that way, of his 'jewels and diamonds,' in New York, Boston, Baltimore, Norfolk, etc.* He

---

* His advertisements for the sale of books by auction, were commonly headed with 'Jewels and Diamonds to be sold or sacrificed, by Robert Bell, humble Provedore to the Sentimentalists.'

was a thorough bookseller, punctual and fair in his dealings; and, as a companion, he was sensible, social and witty.

He left Philadelphia in 1784, with an intention to visit Charleston, South Carolina, where he had sent a quantity of books to sell at auction; but on his way was taken sick at Richmond, Virginia, and died there September 23, 1784, aged nearly sixty years.

JOSEPH CRUKSHANK was born in Philadelphia, and served an apprenticeship with Andrew Steuart. He was one of the society of Friends, and printed books for them as well as for his own sales. He opened a printing house in 1769, and soon after a book and stationery store, in Third street, near Market street, in company with Isaac Collins. Their firm was CRUKSHANK & COLLINS. The partnership continued only one year, when it was dissolved, and Collins removed to Burlington.

Crukshank took a good stand in Market street, and traded very considerably. In 1772, he printed for Bell *Blackstone's Commentaries* in four volumes octavo; also several other works of importance. Fair in his dealings, punctual in his payments, and amiable in his manners, he was greatly esteemed by his fellow citizens.

WILLIAM EVITT, was born in Pennsylvania, and served an apprenticeship with Andrew Steuart. In 1770, he printed 'at the Bible-in-Heart, Strawberry-Alley,' with the press and types which had been Steuart's, which he purchased. He issued proposals for publishing weekly, on Saturday evening, a newspaper, to be entitled *The Pennsylvania Evening Post*. This paper never made its appearance; but one of the same title was, afterwards, published by Benjamin Towne.

I can find no other particulars of Evitt which will be creditable to the trade. He was, for a time, a journeyman; and, afterwards, became a soldier in the American army, and died in the service of his country.

WILLIAM HALL & DAVID HALL Junior, were the sons of David Hall, and were taught printing by their father. After his death, in 1772, they became the partners of Sellers; and the firm of HALL & SELLERS was continued until the death of Sellers. The business was then for several years managed in the names of WILLIAM & DAVID HALL. It was, afterwards, transferred to WILLIAM HALL Junior. William Hall Senior, was for several successive years, a member of the Pennsylvania legislature.

JAMES HUMPHREYS Junior, was the son of James Humphreys, a conveyancer, etc.[19] He was born in Philadelphia, received an education at the college in that city, and was there placed under the care of an uncle, to study physic; but disliking the profession, he became an apprentice to William Bradford, and was by him taught printing. Supplied with good printing materials, he began business 'at the lower corner of Black-horse Alley, in Front Street,' and in January, 1775, he published a newspaper.

Humphreys printed several books before the commencement of the revolutionary war, and among them were Sterne's *Works* in five volumes, duodecimo, Wettenhall's *Greek Grammar*, corrected for the use of the college in Philadelphia; and afterwards, *Strictures on Paine's Common Sense*. Two editions of the last work, consisting of several thousand copies each, were sold in a few months.

Humphreys having acted as clerk in the court of chancery,

and, as a qualification, taken the oath of allegiance to the British king; he, on that account, refused to bear arms in favor of his country, and against the government of England; and was, in consequence, denounced as a tory. His paper, it has been said, was under the influence of the British government, and he was several times in the hands of the *people*. He had done no injury to the individuals who were dissatisfied with his political opinions, and from them he received no essential abuse. Among the whigs he had good friends, one of whom was Doctor Rittenhouse, a literary character well known in our country.

Benjamin Towne, who began the publication of *The Evening Post*, a rival paper, was not friendly to Humphreys, and published a number of pieces calculated to excite the popular resentment against him. November 16, 1776, Humphreys was attacked by a writer in Towne's paper under the signature of A Tory. Not knowing what might be the consequence of these assaults, in those times of commotion, Humphreys discontinued his paper, quitted business, and went into the country. At the very time Towne published these pieces, Humphreys had loaned him the paper on which *The Evening Post* was published, without any prospect of payment.

Humphreys, thus driven from Philadelphia, remained in the country till the British army approached the city; and then returned and remained there while it was possessed by the British troops; with whom he again left the city, accompanied the army to New York, and there continued as a merchant until the establishment of peace. He then went to England, procured a supply of good printing materials, and after some time went to Nova Scotia, and opened a printing house in Shelburne, and published a newspaper called *The Nova Scotia Packet*. Not meeting with sufficient encouragement, the *Packet* was discontinued; he closed his printing and employed himself as a merchant at Shelburne; in this situation he remained until 1797, when, having suffered loss by French privateers, he again returned to Philadelphia, and there opened a printing house. From that time till he died he was employed in book printing, and a number of valuable works have come from his press. He was a good and accurate printer, and a worthy citizen. He died February 10, 1810, aged sixty-three years.

His sons, who succeeded to their father's business, relinquished it in 1812, and the stock was disposed of at auction. Several of his daughters were good compositors, and often worked at the case.

BENJAMIN TOWNE was born in Lincolnshire, and brought up to printing in England. He was first a journeyman to Goddard, and then his partner. He purchased the right which Galloway and Wharton had in the printing house managed by Goddard. This partnership did not continue a year, but ended in 1770. In 1774, Towne opened a printing house on his own account.

James Humphreys had proposed to publish a newspaper, professedly impartial. Towne immediately issued a proposal for another paper. It was supposed that Humphreys's paper would be in the British interest. Towne took opposite ground. Both papers appeared before the public in January, 1775. Suspicion was soon excited against Humphreys's *Ledger*, and was kept awake by the publications in Towne's *Evening Post*. In less than two years Towne succeeded in obliging Humphreys to discontinue the *Ledger*; and, through fear of popular resentment, to leave the city.

Towne remained a whig until the British army took possession of Philadelphia; he then became a royalist. At that time
Humphreys returned and renewed the *Ledger*. Towne continued *The Evening Post*. There was this difference between Humphreys and Towne: the first possessed a candid mind, and was
apparently guided by moral principle; Towne appeared to be
artful, and governed by self interest. When the British troops
evacuated the city, Humphreys went with them. Towne, although proscribed by the state government for joining the
royal standard, remained; and again adopted the language of a
whig; but his conduct gained no friends among the loyalists,
and it lost him the confidence of those who had been his patrons.
But he was permitted, without molestation, to pursue his business, and I believe he continued his paper, which was handsomely executed, till 1782.

When congress first met in Philadelphia, after the British
army evacuated it, Doctor Witherspoon, who was then a member, went into the bookstore of Aitken, where he met with
Towne. After some conversation, Towne requested the doctor
to furnish him with intelligence and essays for the *Evening Post*,
as he formerly had done. The doctor refused, and told him that
it would be very improper for a member of congress to hold
intercourse with a man who was proscribed by law; but he
added, 'if you make your peace with the country first, I will
then assist you.' 'How shall I do it, doctor?' 'Why,' answered
the doctor, 'write and publish a piece acknowledging your
fault, professing repentance, and asking forgiveness.' 'But what
shall I say?' The doctor gave some hints; upon which Towne
said, 'Doctor, you write expeditiously and to the purpose; I will
thank you to write something for me, and I will publish it.'

'Will you? then I will do it,' replied the doctor. The doctor applied to Aitken for paper and ink, and immediately wrote, 'The humble Confession, Recantation and Apology of Benjamin Towne,' etc. It was an excellent production, and humorously ironical; but Towne refused to comply with his promise to publish, because the doctor would not allow him to omit some sentences in it. It, however, made its appearance, some time after, in several newspapers; and, passing for the genuine work of Towne, raised his reputation as a writer. When Doctor Witherspoon's works were published, this recantation was among them.

Towne was not deficient in intellect and was a decent workman. He was a *bon vivant*, but he did not possess the art of accumulating and retaining wealth. He died July 8, 1793.

ROBERT AITKEN[20] was born at Dalkeith, in Scotland, and served a regular apprenticeship with a bookbinder in Edinburgh. He came to Philadelphia, as a bookseller, in 1769; returned to Scotland the same year, came back to Philadelphia in 1771, and followed the business of bookselling and binding, both before and after the revolution. In 1774, he became a printer. In 1775, he published a magazine, and in 1782, an edition of the Bible, small duodecimo, on a brevier type. This edition, said to be the first printed in America, which is, however, a mistake,* was recommended to the public by congress, as a pious and laudable undertaking in the existing state of the country. A copy of this resolve of congress is printed at the end of the Old Testament. Imprint—'Philadelphia, Printed and sold

* See Printers in Cambridge, Boston and Germantown.

by R. Aitken, at Pope's head, above the Coffee House in Market street, MDCCLXXXII.'

After the revolutionary war he printed several valuable works. Among them were the first three volumes, in quarto, of *The Transactions of the American Philosophical Society*. He had a son bred to printing, who was some time his partner.

Aitken died in July, 1802, aged sixty-eight years. For thirty-one years he had been a citizen of Philadelphia. He was industrious and frugal. His printing was neat and correct. In his dealings he was punctual, and he acquired the respect of those who became acquainted with him.

Jane Aitken, his daughter, continued his business. She had in 1810 a printing house in Philadelphia; and printed Thompson's translations of the Bible, in four volumes, octavo. The printing was well and handsomely executed. She obtained much reputation by the productions which issued from her press.

STORY & HUMPHREYS. Enoch Story, the elder, and Daniel Humphreys, were copartners. They began printing 'in Norris's alley, near Front Street,' in 1775. The well known Joseph Galloway, once the partner of Goddard, in order to promote his political views, is said to have procured the materials of a printing house for Story, who took Humphreys, not then engaged in business, into partnership. Their chief employment was a newspaper, which they had published but a few months when their printing house and materials were burnt, and their partnership was in consequence dissolved. Story was bred a merchant, but was unfortunate in mercantile affairs, and unsuccessful in other business.

Daniel Humphreys, son of Joshua Humphreys, served his

time with William Bradford, and was a fellow apprentice with James Humphreys; but they were not related. Daniel, some time after his misfortune by fire, opened another printing house; and from June, 1783, to July, 1784, was a partner of Ebenezer Oswald in the publication of the *Independent Gazetteer*; and afterwards began another newspaper, which he published several years. The typography of this paper was neatly executed. He had a printing house in Philadelphia till 1811; was noted as a good proof reader, and in this business was often employed. He died June 12, 1812.

ENOCH STORY, THE YOUNGER, was the kinsman of Enoch Story, who was the partner of Daniel Humphreys. He served his apprenticeship with William Hall, and began business at Baltimore. In 1775, and for some time after, he was a job printer in Strawberry alley, Philadelphia. He died in Baltimore.

JOHN DOUGLAS MACDOUGALL, printed in Chestnut street, in Philadelphia, in 1775, and probably before that time. He was not, I believe, long or largely in trade. He was born in Ireland, and had, previously to engaging in business in this city, worked in the printing house of John Waterman, Providence, Rhode Island. He died in New York, August, 1787.

SAMUEL DELLAP, printed several small works, which he sold at his shop 'in Front street, between Market and Arch streets,' in 1771, and after. About the year 1792, he sold books by auction in an outhouse belonging to the Black Horse Tavern, in Market street, north side, between Fourth and Fifth streets. In this place he died of the yellow fever in 1793, aged about fifty-three years.

He went frequently to New York, where he advertised his publications, and collected old books; these he sold at auction in Philadelphia.

MELCHIOR STEINER AND CHARLES CIST. Steiner was born in Switzerland. He was the son of the Rev. John Conrad Steiner, who came to Philadelphia, and was, for some time, pastor of the Dutch Presbyterian church in Race street. He served his apprenticeship with Henry Miller, and succeeded him in business. Cist was born in St. Petersburgh, Russia, where he received a good education, and was brought up a druggist and apothecary, and afterwards studied physic. He came to America in 1769, and engaged with Henry Miller as a translator of English into German; by continuing in the employment of Miller several years he acquired a considerable knowledge of printing. These two entered into partnership under the firm of STEINER & CIST. They executed book and job work, in both the German and English languages, 'in Second street, at the corner of Coat's alley.' This copartnership was of short continuance. Not long after the commencement of the revolutionary war, they published a newspaper in the German language; but, for want of sufficient encouragement, it was discontinued in April, 1776.

They left Philadelphia when the British army approached it; and returned when it was evacuated in 1778. In 1779 they published a German newspaper. In 1781 they dissolved their copartnership. Steiner continued the paper three or four years, but by neglecting business, became poor. Cist pursued it prudently, and acquired considerable property. When the seat of government was removed to Washington, Cist carried his press there, remained with it several years, and built two or three houses in that city.

Cist died near Bethlehem, December 1, 1805, and was buried in the Moravian churchyard, in that place.

Steiner ceased to be a master printer, and became a clerk in a public office, in 1794. He died in Washington in the winter of 1807, aged about fifty years.

In 1810 there were in the county and in the city of Philadelphia, fifty-one printing houses, one hundred and fifty-three printing presses, and seven paper mills.*

The first press established west of the Allegany, was in Pittsburg, Pennsylvania, in 1786, by John Scull, under the patronage of Judge Brackenridge.

CHRISTOPHER SAUER, ALIAS SOWER.[21] This eminent printer was born in the town of Lauterburg, in Germany, in the year 1694. The business he was bred to was that of a tailor. He came to America in 1724, and took up his residence in Germantown, where for some time his principal employment was making button molds, which he found to be profitable. He followed various other occupations for fourteen years after his arrival, but had no concern in printing. He left Germantown, and was, at one time, engaged as a farmer; at other times was concerned in casting stoves at a furnace near Reading, in Pennsylvania, and discovered great ingenuity in casting. After being several years absent from Germantown, he returned to that place, and for some time lived with a noted German doctor by the name of Witt, who was commonly called a conjuror. From this man,

* James Mease, *The Picture of Philadelphia* (Philadelphia, 1811), pp. 80–88.

Sower gained some medical knowledge. At length by accident he became a printer.

The Baptists, or Tunkers, in Germany, raised by subscription, a sum of money, in order to purchase religious books and disperse them among their poor friends in Pennsylvania, and to establish a press there to print for the same purpose. Accordingly a press and types, with a quantity of books, were sent out and intrusted to the management of a German Baptist by the name of Jacob Gaus. He was to have the use of, and the emolument arising from the press, on condition that he should distribute a certain number of copies of each of the religious books he should print, among the poor Germans. This person did not possess the ability necessary for the undertaking, and no other person who was thought to have sufficient ability for the purpose was found to take his place. The business was suspended and the press and types viewed as useless lumber. At length Sower appeared, and was so fortunate as to get the press, types, and the books* into his possession, though not without much opposition. He was opposed by the friends of Gaus, and particularly by Alexander Mack, the first minister, and the spiritual father of all the Tunkers, or German Baptists, at that time in Pennsylvania. The transfer of the property being made to Sower, he immediately began business according to the benevolent intentions of those who were at the expense of the establishment. The German books sent over were distributed gratuitously among the poor. The press was set to work on reli-

---

* It is uncertain whether these were from the society formed in England for diffusing religious information among the German settlers, or from a similar society in Germany, but there can be no doubt that one or more presses were established in Pennsylvania by pious friends in Europe; and that not only the press at Germantown, but that at Ephrata, was supported for this purpose.

gious tracts, and a proportion of them given away. Others were sold, and produced a profit to the printer. In a short time, Sower so managed the concern as to gain the approbation even of his opposers. The ingenuity of Sower, his great attention to the establishment, with the aid of some good workmen whom he procured from Germany, soon placed the business on a respectable footing, and it became profitable to him. In 1738 he published a German Almanac. This was the first in that language printed in the country. It was continued annually by him and his successors, for forty years. In the year 1739 he published a small newspaper in German; and in 1743, he issued from his press, on a German long primer type, and in that language, an edition of the Bible, in 4to. This was the second Bible printed in British America. The first was the Indian translation, from the press in Cambridge, Massachusetts, as early as 1663. Sower's edition of the German Bible was nearly three years in the press. The price to subscribers was only fourteen shillings currency, bound; but it was to others twenty shillings. This was the largest work that had issued from any press in that colony, and it was not equalled for many years after. The edition consisted of a thousand copies.[22]

Sower printed a number of minor works in German, and *Juvenal* in English. For those in English he employed a proof reader, as he never could acquire the correct orthography of the language.

After he printed the Bible, he erected a mill for manufacturing paper, and was, for a short time, concerned in that business; and also in that of book binding.

When particular sorts of his types were deficient, he contrived to cast new ones as they were wanted. In short, his ingenuity enabled him to complete the manufacture of any article which he undertook. It is said he was sufficiently adroit at sixteen different trades or avocations, by following either of which he could secure a maintenance. Among them were those of stove caster, farmer, clockmaker, tailor, distiller, farrier, apothecary, paper maker, tanner, tin plate worker, lampblack maker, printers' ink-maker, bookbinder and printer. To the last of these he was particularly attached; as an evidence of which, he desired on his death bed, that the printing business might always continue among his descendants; and that some one or other of them would acquire and practice the art.

He was religious in the temper of his mind, and quiet in his deportment. Although inclining to Mennonism, he was called a Separatist; but in fact, did not join any particular sect.

He married in Germany. His wife died December 24, 1752. He died September 25, 1758, aged sixty-four, and was buried in his own land, at the back of his dwelling house in Germantown. He had but one child, a son, who succeeded him in business.

CHRISTOPHER SOWER JUNIOR,[23] was born in Witgenstein, near Marburg in Germany, and was only three years of age when he arrived in Philadelphia with his father, by whom he was employed in various occupations until 1738, when his father commenced printing; he was then instructed in that art.

He commenced business as a bookbinder some years before the death of his father, but at his decease he succeeded him in the printing house. This was in 1758, when he was thirty-seven years old. He continued the establishment on an enlarged scale, printed many valuable books, and published a weekly newspaper. In 1763, he finished a quarto edition of the Bible, in

German, on a pica type; and completed another in 1776. The types for that last mentioned, were cast at his own foundery. This foundery was the first of the kind in British America. The materials for it he received from Germany in 1772.*

In 1773 he built a paper mill on the Schuylkill, and manufactured both writing and printing paper. He had previously established a bindery. He made printing ink of the best quality, and excellent lampblack for this purpose. His presses were made under his own inspection, in his extensive establishment. Thus the various branches of business necessary to complete a printed book were executed by him, or by his own immediate workmen. Most of these branches he could perform himself, and at some of them he was a first-rate workman. He possessed in this respect the genius of his progenitor. The printing executed at his German press was both neat and correct. His ink was remarkably good.

Besides the various branches of bookmaking, he dealt in drugs and medicines. Of these articles he imported and sold large quantities. He conducted his business with high reputation. His influence in the community, especially among the Germans, was very extensive. No medicines could be esteemed effectual, unless procured at Sower's apothecary shop; no almanac, unless published by him, could be correct in time and weather; and no newspaper promulgated truth but Christopher Sower's *German Gazette*. As an instance of his popularity among his neighbors, it is mentioned that at the time when there was a warm contention between the people of Pennsylvania and the proprietors, the quakers, who were desirous of obtaining some exclusive privileges, had an ascendency in the legislature, to

* See Type Founderies in America, pp. 28–30.

which body they had petitioned. A new election was approaching. The petition of the quakers was unpopular with those who were not of that sect. Sower, in his *German Gazette*, zealously opposed the petition, and at the time of the election of new members, at the head of three hundred qualified voters, proceeded in regular order from Germantown to Philadelphia, and successfully supported the candidates opposed to the quakers. This happened about the year 1760, and appears to be the only instance of his taking such an active part in political affairs.

In 1777 he gave up the management of the printing house to two of his sons. He possessed by inheritance from his father, and from his own exertions, an independent estate, and was inclined to quit the fatigues of business and the further pursuit of wealth, and pass the remainder of his life in religious repose. He is represented as well balanced in his temper; in his disposition, pacific; in his habits, industrious and plodding; in conduct, exemplary; and in religion a saint, commanding respect, and the silent and sullen veneration even of the most profligate. 'Such was the even tenor of his way.' But 'man is born to trouble as the sparks fly upward.' The days of his affliction approached. Often does the mariner, after a long and successful voyage, approach within view of his desired haven, when suddenly, by adverse gales, on an unseen rock, he suffers shipwreck. Sower now began to experience such trying scenes as would prove his fortitude as a man, and test his virtue as a Christian.

It does not appear that he actually declared himself, during the revolutionary struggle, either for or against the colonists. It rather seems that he was disposed 'to submit to the powers that be for conscience sake.' The Tunkers, or German Baptists, were generally rich. Men of property are at all times generally opposed to a revolution. It was supposed that Sower and his Christian brethren wished to remain neutral, and that they consented 'rather to bear the ills they had, than to fly to those they knew not of.' His property was greatly injured by the war; particularly by the battle of Germantown. The war had commenced in favor of the British, and it was uncertain how the contest would end.

His son Christopher had rendered himself obnoxious to the whigs, and had fled to the enemy. He and other friends of Sower had alarmed his fears, and strongly insisted on his going for safety to Philadelphia, then in possession of the British troops. Whatever might lead him to the measure, true it is that on the nineteenth of October, 1777, fifteen days after that battle he deserted his home, and went into the city. He remained there till May 23, 1777, [? 8], when he returned to Germantown. This was twenty-four days before the enemy evacuated Philadelphia. After his arrival he was arrested in his own house. This measure was justified by his having been with the British army. With an inflamed and exasperated populace this was sufficient proof of his being a traitor.

They went to him and demanded his signature to the oath prescribed by congress. He replied that he would cheerfully swear allegiance to the state, but could not, consistently with his religious faith, engage to perform all which that oath required. He was therefore made a prisoner and taken to the American army and confined five days. He was afterwards released on parole, and allowed to reside in Mathatchen, twenty-one miles from Germantown. While in durance, before he reached the army, some ill-disposed persons deprived him of his remarkable and full grown beard, and otherwise maltreated him. Whilst a prisoner with the army he had to endure other indignities from the soldiers. He bore all, however, with Christian resignation.

One circumstance, rather extraordinary, took place at this time, which has often been mentioned, and the fact attested, both by his friends, and those who were then his political enemies. He was denuded at the camp by the soldiers, then arrayed in tattered regimentals, and paraded. His pantaloons were seized by a soldier who put them on his own limbs. A short time after, this soldier was seized with agonizing pains in all parts of his body, and exclaimed: 'I can neither live nor die! I am in torment. Take off the old man's trowsers, that I may die!' They were taken off, and the soldier presently expired. The cause that produced the pains and sudden death of the soldier is not stated. By some of the friends of Sower, who esteemed him a saint, this incident was thought to be a judgment of God for the cruelty with which he had been treated.

He returned to Mathatchen on the twenty-third of June, 1778. While he remained there, the court for the confiscation of estates opened its session in the town of Lancaster, whither all those concerned were, by public advertisement, notified to appear during the month of June, and show cause, if any they had, why final proceedings as to their estates should not be taken. His case came on at this court the very day he arrived in Germantown. A newspaper was rarely seen in Germantown at that time, and not having seen the notification he knew nothing of the sitting of the court until it was too late for him to make his appearance. His estate was confiscated, and neither he nor his friends had faith enough to petition the court on the subject. This was a fatal blow to the fortunes of Sower. Had he appeared in court this stroke might have been arrested. As no overt act could be alleged against him, his property to the amount of 90,000 dollars, might have remained in his hands. It was now seized, and soon after sold at auction at a very low rate. Besides his house, lands, drugs, medicines, paper, and types, all his books, bound and in quires, were sold. Among the books in sheets was the greater part of his edition of the German Bible, consisting of a thousand copies. These went off by the hammer for less than a quarter of the price of a like quantity of ordinary wrapping paper. The books were in the German language, with which the very few persons who attended the sale in order to make purchases were acquainted, and they placed but little value on the articles. His printing materials and book stock were purchased by a printer from the city, who did not know their value. Instead of having the book stock bound, he sold a part of it to be used as covers for cartridges, proper paper for that purpose being at that time not to be obtained. Thus what was, at first, intended for the salvation of men's souls, proved eventually the destruction of their bodies.

Sower's property was seized on the twenty-seventh of July, 1778. When the officers came to his house for this purpose he was at breakfast. They began to take an inventory of his property, and demanded his keys. He delivered them with much composure, only observing that if they had a better right to them than himself, they must take them. The day following he received notice to quit the premises, and he took a final leave of his home and of his effects, and went to the house of his brother-in-law, Henry Sharpnach, in the same town. Here Sower resided two years, and employed himself in binding books. In addition to his misfortunes, having been in extensive trade, he had many debts due to him, which were now cancelled in continental bills. These were a lawful tender, but had depreciated in value at the rate of ninety dollars in bills to one dollar in specie. But he was otherwise treated by some of his Christian brethren. He had considerable sums in their hands and they paid him the full value of the sums which they had borrowed.

His type foundery, having been in the possession of Justin Fox, the master workman, and kept and used in buildings in the neighborhood occupied by him, was on this account supposed to be his property, and thus escaped confiscation.*

It was the opinion of many of Sower's friends, that when the war should end he would be indemnified for the loss he sustained. For this reason neither he nor his friends interfered in the sales of his confiscated property.

A German bookbinder in Germantown, by the name of Siebert, and his son-in-law Michael Billmeyer, who shortly after established himself as a printer in that place, hearing that the Bible sheets were selling for the use already mentioned, went to Philadelphia and repurchased what remained, and also a part of the printing materials. They recommenced the printing business in Germantown. They reprinted such parts of the Bible as had been destroyed, and having completed the purchased copies, they bound and sold them.

The greater part of Sower's types had been wantonly mixed and thrown together in heaps. Several thousand pounds weight were afterwards sold by the person who purchased them at auction, to Justin Fox, Sower's type founder in Germantown.

He had, cast and standing in his printing house, types for the whole of the German hymn book. After he completed his last

* See the article, Type Founderies.

issue of the quarto edition of the Bible, his foundery was engaged in casting types sufficient to keep the whole Bible standing. The battle of Germantown put a stop to this proceeding when the work was nearly complete.

Sower removed from the house of his brother-in-law in 1780 to Mathatchen. He kept house at this place, assisted by his daughters.

He was fond of walking, and preferred that mode of traveling to riding. It is said he usually progressed on foot four miles an hour. Within a fortnight before his death, he walked on a sabbath morning, twelve miles from his home, up to Shippack, to supply the pulpit for his Christian brethren in that place. After the religious services for the day were over, he returned home on foot. On this day, it has been said, he appeared to have a presentiment of his approaching dissolution, as he observed to the congregation, in the course of his preaching, that this was the last time he could perform that service for them.

At the request of a worthy member of congress, the Hon. Frederick Augustus Muhlenburgh, afterwards speaker, he drew up a statement of his sufferings. This was completed eight days before his death, when he observed that he had 'now finished nearly all he had to do.' The minister who preached his funeral sermon mentioned that to him Sower had foretold his death, and that two of his sons would speedily follow him.*

His working hours at Mathatchen were employed in binding books; and this business, it appears, was to be the means by which his pilgrimage on earth was to be ended.

He had undertaken to bind some of the same quarto Bibles which he had last printed, and which had been repurchased. He

* This prediction was fulfilled.

began the process of binding these books by the laborious employment of beating them, as is usual, and imprudently completed as much of this work in half a day as is usually done in a whole day. The weather was warm, and by this exertion he became overheated. He went out to a spring where he drank so freely of water as to produce a fit of apoplexy, which soon after terminated his mortal existence.

He was a rigid and exemplary member of the society called Tunkers, a sect of the German Baptists, and embraced their creed, not by education, but by conversion, and was ordained a minister in their religious assemblies, June 10, 1753. His wife and some of his children were church members of the same society.

He, with a number of his friends of this sect, had at one time agreed not to marry, but to devote their time as much as possible to religious duties. Sower, however, was the first to annul this agreement, and married in 1751. His wife died in 1777.

The rapid emigration of Germans to Pennsylvania may in considerable degree be attributed to Sower and his father. The letters which they wrote and sent to the land of their nativity, gave such a favorable representation of the climate of the province, where land was so easily to be obtained, as induced great numbers of their countrymen, with their families, to emigrate, and settle there.

Sower was a very conscientious printer. The Associate Presbytery of Pennsylvania (or, Seceders, as sometimes called) ordered, about the year 1765, that some of their actions, or something of the kind, should be published, and deputized John Fulton, a papermaker of Oxford township, near Lancaster, to engage the printing. Fulton called on Sower to have it done.

'My friend,' replied Sower, 'I do not print everything. If irreligious, or otherwise dangerous, I always refuse; but if you will leave the piece for my perusal I will give you an answer.' Fulton called again, and Sower informed him he would gladly print the piece.

Sower was remarkably temperate and regular in his habits. He never drank ardent spirits, was very economical, rose at four in the morning, and spent an hour in devotional exercises. At five his whole family were called up and proceeded to their various employments.

He died August 26, 1784, aged sixty-two years, leaving eight children—five sons and three daughters. On his tombstone in the burying ground of the Mennonists in Mathatchen, the following lines are sculptured, viz:

> Death, thou hast conquered me,
>   'Twas by thy darts I'm slain;
> But Christ shall conquer thee,
>   And I shall rise again.

> Time hastens on the hour,
>   We just shall rise and sing,
> O Grave! where is thy power?
>   O Death! where is thy sting?

CHRISTOPHER SOWER, THIRD,[24] was brought up a printer by his father, Christopher Sower Junior, and was for some time concerned with him in business. He was a member of the German Baptist church, and of the sect called Tunkers, from which he withdrew, and left the United States with the British army, at the close of the revolutionary war.

In 1777, his mother dying, his father resigned the management of the printing house to Christopher and his brother Peter. Soon after this connection in business commenced, the troubles occasioned by the war increased, especially in the neighborhood of Germantown, and caused at first temporary suspension, and soon after a total end to their business in Germantown. On the fourth of October, of this year, the day on which the battle was fought in this place, they fled to Philadelphia. Till this time they continued the German newspaper, and had printed the *German Almanack* for 1778. This was the 40th number of this annual publication which had issued from the press of the Sowers. This ended the partnership of these brothers. They had both become obnoxious to their countrymen by speaking and acting in favor of the enemy. Peter remained in Philadelphia till it was evacuated by the British army. He then went to New York, and became a student in physic. At the close of the war he left that city in a vessel for New Providence, where he died soon after his arrival.

Christopher the third did not possess the prudence of his father or his grandfather. At the beginning of the war he warmly espoused the cause of the country, and thus became popular; but he soon turned to the opposite side, and so conducted as to endanger the safety of his person. It is said this change in him was effected by the instigation of Joseph Galloway, who was an intimate in the family, and a notorious adherent to the cause of the British government. He was a man of influence, a member of the Pennsylvania legislature, and had for some years preceding been the silent partner of William Goddard in the publication of the *Pennsylvania Chronicle*.* He was a man who was

* See an account of that public journal in the section on newspapers.

possessed of handsome talents, and he conducted his Gazette with ability, though with severity against his countrymen.

Christopher resumed the publication of the *Germantown Gazette*, in Philadelphia, as soon as he could get his press and German types for the purpose. This business was speedily accomplished, and the paper was published till the British army removed from that city to New York.

Sometime after the battle of Germantown, a detachment of the British army left Philadelphia, and for some forage, or other purpose, proposed to pass through Germantown, and return by the ridge road. Sower 3d, having some private business to transact, took advantage of this escort to proceed to his former residence, to obtain some papers of family importance. He stepped into his house, obtained the papers, and was proceeding to join the detachment, when, unapprehensive of danger, he was apprehended opposite the market house, by Capt. Coleman, an officer in the American army, who was lurking for stragglers. Sower was then taken to the American camp, detained five weeks, and then exchanged.

Capt. Coleman, who took Sower prisoner in his excursion to Germantown, was himself, sometime after Sower's release, taken prisoner by the British, and confined on board a prison-ship in New York, with others from Germantown who were acquainted with Sower. Some time after their confinement, Sower, with some of his British friends, went on board of the prison-ship, but did not know of the capture and confinement of his Germantown acquaintance. Sower soon recognized Coleman and the others, who rather shunned than courted an interview with him. However, Sower went to them, familiarly accosted them, and expressed his surprise at finding them in their present situation. He told them, particularly Coleman, that they had nothing to fear from his resentment, but that, on the contrary, he was disposed to befriend them as much as lay in his power; and for that purpose inquired into their present circumstances. Soon after Sower left the prison-ship he supplied Coleman with linen and other necessaries, and in the course of a few days effected his liberation, and that of the two others, his companions, without an exchange. He lived many years after the war, in Third street, opposite to the Golden Swan tavern.

When Sower 3d was brought to headquarters, General Washington, after some interrogatories, addressed him thus: 'Well, Mr. Sower, you will be likely now to get some *sour* sauce.' Sower would not have been exchanged at all, or at least not so soon as he was, but for the occurrence of a fortunate incident. He had somehow received information of George Lusk, a powder manufacturer, being at a certain place unprotected. Lusk had been a next door neighbor to Sower, and was now the principal person on whom the Americans depended for a supply of gunpowder. Sower knew the estimation in which he was held, and instantly formed the plan for making him a prisoner, in order to effect his own release. The plan succeeded and Lusk was taken prisoner, and some time after exchanged for Christopher, who returned to Philadelphia. Threats were given out against the lives of both; but an even exchange was at length effected. They, perhaps, owed their lives to each other.

Christopher went to New York with the British army, and sometime after embarked in a ship of war for England. He returned to New York, where he remained till the war ended. He visited England again; after remaining there two years, he went with his family to New Brunswick, and there published *The Royal Gazette*. He was appointed postmaster for that province, and he obtained a colonel's brevet from the British government, which entitled him to half pay for life.

In 1779 he left that colony, and went in search of health, and to visit his brothers, to Baltimore, where, shortly after his arrival, he was attacked with apoplexy and died on the third of July of that year, aged forty-six.

DANIEL SOWER, another brother of Christopher 3d, was by profession, a papermaker, and after his apprenticeship was ended, conducted the mill built by his father. This mill was given to Daniel by his father, but the legal conveyance not having been made, the property was confiscated and sold as the property of the father. Daniel purchased another mill, but within a short time after, sold it, and turned his attention to agriculture in Chester county, Pennsylvania.

DAVID SOWER was also brother to Christopher 3d. He acquired a knowledge of the art of printing, and established a printing house in Norristown, Pennsylvania, and there published a newspaper, which he relinquished to his son Charles in 1811. After which David opened a store in Mathatchen; besides which he now pursued the business of a farmer.

SAMUEL SOWER, the youngest brother to Christopher, was brought up a housewright, and settled on Chestnut hill, near Germantown. He then became a printer, and also an apothecary. In 1794, he removed to Baltimore, where he attended to the business of printing and bookselling till 1804, when he commenced a type foundery in copartnership with William Gwynn. He afterwards purchased the foundery which had been owned by his father and worked by Justus Fox. He continues now, [1815] the type making business in Baltimore, under the firm of S. Sower & Co. Samuel is an ingenious mechanician. He cast the diamond type for a small pocket Bible which was lately printed in that city. To this type, he added an italic. Diamond italic has not been, I believe, attempted in Europe, unless very recently.

Of Christopher's three sisters, one died in infancy, another in two or three years after her father, and the third is now [1815] living.

The treaty of peace in 1803 would have enabled Christopher Sower, the second of that name, to have recovered a part of his landed estate, but as the Tunkers will not, in any case, commence lawsuits, he received no benefit from the provision made in the treaty for those in his situation; and it is added that several of the children received some compensation from the British government.

MILLER[25] & HOLLAND were copartners in a printing establishment in Lancaster in 1751. They printed some small works in the German language, and, in 1752, published a newspaper in German and English. This firm was of short continuance. In 1753 I find that a book, then lately published, was advertised for sale 'by Samuel Holland, printer in Lancaster,' and no mention was made of Miller.*

* This was probably Henry Miller, then lately returned from Europe, and who went again to Europe in 1754, but previously worked about twelve months for Bradford in Philadelphia. [See Henry Miller.]

WILLIAM DUNLAP, began printing in Lancaster in 1754, in the English and German languages. He remained there till the beginning of the year 1757, when he removed to Philadelphia. [See pp. 386–387.]

LAHN, ALBRIGHT AND STIEMER, mentioned in the first edition of this work, I am informed did not begin business until the conclusion of the revolutionary war.

FRANCIS BAILEY[26] began business in 1771, in company with Stewart Herbert, but they did not continue a long time in partnership. In 1772, and after, Bailey's printing house was in Spring street, Lancaster. The types with which he began business, were manufactured in Germantown. Afterwards he manufactured types for himself and others. As a mechanician he was celebrated.

Bailey was instructed in printing by Peter Miller at Ephrata, Lancaster county. He removed to Philadelphia in 1778 or 1779, and published a newspaper in that city. He eventually returned to Lancaster. His daughter-in-law in 1818 conducted a press in Philadelphia.

STEWART HERBERT began printing with Francis Bailey in 1771. A separation appears to have taken place soon after, and Herbert opened a printing house 'in Queen street, Lancaster,' and printed there in 1774. He afterwards printed a small newspaper in Hagerstown, Maryland.

Andrew Steuart in 1761, had a shop in Lancaster; but I do not find that he had a press there.

EPHRATA, situated near Cocalico creek in Lancaster county, has been called Dunkardtown, and Tunkardtown, but is now known by the name of Ephrata. It was settled in 1733, by a sect called, by some, Tunkers, and by others, Dunkers or German Baptists, most of whom were from Germany, or of German extraction. They believe in the general redemption and salvation of the human race. They are generally well informed, peaceable in their disposition, simple in their language, and plain in their dress. They neither swear nor fight, nor go to law, nor take interest for money loaned. They commonly wear their beards. At first they kept the first day sabbath, but afterwards the seventh day.

PETER MILLER, a venerable and pious leader and teacher among the Tunkers, began with them the settlement of Ephrata. About the year 1746, Miller opened a printing house, and he and his associates erected a paper mill. Miller printed a number of books in the German language, and a few in English; all on religious subjects, and written chiefly by himself.

In 1748 and 1749, he wrote and printed in Dutch, a work entitled *Blutigen Schau Platzes.** It made fourteen hundred and twenty-eight pages, which he published in two volumes, and then translated it into German. The paper on which it was printed, was manufactured at Ephrata village. This work gave employment to Miller for more than two years. During that time his bed was a bench; his pillow a wooden block of about four inches in thickness and width, and ten inches in length; and he slept but four hours in twenty-four.†

---

* In the title page of each volume is an impression from a cut. One cut is enclosed with a circle, and engraved on wood; the other on type metal.

† This information I received from Mr. Francis Bailey, of Lancaster, Pa., an

'Miller was born in Germany in 1709; had his education in the university of Heidelberg; came to this country in 1730; settled with the Dutch Presbyterians in Philadelphia; and was the same year ordained a preacher among them. In 1735 he embraced the principles of the Baptists; and in 1744 he received another ordination to be the prior or head of the society at Ephrata.'* After Miller left the Presbyterian society in Philadelphia, he removed to Berks county, where he discovered a valuable quarry of agate, and he, in company with one Conrad Weiser, a celebrated Indian interpreter, became concerned in working this quarry, and in exporting large quantities of the agate to Germany. But Miller's religious impressions soon led him to believe that his time and talents should be more usefully employed; and Weiser dying, Miller forsook the business of the quarry, and then associated with the Dunkers, and began the settlement of Ephrata.

---

ingenious and very respectable printer, taught by Miller. Mr. Bailey mentions that he has often witnessed Miller resting in the manner I have represented, and that he has slept in the same room with Miller in a similar way. He also informs me 'that during the time *Blutigen Schau Platzes* was in the press, particular sorts of the fonts of types on which it was printed ran short. To overcome this difficulty, one of the workmen constructed a mold that could be moved so as to suit the body of any type not smaller than brevier, nor larger than double pica. The mold consisted of four quadrangular pieces of brass; two of them with mortices to shift to a suitable body, and secured by screws. The best type they could select from the sort wanted, was then placed in the mold, and after a slight corrosion of the surface of the letter with aquafortis to prevent soldering, or adhesion, a leaden matrix was cast on the face of the type, from which, after a slight stroke of a hammer on the type in the matrix, we cast the letters which were wanted. Types thus cast answer tolerably well. I have often adopted a method somewhat like this to obtain sorts which were short; but instead of four pieces of brass, made use of an even and accurate composing stick, and one piece of iron or copper having an even surface on the sides; and instead of a leaden matrix, have substituted one of clay, especially for letters with a bold face.

* Morgan Edwards, *Materials toward a History of the Baptists in Pennsylvania* (Philadelphia, 1770).

Among the brethren of his religious sect, Miller went by the paternal name of Jabez, alluding to I Chronicles, chap. iv, verses 9 and 10. His chin bore that dignified and characteristic mark of manhood given by the creator, a beard, flowing over his bosom. His countenance, it is said, was continually so serene that all who saw him might pronounce that he had not only made a treaty of peace with himself, but with all the world.

It is not supposed that Miller was bred to printing; but it is understood he obtained a knowledge of the art after he arrived in Pennsylvania from the second Christopher Sower of Germantown. They were of the same religious sect, and in some way associated in the general government of the church of which they were members.

Miller was a good classical scholar, a man of most amiable manners, and highly respected. He died about the year 1790, aged eighty years.

BOOKSELLERS
IN PHILADELPHIA

1692. WILLIAM BRADFORD, sold pamphlets and other small articles.

1718. ANDREW BRADFORD, 'sign of the Bible, in Second-Street.' He was also a printer and binder.

1718. JOHN COPSON, bookseller, but dealt chiefly in other goods; he was concerned with Andrew Bradford in the first newspaper which was published in Pennsylvania.

1729. BENJAMIN FRANKLIN, 'in Market-Street.' He likewise was a printer and binder.

1741. ALEXANDER ANNARD, 'in Second Street, near the Church.'

1742. WILLIAM BRADFORD, the younger, 'in Second-Street.'

1742. JOHN BARKLEY 'at the Sign of the Bible in Second-Street; from Great Britain.'

1742. JAMES REED, 'next door to the Post-Office, in Market-Street.'

1742. JOSEPH GOODWIN, 'in Second-Street, near Black-Horse Alley.' He afterwards, removed into Blackhorse alley. Goodwin was from England, and was a bookseller, binder and stationer. It appears that he was a considerable dealer.

1743. STEPHEN POTTS. 'at the Bible and Crown, in Front-Street.'

1743. J. SCHUPPEY, 'at the Sign of the Book in Strawberry-Alley;' he was a binder, and sold a few books. It is probable that he was a German.

1743. CORNELIA BRADFORD, 'in Second-Street.'

1748. DAVID HALL, 'in Market-Street.' He was a printer, and the partner of Franklin; he dealt largely in books and stationery.

1755. HENRY SANDY, 'Lætitia-Court.'

1757. WILLIAM DUNLAP, 'in Market-Street.' Dunlap was bred to printing, which business he followed, but dealt somewhat extensively as a bookseller. About 1767 he removed to Virginia, and settled there as a minister of the church of England.

1758. BLACK HARRY, 'in Lætitia-Court,' was a binder, and sold small books, &c.

1759. ANDREW STEUART, 'Lætitia-Court;' but removed in 1762, to 'the Bible-in-Heart, in Second-Street.' He was a printer and a dealer in pamphlets.

1760. JAMES RIVINGTON, 'in Second-Street,' by his agent who became his partner the following year.

1761. RIVINGTON & BROWN, 'in Second-Street,' but they some time after took another stand. They were both from England. Rivington soon after opened bookstores in New York and Boston; and resided at New York.

1763. ZACHARIAH POULSON, 'Sign of the Bible in Second-Street between Arch and Race Streets.' He was a bookbinder, bookseller and stationer. This Mr. Poulson who was the father of the proprietor of the *American Daily Advertiser*, was a native of Copenhagen; he arrived in Philadelphia in 1749, when he was at the age of twelve years. Soon after he became an apprentice to the first Christopher Sower, of Germantown, of whom he learned printing. He was an excellent workman and a very respectable citizen. In the latter part of his life he kept a stationer's shop in Second Street, above Arch street. He died January 14, 1804, aged 67, and was buried in the Moravian cemetery, Philadelphia.

1764. WILLIAM SELLERS, 'in Arch-Street, between Second and Third Streets;' he was a printer and bookseller, from England, and became the partner of David Hall.

1764. SAMUEL TAYLOR, 'at the Book-in-hand, corner of Market and Water streets.' He carried on bookbinding and bookselling.

1765. WOODHOUSE & DEAN. This connection lasted less than a year. Dean died, and Woodhouse continued business on his own account.

1766. JOHN DUNLAP, 'in Market-Street,' succeeded to the printing and bookselling business of William Dunlap.

1766. ROBERT BELL, 'at the Union-Library, in Third Street,' in 1770. He was from Ireland; became a printer and was celebrated as a book auctioneer.

1766. WILLIAM WOODHOUSE, 'in Front-Street, near Chestnut-Street;' afterwards 'near Market street, at the Bible and Crown.' He was a binder and bookseller. He began business with Dean. He established in 1782, a slate and slate pencil manufactory, then the only one in the United States. In 1791, he began printing. He died December 28, 1795, and was succeeded by his son of the same name.

1767. LEWIS NICOLA, 'in Second street', removed in 1768, to Market Street. He published a magazine, kept a circulating library, and sold books.

1768. —— TAGGERT, was a very considerable vender of imported books. He also dealt in English and Scotch goods.

1768. JOHN SPARHAWK, 'at the London Bookstore, Market-Street;' afterwards 'at the Unicorn and Mortar, in Second-Street.' He published several books. His widow continued the business.

1768. JOHN ANDERTON, 'at the London Bookstore, in Second-Street.' He was from England; and, was a binder, letter case and pocketbook maker, and, as such, first began business in New York. He sometimes advertised books for sale in his own name, and at other times as connected with Sparhawk.

1768. ROGER BOWMAN, merchant, sold books on consignment from Great Britain.

1768. ROGER BOWMAN, 'in Second-Street near the Market.' He had a good assortment of books for sale.

1769. ROBERT AITKEN, commenced bookselling in Front street; he was from Scotland, to which country he returned in 1770; but in 1771, came back to Philadelphia; and in 1795, removed to, and opened a bookstore and printing house 'in Market Street,' near Front street. He was an excellent binder.

1770. CRUKSHANK AND COLLINS, 'in Third Street,' were a short time partners as printers and booksellers. Afterwards

JOSEPH CRUKSHANK, opened his printing house and a bookstore in Market street.

1770. JAMES STEUART, 'in Second-Street, between Chesnut and Walnut streets,' from Glasgow, shopkeeper, sold Scotch editions on commission.

1770. SEMPLE AND BUCHANAN, 'in Front-Street;' shopkeepers, from Scotland, sold Scotch editions on commission. Semple afterwards sold books and British goods.

1771. ROBERT MACGILL, 'Corner of Lætitia Court,' binder and bookseller. He removed to Second street, below Market street. He left Philadelphia in 1778, and went to New York.

1771. JOHN MACGIBBONS, 'in Front-Street, between Arch and Race Streets.' Not largely in trade. He republished Josephus's works in four volumes, octavo.

1771. SAMUEL DELLAP, 'in Front-Street, between Market and Arch-Streets;' he kept a book and print shop. At one time he resided at the corner of Third and Chestnut streets. He often sold books at auction.

1773. WILLIAM TRICHET, an Englishman, bound and sold books, at No. 5 South Front street. He was in business about eight years.

1773. JAMES YOUNG, 'at his Book-Store, adjoining the London Coffee-House.' He was in business about twelve months.

1773. THOMAS MACGEE, jun. 'Second Street, nearly opposite Christ Church.'

1773.   GEORGE REINHOLD, 'in Market-Street.' He was from Germany, and traded in Dutch books. He was also a binder.

1735.   CHRISTOPHER SOWER, from Germany, printed and sold books in the German language.

1744.   CHRISTOPHER SOWER, jun., succeeded to the business of his father.

1754.   WILLIAM DUNLAP, printer and bookseller. He removed to Philadelphia in 1757.

1767.   CHARLES JOHNSON, 'in King-Street.'

BEFORE the year 1719, only one newspaper was printed in the British North American colonies. It was published at Boston; and, on the 21st of December, in that year, the second American journal appeared at the same place.* On the following day the third paper was brought forward in the capital of this province.[27]

IN 1760, there were only three newspapers published in that city, viz: two in English, and one in the German language. In 1762, two English and two German papers existed; one of the latter was afterwards discontinued; and from that time until the year 1773, only three papers, two English and one German, were printed in Philadelphia.

The first newspaper in Pennsylvania was entitled,

* The Boston Gazette.

THE AMERICAN WEEKLY MERCURY. It was printed on a half sheet of pot. Imprint, 'Philadelphia: Printed by *Andrew Bradford*, and Sold by him and *John Copson*.' May 25, 1721,* Copson's name was omitted in the imprint, which was altered thus—'Philadelphia: Printed and Sold by *Andrew Bradford*, at the BIBLE in Second Street; and also by *William Bradford* in *New York*, where Advertisements are taken in.' William Bradford's name as a vender of the Mercury in New York, was omitted in December, 1725. In January, 1730, an addition was made to the imprint, viz. 'Price 10s. per Annum. All sorts of Printing Work done cheap, and old Books neatly bound.' In 1738, it was printed in 'Front Street,' to which he transferred his sign of the Bible.

The Mercury occasionally appeared on a whole sheet of pot, from types of various sizes, as small pica, pica and english. It was published weekly, generally on Tuesday, but the day of publication was varied. In January, $174\frac{2}{3}$, the day of the week is omitted; and it is dated from January 18 to January 27; after that time it was conducted with more stability.

In No. 22, two cuts, coarsely engraven, were introduced, one on the right, and the other on the left of the title; the one on the left, was a small figure of Mercury, bearing his caduceus; he is represented walking, with extended wings; the other is a postman riding full speed. The cuts were sometimes shifted, and Mercury and the postman exchanged places.

The Mercury of December 13, 1739, was 'Printed by Andrew and William Bradford,' and on September 11, 1740, it had a new head, with three figures, well executed; on the left was Mercury; in the centre a town, intended, I suppose, to represent

* Copson at that time opened the first insurance office in Philadelphia.

Philadelphia; and, on the right, the postman on horseback; the whole formed a parrallelogram, and extended across the page from margin to margin. This partnership continued only eleven months, when the Mercury was again printed by Andrew Bradford alone. The typography of the Mercury was equal to that of Franklin's Gazette.

Andrew Bradford died November 23, 1742, and the next Mercury, dated December 2, appeared in mourning. The paper was suspended one week, on account of the death of Bradford; therefore the first paper, 'published by the widow Bradford,'* contained an extra half sheet. The tokens of mourning were continued six weeks.

The widow entered into partnership with Isaiah Warner, and the Mercury of March 1, 174$\frac{2}{3}$, bears this imprint, 'Printed by Isaiah Warner and Cornelia Bradford.' Warner, in an introductory advertisement, informed the public, that the paper would be conducted by him.

Cornelia Bradford resumed the publication, October 18, 1744, and carried it on in her own name till the end of 1746. It was, I believe, soon after discontinued. The Mercury was well printed on a good type, during the whole time she had the management of it.

THE UNIVERSAL INSTRUCTOR *in all Arts and Sciences; And Pennsylvania Gazette* was the second newspaper established in the province; it has been continued under the title of the Pennsylvania Gazette to the present time, and is now (1810), the oldest newspaper in the United States.

* Andrew Bradford's widow, Cornelia. [No monument marks the place of Bradford's burial. See Jones's address on Andrew Bradford, pp. 28–31. M]

No. 1 was published December 24, 1728, by Samuel Keimer, on a small sheet, pot size, folio. In No. 2 the publisher adopted the style of the quakers, and dated it, 'The 2d of the 11th mo. 1728.' The first and second pages of each sheet were generally occupied with extracts from Chambers's Dictionary; this practice was continued until the 25th of the 7th mo., 1729, in which the article *Air* concludes the extracts.

When the paper had been published nine months, the printer had not procured one hundred subscribers.

Franklin, soon after he began business, formed the design of publishing a newspaper, but was prevented by the sudden appearance of this Gazette; he was greatly disappointed; and, as he observes, used his endeavors to bring it into contempt. He was successful, and the publisher, being obliged to relinquish it, for a trifling consideration resigned it to Franklin. At this time, Franklin was in partnership with Hugh Meredith; they began printing this paper with No. 40, and published it a few weeks on Mondays and Thursdays, on a whole or half sheet, pot, as occasion required. The price 'ten shillings per annum.' The first part of the title they expunged, and called their paper *The Pennsylvania Gazette*. 'Containing the freshest Advices Foreign and Domestick.' The Gazette, under their management, gained reputation, but until Franklin obtained the appointment of post-master, Bradford's Mercury had the largest circulation; after this event, the Gazette had a full proportion of subscribers and of advertising custom, and it became very profitable.

Meredith and Franklin separated in May, 1732. Franklin continued the Gazette, but published it only once a week. In 1733, he printed it on a crown half sheet, in quarto. Imprint, 'Philadelphia: Printed by B. Franklin, Post-Master, at the New

Printing-Office near the Market. Price 10s. a year. Where Advertisements are taken in, and Book-Binding is done reasonably in the best manner.' In 1741, he enlarged the size to a demy quarto, half sheet, and added a cut of the Pennsylvania arms in the title. In 1745, he returned to foolscap, folio. In 1748$\frac{7}{8}$ the Gazette was published 'By B. Franklin, Postmaster, and D. Hall;' it was enlarged to a whole sheet, crown, folio; and afterwards, by a great increase of advertisements, to a sheet, and often to a sheet and a half, demy. On the 9th of May, 1754, the device of a snake, divided into parts, with the motto, 'Join or die,' I believe, first appeared in this paper. It accompanied an account of the French and Indians having killed and scalped many of the inhabitants in the frontier counties of Virginia and Pennsylvania. The account was published with this device, with a view to rouse the British colonies, and cause them to unite in effectual measures for their defence and security against the common enemy. The snake was divided into eight parts, to represent, first, New England; second, New York; third, New Jersey; fourth, Pennsylvania; fifth, Maryland; sixth, Virginia; seventh, North Carolina; and eighth, South Carolina. The account and the figures appeared in several other papers, and had a good effect.

The Gazette was put into mourning October 31, 1765, on account of the stamp act, passed by the British parliament, which was to take effect the next day. From that time until the 21st of November following, the publication of it was suspended. In the interim, large handbills, as substitutes, were published, headed 'Remarkable Occurrences,' 'No Stamped paper to be had,' &c. When revived, it was published without an imprint until February 6, 1766; it then appeared with the name of David Hall only, who now became the proprietor and the printer of it.* In May following, it was published by Hall & Sellers, who continued it until 1772, when Hall died, but was succeeded by his sons; and the firm of Hall & Sellers continued, and the Gazette was published until 1777, when, on the approach of the British army, the publishers retired from Philadelphia, and the publication was suspended while the British possessed the city. On the evacuation of Philadelphia the Gazette was again revived, and published once a week until the death of Sellers, in 1804. After this event, it was printed by William and David Hall, and in 1810, published by William Hall, Jr., and George Pierie, every Wednesday.[28] William Hall, Jr., died in 1813, and George Pierie in 1814.

THE PENNSYLVANIA JOURNAL *and the Weekly Advertiser* was first published on Tuesday, December 2, 1742. It was printed on a foolscap sheet. The day of publication was changed to Wednesday. Imprint, 'Philadelphia: Printed by William Bradford, on the West side of Second Street, between Market and Chesnut Streets.' But soon after, 'at the Corner of Black-Horse-alley.'

About the year 1766, the imprint was, 'Philadelphia: Printed and sold by William and Thomas Bradford, at the corner of Front and Market-Streets, where all persons may be supplied with this Paper at Ten Shillings a year.—And where Advertisements are taken in.' In 1774, it had in the title, a large cut, the device, an open volume, on which the word 'JOURNAL' is very conspicuous; underneath the volume appears a ship under sail, inclosed in an ornamental border; the volume is supported by

* See account of Franklin and Hall, p. 368.

two large figures; the one on the right represents Fame, that on the left, one of the aborigines properly equipped. This device remained as long as the Journal was published, excepting from July 1774 to October 1775, during which time the device of the divided snake, with the motto, 'UNITE OR DIE,' was substituted in its room.

This paper was devoted to the cause of the country; but it was suspended during the period that the British army was in possession of Philadelphia. About the year 1788, it was published semi-weekly; but its title was not altered. It continued to be headed *The Pennsylvania Journal and Weekly Advertiser*. William Bradford died in 1791; the Journal was published by the surviving partner, until 1797, when it was finally discontinued, and the *True American*, a daily paper, was published in its stead.

THE PENNSYLVANIA CHRONICLE, *and Universal Advertiser*. In the middle of the title was placed a handsome cut of the king's arms. The Chronicle was published weekly, on Monday. The first number appeared January 6, 1767, well printed from a new bourgeois type, on a large medium sheet, folio. Imprint, 'Philadelphia: Printed by William Goddard, at the New-Printing Office, in Market-Street, near the Post-Office. Price Ten Shillings per Annum.'

This was the fourth newspaper in the English language established in Philadelphia, and the first with four columns to a page, printed in the northern colonies. The second to third years the Chronicle was printed in quarto, and the fourth year again in folio, but on a smaller sheet. It was ably edited; in all respects well executed; and it soon gained an extensive circulation. Joseph Galloway, a celebrated character at the commencement of the American revolution, and a delegate to the continental congress from Pennsylvania, before the declaration of independence, and Thomas Wharton, a wealthy merchant, but neither of them in the whig interest, were silent partners with Goddard. The Chronicle was established under their influence, and subject to their control, until 1770. Benjamin Towne, afterwards printer of *The Pennsylvania Evening Post*, was also, for a short time, a partner in the Chronicle establishment; he was introduced to this concern by Galloway and Wharton, who sold him their right in it. In 1770, Goddard separated from his partners, and the politics of the Chronicle became somewhat more in favor of the country. A portion of it was, however, for a long time, devoted by Goddard to the management of a literary warfare which took place between him and his late partners.

The Chronicle was published until February, 1773. It was then discontinued, and the publisher of it removed to Baltimore.

THE PENNSYLVANIA PACKET, *or the General Advertiser* was first issued from the press in November, 1771. It was well printed on a sheet of demy, by John Dunlap, in Market street, Philadelphia. The day of publication was Monday. A well executed cut of a ship divided the title.

From September, 1777, to July, 1778, when the British army was in possession of Philadelphia, the Packet was printed in Lancaster. On the return of the proprietor to Philadelphia, it was published three times in a week; but it was again reduced to twice a week, in 1780. In 1783, and until September 1784, it was

published three times a week by D. C. Claypoole;[29] it then
became a daily paper, and was published by John Dunlap and
David C. Claypoole, and called the *Pennsylvania Packet and
Daily Advertiser*. It was continued till the end of the year 1790
without alteration. In January, 1791, its size was enlarged; it was
printed with new type, on a super royal sheet, five columns in
a page, and published by John Dunlap. In December, 1793, it
was again printed and published by John Dunlap & David C.
Claypoole. In January, 1796, it is called *Claypoole's American
Daily Advertiser*; and printed by David C. and Septimus Claypoole. In 1799, it is by D. C. Claypoole only, as proprietor; and
October 1, 1800, Claypoole sold his right in the paper to Zachariah Poulson; who continued its publication with great reputation.[30] This was the first daily paper published in the United
States. [See p. 428.]

THE PENNSYLVANIA LEDGER; *or, The Virginia, Maryland,
Pennsylvania and New-Jersey Weekly Advertiser* was first published January 28, 1775. It had a cut of the king's arms in the
title. It was printed on a demy sheet, folio, with new types; the
workmanship was neat and correct, and it appeared on Saturdays. Imprint, 'Philadelphia: Printed by James Humphreys,
Jun., in Front-Street, at the Corner of Black-horse Alley;—
where Subscriptions are taken in for this Paper, at Ten Shillings
per Year.'

The publisher announced his intention to conduct his paper
with political impartiality; and, perhaps, in times more tranquil
than those in which it appeared, he might have succeeded in
his plan. He had, as has been stated, taken the oath of allegiance
to the king of England; he pleaded the obligations of his oath,

and refused to bear arms against the British government;* in consequence of which, he was deemed a tory, and his paper denounced as being under corrupt influence. The impartiality of the Ledger did not comport with the temper of the times; and, in November, 1776, Humphreys was obliged to discontinue it, and leave the city.

A few weeks before the British troops took possession of Philadelphia, in September, 1777, Humphreys returned, remained in the city whilst it was in their possession, and renewed the publication of the Ledger; but, when the royal army evacuated the place, it was again discontinued, and never afterwards revived. Whilst the British remained in Philadelphia, the Ledger was published twice a week, on Wednesday and Saturday, market days, and was called *The Public Ledger and Market Day Advertiser*. The last number was published May 23, 1778, and the British army quitted the city about the middle of the following month.

THE PENNSYLVANIA EVENING POST was first published January 24, 1775, by Benjamin Towne. It was well printed on half a sheet of crown paper, in quarto, and published three times in a week, viz; on Tuesday, Thursday, and Saturday evenings; 'Price two pennies each paper, or three Shillings the quarter.' This was the third evening paper which made its appearance in the colonies; the first was *The Boston Evening Post*, and the second *The New York Evening Post*. The Rev. Dr. Witherspoon, member of congress, and some other distinguished personages of that day, it has been said, furnished the Evening-Post occasionally, with intelligence and essays. Although the printer of

* See pp. 397-399.

the paper had been the agent of Galloway and Wharton, he was
on the side of the country until the British army entered the city
in 1777. He remained in Philadelphia after that event, and continued the Evening Post under the auspices of the British general, until the city was evacuated. Towne was proscribed by a
law of the state of Pennsylvania; he did not, however, leave
Philadelphia, but again changed his ground; and, without
molestation, continued his paper until 1782, about which time
the publication of it terminated. After this he occasionally published handbills, headed 'All the News, for two coppers.' These
were hawked in the streets by himself.

STORY AND HUMPHREYS'S PENNSYLVANIA MERCURY
and Universal Advertiser first came before the public, in April,
1775; and was published weekly, on Friday, printed on a demy
sheet, folio, with types said to be manufactured in the country.
A large cut decorated the title; Britain and America were represented by two figures, facing each other, and in the act of shak-
ing hands; underneath the figures was this motto: 'Affection
and Interest dictate the Union.' Imprint, 'Philadelphia; Printed
by Story and Humphreys, in Norris's-Alley, near Front-Street,
where Subscriptions, (at Ten Shillings per Annum), Advertisements, Articles and Letters of Intelligence, &c. are gratefully
received.'

The Mercury was short lived. The printing house whence it
was issued, and all the printing materials therein contained,
were destroyed by fire in December, 1775; and, in consequence
of that event, the paper was discontinued.

This was the last attempt to establish a newspaper in the city
before the American revolution. At the conclusion of the war

another paper by the same title was published by Humphreys, handsomely and correctly executed, and was continued for several years.

A NEWSPAPER in the German language was published weekly, in Philadelphia, as early as May, 1743. The printer of it was Joseph Crellius, who first lived in Market street, but during the year removed to Arch street, where the paper was probably printed and published several years. In November, 1743, Crellius advertised in the Pennsylvania Journal, that he had opened his 'Winter Evening German School, and continued to print his Weekly German Newspaper,' the title of which, I am informed, was *The High Dutch Pennsylvania Journal*. I have not been able to procure a copy of this newspaper, but I believe it was the first that was printed in Philadelphia in the German language.

In February, 1748, Godhart Armbruster commenced the publication, once in a fortnight, of a newspaper in the German language. His printing house was then in Race street.

By an advertisement in *The Pennsylvania Gazette* of September, 1751, I find there was at that time, 'A *Dutch* and *English* Gazette, containing the freshest Advices, foreign and domestick, with other entertaining and useful Matters in *both Languages*, adapted to the Convenience of such as incline to learn *either*,' printed 'at the *German Printing-Office*, in Arch-street; price five shillings per annum.' 'At the same place Copper-plate Printing was performed in the best Manner.' The title of the newspaper was *Die Zeitung*. The name of the publisher of this paper is not mentioned; but it is ascertained to have been Godhart Armbruster, who, in 1747, went to Europe. He returned in 1748, and brought with him a copper plate printer by the name of Behm, and a supply of new German types. This Gazette was probably that which he first published in 1748. It is mentioned in his Almanac for 1749, and was then published weekly, at ten shillings per annum. In 1751 it was printed only once in a fortnight, as at first.

A press for the German language had been established in that city, for some years, at the expense of a society in London, formed for the benevolent purpose of 'promoting religious knowledge among the German emigrants in Pennsylvania.' School books, and religious tracts in the German language, were printed at this press; and, in order to convey, with the greater facility, political and other information to the German citizens, a newspaper was published at the establishment. The title of the paper I have not been able to ascertain. It was printed by Anthony Armbruster;* with whom, at that time, Franklin was a silent copartner.

The Rev. Dr. William Smith, provost of the college at Philadelphia, was agent for the English society, and had the direction of the press, and of the newspaper.

Formal complaints having been made to the house of assembly respecting the official conduct of William Moore, president of the court of common pleas for the county of Chester, the assembly applied to the governor to remove him from office. Moore, in his vindication, presented 'a humble address' to the governor, which was expressed in terms that proved offensive to the assembly. It was published both in the Gazette and

---

* Since the first edition of this work was published, I have been informed that the newspaper here mentioned was the continuation of that published in 1748, and after by Godhart Armbruster.

in the Journal; and application was made to Dr. Smith to publish a German translation of it in the German newspaper, with which he complied. The house of assembly considered this address as a high reflection on the proceedings of their body, and resolved that 'it was a libel.'

The assembly were desirous of discovering the author of the German translation. They were suspicious of Dr. Smith. The three printers of newspapers, and several other persons, were summoned to give their testimony before the assembly. Hall and Bradford, printers of the English newspapers, knew nothing of the German translation, and were dismissed. Armbruster was interrogated, and committed to the custody of the sergeant at arms, for a contempt to the house in prevaricating in his testimony, and refusing to answer a question put to him; but he was the next day discharged, on his asking pardon, giving direct answers, and paying fees.

The Rev. Dr. Smith, the editor of the German paper, and Judge Moore, were on the 6th of January, 1758, apprehended and brought before the house. Moore was charged by the assembly with mal-administration in his office as a magistrate, and with writing and publishing the address. In respect to the first charge, he denied the jurisdiction of the house; at the same time declaring his desire to obtain an impartial hearing before the governor, the usual tribunal in such cases; or, before a court of justice, where he could be acquitted or condemned by his peers. To the second charge he acknowledged that he wrote and published the address to the governor, and claimed a right to do it. He was imprisoned for refusing to acknowledge the jurisdiction of the house, and for writing the address. Dr. Smith was also committed for printing and publishing the address, although he pleaded 'that the same thing had been done four weeks before by Franklin & Hall, printers to the house, in the Pennsylvania Gazette; and, afterwards, by Bradford, printer of the Pennsylvania Journal; neither of whom had been molested.'

The house, by two resolves, fixed the nature of the crime, and their own authority to try it. Smith, before he left the house, offered to appeal to the king in council; but this was not taken notice of by the assembly. It was intimated to Smith, that he could escape confinement only by making satisfactory acknowledgement to the house; to this he replied, 'that he thought it his duty to keep the Dutch press as *free* as any other press in the province; and, as he was conscious of no offence against the house, his lips should never give his heart the lie; there being no punishment, which they could inflict, half so terrible to him as the thought of forfeiting his veracity and good name with the world.' He spoke more to the same purpose, which was so highly approved by a large audience that on that occasion had crowded into the hall of the assembly, as to produce a burst of applause. Some gentlemen who gave this token of their approbation, were taken into custody, examined, reprimanded and discharged. Smith and Moore determined to petition the king for redress.*

This German paper was published about the year 1759, by Weiss and Miller, conveyancers. It was printed for them about two years by Armbruster.

In 1762, Anthony Armbruster printed this German paper on his own account, and, in 1764, published it weekly in Arch street.

* See *American Magazine* for January, 1758. See also, *Journals of the House of Assembly of Pennsylvania*, for 1757 and 1758.

H. Miller's German paper was commenced also in 1762; and for some time there were two German and two English newspapers published in Philadelphia.

DER WOCHENTLICHE PHILADELPHISCHE STAATSBOTE was first published in the German language at Philadelphia, in January, 1762; printed by Henry Miller, with German types, very similar to, though handsomer than English blacks. It was, as occasion required, printed on a whole or half sheet of foolscap; the size of the paper was afterwards enlarged to a crown sheet. The day of publication, at first, was Monday, but it was frequently changed.

In 1775, the paper was enlarged to a demy size, and published twice a week, on Tuesday and Friday; in 1776, only once a week, on Tuesdays, at 6s. per annum. In 1765, a cut of a postman on horseback, was introduced into the title; the postman was on a gallop, and held in his left hand a newspaper, on which appeared the word *Novæ*. In 1768, the title was altered to *Pennsylvanische Staatsbote*. In 1775, the cut was omitted, and the paper entitled *Henrich Miller's Pennsylvanischer Staatsbote*. With this alteration in the title, it was printed until the British army took possession of the city in 1777; the publication of it was then suspended, but was revived soon after that army evacuated Philadelphia, and continued till May, 1779, when the publisher retired from business, and his paper was continued by Steiner & Cist, for a few months, and then by Steiner only, until 1794; and after that time by H. & J. Kammerer, and others, until 1812, when it was discontinued. [See pp. 387–389.]

James Robertson, who before 1775 printed at Albany, and afterwards at Norwich and New York, published in Philadel-

phia, whilst the British army occupied the city, a paper entitled
The Royal Gazette.

A PUBLIC journal was printed in the German language
at Germantown, as early as the summer of 1739, by
Christopher Sower.[31] The title of it in English was

THE PENNSYLVANIA GERMAN RECORDER OF EVENTS.[32]
At first this paper was printed quarterly, at three shillings per
annum; it was afterward published monthly, and continued for
several years. This was, undoubtedly, the first newspaper printed in the German language in America.

GERMANTOWNER ZEITUNG (*Germantown Gazette*) was
printed by Christopher Sower, jun., and, probably, as a substitute for the *Germantown Recorder*, which had been published by
his father. It was a weekly paper, and commenced about 1744.
As an appendage to it, Sower for some time published, every
fortnight, a small magazine of eight, 8vo. pages, containing,
chiefly, moral and religious essays; with which, it is said, he, for
some time, supplied his newspaper customers gratis. It was
entitled *Ein Geistliches Magazin.*[33] The *Zeitung* was continued
until the troubles occasioned by the revolutionary war obliged
the publisher to drop it. It had an extensive circulation among
the Germans settled in Pennsylvania. Its publication was continued till 1748.

A NEWSPAPER in the English and German languages
was published in Lancaster, by Miller and Holland, in

January, 1751. What the title of it was I cannot learn, nor the time at which it was discontinued.

Francis Bailey, it is said, published a paper in English soon after the beginning of the war, but this fact is doubted by some. He afterwards removed to Philadelphia, in 1778, and there published the *Freeman's Journal*.

THE GENERAL MAGAZINE, *and Historical Chronicle, for all the British Plantations in America* was published monthly. No. 1 appeared in January, 1741. It has for a frontispiece, the prince of Wales's coronet and feather, with the motto, *Ich Dien.* It was published only six months. Imprint, 'Philadelphia: Printed and sold by Benjamin Franklin.' 12*s.* per annum. 12mo.

THE AMERICAN MAGAZINE, *or a Monthly View of the British Colonies* was first published January, 1741. Foolscap 8vo., forty-eight pages. 12*s.* per annum. Imprint, 'Philadelphia: Printed and sold by Andrew Bradford.'

This work was edited by, and published for, John Webbe, who having issued the prospectus from the American Mercury of November 6, 1740, gave offence to Benjamin Franklin, and produced a short, but smart paper war between Franklin, Webbe, and Bradford. Webbe had employed Bradford to print the work. Franklin asserted that it had previously been engaged to him. This was contradicted by Webbe; but he acknowledged that he had conversed with Franklin on the subject, who had given to him, in writing, the terms on which he would print and publish it. The consequence was, that Franklin began the magazine above mentioned, and published it a month sooner than Webbe could bring his forward. I cannot find that Bradford and Webbe printed more than two numbers of this work.

THE AMERICAN MAGAZINE, *or Monthly Chronicle for the British Colonies* was first published in October, 1757. Imprint, 'Philadelphia: Printed by William Bradford.' Price 12s. per annum. It was discontinued soon after the appearance of *The New American Magazine*, printed in January, 1758, by Parker, and edited by Nevil, at Woodbridge. I cannot find that Bradford published more than three numbers.

THE PENNY POST was a small work of a few pages 12 mo. published for a short time by Benjamin Mecom, in 1769. I have not seen a copy of it. His design was to print it weekly; but it came from the press in an irregular manner.

THE AMERICAN MAGAZINE was published monthly, through the year 1769, for its author Lewis Nicola; each number contained forty-eight pages. To this magazine were subjoined the transactions of the American Philosophical Society, of which Nicola was a member. The work was begun and ended with the year. It was printed in octavo, price 13s. per annum.

Nicola was born at Rochelle, in France, and educated in Ireland. He had some appointment in the British army, but quitted it. He was the author of one or more small military treatises, written about the commencement of our revolution, to which he was friendly. He obtained military rank in Pennsylvania, and eventually became a general officer in the militia.

THE ROYAL SPIRITUAL MAGAZINE, *or the Christian's Grand Treasury* was begun in 1771, and published monthly, for a few months only, by John MacGibbons, in Front street, between Arch and Race streets.

THE PENNSYLVANIA MAGAZINE, *or American Monthly Museum* was first published in January, 1775, by Robert Aitken. The celebrated Thomas Paine, author of *Common Sense,** &c., was one of the principal compilers and writers of the Museum. It was a work of merit; each number contained forty-eight pages, octavo, with an engraving. The war put an end to it.

Aitken contracted with Paine to furnish, monthly, for this work, a certain quantity of original matter; but he often found it difficult to prevail on Paine to comply with his engagement. On one of the occasions, when Paine had neglected to supply the materials for the Magazine, within a short time of the day of publication, Aitken went to his lodgings, and complained of his neglecting to fulfil his contract. Paine heard him patiently, and coolly answered, 'You shall have them in time.' Aitken expressed some doubts on the subject, and insisted on Paine's accompanying him and proceeding immediately to business, as the workmen were waiting for copy. He accordingly went home with Aitken, and was soon seated at the table with the necessary apparatus, which always included a glass, and a decanter of brandy. Aitken remarked, 'he would never write without *that.*' The first glass put him in a train of thinking; Aitken feared the second would disqualify him, or render him

* There was a political paper published in London, in 1739, which I have seen, that bears the title *Common Sense.*

untractable; but it only illuminated his intellectual system; and when he had swallowed the third glass, he wrote with great rapidity, intelligence, and precision; and his ideas appeared to flow faster than he could commit them to paper. What he penned from the inspiration of the brandy, was perfectly fit for the press without any alteration, or correction.*

* Aitken was a man of truth, and of an irreproachable character. This anecdote came from him some years before his death. Paine, when he edited the Magazine for Aitken, was suspected of toryism.

NOTES TO CHAPTER VI

Chief among works published after Thomas's pioneering book are: C. R. Hildeburn, *A Century of Printing; Issues of the Press in Pennsylvania, 1685–1784* (Philadelphia, 1885–1886), 2 vols.; 'William McCulloch's Additions to Thomas's *History of Printing*' edited by C. S. Brigham and published in *The Proceedings of the American Antiquarian Society*, XXXI, 89–247 (April 1921), is a most interesting appendix to Thomas on Pennsylvania printing; Oswald Seidensticker, *The First Century of German Printing in America, 1728–1830* (Philadelphia, 1893); D. C. McMurtrie, *A History of Printing in the United States* (New York, 1936), II, 1–98.

For works on printing in Philadelphia, see Carl Bridenbaugh, 'The Press and the Book in Eighteenth Century Philadelphia,' in *The Pennsylvania Magazine of History and Biography*, LXV, 1–30 (Jan. 1941); H. G. Brown, *A Directory of the Book-Arts and Book Trade in Philadelphia to 1820* (New York, 1950); J. W. Wallace, 'Early Printing in Philadelphia,' in *Pennsylvania Magazine of History and Biography*, IV, 432–446 (1880).

1. The inscription on Bradford's tombstone, in Trinity church yard, New York, says: 'He was born in Leicestershire, in old England, in 1660.' But *The American Almanack for 1739*, printed by him, has in the record of events which have occurred in the month of May: 'The printer born the 20th 1663.' That day was accordingly selected for commemoration in 1863. H See also J. W. Wallace, *An Address delivered ... May 20, 1863, on the Two Hundredth Birth Day of Mr. William Bradford*

(Albany, N.Y., 1863); A. J. Wall, Jr., 'William Bradford, Colonial Printer,' in *Proceedings of the American Antiquarian Society*, LXXIII, 361–384 (Oct. 1963); *Dictionary of American Biography*, II, 563–564.

2. Mr. Wallace, in his commemorative address, says: 'The earliest issue of Bradford's press, known to me, is an Almanack for the year 1686, produced of course in 1685. It was called *Kalendarium Pennsylvaniense or America's Messenger, an Almanack.*

'In 1686 he produced Burnyeat's Epistle. The title is *An Epistle from John Burnyeat to friends in Pennsylvania, to be by them dispensed to the Neighboring Provinces, which for Convenience and Dispatch was thought good to be Printed, and so ordered by the Quarterly meeting of Philadelphia the 7th of 4th Month 1686.* Printed and Sold by William Bradford, near Philadelphia, 1686.'

The fact that in 1688 Bradford issued proposals for printing 'a large Bible' was accidentally discovered by Mr. Nathan Kite of Philadelphia, one hundred and fifty years afterwards, he having found a copy of the proposals in print serving as the inner lining paper of the cover of a book. The proposals are given in full in the appendix to Mr. Wallace's address. H

3. These extracts from the printed contemporaneous accounts of Bradford's trial are not literal transcripts of the original; but the forms of expression were sometimes condensed, and sometimes paraphrased, by Thomas, while meaning always to preserve the sense. H

4. *Dictionary of American Biography*, IX, 611–612.

5. A. J. DeArmond, *Andrew Bradford, Colonial Journalist* (Newark, Del., 1949).

6. In *Andrew Bradford, Founder of the Newspaper Press in the Middle States of America* (Historical Society of Pennsylvania, 1869), the 1869 annual address by Horatio Gates Jones, it is said that Bradford's paper, the *Weekly Mercury* of April 4, 1728, has a statement that 'the Post Office will be kept at the house of Andrew Bradford.' He may therefore have had the appointment that early. H

7. Mr. Jones in his discourse controverts this charge of illiteracy against Bradford [which originated with Franklin]. H

8. Mr. Jones, p. 21, enumerates seven almanacs printed by Bradford, rivals of Poor Richard, besides a sheet almanac. M

9. Mr. Jones in his discourse on Andrew Bradford says he died 'on the night of the 24th of November.' M

10. *Dictionary of American Biography*, X, 288–289.

11. Of a very large body of literature concerning Franklin, see particularly *The Papers of Benjamin Franklin* (Yale University Press,

1959–), 14 vols.+; *The Autobiography of Benjamin Franklin* (Yale University Press, 1964); *Account Books kept by Benjamin Franklin*, ed. by G. S. Eddy (New York, 1928–1929), 2 vols; *Dictionary of American Biography*, VI, 585–598.

12. The reader will call to mind the fact that a translation of the last ten books of Ovid's Metamorphoses was made in Virginia by George Sandys, the colonial treasurer, between 1621 and 1626. It was printed in London in 1626. H

13. The birthday of Deborah Read cannot now be ascertained; she was married to Franklin Sept. 1, 1730, and died Dec. 19, 1774. The head-stone of John Read, who died Sept. 2, 1724, found under the Franklin monuments, is supposed to be that of her father. The two are always mentioned as Mr. and Miss Read in the notices of them. There is a pedigree of Franklin's descendants in *The Papers of Benjamin Franklin*, I, lxii–lxvi. M

14. They printed the journals of Congress in 1776. M

15. *Dictionary of American Biography*, VIII, 123.

16. *Dictionary of American Biography*, XII, 631–632.

17. *Dictionary of American Biography*, II, 558–559.

18. *Dictionary of American Biography*, V, 514–515; A. M. Lee, 'Dunlap and Claypool,' in *Journalism Quarterly*, XI, 160–178 (June 1934).

19. *Dictionary of American Biography*, IX, 375–376.

20. W. Spawn, 'The Aitkin Shop,' in *Papers of the Bibliographical Society of America*, LVII, 422–437 (4th qtr. 1963).

GERMANTOWN

21. F. Reichmann, *Christopher Sower, Sr., 1694–1758* (Philadelphia, 1943); *Dictionary of American Biography*, XVII, 415–416; E. W. Hocken, *The Sower Printing House of Colonial Times* (Pennsylvania German Society, 1948).

22. For a bibliographical account of this edition of the German Bible, see E. B. O'Callaghan's *List of Editions of the Holy Scriptures*, pp. xii, 32 *et seq.* M

23. *Dictionary of American Biography*, XVII, 416–417.

24. J. O. Knauss, 'Christopher Saur the Third,' in *Proceedings of the American Antiquarian Society*, XLI, 235–253 (April 1931); *Dictionary of American Biography*, XVII, 417–418.

LANCASTER

25. See L. M. Bausman, *A Bibliography of Lancaster County, 1745–1912* (Philadelphia, 1916).

26. *Dictionary of American Biography*, I, 494–495.

27. There were 14 newspapers printed in the state of Pennsylvania in 1790, and it was supposed about five times that number in the whole country. The first stage between New York and Philadelphia commenced running in 1756, and occupied three days in the transit. Newspapers were carried in the mail free of charge, until 1758, when, by reason of their great increase, they were charged with postage at 9*d.* a year for fifty miles, and 18*d.* for 100 miles. M

28. There is a complete file of this paper from 1728 to 1804, in the collection of the Library Company of Philadelphia. Its publication was suspended for a short time in 1815; but it was resumed, and survived until 1823 or 1824, when it was the oldest paper in the country. M

29. Mr. Claypoole was a gentleman of the old school, supposed to have been a descendant from Oliver Cromwell, whom he is said to have resembled in feature. The debates in Congress, from 1783 to 1799, were printed in his paper. He also published the first edition of Washington's *Farewell Address*, and had permission to preserve the manuscript, which was sold Feb. 15, 1850, by auction, and purchased by Mr. James Lenox, of New York, for upwards of $2,000. It consists of about 30 pages, in Washington's hand writing. Mr. Claypoole died March 19, 1849, aged 92. M

30. Zachariah Poulson was the son of Zacharia, who was born in Copenhagen, Denmark, June 16, 1737. He was the only son of Nicholas Paulsen, a printer, who left his native country to enjoy liberty of conscience. They arrived in Philadelphia in 1749. Zacharia learned printing of Christopher Saur, the noted German printer at Germantown, and married Anna Barbara Stallenberg. He was a man of the most exemplary piety and manners; his 'countenance, on which nature had shed its bounty, was ever enhanced and lit up by the evidences of a happy train of mental associations. ... His apparel was a light drab, plain cut coat, and breeches in old-time fashion.' He died on the 4th of June, 1804, aged 67. It is recorded of him that he had always been esteemed, by those who knew him, for his integrity, for the sincerity and ardor of his friendship, and for his amiable and inoffensive deportment. His remains were borne to the cemetery of the Moravian church by his brethren of the typographic art [Abraham Ritter, *History of the Moravian Church of Philadelphia* (Philadelphia, 1857), pp. 90–91]. The son, Zachariah junior, mentioned above, was born in Philadelphia, Sept. 5, 1761. He served his apprenticeship with Joseph Cruikshank, was eminent as a printer, and was for many years elected printer for the senate of the state. On the 1st of October, 1800, he undertook to conduct a daily paper, having

purchased Mr. Claypoole's establishment for $10,000. Poulson continued his paper under the title of *Poulson's Daily Advertiser*, until Dec. 18, 1839, when it was merged in another concern. He died July 31, 1844, aged 83, 'being the last link connecting the publishing fraternity with that of the days of Franklin.' He had acquired a large fortune by his paper. His portrait is given in Henry Simpson, *The Lives of Eminent Philadelphians* (Philadelphia, 1859). His son, Charles A. Poulson, died Feb. 15, 1866, aged 77. The *Philadelphia North American*, with which the *Advertiser* was united, announced in 1867, that it had entered upon its one hundredth year, and was never more prosperous. M

31. This person was a native of Germany, born 1693, and immigrated 1724. He wrote his name Saur (pronounced *sour*), for which reason, it is probable, his son altered the orthography of his own name to Sower. For a particular description of Saur and his enterprises, see Simpson's *Lives of Eminent Philadelphians*, p. 902; *Printer's Circular*, VII, 356 (Dec. 1872); O'Callaghan's *List of Editions of the Holy Scriptures*, passim. M

32. This paper was entitled *Der Hoch-Deutsch Pennsylvänische Geschicht-Schreiber, oder Sammlung wichtiger Nachrichten aus dem Natur- und Kirchen-Reich*, signifying in English, the High-Dutch Pennsylvania Historiographer, or collection of Impartial Intelligence from the Kingdoms of Nature and the Church. Saur designed it to serve as a journal for the sect of Tunkers, with whom he was identified, and at first published it only occasionally on one side of a sheet for gratuitous distribution. It took a more definite form in 1736, as a folio, 9 by 13 inches. See *Printer's Circular*, VII, 356. M

33. For a more correct account of this work see Simpson's *Lives of Eminent Philadelphians*, pp. 903–904, note. M

NEW YORK

THIS colony was settled by the Dutch, and remained in their possession until 1664, when it was surrendered to the king of England, and by him granted to the duke of York. No press was established under the Dutch government.

In 1665, *The Conditions for New Planters in the Territories of His Royal Highness the Duke of York*, who was afterwards king of England, were printed on one side of a foolscap half sheet. A gentleman,* who possessed one of the printed copies of these conditions, informed me that, on its margin, in ancient writing, were these words, 'This was printed at Boston in May 1665.' Cambridge was undoubtedly meant, as a press was not established in Boston till some years after this time. This writing is, however, proof that in 1665 there was no printing press in New York. The small quantity of printing necessary for the colony was probably done at Cambridge, or at Boston, until about 1684, when William Bradford began printing in Pennsylvania. It does not appear that any printing was executed in New York until 1693.

In 1700, some gentlemen in Boston applied to Bartholomew Green of that town, to print a pamphlet, entitled, 'Gospel Order Revived, Being an Answer to a Book lately set forth by the Reverend Mr. *Increase Mather*, President of *Harvard* College,

* Hon. Ebenezer Hazard, of Philadelphia; late postmaster general.

&c. entituled, *The* Order of the Gospel, *&c.* Dedicated to the Churches of Christ in *New-England. By sundry Ministers of the Gospel in New-England.*' Green declined printing the pamphlet before it had been submitted to the licensers of the press, to which the authors would not consent. Some months after, the pamphlet was published, and appeared without the name of the printer, or the place of his residence. The imprint was, 'Printed in the year 1700.' To the pamphlet was prefixed the following advertisement, viz.

'The reader is desired to take Notice, that the Press in Boston is so much under the *aw* of the Reverend Author whom we answer, and his Friends, that we could not obtain of the Printer there to print the following sheets, which is the only true Reason why we have sent the Copy so far for its Impression.'

The pamphlet, on its appearance in Boston, particularly the advertisement attached to it, produced considerable agitation. Green to clear himself of the aspersion, as he termed it, of his press being under control, etc., published a handbill, a newspaper was not then published in English America. In this handbill, Green asserts that the pamphlet was printed at New York.

This pamphlet, of which I have a copy, contains fifty two pages, small quarto, incorrectly and badly printed, and is, the laws excepted, the only book printed in New York as early as 1700, which I have seen, that contained more than thirty-eight pages.[1]

WILLIAM BRADFORD,[2] the first who printed in Pennsylvania, introduced the art into New York. He continued his printing in Philadelphia until some time in the year 1693, when he set up a press in New York, and was appointed printer to the government. The first book from his press was a small folio volume of the laws of the colony, bearing the date of that year. In the imprint he styles himself 'Printer to their Majesties,' and directs to his printing house 'at the Sign of the Bible.'

In 1698, he printed *The Proceedings of His Excellency Earle Bellemount, Governor of New York, and his council, on the 8th of May 1698*, one sheet folio, New York, printed by William Bradford, printer to the King, 1698.

His imprint to 'an account of the illegal trial of Nicholas Bayard in $170\frac{1}{2}$,' is, 'Printed by William Bradford at Sign of the Bible New York, 1702.'

In 1709, November 12, the general assembly of the colony ordered, 'that Mr. Bradford do print all the acts of the general assembly of this colony now in force.' A warrant from the speaker, of the same date, '*appoints* and *orders* William Bradford' to print the laws in conformity to the resolve of the general assembly. The laws were printed by him accordingly, and he completed them in the year following, with this imprint. 'Printed by *William Bradford*, printer to the Queen's most excellent majesty for the colony of New York, 1710.'*

I have a pamphlet printed in that city in 1711, by 'William and Andrew Bradford,' from which it appears that, at that time,

---

* Wm. Smith in his *History of the Province of New-York* (Philadelphia, 1792), p. 124, mentions that in 1703, the governor proposed to the assembly to lay a duty of ten per cent. on certain articles, but they resolved to the contrary. On which 'the very printer, clerk, and door keeper, were denied their salaries.' He also says, p. 132, 'the assembly of 1709, agreed to raise money for several designated purposes, among which were small salaries to the printer, clerk of the council, and Indian interpreter.'

there was some connection in business between Bradford and
his son Andrew; but that concern could have been only for a
year or two, for Andrew, in 1712, removed to Philadelphia.

Franklin* mentions that when he first visited New York
about 1723, William Bradford was a printer, and it appears the
only printer, in that city. Franklin applied to him for work;
Bradford having but little business could not employ him; but
he recommended him to his son, who then printed in Philadelphia, and Franklin accordingly went there.

Franklin observes, that Bradford was the first who printed in
Pennsylvania, but had 'quitted that province on account of a
quarrel with *George Keith*, the governor,' etc. He must have
made a mistake; there had been no governor of Pennsylvania by
the name of *George Keith*. Sir William Keith was appointed
governor in 1717; but Bradford had settled in New York
twenty four years prior to that event. There was a George
Keith,† who has already been taken notice of as a man of
abilities, a schoolmaster, and preacher among the quakers, and
the author of several tracts in their defence, which were printed
by Bradford when he resided in Philadelphia. This George

---

* *Autobiography*, p. 71.

† George Keith repelled the attack of Increase and Cotton Mather upon the
quakers, and then differed with his brethren, who in consequence disowned
him; afterwards he went to England, took holy orders, returned to America,
as a missionary from the Society for propagating the gospel in foreign parts,
and, in 1702, preached a sermon 'at her Majesties Chapel, at Boston in New
England,' entitled 'The Doctrine of the Holy Apostles and Prophets the Foundation of the Church of Christ.' This sermon was printed, at Boston, the same
year. He again returned to England, and in 1706, published 'a journal of [his]
travels from New Hampshire to Caratuck, on the continent of America.' At
this time he was rector of Edburton in Sussex, England. It was posterior to this
event that he became a Baptist, and the founder of a sect called Keithian
Baptists.

Keith was violently hostile to President Lloyd, who governed Pennsylvania in the absence of the proprietor.* Bradford as has been stated became interested in the quarrel, and he, with Keith and others, seceded from the quakers, which eventually caused Bradford's removal to New York.

Bradford continued to print for the government of New York; and during thirty years was the only printer in the province. On the 16th of October, 1725, he began the publication of the first newspaper printed in that colony.

Bradford is characterized by Franklin as 'a cunning old fox.' Be this as it may, he was very kind to Franklin when the latter was a young and needy adventurer, as is apparent from the account which Franklin himself gives of their first and second interviews. He had two sons, Andrew and William, and a daughter, all by his first wife; both sons were brought up to printing. Andrew, who was named after his grandfather Andrew Sowles, printer in London, settled in Philadelphia. William not enjoying health on land, soon after he became of age adopted the life of a seaman. Tacey, his daughter, who was named after her grandmother, the wife of Andrew Sowles, was married to Mr. Hyat, who was several years sheriff of Philadelphia county.

Bradford, having buried his first wife, married a widow in the city of New York, of the name of Smith, who had several children by her former husband. This marriage, it has been said, was attended with no small injury to his pecuniary interests. He continued his residence in the city, and enjoyed a long life without experiencing sickness or the usual infirmities

* See William Bradford, under the head of Philadelphia.

of age. Several years before his death he retired from business,
and lived with his son William, in Hanover square. As early as
1728, he owned a papermill at Elizabethtown, New Jersey.
When this mill was built, I cannot determine; but probably it
was the first that was erected in New Jersey.

On the morning of the day which closed his life, he walked
over a great part of the city. He died May 23, 1752, aged
ninety two years. The *New York Gazette* which announced his
death on the Monday following, mentions, 'that he came to
America seventy years ago; was printer to the government upwards of fifty years, and was a man of great sobriety and industry; a real friend to the poor and needy, and kind and affable
to all. His temperance was exceedingly conspicuous; and he was
almost a stranger to sickness all his life. He had left off business
several years past, and being quite worn out with old age and
labor, his lamp of life went out for want of oil.' He was buried
in Trinity churchyard, where his tombstone yet remains. The
inscription on this stone concludes thus.

> Reader, reflect how soon you'll quit this stage,
> You'll find but few attain to such an age;
> Life's full of pain; lo, here's a place of rest;
> Prepare to meet your God, then you are blest.

'Here also lies the body of Elizabeth, wife to the said William
Bradford, who departed this life July 8, 1731, aged 68 years.'
[See pp. 340–355.]

JOHN PETER ZENGER[3] was established in New York as early
as 1726, and printed in Smith street. Afterwards, in 1734, he
removed 'to Broad-Street near the upper End of the Long
Bridge.' It appears that his business for several years was con-

fined to printing pamphlets for the authors of them, and some small articles for himself.

In the latter part of the year 1733 he began the publication of a newspaper. Until this time only one had been printed in the city, and there was no other paper issued from any press between Philadelphia and Boston.

Zenger's *Journal* soon assumed political features which excited general attention in the colony; several writers in this paper attacked the measures of government with a boldness which was unusual in those days. Zenger was, in consequence, arrested, confined in prison for several months, debarred the use of pen, ink and paper, denied the conversation of his friends, and finally tried upon a charge of libellous publications in his Journal; but he was acquitted by the jury, to the great mortification of the officers of the government, and to the no less gratification of the citizens.*

Zenger was poor.[4] Sometime after his commitment his counsel moved that he might be admitted to bail; but the court demanded bail which was deemed to be excessive. Zenger was examined respecting his property; and he made oath 'that, his debts being paid, he was not worth forty pounds, the tools of his trade and his wearing apparel excepted.' Notwithstanding this oath, the court 'ordered that he might be admitted to bail, himself in 400*l.* with two sureties, each in 200*l.*, and that he should be remanded till he gave it.' Zenger 'knowing this sum to be ten times the amount of what indemnity he could give to any person to whom he might apply to be his bondsman, declined to ask that favor of his friends, and submitted to further confinement.'

* See pp. 487–491.

Zenger was a German. In one of his newspapers, published during his imprisonment, he mentioned, that 'tho' he was a poor printer, he should remember that he had good German blood in his veins.'[5] He and Bradford were, for a number of years, the only printers in New York, and for a long time they carried on a paper war against each other. In December, 1734, a writer in *Bradford's Gazette* accused Zenger of publishing 'pieces tending to set the province in a flame, and to raise sedition and tumults;' and deridingly upbraided him with being brought to America at the expense of government, etc. Zenger, in his *Journal*, refutes the charges of criminality brought against him. He was then in confinement, and dates '*From my prison*, December 20, 1734.' Respecting his being sent to America at the expense of the government, he observes: 'That I was brought over at the charitable expense of the crown is the only truth that groaping fumbler found when he studied that clumsy performance.—I acknowledge it; thanks to Queen Anne, whose name I mention with reverence, her bounty to me and my distress'd country folks will be gratefully remembered,' etc. The writer in the *Gazette* had made some remarks on Zenger's sword; and stated that the sheriff had no private orders relative to his confinement. To these remarks Zenger replied—'My sword was never intended to protect me against a sworn officer in the discharge of his duty: But since this scribbler must needs make himself merry with it, I think it may not be amiss to tell my readers a serious but true story. About eight weeks ago the Honorable Francis Harrison [one of the council] came to my house, and swore by the God that made him he would lay his cane over me the first time he met me in the street, with some other scurrilous expressions more fit to be uttered to a drayman than a gentleman. Against such Assaults my sword not only could but would have protected me, and shall while I have it against any man that has impudence enough to attempt any thing of that nature.— *Vim vi repellere licet*. What private orders the sheriff had concerning me are best known to himself. This I know that from the time of my being apprehended till the return of the precept by virtue of which I was taken, I was deny'd the use of pen, ink, and paper; alterations were purposely made on my account, to put me into a place by myself, where I was so strictly confined above fifty hours that my wife might not speak to me but in presence of the sub-sheriff; to say this was done without orders is lybelling the sheriff, and I hope he will resent it.'

It appears that Zenger was a good workman, and a scholar; but not a correct printer of English. He had a family, and two of his sons were his apprentices. He continued in business till about August, 1746, when he died, and was succeeded by his widow.

One of his daughters was mistress of a tavern in New York in 1758, and her house was frequently resorted to by printers who respected her father.

JAMES PARKER[6] was born in Woodbridge, New Jersey, and served his apprenticeship with William Bradford in New York. He began business about the year 1742, when Bradford quitted it. Bradford's *New York Gazette* being discontinued, Parker established another newspaper of the same title, with the addition of *Post Boy*.

Parker was well acquainted with printing, a neat workman, and active in business. By the aid of partners, he established a press at New Haven; and, conducted one in New York, and another in Woodbridge. In 1752, he began the publication of a periodical work, entitled, *The Reflector*.[7] In January, 1753, Parker commenced a partnership in New York with William Weyman, under the firm of PARKER & WEYMAN. Weyman managed the concerns of the firm. They published several books, and printed for government. Their newspaper was in good repute; it had an extensive circulation, and they acquired property.*

Parker purchased the press and types which had been owned by Zenger; and, in 1755, he opened a printing house in New Haven, in partnership with John Holt. During his connection with Weyman, Parker resided for the greater part of his time at Woodbridge, and managed the press in that place on his own account. In January, 1759, Parker and Weyman dissolved their partnership. Parker continued the business a few weeks, and then assigned it over to his nephew Samuel Parker. In July, 1760, James Parker resumed his printing house and newspaper in New York. Holt, having closed his concerns at New Haven, came to New York, and Parker and he formed a partnership under the firm of JAMES PARKER & COMPANY. This partnership ended in April, 1762, when Parker, who still resided in New Jersey, leased his newspaper and printing house to Holt.

In 1766, Holt quitted the premises, and Parker again resumed them, and carried on the business of the printing house, in connection with his son, until a few months before his death. He had long been an invalid. It was his intention when he separated from Holt, to have resided wholly in the city; but his declining health obliged him to be a great part of his time at Woodbridge, and finally to retire from business. In 1770, he closed all his earthly concerns.

* See Newspapers, and other periodical works, under the head of New York.

A paper addressed 'To the Betrayed Inhabitants of New York,' signed '*A Son of Liberty*,' was printed privately in Parker's printing house, in December, 1769. This paper was laid before the general assembly, which resolved that it was 'a false, seditious and infamous libel;' and, in an address, requested the lieutenant governor, to issue his proclamation, offering a reward of one hundred pounds, New York currency, for the discovery of the author. A journeyman in Parker's printing house, one Michael Cummings, from Cork, in Ireland, allured by the proffered reward, lodged a complaint against Parker, as the printer; in consequence of which, he was taken into custody, on the 7th of January, 1770, by virtue of a warrant from the chief justice Horsmanden, in which he was charged with being the printer of the libel, and made amenable, before the lieutenant governor and council, to be examined concerning the premises. This process was strictly executed. While he was detained in a course of examination before the lieutenant governor and the council, the sheriff returned to Parker's house, and took all his apprentices into custody, and immediately conducted them to the lieutenant governor and council. Upon their entrance, their master, who had not the least opportunity of seeing them after he was arrested, was ordered into another apartment under the custody of the sheriff, and was not present at their examination. The eldest apprentice was first examined, and the paper in question being produced, he was asked whether he had seen it before? To which he answered, that he had frequently seen it, as printed copies of it had been dispersed about the city. He further alleged, that, though repeatedly pressed to declare whether it was printed at his master's printing house, he refused to make any such declaration. But at length being threatened with a commitment, he confessed that it was printed by Parker; and, at the same time, assured the lieutenant governor and council that he was ignorant who was the author. The younger apprentices corroborated his evidence; after which they were all dismissed. Further proof being thus procured against Parker, he was again brought before the lieutenant governor and council, and reexamined on the subject; and though he repeatedly refused to discover the author, yet being at length wrought upon by threats, that application would be made to his superiors to procure his dismission from his employment in the postoffice, and that he must either give bail or be committed, unless he would discover the author; and, not having had it in his power to consult with the author about an indemnification from him, he resolved to make the discovery, provided he could procure an engagement on the part of the government, that he should not be prosecuted. This indemnity his honor and the council, after some consideration, thought proper to give to him; upon which he submitted to an examination on oath, and was discharged upon his single recognizance, to appear and give evidence against General Alexander MacDougall, whom he charged as being the author of the paper in question. Early the next morning the sheriff went to the house of MacDougall, and took him into custody, on a warrant issued by his honor the chief justice, wherein he was charged with causing the paper to be printed, which in the warrant was said to be a 'false, seditious, and infamous Libel;' and the sheriff, according to the command of the precept, conducted him to the chief justice's chamber, to be examined concerning the premises, and to be dealt with according to law. When MacDougall was brought into the chamber of the chief justice, his honor said to him, 'So you have brought yourself into a pretty scrape.' To which MacDougall replied, 'May it please your honor, that must be judged of by my peers.' The chief justice then told MacDougall, that there was full proof that he was the author, or publisher, of the above mentioned paper, which he called a '*false*, vile, and scandalous libel.' MacDougall again replied, 'this must also be tried by my peers.'

His honor thereupon informed him 'that he must either give bail, or go to gaol.' To which MacDougall replied, 'Sir, I will give no bail.' His honor then ordered the sheriff to take him to gaol, and made out a mittimus charging him with being the author and publisher of a 'certain false, scandalous, seditious and infamous paper,' addressed 'to the Betrayed Inhabitants of the City and Colony of New York,' and subscribed, '*A Son of Liberty*;' and commanding the sheriff 'therewith to receive him, and safely keep him in gaol, until he should thence be delivered by due course of law.'

MacDougall remained in prison till April term following, when the grand jury found a bill against him, as the author of a libel against the general assembly; but it being late in the term, the trial was put off till another session, and MacDougall was admitted to bail. Before the next term, Parker died, and of course the evidence against MacDougall was lost. In consequence of which, MacDougall on the 13th of December, 1770, was, by an order of the assembly, taken before that body by the sergeant at arms, and placed at the bar of the house; he was then informed by the speaker, that he was charged by a member of that house, with being the author of the libel before mentioned, and that he was by an order of the house to answer to the question, 'Whether he was guilty or not.' MacDougall asked who were his accusers, and what evidence was adduced against him? These were questions for which the house was not prepared; and MacDougall was interrupted by Mr. De Noyellis, who was supported by the speaker. The latter informed Mac- Dougall that he had no right to speak until he had obtained leave of the house. After some objections and difficulties had been surmounted, MacDougall obtained leave to state his reasons why he ought not to answer the question put to him, or the charge against him. He declined answering it for two reasons which rendered it improper for him to do so. One was, because the paper which had just been read to him, was declared by the honorable house to be a libel; the grand jury of the city and county of New York had also declared it to be libellous, and found a bill of indictment against him, as the author of it. The second reason arose from the fact, that the honorable house had addressed the lieutenant governor to issue his proclamation, offering a reward of one hundred pounds for discovering the author or publisher of the paper signed 'A Son of Liberty,' in order that he might be proceeded against according to law; in consequence whereof information had been given; and a prosecution against him was then pending before the supreme court, where he should be tried by a jury of his peers. He stated further, that as the honorable house was a party in the question, the prosecution being commenced at the instance and recommendation thereof, he conceived it ought not to take cognizance of the matter; and questioned if any precedent could be found on the journals of the house of commons, to shew it had taken cognizance of any supposed libel, when the reputed author of it was under prosecution. Such a proceeding would be an infraction of the laws of England, which forbid that any

British subject should be punished twice for the same offence. For these reasons MacDougall declined either to affirm or to deny anything respecting the paper before the house.

A debate arose in which Mr. De Noyellis insisted that the house had the same power to make a person accused deny or acknowledge a fact, as the courts below had to oblige a prisoner to plead guilty or not guilty. This doctrine was opposed by Mr. Clinton; who said the house had the power to throw the accused over the bar, or out at the window—but the public would judge of the action. It was finally agreed to call in evidence as to the facts, whether a prosecution against MacDougall had been instituted, and to determine if the house was a party to the prosecution. A dispute arose about the manner of entering MacDougall's two reasons on the journals. He conceived justice had not been done to the second; and after some debate, he was ordered to commit it to writing. It was contended by the speaker, and several other members, that his written statement reflected on the honor and dignity of the house. After the subject had been debated, it was decided that he was guilty of a breach of the privileges of that house, and he was ordered to ask pardon of the same. With this order MacDougall refused to comply, alleging that he had not been guilty of any crime; and he asserted, that rather than resign the rights and privileges of a British subject, he would suffer his right hand to be cut off at the bar of the house. He was committed to prison by the sergeant at arms, where he remained several months. [See pp. 519–520.]

CATHARINE ZENGER. She was the widow of John Peter Zenger. Her printing house was 'in Stone-street, near Fort George.' Catharine Zenger continued the printing business, and

The New York Weekly Journal, after her husband's death in
1746. In December 1748, she resigned her printing house to her
son John Zenger; and, about two years after, removed to
'Golden-Hill, near Hermanus Rutgers,' where she sold pamphlets, etc.

HENRY DE FOREEST was born in New York,* and served
his apprenticeship with either Bradford or Zenger, probably
with the latter. I can learn but little respecting him. In 1746, he
published a newspaper, entitled, *The New York Evening Post*. I
cannot ascertain how long before or after 1746, this paper was
published. But De Foreest was not many years in business. He
printed several pamphlets, which I have seen advertised for
sale by him in Zenger's *Journal*; also, *The Whole Book of Forms,
and the Liturgy of the Dutch Reformed Church*, etc., an octavo
volume of 216 pages.

JOHN ZENGER was the eldest son of John Peter Zenger, and
was taught printing by his father, who died before he became of
age, and he completed his apprenticeship with his mother. His
mother resigned her printing house to him in 1748. He published a few pamphlets, and printed blanks for his own sales; but
it does not appear that his press was employed in any thing of
more consequence than the newspaper, which was begun by
his father, continued by his mother, and now published by him.
He printed the *Journal* till January 1751. How long after that
time he remained in business, I cannot determine. His printing

---

* I formerly heard that he was a foreigner, but a grandson of his name, now
living in Philadelphia, has since informed me, that his grandfather was born in
New York, although he can give no account of him as a printer.

house was 'in Stone-Street.' He printed with the types that were used by his father, which, in 1750, appeared to be much worn. His work is not so well executed as that done by his father.

HUGH GAINE[8] was born in Ireland. He served his apprenticeship with James Macgee, printer in Belfast, by whom Andrew Steuart, who has been mentioned as a printer in Philadelphia, was also taught printing. After his arrival in New York he worked several years as a journey-man to James Parker.

Gaine set up a press in New York, about the year 1750, and in 1752 published a newspaper, entitled, *The New York Mercury*. He was industrious and economical, and he experienced the advantages which usually result from such habits. Having acquired a small property, he took a house in Hanover square, opened a book and stationery store, and increased his printing, etc., until his business soon became extensive and lucrative. He kept the stand in Hanover square above forty years, where he published several duodecimo and octavo volumes for his own sales, and a number of pamphlets for himself and others. In 1764 and 1765 he printed for government, *the Journal of the Votes and Proceedings of the House of Assembly*, from 1691 to 1765, in two large folio volumes of one thousand pages each. He continued to print and sell books until the close of a long life.

Gaine's political creed, it seems, was to join the strongest party. When the British troops were about to take possession of New York in 1776, he left the city, and set up his press at Newark; but soon after, in the belief that appearances were against the ultimate success of the United States, he privately withdrew from Newark, and returned to New York. At the conclusion of the war, he petitioned the state legislature for leave to remain in the city, and having obtained permission, his press was employed in book printing, etc., but his newspaper was discontinued when the British army left.

Gaine was punctual in his dealings, of correct moral habits, and respectable as a citizen. He began the world a poor man, but by close application to successful business through a long period of time, he acquired a large property. He died April 25, 1807, aged eighty-one years.[9] [See pp. 496–498.]

WILLIAM WEYMAN, born in Pennsylvania, was the son of an episcopal clergyman, who was rector of the church in Oxford, county of Philadelphia. He served his apprenticeship with William Bradford, in Philadelphia. He has already been taken notice of as the partner of James Parker. Parker was the proprietor of the newspaper published by the company, and the owner of the printing materials. They printed for the government six years; and, in the various branches of their profession, did more business than any other printers in the city. Weyman was the principal manager of their press from the commencement of their connection, and of course was well known to the public. These circumstances rendered it easy for him to form an establishment of his own.

The partnership of Parker and Weyman ended in 1759, and Weyman, having provided himself with new types and other necessary materials, opened a printing house; and, in February of that year, introduced another newspaper to the public, by the title of *The New York Gazette*. It appears that Parker and Weyman were not on friendly terms after they separated.

Weyman's business was principally confined to his newspaper, and it yielded him only a maintenance. He died July 18, 1768. His death was thus announced in the Mercury. 'Died at his house in this city, of a lingering illness, which had for some time rendered him incapable of business, Mr. William Weyman, for many years past a printer of note.'[10] [See pp. 498–502.]

JOHN HOLT[11] was born in Virginia. He received a good education, and was instructed in the business of a merchant. He commenced his active life with commercial concerns, which he followed for several years, during which time he was elected mayor of Williamsburg, in his native province. In his pursuits as a merchant he was unsuccessful, and in consequence he left Virginia, came to New York, and formed a connection with James Parker, who was then about setting up a press in New Haven. Holt went to New Haven, and conducted their affairs in that place under the firm of James Parker & Company, as has been related. After the business at New Haven was discontinued, Holt, in the summer of 1760, returned to New York, and there, as a partner, had the direction of Parker's *Gazette* about two years. During the four succeeding years he hired Parker's printing materials, and managed *The New York Gazette and Post-Boy*, as his own concern. In 1765, he kept a bookstore. In 1766, he left Parker's printing house, opened another, and began the publication of *The New York Journal*, in the October following, and retained a large number of the subscribers to the *Gazette*.

Holt was a man of ardent feelings, and a high churchman, but a firm whig, a good writer, and a warm advocate of the cause of his country. A short time before the British army took possession of New York, he removed to Esopus, and thence to Poughkeepsie, where he remained and published his *Journal* during the war. He left at New York a considerable part of his effects, which he totally lost. Another portion of his property, which had been sent to Danbury, was pillaged or burnt in that place by a detachment of the British army; and a part of his types, with his household furniture, etc., were destroyed by the enemy at Esopus. In the autumn of 1783, he returned to New York, and there continued the publication of the *Journal*.

He was printer to the state during the war; and his widow, at his decease, was appointed to that office. Holt was brother-in-law to William Hunter, printer at Williamsburgh, who was deputy postmaster general with Franklin. Soon after his death, his widow printed the following memorial of him on cards, which she dispersed among her friends and acquaintances, viz.

A Due Tribute

To the Memory of

JOHN HOLT,

Printer to this State,

A Native of Virginia,

Who patiently obeyed Death's awful Summons

On the 30th of January, 1784,

In the 64th year of his Age.

To say that His Family lament Him,

Is Needless;

That His Friends Bewail Him,

Useless;

That all Regret Him,

Unnecessary;

For, that He merited Every Esteem

Is certain.

The Tongue of Slander can't say less,

Tho' Justice might say more.
In Token of Sincere Affection
His Disconsolate Widow
Hath caused this Memorial
To be erected.

SAMUEL PARKER was the nephew of James Parker, with whom he served his apprenticeship. He was only seventeen months in business which he did not manage to the best advantage. He was, however, an expert workman. His uncle assigned his printing house to him in February, 1759; but resumed it in July, 1760. Parker died at Wilmington, North Carolina, previous to the revolution.

SAMUEL FARLEY came from Bristol, England. He was the son of Felix Farley, formerly the proprietor and printer of the *Bristol Journal*. He settled in New York in 1760, and published a newspaper in 1761, when William Goddard and Charles Crouch were his journeymen. In 1762, his printing house was burnt, in which calamity most of his printing materials were destroyed. Some time after this event, he went to Georgia, and having passed through the preparatory studies, he there commenced the practice of law. He left Georgia about the year 1775. When he died I cannot say.

JAMES ROBERTSON[12] & COMPANY had a printing house in Broad street in 1768, and in 1769 removed to 'the corner of Beaver street, opposite to his Excellency Governor Gage's.' Robertson was the son of a printer in Scotland, and, as has elsewhere been stated, went from thence to Boston with John

Fleming. When Robertson was in New York, the firm of the
company was altered to ALEXANDER & JAMES ROBERTSON,
who were brothers, and royalists. They published a newspaper;
but after a trial of some months it was discontinued; and they
removed to Albany, and printed a newspaper in that city. They
afterwards, in connection with John Trumbull, opened a printing house in Norwich. The Robertsons returned to New York
when it was in possession of the royal army, in the time of the
war. On the establishment of peace, they removed to Shelburne, Nova Scotia. [See p. 303.]

SAMUEL F. PARKER, the son of James Parker, had an interest
in the printing house and business of his father in New York
several years before his father died. Not long after the death of
James Parker, Samuel leased his printing house, with the apparatus and the Gazette, to Inslee & Carr, and otherwise disposed
of the press and types in Woodbridge. Being infirm in health,
he did but little business at printing, after his father's death. In
1773, he, in company with John Anderson, endeavored to re-
establish *The Gazette and Post Boy*, which had been discontinued
by Inslee & Carr, but did not succeed. He died some time after.

SAMUEL INSLEE & ANTHONY CARR were copartners, and
had for some time been in the printing house of James Parker,
with whom Carr served his apprenticeship. In 1770, soon after
Parker died, they took his printing house and materials on a
lease from his son, and continued *The New York Gazette and
Post Boy* for more than two years, but did little other printing.
Inslee was afterwards employed by Collins at Trenton, and
died suddenly in his printing house.

JAMES RIVINGTON, was from London. He was bred a book-seller,[13] and as such went extensively into business in that city. No man in the trade was better acquainted with it than he. He possessed good talents, polite manners, was well informed, and acquired so much property as to be able to keep a carriage. He formed an acquaintance with many of the nobility, which led him into a dissipated and expensive course of life. Rivington became fond of amusements, and regularly attended the horse races at Newmarket; at one of which he lost so much money as to conceive himself to be ruined. He was, therefore, induced to persuade one of his principal creditors to take out a commission of bankruptcy against him. After due examination into his affairs, his creditor assured him that it was unnecessary, as he possessed property more than sufficient to pay all demands against him. Rivington, however, persisted in his request, and went through the process required by the bankrupt act. He eventually paid twenty shillings in the pound, and had some-thing left.*

This event determined Rivington to remove to America, where he arrived in 1760, and settled as a bookseller in Phila-delphia. The year following he left his business in Philadelphia with a partner by the name of Brown, and went to New York, opened a bookstore at the 'Lower end of Wall street,'[14] and made that city his place of residence. In 1762, he commenced bookselling in Boston, by an agent, William Miller, who the same year became his partner, but died in 1765; and, in conse-quence, the bookstore in Boston was discontinued.

After some years he failed; but very speedily settling his

* This information was received from one of his assignees by a gentleman, who communicated it to me.

affairs, he recommenced business, which he confined to New York. He eventually adopted printing; and in April, 1773, published a newspaper, which was soon devoted to the royal cause. Rivington printed several books for his own sales, among which was *Cooke's Voyage*, in two volumes 12mo., and dealt largely as a bookseller and stationer. He knew how to get money, and knew as well how to spend it; being facetious, companionable, and still fond of high living; but, like a man acquainted with the world, he distinguished the guests who were his best customers.

Rivington, in his Gazette, fought the *Rebels*, a term of which he made very frequent use while he entertained the opinion that the Americans would be subjected by the British arms; but, when he despaired of this event, and believed that Great Britain would, herself, acknowledge the independence of the United States, he deemed it prudent to conciliate the minds of some of the leading Americans. To this end, it is said, he sent out of the city such communications as he knew would be interesting to the commanders of the American army, and he ventured to remain in New York when the British troops evacuated it, at the conclusion of the war. Rivington, in consequence of his peace offerings, was protected from the chastisement he might otherwise have received on the part of those whom he had personally abused in his paper; among whom were several officers of the American army.[15] Rivington, at this period, quitted printing; and discontinued his Gazette, which failed for want of customers to support it; but he uninterruptedly, and to a large extent, traded in books and stationery several years after the establishment of peace. He finally failed again, and being advanced in years, closed his business, and soon after his life. He died at the age of seventy-eight years, in July, 1802.[16]

It is but justice to add, that Rivington, for some time, conducted his Gazette with such moderation and impartiality as did him honor. To the other qualities of a gentleman he added benevolence, vivacity, and with the exceptions already mentioned, punctuality in his business. Interest often produces a change of opinion, and the causes which induced Rivington to support the measures of the British cabinet were sufficiently apparent. And the visit made to him by a party of men from Connecticut, who destroyed his press, etc., as will be hereafter related, doubtless tended to prejudice his mind against the American cause; and prompted him, after he was appointed printer to the king, and placed under the protection of the royal army, boldly, and without disguise, to carry his resentment beyond the bounds of truth and justice. [See pp. 508–511.]

ROBERT HODGE was born in Scotland, served his apprenticeship with a printer in Edinburgh, and, when out of his time, went to London, where he worked as a journeyman two years. In 1770, he came to America, and was employed in the printing house of John Dunlap, in Philadelphia. Hodge was industrious, prudent, and a good workman. He became acquainted with a young printer possessing similar qualifications. By their industry and economy they soon acquired sufficient property to purchase printing materials. With these, in 1772, they began business in Baltimore, where they intended to have published a newspaper; but, not meeting with the encouragement they expected, before the end of the year they left Baltimore, and settled in New York. Here they opened a printing house in Maiden lane, and commenced business under the firm of HODGE & SHOBER. Their partnership continued for more than two years. Early in 1775, Hodge sold his part of the press and types to his partner, and they separated.

During their partnership they printed the greater part of an edition of *Josephus's Works*, in four volumes octavo, for a book- seller in Philadelphia. But it appearing in the event, that he was not able to support the expense of the whole of the edition through the press, Hodge completed the impression. On the approach of the British troops, who in 1776 took the city, Hodge removed into the country, but could not take with him all his books; he left in the city one half of them in sheets, and those he lost. He remained in the country in the state of New York for a year or two, when he went to Boston, and there, in connection with others, opened a printing house.

When peace was restored to the country, he returned to New York, and began the business of a bookseller. Soon after he entered into partnership with two other booksellers, who were his countrymen, and they opened a printing house of which he had the management. This company continued in business for more than three years. During this period, Hodge's dwelling house and bookstore were consumed by fire, by which unfortunate event he lost a considerable part of his property; and, soon after, the partnership was dissolved.

Hodge continued the business of a bookseller for several subsequent years; he then sold his stock in trade, purchased an estate in Brooklyn, on Long Island, to which he retired. He died in August, 1813, aged 67 years.

FREDERICK SHOBER was born in Germany, but served an apprenticeship with Anthony Armbruster, a German printer, in Philadelphia. He worked as a journeyman for two or three years, was attentive to business, and very prudent. In 1772, he entered into partnership with Robert Hodge, and they opened a printing house in Baltimore. They remained in Baltimore a few months, and then removed to New York. In 1775, they closed the concerns of the company. Shober purchased the property of Hodge in the printing house, and sold it to Samuel Loudon, who became his partner. The name of the company was, SHOBER & LOUDON. The confusion into which business of every kind was thrown by the commencement of hostilities alarmed Shober; and, before the close of the year 1775, he sold his right in the printing materials to Loudon, retired to the country, purchased a farm, engaged in the business of agriculture, and never resumed printing. He died about 1806, at, or near, Shrewsbury in New Jersey.

SAMUEL LOUDON,[17] was born in Ireland, and settled in New York some years before the revolution as a ship chandler. In 1775, he purchased a part of the printing materials owned by Shober; in company with whom he began printing. They were but a few months together before Shober judged it prudent, from the existing situation of public affairs, to leave New York, and retire to a farm. Loudon purchased the remainder of the printing materials, and opened a printing house 'in Water street, between the Coffee house and the Old Slip.'

Loudon was decidedly a whig, and in the first week in January, 1776, published a newspaper devoted to the cause of the country. A short time before the British army took possession of the city, in 1776, he removed with his press to Fishkill, and there published *The New York Packet* until the establishment of peace; when he returned to the city, and remained in business long after.

Loudon printed a few books, and kept a book store; he was an elder in 'the Scotch Seceder church.' He died at Middletown Point, New Jersey, February 24, 1813, aged eighty-six years.

JOHN ANDERSON was the partner of Samuel F. Parker in 1773; and, having made an unsuccessful attempt to revive Parker's *New York Gazette*, they separated; after which Anderson opened a printing house 'on Beekman's-Slip;' and issued some inconsiderable articles from his press. In 1775, he published a small newspaper.

I have been informed that he was from Scotland.

ALEXANDER AND JAMES ROBERTSON. James Robertson first set up his press in New York, in 1768. After remaining there a short period, he entered into partnership with his brother. They published in that city *The New York Chronicle*, which, after a trial of about two years, was discontinued, and they removed to Albany. Until that time, New York was the only place in the colony where printing had been introduced.[18]

The Robertsons were the first who opened a printing house in Albany. They were patronized by Sir William Johnson, then superintendent of Indian affairs, who advanced them money to purchase a press and types. They began business there about the year 1771, and soon after published a newspaper.

They set up a press in Norwich, Conn., in 1775, in company with John Trumbull, but continued their printing house in Albany until the commencement of the revolutionary war; when, being detected in publishing and circulating in a private manner, highly obnoxious handbills, etc., in support of the royal cause which they decidedly espoused, they judged it expedient hastily to leave the city, and went to Norwich. They left their press and types in the care of a friend who resided in the vicinity of Albany. This friend removed them privately to his farm, and there buried them. They were afterwards taken up and sold to Solomon Balantine, who began the establishment of a second newspaper in that city in 1782.

The Robertsons remained in Norwich until the British army, in 1776, took possession of New York, when they went to that city, and there published *The Royal American Gazette*. [See pp. 303, 476–477.]

1743. CATHARINE ZENGER, sold pamphlets and some articles of stationery.[19]

1747. ROBERT CROMMELIN, 'near the Meal-Market;' he was from Scotland, and became a dealer in books, and in English and Scotch goods.

HUGH GAINE, 'at the Bible and Crown in Hanover-Square.' He was from Ireland, where he had been brought up a printer. He came to New York about 1745, and worked as a journeyman about six years in Parker's printing house; first, at 9s. currency (one dollar and an eighth) per week, and found himself; and afterwards he had a small allowance for board. His economy was such that from these wages he contrived to lay up money; having accumulated the sum of seventy-five pounds, he found a friend who imported for him a press and a few types, the cost of which exceeded the sum he had saved about one hundred dollars. With these materials he opened a printing house, and by persevering industry and economy was soon enabled to discharge the debt he had contracted for his press and types, and to open a bookstore. Eventually he acquired a large fortune.

1761. GARRAT NOEL, 'near the Meal Market,' afterwards 'next door to the Merchant's Coffee-House.' He was a publisher, and dealt largely, for a bookseller of that time, in imported books and stationery. After he had been in business a number of years, Ebenezer Hazard became his partner, under the firm of Noel & Hazard.

1761. RIVINGTON & BROWN, 'Hanover-Square.' After a lapse of several years this partnership was dissolved, and the business was continued by

JAMES RIVINGTON, who dealt largely in books and stationery. He commenced printing in 1773.

1765. JOHN HOLT, 'Broad-Street, near the Exchange;' his principal business was printing, but he sold books several years.

1768. NICHOLAS BOGART, 'near Oswego-Market,' sold Dutch books, and published a Dutch version of the Psalms, &c.

1759. ROBERT MACALPINE, 'book-binder, in Beaver Street;' he also sold books.

1772. NOEL & HAZARD. Garrat Noel entered into partnership with Ebenezer Hazard; they dealt largely in books and stationery.

1773. SAMUEL LOUDON, 'at his shop on Hunter's-Quay,' was not brought up to bookselling; but about this time he commenced the business, and afterwards that of printing.

1774. VALENTINE NUTTER, 'opposite the Coffee-House Bridge,' bookbinder and bookseller.

WHEN treating of the introduction of printing into New York, I should have mentioned, that in 1668, Governor Lovelace was desirous of having a press established in that province; and it appears by a record made at the time, that he sent to Boston to procure a printer, but did not succeed in his application. In 1686, among other articles of instruction sent by King James to Governor Dongan, one was, that he should 'allow no printing press in the province.' And, consequently, the pamphlets which appeared in the famous dispute respecting the unfortunate colonel Leisler, in 1689 and 1690, are supposed to have been printed in Boston.

THE first newspaper published in the city was printed by William Bradford. It made its appearance October 16, 1725, and, entitled

THE NEW-YORK GAZETTE, was published weekly, on Monday. I have a few numbers of this Gazette, published in 1736. They are printed on a foolscap sheet, from a type of the size of english, much worn. In the title are two cuts, badly executed; the one on the left is the arms of New York, supported by an Indian on each side; the crest is a crown. The cut on the right is a postman, on an animal somewhat resembling a horse, on full speed. The imprint, 'Printed and Sold by William Bradford, in New York.'

Bradford was near seventy years of age when he began the publication of the Gazette; he continued to publish it about sixteen years, and then retired from business. James Parker began The New York Gazette anew in January, 1742–3.

THE NEW-YORK WEEKLY JOURNAL was the second newspaper established in the province; it made its appearance November 5. 1733.* The Journal was of the small size usually
printed at that time, that is foolscap; generally a whole sheet,
printed chiefly on pica. It was published every 'Munday.' Imprint, 'New York: Printed and Sold by John Peter Zenger: By
whom Subscriptions for this Paper are taken in at Three Shillings per Quarter.'

The Journal was established for a political purpose. For three
years it was in a state of warfare with the administration of
Governor Crosby, and his successor Lieutenant-Governor
Clarke. It was supposed to be published under the patronage of
the Honorable Rip Van Dam, who had been president of the
council, and opposed the governor and his successor. The *New
York Gazette*, printed by Bradford, was then under the control
of the governor.

Newspapers were not at that time burthened with advertisements. I have seen several numbers printed after the paper had
been established seven or eight years, with only one or two
advertisements. It was well printed. Zenger appears to have
understood his business, and to have been a scholar, but he was
not correct in the English language, especially in orthography.

On Sunday, the 17th of November, 1734, Zenger was arrested and imprisoned by virtue of a warrant from the governor
and council, 'for printing and publishing several seditious libels,' in the *New York Weekly Journal*, viz: in Numbers 7, 47,
48 and 49. The governor and council by message requested the

* Zenger, by some mistake, dated his first paper *October* 5, 1733, instead of
November 5. In the account of his trial, he mentions that he began the Journal
Nov. 5, 1733, and so it appears from the numbers. No. 2 is dated November 12,
1733.—*Munday*, was so spelled by Zenger, and others at that time.

concurrence of the house of representatives in prosecuting Zenger, and a committee of conference on the subject was chosen by the house and by the council. The house finally ordered the request of the governor and council to lie on the table, and would not concur. The governor and council then ordered the mayor and magistrates, at their quarter session in November, 1734, to attend to the 'burning by the common hangman, or whipper, near the pillory, the libellous papers.' The mayor's court would not attend to the order; the papers were therefore burnt by the order of the governor, not by the hangman or whipper, who were officers of the corporation, but by the sheriff's servant. At the next term of the supreme court, the grand jury found the presentment against Zenger *ignoramus*. The attorney general was then directed to file an *information* against him for printing the said libels, and he remained in prison until another term. His counsel offered exceptions to the commissions of the judges, and prayed to have them filed. The judges would not allow, or even hear the exceptions, and they excluded Zenger's counsel, Mr. Alexander and Mr. Smith, from the bar. Zenger obtained other counsel, viz: Mr. John Chambers, of New York, and Andrew Hamilton, Esq., of Philadelphia. Mr. Hamilton made the journey from Philadelphia to New York for the sole purpose of defending Zenger. Zenger being put to trial pleaded *not guilty*. The printing and publishing the papers were acknowledged by Zenger's counsel, who offered to give the truth in evidence. This the court would not admit. Mr. Hamilton argued the cause in a most able manner, before the court and a numerous and respectable assemblage of people. The judges observed, that the jury might find that Zenger printed and published the papers in question, and leave it to the court to determine whether they were libellous. Mr. Hamilton remarked, that they *might* do so, but they had a right, beyond all dispute, to judge of the *law* as well as the *fact*, &c. The jury having retired a short time, returned with a verdict, *not guilty*, to the great mortification of the court, and of all Zenger's prosecutors; but which was received by the audience with loud bursts of applause, concluding with three cheers. The next day Zenger was released from prison, after having been confined eight months.

At the common council of the city of New York, holden on the 29th of September following, the mayor, alderman and assistants, presented Mr. Hamilton with the freedom of the city, and the thanks of the corporation expressed in the following manner.

'*City of New York*, ss.: Paul Richards, Esq., Mayor, the Recorder, Aldermen, and Assistants of the City of *New York*, convened in Common Council, to all to whom these Presents shall come, Greeting. Whereas, Honour is the just Reward of Virtue, and publick Benefits demand a publick Acknowledgment. We therefore, under a grateful Sense of the remarkable Service done to the Inhabitants of this City and Colony, by *Andrew Hamilton*, Esq; of Pennsylvania, Barrister at Law, by his learned and generous Defence of the Rights of Mankind and the Liberty of the Press, in the Case of *John-Peter Zenger*, lately tried on an Information exhibited in the Supreme Court of this Colony, do by these Presents, bear to the said Andrew Hamilton, Esq; the publick Thanks of the Freemen of this Corporation for that signal Service, which he cheerfully undertook under great Indisposition of Body, and generously performed, refusing any Fee or Reward; and in Testimony of our great

Esteem for his Person, and Sense of his Merit, do hereby present him with the Freedom of this Corporation. These are, therefore, to certify and declare, that the said *Andrew Hamilton*, Esq; is hereby admitted and received and allowed a Freeman and Citizen of said City; To Have, Hold, Enjoy and Partake of all the Benefits, Liberties, Privileges, Freedoms and Immunities whatsoever granted or belonging to a Freeman and Citizen of the same City. *In Testimony* whereof the Common Council of the said City, in Common Council assembled, have Caused the Seal of the said City to be hereunto affixed this Twenty-Ninth Day of *September*, *Anno Domini* One Thousand Seven Hundred and Thirty-Five.

'By order of the Common Council,

William Sharpas, Clerk.'

The foregoing grant of the freedom of the city was, by order of the corporation, sent to Mr. Hamilton by Stephen Bayard, one of the aldermen, in a gold box weighing five and a half ounces, made for the occasion. On the lid of the box was engraved the arms of the city, with this motto: 'DEMERSÆ LEGES TIMEFACTA LIBERTAS HÆC TANDEM EMERGUNT.' On the inner side of the lid: 'NON NUMMIS— VIRTUTE PARATUR.' On the front of the rim of the box, a part of Tully's wish: 'ITA CUIQUE EVENIAT, UT DE REPUBLICA MERUIT.'[20]

Zenger published the Journal on Mondays, till he died in the summer of 1746. It was continued by his widow, Catharine Zenger, till December, 1748, when she resigned the publication to her son John Zenger. Her imprint was, 'New York: Printed by the Widow *Cathrine Zenger*, at the Printing-Office in Stone-Street; Where Advertisements are taken in, and all Persons may be supplied with this paper.' She spelled her name *Cathrine* in all her imprints and advertisements.

John Zenger, in January, 1748–9, new modelled the title of the Journal, and added a cut, coarsely executed, of a section of the royal arms, containing three lions gardant, encircled with the usual motto, '*Honi soit* qve *mal y pense*;' surmounted by a crown. The imprint, 'New York: Printed by John Zenger, in Stone-street, near Fort George; Where Advertisements are taken in at a moderate rate.' John Zenger published this paper until about 1752, when it was discontinued, but in 1766, the title was revived by John Holt.

In *The New York Journal* of February 25, 1751, is the following advertisement: 'My country subscribers are earnestly desired to pay their arrearages for this Journal, which, if they don't speedily, I shall leave off sending, and seek my money another way. Some of these kind customers are in arrears upwards of seven years! Now as I have served them so long, I think it is time, ay and high time too, that they give me my outset; for they may verily believe that my every-day cloathes are almost worn out. N. B. Gentlemen, If you have not ready money with you, still think of the Printer, and when you have read this Advertisement, and considered it, you cannot but say, Come Dame, (especially you inquisitive wedded men, let the Batchelors take it to themselves) let us send the poor Printer a few Gammons or some Meal, some Butter, Cheese, Poultry, &c. In the mean time I am Yours, &c.

J. Zenger.'

THE NEW YORK GAZETTE, *or, Weekly Post-Boy,* was established by James Parker, in January, 1742–3, about the time that

Bradford discontinued his Gazette, and he probably retained the subscribers for that paper.

I have a few numbers of this Gazette published several months after its establishment, the title of which reads thus, '*The New York Gazette Revived in the Weekly Post-Boy*. Containing the freshest Advices, Foreign and Domestick.' It was printed on Thursdays, on a foolscap sheet, folio. Imprint, 'New York: Printed by James Parker, at the New Printing-Office in Beaver-Street, where Advertisements are taken in, and all Persons may be supplied with this Paper.'

Two letters appeared in the Gazette of February, 1748, reflecting upon some respectable quakers in Philadelphia. These letters were not genuine, and gave offence to some of Parker's readers. He, therefore, the 29th of that month, thus addressed the public,

'Poor Printers are often under a very unhappy dilemma, of either displeasing one Part of their Benefactors, or giving Offence to others; and sometimes get the Ill-will of both sides; It has indeed been much against my Will to print any Thing, that savour'd of Forgery, Invective, or Partyism; but being too dependent, can't always avoid it: The Press is looked on as the grand Bulwark of *Liberty Light*, *Truth* and *Religion*; and if at any Time the Innocent is attack'd unjustly, the Gospel pronounces such *Blessed*; and common Sense tells us *their Innocence will shine the more conspicuously thereby*: But on the other Hand, it often is noted that Persons are too apt to be touch'd at having any of their Faults exposed. However, if I have openly injur'd any, I am willing as openly to vindicate them, or to give them all the Satisfaction that Reason requires without being sway'd with either their high Words or low Promises:

But let the stricken Deer go weep, the Hart
Ungall'd go play.   —*Shakespear*'

In 1753, William Weyman became the partner of Parker, and the principal manager of the paper. It was enlarged to a crown sheet, and bore this title, *The New York Gazette; or, The Weekly Post-Boy*. A cut of the colony arms divided the title.

A stamp act was passed by the legislature of New York, December 1, 1756, which was continued until January, 1760, but during that period this paper was sometimes published with a stamp, and sometimes without; and it often appeared without an imprint.

Parker & Weyman having published in the Post-Boy some 'Observations on the Circumstances and Conduct of the People in the Counties of Ulster and Orange in the Province of New York,' which gave offence to the assembly, they were taken into custody by the sergeant at arms; Weyman on the 18th, and Parker on his return from Woodbridge to the city, on the 23d of March, 1756. They were discharged on the 30th of the same month, after acknowledging their fault, begging pardon of the house, giving up the name of the writer, and paying fees. The writer was the Reverend Hezekiah Watkins, missionary from the society for propagating the gospel in foreign parts. He lived at Newburg, in Orange county, and, by order of the house, at their next session, he was taken into custody by the sergeant at arms, brought to New York, and voted 'guilty of a high misdemeanor, and contempt of the authority of the house.' In a petition presented to the house he asked pardon, and promised to be more circumspect in future. He was, in consequence, brought to the bar, and there received a severe reprimand from the speaker; and, after paying the fees, was discharged.*

* See Journal of the Assembly of New York for 1756.

This paper was ably conducted. It often contained original, well written essays, moral and political; and the circulation of it was for many years very extensive.

The partnership between Parker and Weyman expired in February, 1759, at which time Weyman began another paper. Parker, having assigned his paper to his nephew Samuel Parker, resided principally in New Jersey after his connection with Weyman ceased. The nephew printed the Post-Boy until July, 1760, when his uncle returned to New York, and resumed the publication. The imprint, 'Printed by James Parker and Co.' John Holt was the partner; but his name was not mentioned in the firm. This partnership ended in April, 1762, and Holt then printed the Post-Boy, on his own account, till October, 1766, when he relinquished it to Parker, who again resumed its publication on the 27th of November, 1766, and continued it, with some intermissions, on a demy sheet well printed, until near the time of his death in 1770.

The Gazette and Post-Boy, like many other American newspapers published at that time, appeared in mourning on the 31st of October, 1765, on account of the stamp act; it was, however, carried on as usual, without any suspension, and without stamps. The Gazette dated November 7, 1765, contained an anonymous letter, directed to the publisher Holt, which he informed the public, was thrown into his printing house, and a copy of it set up at the coffee-house. The contents of the letter were as follows,

'*Dulce et decorum est pro Patria mori.*

'Mr. Holt, As you have hitherto prov'd yourself a Friend to Liberty, by publishing such Compositions as had a Tendency to promote the Cause, we are encouraged to hope you will not be deterred from continuing your useful Paper, by groundless Fear of the detestable Stamp-Act. However, should you at this critical Time, shut up the Press, and basely desert us, depend upon it, your House, Person and Effects, will be in imminent Danger: We shall therefore, expect your Paper on Thursday as usual; if not, on Thursday Evening ——— take CARE. Signed in the Names and by Order of a great Number of the Free-born Sons of New-York.

'JOHN HAMPDEN.

'On the Turf, the 2d of November, 1765.'

To the title of the Gazette of November 7, 1765, was added in a large type this motto: 'The United Voice of all His Majesty's *free* and *loyal* Subjects in America—LIBERTY, PROPERTY, and *no* STAMPS.'

On August 27, 1770, Samuel Inslee and Anthony Carr published this paper, and continued it two years. The publication was then suspended for several months; but in August, 1773, it was renewed by Samuel F. Parker and John Anderson. They printed the Post-Boy but a short time, when it was discontinued; having completed a period of thirty years from its first appearance before the public.

THE NEW YORK EVENING POST was the fourth newspaper established in that city, and it was printed by Henry De Foreest. It appeared before the year 1746, and was continued until 1747. Thus far I speak with certainty; but how long before 1746, and how long after 1747, it was published, I have not been able to ascertain. It was printed weekly, on Monday.

If we may judge of the editorial abilities, and the correctness of the printer, by the following extract from the Evening Post of October 13, 1746, we shall not be led to rank him with the editor of the present New York Evening Post,* who is one of the most able and celebrated conductors of a public journal in the United States.

'Last Friday arrived here Capt. Griffin from Boston, who informs us, that as soon as they heard of the French Fleet, the Bostoneers was in the greatest hurrey imaginable to Fortifie the Place, which they have done in a very strong manner; that there *wat* 30,000 fighting men, wereof was 700 Horse; they are very well provided with all manner of war like stores, and ready if *Monsieaur* should pay them a Visit, to give him a very warm Reception.'†

Fleet, who republished the above paragraph in the Boston Evening Post of October 20, 1746, thus commented upon it. 'Here's *Veracity*, *Orthography* and *Grammar*, all in the Compass of a few Lines; and Brother Type may well expect the Thanks of *some* Gentlemen, for the great Honour he has done *them* in his inimitable Piece.'

After this paper was discontinued, there were only two published in that city until 1759, viz: Parker's Gazette, and Gaine's Mercury.

THE NEW YORK MERCURY was first introduced to the public on the 3d of August, 1752.‡ It was published weekly, on

---

* William Coleman, born 1766, died 1829.

† A fleet from Brest was then on the coast, destined, as supposed, to attack Boston or New York.

‡ If the numbers of Gaine's paper in 1763 and 1764 are correct, the Mercury must have been first published in October, 1752; but the above date is from a record, and I believe is as it should be.

Monday, on a crown sheet, folio; a cut of the king's arms was early introduced into and divided the title; this cut, in the year 1763, was exchanged for a figure of Mercury; some years after, the arms of the province took the place of Mercury, when the title was altered to *The New York Gazette and the Weekly Mercury*; and, in 1777, the king's arms again appeared in the title. The usual imprint for many years was, 'Printed by Hugh Gaine, Printer, Bookseller and Stationer, at the Bible and Crown, in Hanover-Square.'

For a few years, the collection of intelligence in this paper was not inferior to that of any paper published in the city. Its circulation became extensive, and it gained many advertising customers.[21]

On the 12th of May, 1753, Gaine published in the Mercury a part of the proceedings of the assembly of New York, and the king's instructions to governor Osborne, I believe without permission, and not correctly; for which he was called to the bar of the house on the Wednesday following. On asking pardon, he was merely reprimanded by the speaker, and dismissed.

In 1775, a series of well written essays, under the title of The Watch Tower, were published in this paper.

During the political contest with Great Britain, the Mercury appeared rather as a neutral paper. Gaine seemed desirous to side with the successful party; but not knowing which would eventually prevail, he seems to have been unstable in his politics. After the war commenced, he leaned toward the country. When the British army approached New York in 1776, Gaine removed to Newark, in New Jersey, and there, during a few weeks, published the Mercury. Soon after the British gained possession of the city of New York, he returned, and printed under the protection of the king's army; and, like Rivington, devoted his paper to the royal cause.

During the war both Gaine and Rivington were taken notice of by a poet to whom the muses were auspicious.* Several poetical essays, of which Gaine and Rivington were the heroes, appeared in the newspapers, and afforded no small degree of amusement to those who were acquainted with these noted typographers; particularly a versification of Gaine's petition to the republican government of the state, at the close of the war.[22]

Gaine published the Mercury until peace was established, and it was then discontinued, after an existence of about thirty-one years.

THE NEW YORK GAZETTE made its first appearance February 17, 1759. It was printed on a crown sheet, folio, every Monday, with the king's arms in the title; and the typography was not inferior to that of the other newspapers published in the city.

Weyman, who had been many years the partner of Parker, and manager of the Gazette and Post-Boy, was encouraged and handsomely supported by subscribers; and for some time he had a share of advertising customers. After publishing this paper several years, his subscribers dropped off, his advertising customers decreased, and the publication of the Gazette was several times suspended.

Weyman, who was printer to the colony, in November,

---

* Philip Freneau, born in New York, 1752; died at Monmouth, N.J., 1832. He was at different times editor of papers in New York, Philadelphia and New Jersey.

1766, published in his Gazette, the address of the house of representatives to his excellency the governor, in answer to his speech at the opening of the session of the general assembly; in doing which, he neglected, contrary to the rules of his profession, to read by copy, and to revise his proof sheet; in consequence of this neglect two gross errors escaped from his press. One was, the insertion of the word *never* instead of *ever*; the other was the omission of the word *no*. The sentence in which the word was omitted, should have read thus—'Your excellency has done us *no* more than strict justice in supposing that we will cheerfully cooperate with you.' Two days after the publication of this address in the Gazette, the printer was ordered to attend the house, and he attended accordingly. Being asked by the speaker, 'Whether he printed *The New York Gazette,*' which was shown to him; and answering in the affirmative, he was asked, 'Why he had in his said Gazette, reprinted the address to his excellency Sir Henry Moore, in a manner injurious to the honor and dignity of the house?' He replied, that 'he was very innocent of the alteration made in the said address, till a number of the Gazettes had been distributed; that upon discovering the mistakes he immediately corrected the press, and endeavored to get back all the erroneous copies; that he had charged one of his journeymen with making the alterations, but could not prove the fact upon him; and that as the same had not been printed with any design by him, he hoped the house would pardon his inadvertency.' Weyman was directed to withdraw; and, the house proceeded to the consideration of the excuse he had offered; after which he was ordered to attend the house, with his journeyman, William Finn, the next morning at ten o'clock. Weyman and his journeyman attended according to order, and being placed at the bar of the house, Weyman was further examined; the house then resolved, that the errors made in reprinting the address, 'appeared to be done through the carelessness and inadvertency of the said Weyman, without any design in him of reflecting on the house.' Weyman thereupon made an acknowledgment of his fault, asked pardon of the house, and promising to behave more circumspectly for the future, was discharged from further attendance.*

Weyman made several severe attacks on Parker, his late

---

* Extract from the journals of the general assembly of New York, 1766.

Weyman, in his next New York Gazette, apologized to the public for the errors he had committed when 'reprinting' the address; and in his apology inserted the story of the blunder made in an edition of *The Book of Common Prayer,* as follows.

'A printer in England, who printed The Book of Common Prayer, unluckily omitted the letter *c* in the word *changed* in the following sentence—"We shall all be CHANGED in the twinkling of an eye." A clergyman, not so attentive to his duty as he should have been, read it to his congregation as it was printed, thus—"We shall all be HANGED in the twinkling of an eye." ' 'Hence,' said Weyman, 'must appear what a most significant alteration is made in the sense when only a single letter is either added or omitted in a word in printing or reading; and evinces the great necessity of the utmost care being taken in both.'

Sentences of authors have often been rendered ludicrous by the errors of the press. Even the Bible has not escaped. In an edition of Brackenridge's *Law Miscellanies,* 'the *younger* practitioner of the bar,' was rendered 'the *young cur* practioner.'

In Scotland, that land proverbial for its correct Biblical typography, in the pocket Bible, printed there about 1760, this sentence in Jude, 'Suffering the vengeance of eternal *fire,*' was rendered, 'Suffering the vengeance of eternal *life.*' In a quarto Bible printed in Scotland, thousands of copies of which were sold in America, in the prohibition for marriages was the following, 'A man may not marry his wife's mother's brother.' In a Bible printed in England, the negative *not* was omitted in the seventh commandment. Numerous errors of the like kind with these have been discovered in various editions of the Bible. In an 8vo edition printed for me, in 1802, in the third of Job, instead of '*sighing* cometh before I eat,' it was printed '*fishing* before I eat.' In the small Bible printed by Aitkin in Philadelphia, during the revolutionary war; in 2d Kings, 7, 12, 'I will *now* shew you what the Syrians,' etc., it was printed 'I will *not* shew,' etc. [23]

partner, who was comptroller of the post office, and indirectly accused him of giving orders to postriders not to circulate *The New York Gazette*; but it does not appear that the comptroller of the post office did anything more, at that time, than to require the publishers of newspapers to furnish saddlebags for postriders, in which newspapers might be carried separate from the mail, the contents of which, it was said, often received injury from the dampness of newspapers. By several of Weyman's remarks, it is evident he was not on good terms with Parker after they separated; and Weyman, in some of his addresses to the public, mentioned that he had 'to struggle hard against many inconveniences, joined to his incumbrance occasioned by the *short circulation of cash*, and the arrearages of his customers.' We do not often exhibit liberality toward those of the same profession with ourselves, who, as we imagine, enjoy a degree of prosperity superior to that which falls to our lot, or consider whether the cause of our inferiority may not be negligence or misfortune. Parker, by a long course of business, and good management of his affairs, possessed a very handsome property. Weyman, from various causes, was not so fortunate, and therefore, probably, did not feel that cordiality toward his former partner, he otherwise might. However this may have been, Weyman actually brought the following charge against one of the postmasters general, and the comptroller of the post-office, both of whom were publishers of newspapers, viz: of 'endeavoring to stop the circulation, by post, of any newspapers but their own, under a base conclusion, that *every government ought to take its own newspapers.*'

Weyman's valedictory gives us an idea of his circumstances, his feelings, and his editorial abilities. It is as follows.

'The Subscriber having lately given a Hint of his Intention to Stop this Gazette, from a *base* we may say *villainous* Attempt to suppress the Distribution of News-Papers, from one Government to another, made by a P. Master General 10 or 12 years ago, and lately put into Execution by one of his Servants, (who with his Colleague first Schem'd the Matter). This egregious Attack on the Usefulness of the Press (which seems to be prosecuted) joined with the Printer's private Affairs, obliges him to inform the Publick of a *total stop* this Day. All other Work will still be performed with that Dispatch and Care the Nature of the Business will admit of.—He gives Thanks from his *Heart* and not from his *Tongue* to all his good Encouragers, at times, hitherto.—A singular Paper may appear at Times, with the best Intelligences, to be sold cheap without Subscription, *English Method*. Advertisements whose Times are not expired, their Money shall be returned, if demanded, after a proper Allowance. From such an unparalleled Oppression, as mentioned at first, and my innate Concerns, I am obliged to subscribe myself, The Publick's Most Thankful and Most Obedient Humble Servant, *W. Weyman*.'

This Gazette terminated December 28, 1767, after it had been published about nine years. The publisher died in July following.

THE AMERICAN CHRONICLE was published, if I recollect aright, rather short of two years. I cannot be certain that I am altogether correct as to the title. I once owned a file of this paper, but lost it many years since. It was handsomely printed, on a crown sheet, folio. The title was in German text, well engraved on a block. Samuel Farley, the printer and publisher of it, was an Englishman.* Before the Chronicle had fully gained an establishment, the house in which it was printed took fire and was consumed. The paper was first printed in 1761, and was discontinued, in consequence of the fire, in 1762.

THE NEW YORK PACQUET was published in New York in the year 1753. How long before this period the paper was in circulation, or how long after, I am unable to say. I cannot discover any one who is able to give me information respecting it. It was published but a short time.

THE NEW YORK JOURNAL, *or General Advertiser.* Holt, the editor of this Journal, began the publication of it May 29, 1776, with new types, &c., but issued only 'Numb. 1,' when it was suspended, and he resumed printing Parker's New York Gazette, which he had relinquished the preceding week.† He continued to publish the Gazette till the 9th of October following, when he again resigned the Gazette to the proprietor, and on the 16th of that month recommenced publishing the Journal, which he did not again lay aside; he, however, began this second publication of the Journal with 'Numb. 1241,' following that of Parker's Gazette. Of course Parker's Gazette and Holt's Journal had the same number weekly at the head of their respective papers, and both were published on Thursday. The imprint to the Journal was, 'New York: Printed and Published by John Holt, near the Exchange, (For six years last past, publisher of

* See p. 476.
† See *New York Gazette; and Weekly Post-Boy.*

the New York Thursday's Gazette and Weekly Post-Boy).' At
first the title was without a cut, but in a short time it appeared
with the king's arms; which, until 1775, decorated the titles of
many of the newspapers on the continent of North America, as
well as those of the West India islands.

In 1774, Holt discarded the cut of the king's arms from the
title of the Journal, and in its place introduced that of a snake
divided into parts, with the motto 'Unite or die.' In January,
1775, the snake was united, and coiled with the tail in its mouth,
forming a double ring; within the coil was a pillar standing on
Magna Charta, and surmounted with the cap of liberty; the
pillar on each side was supported by six arms and hands, fig-
urative of the colonies.[24] On the body of the snake, beginning
at the head, were the following lines,

> United now, alive and free,
> Firm on this basis Liberty shall stand,
> And, thus supported, ever bless our land
> Till Time becomes Eternity.

Holt had published Parker's Gazette, first in company with
Parker, and afterwards on his own account, from 1760 to 1766.
As I have before observed, he began the second publication of
the Journal with No. 1241, following in order the number of
the Gazette which he published the preceding week. For this he
assigned as a reason, that he should be able the more readily to
settle with his customers. He seemed to consider the subscribers
to Parker's Gazette as his customers, and the Journal as a continuation of the Gazette, which he had lately published. He
mentioned his 'having occasion to *alter* the title of *his* paper,'

meaning Parker's Gazette; 'and, that he had altered it, first for the sake of distinction, as he was informed Parker intended publishing a paper under the former title; and, secondly, because, as Parker formerly published a paper under that title, he, Holt, would not avail himself of any advantages from a *name* originally assumed by Parker.' The fact was, Parker ever had been the proprietor of the Gazette and Post-Boy, and had taken Holt as a partner; and, two years after, when the copartnership ended, leased to him his paper and establishment. Holt could not command any property when he became the partner of Parker, who had been many years in business, and had acquired much celebrity as a printer, of which Holt as his partner was a partaker, and derived much benefit from it; but after his partnership and the subsequent lease of Parker's establishment had expired, and he began business for himself, he appeared disposed to retain both Parker's Gazette, and the purchasers of it, without due compensation.

Holt procured a new printing-apparatus at the time he began the Journal. This paper soon had a very extensive circulation; it was sent to all who had been customers to the Gazette; and was generally received.

The Journal was a zealous advocate for the American cause; it was supported by many able writers besides the editor; and it maintained its ground until the British army took possession of the city of New York, in 1776, when the publisher of it removed to Kingston (Esopus), and the Journal was discontinued several months; but was revived at that place in July, 1777. Esopus was burned by the British in October of that year, and Holt removed to Poughkeepsie, where he published the Journal until the termination of the war.

In the Autumn of 1783, it was again printed in the city of New York, with an alteration in the title, as follows: *The Independent Gazette; or The New York Journal Revived.* In January, 1784, it was printed, from a new and handsome bourgeois type, 'at No. 47, opposite the Upper Corner of the Old-Slip, Hanover-Square;' and was published twice a week, on Thursdays and Saturdays; but before the close of that month the editor, Holt, died.

Elizabeth Holt continued the Journal, after her husband's decease, until 1785, but it appeared only on Thursdays.*

In January, 1787, Elizabeth Holt and Oswald† sold their right in the Journal, and their establishment, comprising the whole of their printing materials, to Thomas Greenleaf.

Greenleaf, soon after he came into possession of the Journal, printed it daily, or rather, he made the establishment the foundation of two papers. One he published with the same title, weekly, on Thursday, for the country; the other, intended for circulation in the city, bore the title of *The New York Journal, and Daily Patriotic Register.* The titles of these papers were afterwards altered. That printed daily was called *The Argus, or Greenleaf's New Daily Advertiser*; and the weekly paper was published twice a week, and entitled *Greenleaf's New York Journal and Patriotic Register.*

---

* For a few months, in 1781, it was published by Eleazer Oswald for Elizabeth Holt; and afterwards, to January, 1787, it was printed in the name of Eleazar Oswald.

† Oswald was the kinsman of Mrs. Holt. He had been a colonel in the American army. In 1782, he commenced the publication of the Independent Gazetteer, in Philadelphia. This paper was continued during his connection with the New York Journal, and for several years after. He died in September, 1795.

When the two great political parties were forming, subsequent to the organization of the federal government, that which opposed the administration, attacked the measures of the venerable Washington with a great degree of virulence, in Greenleaf's paper.

Greenleaf was born at Abington, in Massachusetts, and was taught printing in Boston, by Isaiah Thomas. He was the son of Joseph Greenleaf, who, at an advanced age, in 1774, engaged in the printing business at Boston.

He continued the papers above mentioned until 1798; at which time the yellow fever raged in New York, and great numbers left the city to escape that pestilence; but Greenleaf remained at his post, took the disease, and fell a victim to it at the age of forty-two years. He was well acquainted with his business, enterprising, and amiable in his manners. After his decease, his widow, Ann Greenleaf, published both the semi-weekly and daily paper for a time; but eventually sold her establishment to James Cheetham, who altered the title of both papers. The one published semi-weekly was now called, *The American Watch-Tower*, and the daily paper bore the title of *The American Citizen*. Cheetham was born and brought up in England. He was not bred to printing, but he was a very able editor, and a distinguished writer. Occasionally the vigor and pungency of his style remind his readers of the productions of the renowned Junius.[25]

THE NEW YORK CHRONICLE. I have not been able to ascertain, accurately, when this paper first made its appearance, or when it was discontinued; but it was published by Alexander and James Robertson, and commenced either in 1768 or 1769.

Not long after the close of the year 1770, the printers of the Chronicle removed to Albany, and the publication of it ceased.

508   RIVINGTON'S NEW-YORK GAZETTEER; *or The Connecticut, New-Jersey, Hudson's River, and Quebec Weekly Advertiser,* commenced its career April 22, 1773, on a large medium sheet, folio. It was printed weekly, on Thursday; and when it had been established one year, this imprint followed the title, 'Printed at his EVER OPEN and uninfluenced press, fronting Hanover-Square.' A large cut of a ship under sail was at first introduced into the title, under which were the words *New York Packet.* This cut soon gave place to one of a smaller size. In November, 1774, the ship was removed and the king's arms took the place of it. In August, 1775, the words '*Ever open and uninfluenced*' were omitted in the imprint.

The Gazetteer was patronized in all the principal towns by the advocates of the British administration who approved the measures adopted toward the colonies; and it undoubtedly had some support from 'his Majesty's government.' The paper obtained an extensive circulation, but eventually paid very little respect to 'the majesty of the people;' and, in consequence, the paper and its publisher soon became obnoxious to the whigs.

Rivington continued the Gazetteer until November 27, 1775; on which day a number of armed men from Connecticut entered the city, on horseback, and beset his habitation, broke into his printing house, destroyed his press, threw his types into heaps, and carried away a large quantity of them, which they melted and formed into bullets. A stop was thus put to the Gazetteer.[26]

Soon after this event, Rivington went to England, where he

supplied himself with a new printing apparatus, and was appointed king's printer for New York. After the British gained possession of the city, he returned; and, on October 4, 1777, recommenced the publication of his Gazette under the original title; but in two weeks he exchanged that title for the following, *Rivington's New York Loyal Gazette*; and on the 13th of December following, he called his paper *The Royal Gazette*. Imprint, 'Published by James Rivington, Printer to the King's Most Excellent Majesty.' The Royal Gazette was numbered as a continuation of the Gazetteer, and Loyal Gazette, and was published on Wednesdays and Saturdays; printed on a sheet of *royal* size, with the *royal* arms in the title.

Rivington could not consistently have given the Royal Gazette the motto selected by our brethren, the printers of the (Boston) Independent Chronicle—'*Truth its Guide, and Liberty its Object.*' This Gazette was, by some, called The *Brussels Gazette** of America; but it commonly went by the name of Rivington's lying Gazette. Even the royalists censured Rivington for his disregard to truth. During the war, a captain of militia at Horseneck, with about thirty men, marched to Kingsbridge, and there attacked a house within the British lines, which was garrisoned by refugees, and took most of them prisoners. Rivington published an account of this transaction which greatly exaggerated the affair in favor of the refugees; he observed that a large detachment of rebels attacked the house, which was bravely defended by a refugee colonel, a major, a quartermaster, and fifteen privates; and that after they were taken and carried off, another party of refugee dragoons,

* A paper published at Brussels many years since, which was notorious for falsehood.

seventy-three in number, pursued the rebels, killed twenty-three of them, took *forty* prisoners, and would have taken the whole rebel force, had not the refugee horse *'been jaded to a stand still.'* Several times did Rivington apologize for *mistakes* made in paragraphs which he himself had manufactured for his Gazette.

The following appeared in the Royal Gazette of July 10, 1782, when there was a prospect of peace.

'To the Public.—The publisher of this paper, sensible that his zeal for the success of his Majesty's arms, his sanguine wishes for the good of his country, and his friendship for individuals, have at times led him to credit and circulate paragraphs without investigating the facts so closely as his duty to the Public demanded; trusting to their feelings, and depending on their generosity, he begs them to look over past errors, and depend on future correctness. From henceforth he will neither expect nor solicit their favors longer than his endeavors shall stamp the same degree of authenticity and credit on the Royal Gazette of New York as all Europe allow to the Royal Gazette of London.'[27]

During the war, a newspaper was published daily in the city of New York under the following arrangement: Rivington's Royal Gazette on Wednesday and Saturday, Gaine's Gazette or Mercury on Monday, Robertson's, Mills & Hick's Royal American Gazette, on Thursday—and Lewis's New York Mercury and General Advertiser on Friday. These papers were all published under the sanction of the British commander in chief; but none of the printers assumed the title of 'Printers to the King' except Rivington, who had an appointment.

When the war ended, Rivington discarded from his paper

the appendages of royalty. The arms of Great Britain no longer appeared. It was no more The Royal, or a Loyal Gazette, but a plain republican newspaper, entitled *Rivington's New York Gazette and Universal Advertiser*. It was, however, considered as a wolf in sheep's clothing, and, not meeting with support, the publication of it terminated, and the editorial labors of Rivington ended, in the year 1783. Few men, perhaps, were better qualified than the editor of the Royal Gazette to publish a newspaper.

It has been remarked (page 480), that for some time Rivington conducted his paper with as much impartiality as most of the editors of that period; and it may be added, that no newspaper in the colonies was better printed, or was more copiously furnished with foreign intelligence. In October, 1773, Rivington informed his readers that each impression of his weekly Gazetteer, amounted to 3,600 copies.

THE CONSTITUTIONAL GAZETTE was first issued from the press of John Anderson, in August, 1775; the publication of which was on Mondays and Thursdays, and continued but a few months. It was printed on a half sheet, quarto, of crown paper. It seems to have borrowed its title from a political paper published in New Jersey ten years before; but it resembled that paper in name only.

THE NEW YORK PACKET, *and the American Advertiser*, commenced the first week in January, 1776. It was printed Thursdays, on a sheet of royal folio, with a new long primer type. Imprint: 'Printed by Samuel Loudon, in Water-Street, between the Coffee-House and the Old Slip.'

I take notice of this paper, although it originated after the war began, because it was the last established in the city before the declaration of independence. Loudon died at Middletown Point, New Jersey, February 24, 1813, in the ninetieth year of his age.

During the war it was published at Fishkill; after the return of peace it was again printed in the city; it was finally changed to a daily paper, and continued several years.

NEWSPAPERS
IN ALBANY

THE ALBANY POST-BOY was first published in this city in 1772.[28] Alexander and James Robertson were its publishers. The publication of it ended in 1775. The Robertsons, as has been observed under the head Connecticut, &c., were, in 1773, concerned in printing *The Norwich Packet*; and it is not improbable that, at the same time, one of them resided in Albany and conducted the Post-Boy. In 1776, they joined the royalists in the city of New York.

OTHER PERIODICALS

THE INDEPENDENT REFLECTOR was a neatly printed paper, published weekly on Thursday, on a sheet of foolscap writing, folio, by James Parker. It contained moral and political essays, but no news. It first appeared on November 30, 1752, and the publication of it was supported two years. The pieces in it were written by a society of literary gentlemen, in and near New York; several of whom were afterwards highly distinguished in public life. The late Governor Livingston, the Rev. Aaron Burr, president of New Jersey College, John Morin Scott,

Gen. William Alexander, known afterwards as Lord Stirling, and William Smith, who died chief justice of Canada, were reputed to be writers for the Reflector.

This work, it has been said, ultimately gave much offence to men in power, by whom the writers for it were silenced. Parker appeared to be intimidated, and declined being further concerned in the publication. 'The authors applied to him to publish, by way of supplement, a vindication of the work, with an account of its origin and design, and the cause of its being discontinued. He refused, and some suspected that he was *drawn off* by those in office, instead of being alarmed into a relinquishment of the work. After Parker declined, De Foreest was applied to, who consented to print the supplement; and in an advertisement said, or was made to say, that "the writers of the Reflector, on this occasion, were obliged to employ the worst printer in the city." ' These were not, I believe, the identical words used on the occasion, but it is the import of them.

JOHN ENGLISHMAN, *in Defence of the English Constitution* was printed on a half sheet, foolscap, and published weekly, on Friday, by Parker and Weyman. It was continued about three months.

NOTES TO CHAPTER VII

See W. Eames, *The First Year of Printing in New York; May, 1693 to April, 1694* (New York Public Library, 1928); C. R. Hildeburn, *List of the Issues of the Press in New York, 1693–1784* (Philadelphia, 1889) and *Printers and Printing in Colonial New York* (New York, 1895); D. C. McMurtrie, *A History of Printing in the United States* (New York, 1936),   NEW YORK

II, 132–220; G. L. McKay, *A Register of Artists ... Printers & Publishers in New York City, 1633–1820* (New York Public Library, 1942); M. W. Hamilton's *The Country Printer, New York State, 1785–1820*, 2nd edn. (New York, 1964), is also a useful work.

NEW YORK CITY

1. The first printing done in New York was Gov. Fletcher's proclamation, printed by Bradford in 1693, and dated Aug. 25. The *Laws* noticed above were printed the same year. M

2. See J. W. Wallace and A. J. Wall, Jr., *op. cit.*

3. L. Rutherford, *John Peter Zenger, His Press, His Trial, and a Bibliography of Imprints* (New York, 1904); Jas. Alexander, *A Brief Narrative of the Case and Trial of John Peter Zenger*, ed. by S. N. Katz (Harvard University Press, 1963); *Dictionary of American Biography*, XX, 648–650.

4. E. B. O'Callaghan, ed., *Documentary History of the State of New-York*, 4to edn. (Albany, 1850–1851), IV, 630; W. A. Duer, *The Life of William Alexander, Earl of Stirling* (New Jersey Historical Society, 1847), pp. 4–5; Wm. Smith, *History of the late Province of New-York* (New-York Historical Society, 1830) II, 16 *et seq.* M

5. Among the Palatines that arrived in New York in 1710 were Johanna Zangerin, aged 33, and her son John Peter, aged 13. On Oct. 26, of that year, the latter was apprenticed to William Bradford, the printer, by Gov. Hunter, when his mother's name was written Hannah Zenger (*in* being a common termination to feminine names in German). See *Documentary History*, III, 340–341. His indentures can be found in *The Historical Magazine*, VIII, 35–36 (Jan. 1864). M

6. For a more extended sketch of Parker see *Documents Relative to the Colonial History of the State of New-York* (Albany, 1856–1883), 14 vols., VIII, 221, note by Dr. O'Callaghan; also his *Documentary History*, III, 323. M See also *Dictionary of American Biography*, XIV, 226–227.

7. Gov. Clinton, by a written order under his hand, dated Oct. 20, 1747, forbade James Parker, who usually printed the journals of the house of assembly, to publish the assembly's remonstrance to his message and proceedings. Smith, II, 150. M

8. See Gaine's *Journals*, ed. by P. L. Ford (New York, 1902), 2 vols.; *Dictionary of American Biography*, VII, 91–92.

9. See O'Callaghan's *Documentary History*, IV, 384–387. M

10. In 1763 Weyman began the printing of a new edition of the Indian *Common Prayer Book*, under the patronage of Sir William Johnson, the Rev. Dr. Barclay having undertaken to superintend it. It absorbed certain *sorts* to such an extent, that after borrowing all he could get from the other offices, he was enabled to set up but half a sheet, and the

work went on with the *safest haste*. The death of Dr. Barclay in 1764, brought the work to a stand. In a letter to Sir William, dated March 25, 1764, he wrote that the work 'still lies dead,' and suggested that the Rev. Mr. Ogilvie should be engaged to go on with its supervision. Mr. Weyman having died in July, 1768, Hugh Gaine was induced to investigate the condition and progress made by Weyman, who reported that 74 pages had been printed; that by reprinting two sheets, 400 copies could be made up; that Weyman was indebted to him £300, and was involved several hundred pounds more than his estate could pay. (See O'Callaghan, *Documentary History*, IV, 327–384.) Weyman also printed for the Rev. Theodorus Frielinghuysen, of the Dutch Reformed church at Albany, a Catechism in Low Dutch, without date of publication but bearing the date to the preface of 1747. M

11. V. H. Paltsits, *John Holt* (New York Public Library, 1920); *Dictionary of American Biography*, IX, 180–181.

12. *Dictionary of American Biography*, XVI, 23–24.

13. *Dictionary of American Biography*, XV, 637–638. The house of Rivington, still extant in London, was established in 1711 by Charles Rivington, who succeeded Richard Chiswell in Paternoster row in that year, and it has ever since been familiar to the readers of religious books in every part of the world wherever the English language is spoken. He was succeeded in 1742 by his sons John and James, the latter of whom is the subject of this sketch. John died in 1792, and the business is still continued by his descendants. James was the original publisher of Smollett's *History of England*, by which it is said that he made £10,000, a larger sum than had ever before been made by one book. M

14. In September 1760, Rivington advertised that he had just opened in Hanover square, and is styled the only London bookseller in America. M

15. He used to relate a story of his interview with the noted Ethan Allen, who paid him a visit for the purpose of administering chastisement. He says, 'I was sitting alone, after a good dinner, with a bottle of Madeira before me, when I heard an unusual noise in the street and a huzza from the boys. I was in the second story, and stepping to the window, saw a tall figure in tarnished regimentals, with a large cocked hat and an enormous long sword, followed by a crowd of boys, who occasionally cheered him with huzzas of which he seemed insensible. He came up to my door and stopped. I could see no more, my heart told me it was Ethan Allen. I shut my window and retired behind my table and my bottle. I was certain the hour of reckoning had come. There was no retreat. Mr. Staples, my clerk, came in paler than ever,

and clasping his hands, said, "Master, he has come!" "I know it." "He entered the store and asked if James Rivington lived there, I answered yes, sir. Is he at home? I will go and see, sir, I said, and now master what is to be done! There he is in the store and the boys peeping at him from the street." I had made up my mind. I looked at the Madeira—possibly took a glass. Show him up, said I, and if such Madeira cannot mollify him he must be harder than adamant. There was a fearful moment of suspense. I heard him on the stairs, his long sword clanking at every step. In he stalked. "Is your name James Rivington?" It is, sir, and no man could be more happy to see Colonel Ethan Allen. "Sir, I have come —" Not another word, my dear Colonel, until you have taken a seat and a glass of old Madeira. "But, sir, I don't think it proper—" Not another word, Colonel; taste this wine, I have had it in glass for ten years; old wine you know, unless it is originally sound, never improves by age. He took the glass, swallowed the wine, smacked his lips and shook his head approvingly. "Sir, I come—" Not another word until you have taken another glass, and then, my dear Colonel, we will talk of old affairs, and I have some queer events to detail. In short, we finished two bottles of Madeira, and parted as good friends as if we had never had cause to be otherwise.' See *Documents Relative to the Colonial History of the State of New York*, VIII, 568; L. Sabine, *Biographical Sketches of Loyalists of the American Revolution* (Boston, 1864), 2 vols., II, 215–219. M

16. Rivington was twice married, first to Miss Minshull in England, and second to Miss Elisabeth Van Horne, of New York. The latter died in July 1795, leaving descendants. Susan Rivington, daughter of James, died June 16, 1843, aged 74. His portrait is preserved in the gallery of the New-York Historical Society, and one of the streets in that city still bears his name. M

17. *Dictionary of American Biography*, XI, 427.

18. D. C. McMurtrie, ... *A Check List of Eighteenth Century Albany Imprints* (Albany, New York State Library, 1939), Bibliography Bulletin 80.

19. See especially McKay's *Register, op. cit.*

20. The first motto is altered from Cicero *De officiis*, lib. 2, cap. 7. H

21. In August 1769, Gaine, in transmitting his statement of account with Sir William Johnson, for books, and printing the *Common Prayer Book* in the Mohawk language, writes that he has not included the amount for the newspaper, for the reason that he does not remember

how much is due, but he thinks it is not less than *ten years*; showing that the memory of man was not commensurate with the length of credit given by the old printers! M

22. We have omitted a long poem by Philip Freneau, 'Hugh Gaine's Life,' which Thomas printed in the Appendix to the second edition. It may be found in Freneau's *Poems* (Princeton University Library, 1903), II, 201–214.

23. Weyman began in 1764 to print *The Book of Common Prayer*, by order of Sir William Johnson. The work met with so many hindrances that in 1768, when Weyman died, only 74 pages had been completed. The printing of the work was finished by Hugh Gaine. An account of the origin and progress of this work is given by Dr. O'Callaghan in *Documents Relative to the Colonial History of the State of New-York*, VIII, 815–817. In O'Callaghan's *List of Editions of the Holy Scriptures*, a table is given of the errors and variations in noted editions of Catholic Bibles and also in a large number of American Bibles. M

24. On this occasion the following lines appeared in Rivington's Gazette. One of the allusions will be better understood by reference to the original cut; it cannot be explained here. See Winthrop Sargent's *Loyalist Poetry of the Revolution* (Philadelphia, 1857), p. 147. M

'Tis true Johnny Holt you have caused us some pain,
By changing your *Head-piece* again and again:
But then to your praise it may justly be said,
You have giv'n us a notable *Tail-piece* instead.
'Tis true, that the Arms of a good British King
Have been forced to give way to a Snake—with a Sting;

Which some would interpret as tho' it implied
That the King by the wound of that Serpent had died.
But now must their Malice all sink into Shade,
By the happy device which you lately displayed;
And Tories themselves be convinced you are slandered
Who see you've erected the Right Royal Standard!

25. He died September 19, 1810, aged 37, and the *Citizen* was discontinued in November following. M

26. For an account of this affair, see J. W. Barber, *Historical Collections of the State of New York* (New York, 1851), pp. 169–170. M

27. In the appendix Thomas printed 'Lines on Mr. Rivington's new engraved King's Arms to his Royal Gazette,' and 'Rivington's Confessions,' both poems by Philip Freneau and which appear in Freneau's

Poems, II, 125, 229–238. To rub salt into the wound, Thomas also quoted in the same appendix the Rev. Dr. John Witherspoon's satyrical 'Supplication of J**** R********' which is printed in Witherspoon's *Works*, 2nd edn. (Philadelphia, 1802), IV, 387–396.

28. Albany was the second city in the State of New York, into which printing was introduced. It is inferred that the Robertsons were not established here till late in the season, from the fact that the city charter was printed this year in New York by Hugh Gaine. The copies of their paper are entitled *The Albany Gazette* as far as they can be found. The publication seems to have begun in November 1771. The earliest copy that has been discovered after a search of many years, is No. 8, dated Jan. 20, 1772, and there are a few copies of about that date preserved in the collection of the Albany Institute. In one of these the publisher, 'from motives of gratitude and duty,' apologized to the public for the omission of one week's publication, and hoped that the irregularity of the mail from New York, since the first great fall of snow, and the severe cold preceding Christmas, which froze the paper prepared for press, so as to put a stop to its operation, would sufficiently account for it. The only other work that I have seen of their printing is the city ordinances of 1773, which is better executed than the charter by Gaine. Alexander Robertson died at Port Roseway, Nova Scotia, Nov. 1784, aged 42. James returned to Edinburgh, and was in business there in 1810, and although I have endeavored to trace him since, all effort has failed.

A book store was kept before the revolution by Stuart Wilson, in a Dutch house on the upper corner of North Pearl and State streets.

The next paper here was the *New York Gazetteer and Northern Intelligencer*, which was first published in May 1782, by Balentine & Webster. It was printed on a sheet of short demy, with pica and long primer types, at 13s. ($1.62½) a year. Advertisements of subscribers were to be inserted three weeks gratis. Balentine was addicted to intemperance, and Webster separated from him at the end of a year. The former then enlarged the size of his paper, but abandoned it after one year, when Webster returned from New York, and began the publication of the *Albany Gazette*, which was continued until 1845. The only works printed by Balentine & Webster, that have come to light, are a pamphlet, by the Rev. Thomas Clarke, of Cambridge, Washington county, entitled *Plain Reasons*, being a dissuasive from the use of Watt's version of the Psalms, in worship, and an Almanac for 1783. The only work known of Balentine's press, is an Almanac of 1784. Mr. Webster began an Almanac in 1784, for the year following, entitled *Webster's Calendar, or the Albany Almanac*, which is still published, and is the oldest almanac extant in the United States. M

★ VIII ★

NEW JERSEY

SEVERAL presses were occasionally set up in this
province by Keimer, and others, from Philadelphia and
New York, to print the bills of credit, or paper currency, and to do other occasional printing for the government;
and, when the particular business was accomplished, the printers returned to the place of their permanent residence with their
presses.

THE first press established in New Jersey, it appears, was
at Woodbridge, and for many years this was the only one
in the colony.

The printing which had been done for government by presses
set up occasionally, as mentioned above, was executed at
Burlington. It was there that Keimer, in 1727, sent Franklin to
print the bills of credit; for which, Franklin observes, he 'engraved various ornaments, and performed the business to general satisfaction.'

JAMES PARKER,[1] who has been mentioned among the printers
of New Haven and New York, was born in that borough, and
there began business about the year 1751. He had for several

years conducted a press and a newspaper in New York, but having taken William Weyman as a partner in his concerns in that city, he intrusted the management of the establishment to him, and returned himself to the place of his nativity. There he printed a folio edition of the *Law of the Province*,* and, from time to time, the votes and resolves of the legislature, and did other work for government. There also he published, monthly, more than two years, a magazine, and otherwise employed his press on his own account.

To accommodate the printing of Smith's *History of New Jersey*, in 1765, Parker removed his press to Burlington, and there began and completed the work, consisting of 570 pages, demy octavo, and then returned with his press to Woodbridge.

Parker was a correct and eminent printer. Besides his professional concerns, he was much employed in the public transactions; he was a magistrate, a captain of a troop of horse, in New Jersey, and comptroller and secretary of the general post-office for the northern district of the British colonies. He possessed a sound judgment, and a good heart; was industrious in business, and upright in his dealings.

He died July 2, 1770, at Burlington, where he had resided a short time for the benefit of his health. His funeral was attended five miles from Burlington, by a number of gentlemen of that city, and was met at Amboy by others, who then joined the procession to his house in Woodbridge, where a numerous concourse was collected, and accompanied his remains to the cemetery where those of his ancestors reposed. [See pp. 464–470.]

---

* The copies of this edition of *The Laws of New Jersey*, were sold for five dollars each. The editor was Judge Nevill, who had it printed on his own account.

SAMUEL F. PARKER has been mentioned, as connected with his father in the printing business, during several years; and, afterward, with John Anderson, in New York.

After the death of his father, he became possessed of a large printing apparatus; but from it he derived very little benefit, as he leased the establishment at New York, not much to his advantage, and sold that at Woodbridge, in the course of a few years. He did not improve either his time or his talents; his health decayed; and he slept with his fathers, before he had attained the number of years to which they arrived.

SOME suppose that William Bradford introduced printing into that city before the settlement of Philadelphia; but that opinion is so far from being certain it is not even probable.

ISAAC COLLINS,[2] was a native of Delaware. His parents were from England, and died in early life. He served his apprenticeship, until he was twenty years of age, with James Adams, at Wilmington. He then went, by the consent of Adams, who had but little business, and finished his apprenticeship with William Rind at Williamsburg, Virginia. When of age, he was employed by Goddard and others in Philadelphia; and for his extraordinary attention to business, received twenty-five per cent. more wages than other journeymen in the same printing house. For a short time he was the partner of Joseph Crukshank, in that city.

By the death of James Parker, there was an opening for the settlement of a printer in that colony. Collins embraced the opportunity; and, being supplied with a press, types, etc., by his late partner, he removed to, and began business in Burlington in 1770, and resided there for several years after the commencement of the war. In 1770 he was appointed printer to the government, or, 'to the King's Most Excellent Majesty,' as appears from the imprint of proclamations, etc., which issued from his press. In 1777 he began a newspaper.

He afterwards removed to Trenton, and there prosecuted his business for a number of years. He continued to be printer to the state, and at Trenton he printed a handsome and very correct quarto edition of the Bible; also, an edition in octavo of the New Testament; and several other books.

Collins was of the society of Friends, and was a correct and neat printer. He received much assistance from the quakers in printing the Bible, particularly from those in Philadelphia, New Jersey, and New York. He subsequently removed to New York, there set up his press, and continued active in book printing for some years. His parents dying when he was very young, he had nothing on which he could depend for his advancement in life, but his own exertions. After an attention to business for thirty-five years, he was enabled to retire and enjoy, in the society of his friends, the reward of his industry. He brought up, and educated in a reputable manner, a large family, and had a son a printer in New York. He died in March, 1817, in Burlington aged 71 years.

NEWSPAPERS THE NEW JERSEY GAZETTE was published at Burlington, December 3, 1777. It was printed weekly, on Wednesday, with a good, long primer type, and on a sheet of crown paper, folio. Imprint: 'Burlington: Printed by Isaac Collins. All Persons may be supplied with this Gazette for Twenty-Six Shillings per Annum. Advertisements of a moderate Length are inserted for Seven Shillings and Six Pence the first Week, and Two Shillings and Six Pence for every continuance; and long Ones in proportion.' This paper was neatly printed, and well conducted. Its publisher, although of the society of Friends, was a firm supporter of the rights of his country; and he carefully avoided publishing anything which tended to injure the religious, civil, or political interests of his fellow citizens. It was discontinued in 1786.[3]

NEW AMERICAN MAGAZINE was begun at Woodbridge by James Parker, in January, 1758, and was continued monthly more than two years. Each number contained forty pages, octavo. Although this was a valuable literary work, and but one of the kind was then published in the colonies,* there was not a sufficient number of copies sold to defray the expense of printing, &c. It was, therefore, discontinued, after being published twenty-seven months. Ten years after, a large number of the copies were sold by the printer for waste paper.

The editor was the honorable Samuel Nevil, under the signature of *Sylvanus Americanus*. Judge Nevil was from England, and had been editor of *The London Evening Post*. He had re-

---

* *The American Magazine or Monthly Chronicle*, printed at Philadelphia; but which was discontinued soon after the appearance of this from the press at Woodbridge.

ceived a liberal education, his knowledge was extensive, and his writings commanded considerable attention. He was a judge of the supreme court of New Jersey, speaker of the house of assembly, and mayor of the city of Amboy. He died at Perth Amboy, in November, 1764, aged sixty-seven years.

THE CONSTITUTIONAL COURANT. After the American stamp act was passed by the British parliament, and near the time it was to be put in operation, a political paper was privately printed in Woodbridge, which attracted much notice. It was entitled 'The Constitutional Courant, containing Matters interesting to Liberty—but no wise repugnant to Loyalty.' Imprint, 'Printed by Andrew Marvel, at the Sign of the Bribe refused, on Constitution-Hill, North America.' In the centre of the title was a device of a snake, cut into parts, to represent the colonies. Motto—'Join or die.' After the title, followed an address to the public from the fictitious printer and publisher, Andrew Marvel. This paper was without date, but was printed in September, 1765. It contained several well written and spirited essays against the obnoxious stamp act, which were so highly colored, that the editors of newspapers in New York, even Holt, declined to publish them.

A large edition was printed, secretly forwarded to New York, and there sold by hawkers selected for the purpose. It had a rapid sale, and was, I believe, reprinted there, and at Boston. It excited some commotion in New York, and was taken notice of by government. A council was called, and holden at the fort in that city, but as no discovery was made of the author or printer, nothing was done. One of the council demanded of a hawker named Lawrence Sweeney, 'where that incendiary paper was printed?' Sweeney, as he had been instructed, answered, 'At Peter Hassenclever's iron-works, please your honor.' Peter Hassenclever was a wealthy German, well known as the owner of extensive iron works in New Jersey. Afterwards, other publications of a like kind frequently appeared with an imprint, 'Printed at Peter Hassenclever's iron-works.'

Only one number of the Constitutional Courant[4] was published; a continuance of it was never intended. It was printed by William Goddard, at Parker's printing house in Woodbridge, Goddard having previously obtained Parker's permission occasionally to use his press.

This political paper was handsomely commended in some of the periodical works published in England, after the repeal of the stamp act.

NOTES TO CHAPTER VIII

For recent works on the history of printing in New Jersey, see D. C. McMurtrie, *History of Printing in the United States* (New York, 1936), II, 221–243; Wm. Nelson, 'Some New Jersey Printers and Printing in the Eighteenth Century,' in *Proceedings of the American Antiquarian Society*, XXI, 15–56 (April 1911) and his *Check-List of the Issues of the Press of New Jersey 1723, 1728, 1754–1800* (Paterson, N.J., 1899); C. H. Humphrey, 'Check-List of New Jersey Imprints to the End of the Revolution,' in *Papers of the Bibliographical Society of America*, XXIV, 43–149 (1930).   NEW JERSEY

1. W. H. Benedict, 'James Parker, the printer, of Woodbridge,' in *Proceedings of the New Jersey Historical Society*, 4th ser., VIII, 194–199 (July 1923).   WOODBRIDGE

2. R. F. Hixon, *Isaac Collins* (Rutgers University Press, 1968).   BURLINGTON

NEWSPAPERS   3. *The New Jersey Journal* was printed on a cap sheet by Shepard Kolloch at Chatham, of which no. 71 is dated June 21, 1780. M

MAGAZINES   4. See J. T. Buckingham, *Specimens of Newspaper Literature* (Boston, 1850), II, 246. There is a copy of this paper in the University library, at Cambridge. M

★ IX ★

DELAWARE

PRINTING had a late introduction into Delaware; it was, Georgia excepted, the last of the thirteen colonies where a press was established. The laws, etc., were printed in Philadelphia previous to the year 1761.

THE first printing house introduced into that colony was WILMINGTON opened in that town only about fourteen years before the commencement of the war, by

JAMES ADAMS, who was born in Ireland, and learned the art of printing in Londonderry. When of age, he came to Philadelphia, and was there employed seven years by Franklin & Hall.

He began business for himself, in that city, about the year 1760; but, in 1761, he removed his press to Wilmington, and established himself there. In 1762, he published proposals for printing a newspaper; but not meeting with encouragement, it was discontinued after being published six months.

He printed for government, and although his business was not extensive, he acquired considerable property. Several works on religious subjects, came from his press; and he published one or more almanacs annually, and bound and sold books.

Adams was a good workman, an exemplary Christian, and much esteemed. When the British army were approaching Philadelphia, in 1777, he removed his printing materials, family, etc., to the vicinity of Doylestown, Bucks county, Pa. There he printed an Almanac, but otherwise his press was not employed. When the British evacuated Philadelphia, in 1778, he returned with his press, etc., to Wilmington.

He died near the close of the year 1792, aged sixty three years. He left a large family; four sons and six daughters. The sons were all brought up to printing. Two of them succeeded their father, but were not successful in business.

The following anecdote finds a place here. Adams had hired a man to pull a press, while an apprentice was employed to beat the form. The man had engaged at a shilling a token. The boy was repeatedly, in the course of a day, called by the mistress for culinary and house purposes, whereby the man was much injured. Finding his bill, each week, to fall short of his maintenance, he fell upon a plan to augment his wages, and at the same time fulfil his engagement. When the boy was called away he would still pound and pull the sheets as usual, leaving sufficient time between each for the form to be inked. Adams on inspecting the heap, and perceiving so many faintly impressed copies, asked the meaning. 'I suppose the boy has not beat them;' replied the man, 'and I am sure I leave him time enough and have also performed my duty in pulling.' Adams was diverted with the humor of the man, and ordered the boy to be no more called from the press.

Adams was the only printer who settled in Delaware before 1775.

THE district of country which composes the state of Delaware, was, previously to the revolution, distinguished as 'The Counties of Newcastle, Kent, and Sussex, on Delaware.'

THE first and only newspaper published before 1775, in what is now the state of Delaware, made its appearance in Wilmington about the year 1762, entitled, if my information is correct, *The Wilmington Courant*, printed and published by James Adams, for the short period of six months; when, for want of encouragement, it was discontinued. About the year 1787, Adams commenced the publication of another paper, entitled *The Wilmington Courant*. Its continuance was only two or three years.

NOTE TO CHAPTER IX

See Evald Rink, *Printing in Delaware, 1761–1800* (Eleutherian Mills Historical Library, 1969) and D. C. McMurtrie, *History of Printing in the United States*, II, 244–253.

* X *

MARYLAND

A PRINTING HOUSE was not established in Maryland for more than ninety years after the province was
granted by King Charles I, to George Calvert, baron
of Baltimore, in Ireland.

ANNAPOLIS THE first press was set up in Annapolis in 1726.[1] Before
that time the printing for the colony was done at Philadelphia, by Andrew Bradford.

WILLIAM PARKS.[2] The earliest book I have met with, printed
in Maryland is, *A complete Collection of the Laws of Maryland.
Collected by Authority.* This work is dedicated to Lord Baltimore. Imprint—'Annapolis, Printed by William Parks, 1727.'

Parks began a newspaper either in 1727 or in 1728, most
probably the year last mentioned. This paper, it appears from
the best information, was carried on about eight years, when it
was discontinued, and Parks established himself in Virginia. He
had, in 1729, printed at Williamsburg, the *Laws of Virginia*, etc.
During several years he printed for both colonies, and had a
press in each.

About the year 1733, he quitted Maryland; and, some time
after, the government of the colony procured another printer.
By Keimer's account, the government of each colony paid

Parks a salary of two hundred pounds per annum in country produce.*

JONAS GREEN[3] was born in Boston; he was the son of Timothy Green, who, in 1714, removed from Boston to New London. The government of Maryland having offered a generous consideration to a printer who would establish a press in Annapolis, he closed with the proposal and in 1740 opened a printing house in that city. He was appointed printer for the colony, and had granted to him an annual salary of 500*l.* currency. For this sum he printed the laws as they were made from session to session, proclamations, etc., he being paid the cost of paper used in the work. In 1745 he began a newspaper which was continued by his successors. He printed in 1755 a revised edition of the Laws; and in 1765, Bacon's *Laws of Maryland*, in a large folio volume. His printing was correct, and few, if any, in the colonies exceeded him in the neatness of his work. Green possessed handsome talents, was respected for his conduct in private life, and, in the circle of his acquaintance, was celebrated for his wit and urbanity.

A few years before he died he received William Rind as a partner. The firm of the company was, GREEN & RIND. In 1765, Rind removed to, and settled in, Virginia.

Green died April 7th, 1767, aged fifty-six years.

ANNE CATHARINE GREEN, was born in Holland, and came when an infant, with her parents, to Maryland. She married

* See Keimer's poetical address to his customers at Barbadoes, extracted from the *Barbadoes Gazette* of May 4th, 1734. Keimer had been a printer in Philadelphia, and must have been acquainted with the public and private concerns of the few printers then in the colonies.

Jonas Green; and, in 1767, succeeded him in his business. She printed for the colony, and published the Gazette. William Green, her son, became her partner in 1768; the firm was, ANNE CATHARINE GREEN & SON. William died in August 1770, and Anne Catharine continued the business in her own name. She was the mother of six sons and eight daughters. She died March 23, 1775, aged forty-two years.

FREDERICK GREEN, the son of Jonas and Anne Catharine, was born in Annapolis, and brought up to printing by his father. He succeeded his mother as printer to the colony, and in other business, in 1775; and about the year 1777 he entered into partnership with his brother Samuel, under the firm of FREDERICK & SAMUEL GREEN. They then printed, and kept the postoffice, 'in Charles-Street.' They were the fifth generation of a regular descent of printers in this country. Their great-great grandfather began printing at Cambridge, Massachusetts, about 1649; as has been mentioned in the account given of him and his other descendants.

After the decease of Frederick and Samuel Green, the business was continued by —— Green, son of the last mentioned Green, a great-great-great grandson of Samuel Green printer in Cambridge.

BALTIMORE was but a small village in 1755. Printing was not introduced there till several years after that time.

NICHOLAS HASSELBAUGH was born in Pennsylvania, of parents who were of German extraction. He was taught printing by Sower, in Germantown, and also acquired a knowledge of papermaking. This last branch of manufacturing he followed some time near that place; but, eventually, removed and established a printing press in Baltimore.

He was well supplied with types, manufactured in Germantown, for printing both in the German and English languages; and was the first who printed in that city. He issued school and other small books, etc., from his press, in both languages; and contemplated publishing a German translation of the Bible. The following anecdote, which many years since was circulated in Maryland, gives strength to the supposition that he was actually engaged in that work.

A missionary for propagating the gospel among the Indians, was engaged in that benevolent design in the back settlements of Maryland; and, at a time when a number of Indians were assembled to hear him unfold and explain the doctrines of the Christian religion, he had a Bible in his hand, which he held forth, and with much zeal pronounced it to be 'the gospel—the truth—the work of God!' He was interrupted—'What!' said one of them, 'did the great all powerful spirit *make this book?*' 'Yes,' replied the missionary, 'it is his work.' The Indian, taking the expression according to the literal import of the words, answered indignantly—'I believe it to be a great lie! I go to Baltimore last month, where I *see* Dutchmen *make him*. Great Spirit want no Dutchman to help him.' With these words the savage took an abrupt leave of his instructor.

This anecdote might have given rise to the opinion that Hasselbaugh had printed a part of the Bible. It was related when there was no other printer in Baltimore. The fact, after all, might have been, that the Indian, when at Baltimore, had seen some printing performed; perhaps a spelling book was at the time in the press, and probably he did not know one book from another.

Hasselbaugh was an inhabitant of Baltimore for several years. He possessed a spirit of enterprise, was fertile in invention, and acquired a handsome property. To facilitate some plan of business which he had newly formed, he went abroad and was lost at sea. His widow, in 1773, sold his printing materials to William Goddard, who again sold part of them to Bailey, printer in Lancaster, Pennsylvania.

ENOCH STORY, THE YOUNGER, was born in Pennsylvania, and served an apprenticeship with Hall & Sellers in Philadelphia, as has been related in treating of the printers of that city. He began printing in Baltimore previous to the year 1773. Story sold his types to Goddard, returned to Philadelphia, and printed in Strawberry alley.

HODGE AND SHOBER opened a printing house in Baltimore, in 1772; and issued proposals for publishing a newspaper; but, before the end of the year, they removed to New York.

WILLIAM GODDARD has been mentioned as the first printer in Providence, Rhode Island; and, afterwards, as the publisher of the *Pennsylvania Chronicle* in Philadelphia. In 1773 he removed to Baltimore.

I have already observed that Goddard was a good printer, and an able editor; but he, in many instances, was unsuccessful. The partnership with Galloway and Wharton in Philadelphia proved very unfortunate, and terminated unprofitably for

Goddard, and the parties separated much dissatisfied with each
other. After two trials to establish himself in business, he began
'anew,' as he relates, 'on the small capital of a *single, solitary*
guinea.' He made interest to purchase the materials in the printing house of Hasselbaugh, and added to them the few owned by
Enoch Story. He again began a newspaper, the third attempted
in the province; but at this time there was only one published,
the *Maryland Gazette*. After remaining at Baltimore nearly two
years, he found it necessary to devote some time to the settlement of his former concerns.

Another object at this period attracted his attention. A plan
was formed to abolish, in effect, the general postoffice under the
direction of the British government, by establishing, in opposition, a line of postriders from Georgia to New Hampshire.
This system was to have been supported from a fund to be
raised by the subscriptions of individuals. Goddard left his
printing house in the care of his sister, and went through the
colonies with a view to carry this plan into operation. A large
sum was subscribed, and the scheme was in a rapid state of
progression, when the revolutionary war began.

When congress superseded the British government in the
management of the post office, Franklin was continued as postmaster general, with the privilege of giving commissions to all
other officers in the department. The services rendered by Goddard to this establishment, led him to believe, and his friends to
expect, that he would receive the appointment of secretary and
comptroller of the post office; but Franklin thought proper to
give this office to Richard Bache, his son-in-law, and tendered
to Goddard the choice of surveyorship of post roads, or the
office of deputy postmaster for Baltimore and Norfolk. God-

dard was greatly disappointed, but the state of his affairs made it expedient that he should accept either the one or the other of these places, and he chose that of surveyor of post roads. In 1776, Franklin was sent on an embassy to Europe; and his son-in-law, Bache, succeeded him as postmaster general. Goddard again expected the office of comptroller, but being again disappointed he resigned his surveyorship; and it was apprehended that there was, from that time, some change in his political principles.

Goddard, after having resigned his commission, returned to Baltimore, and there resided; but the business of the printing house continued to be under the management, and in the name of his sister. It was, however, well known that he was interested in the *Maryland Journal*, and had the control of it.

A number of zealous advocates for the American cause had associated in Baltimore, and were called the Whig club. Of this club Commodore Nicholson, then commander of the frigate Virginia, belonging to the United States, was president. In February, 1777, a report was circulated that the British general Howe had offered the most eligible terms of accommodation to congress, which had been rejected and concealed from the people. To ridicule this false and idle report, an ironical piece, signed Tom Tell Truth, written by a member of congress,* appeared in Goddard's paper, published by his sister; but for fear this piece might be misconceived by some, and produce a serious belief in them that these offers had actually been made to congress, another piece was published in the same paper to counteract any bad tendencies of the first. Both pieces were written by the same person. The Whig club was alarmed; the

* Judge C***e, as I am informed.

members of it believed these pieces would produce dangerous effects, and supposed that they were written by some British emissary. They enquired of Miss Goddard who was the author; she referred them to her brother. Goddard was applied to, and refused to give up the author, who was not in town, and could not then be consulted. Some warm words passed between Goddard and the deputed members of the club. The deputation was renewed, with a written mandate ordering him to appear before them the next evening. Goddard treated the mandate and the deputies who bore it rather cavalierly, and did not obey. The club then deputed a committee of six of its members to bring him before them, and if necessary, to use force. Goddard refused to accompany the committee; some of them were armed, and they seized him, and by violence carried him to the club room; here he was refractory, and would not discover the author. The club, in consequence, passed the following resolution, viz.

'In Whig Club, March 4, 1777.

'*Resolved*, that William Goddard do leave this town by twelve o'clock to-morrow morning, and the county in three days. Should he refuse due obedience to this notice, he will be subject to the resentment of a   LEGION.'

Goddard went the next day to Annapolis, where the general assembly was then in session, and presented a memorial to the legislature, detailing his case, and praying for protection. The house referred the case to their committee of aggrievances, which reported, that 'the proceedings of the whig club were a manifest violation of the constitution, and directly contrary to the declaration of rights assented to by the representatives of the freemen of the state. The club published a vindication of their proceedings. Goddard, in reply, published a pamphlet, giving an account of the whole transaction, and satirizing the members of the club with some severity. This pamphlet increased the violence of the club, and Goddard thought himself in danger from their resentment. He therefore presented a second memorial to the house of delegates; in consequence of which, the house, on the 11th of April, 1777, passed the following resolutions.

'*Resolved*, That the proceedings of the persons in Baltimore town, associated and stiled, The Whig Club, are a most daring infringement and a manifest violation of the constitution of this state, directly contrary to the *Declaration of Rights*, and tend, in their consequences, unless timely checked, to the destruction of all regular government.

'*Resolved unanimously*, That the governor be requested to issue his proclamation, declaring all bodies of men associated together, or meeting for the purpose, and usurping any of the powers of government, and presuming to exercise any power over the persons or property of any subjects of this state, or to carry into execution any of the laws thereof, unlawful assemblies, and requiring all such assemblies and meetings instantly to disperse.

'*Resolved*, That the governor be requested to afford William Goddard the protection of the law of the land, and to direct the justices of Baltimore county to give him every protection in their power, against all violence or injury to his person or property.'

Governor Johnson, on the 17th of April, 1777, issued his proclamation conformably to the above resolutions. The interposition of government in favor of Goddard, did not immediately secure to him a state of tranquility. He was accused of toryism, but the accusation did not appear to be supported. It was, however, sometime before his enemies ceased to be troublesome.

In June, 1779, Goddard and Eleazar Oswald advertised that they had formed a partnership as printers, booksellers and stationers; but this connection was of very short duration. Goddard's sister continued to publish the Journal. On the 6th of July, 1779, appeared in that paper certain 'Queries political and military,' written by General Charles Lee. These were sent to the press by Goddard, and when published they occasioned great commotion in Baltimore. An assembly of 'the people' was holden, and a committee consisting of about forty was chosen to wait on Goddard and demand the author of the queries.

This occasioned a considerable ferment, and the disagreement between Goddard and the Whig Club rose to a very high pitch. The violence of the clubists was excessive; but he resisted them with much energy. However, after a long and arduous contest, in which Goddard was, agreeably to the language of the day, 'several times mobbed, and grievously insulted,' the 'rage of the people' subsided; and he finally quitted Baltimore on good terms with *Legion* and the *profanum vulgus*.

Goddard was variously employed until 1784, when he resumed his printing house, and recommenced the publication of the Journal. About this time a rival paper was published by Hayes, which produced, occasionally, a little typographical sparring from each of the editors. In 1787, an almanac published by Goddard was ridiculed by Hayes. This produced a fierce paper war, in which neither party spared the other; but Goddard appeared to be fully a match for his antagonist.

Goddard continued in active business until 1792;* he then sold his printing establishment to his brother-in-law, who, although not a printer, had been in partnership with him. He published, in the Journal, a valedictory address to the citizens of Maryland, whom he left in friendship, and retired himself in peace to a farm in Johnston, near Providence, in the state of Rhode Island.

MARY KATHARINE GODDARD was born in Connecticut, and was the sister of William Goddard. She was an expert and correct compositor of types, and ably conducted the printing house of her brother during the time he was engaged in other concerns. For a period of about eight years, the Journal and every work which issued from that press, were printed and published in her name, and partly on her account. She kept the postoffice, and continued the newspaper, until her brother resumed its publication in 1784.

1774. WILLIAM AIKMAN.

A NEWSPAPER was published at Annapolis, in this colony, as early as 1728. Three papers only had been printed before the revolutionary war, and two of them were published when it commenced.

---

* Goddard loaned a press and types to George Richards, who first published a newspaper in Richmond, entitled *The Virginia Gazette*.

THE MARYLAND GAZETTE. I cannot determine the exact
time when this paper was first introduced to the public; but the
best information I can obtain dates its origin from 1727. I have
ascertained that it was published in June, 1728, by the following
record of the vestry of the parish church in Annapolis, dated in
June, 1728, directing 'the register of the vestry to apply to the
printer to have an advertisement inserted in the *Maryland Gazette*;' and, by a subsequent record of an account 'rendered by
the Printer for publishing an advertisement in the Gazette, and
printing hand-bills.' These and other facts indicate that it was
established the previous year; and I have reason to believe that
it was published irregularly until 1736. I have seen extracts from
it dated in August, 1729.

It was printed by William Parks.

THE MARYLAND GAZETTE was the second newspaper published in the colony. The first had been discontinued about nine
years, when the second of the same title came before the public
in April, 1745, printed by Jonas Green. It was published weekly,
on Thursday, on paper of foolscap size, folio, but it was enlarged, some years after, to a crown sheet. The typographical
features of this Gazette were equal to those of any paper then
printed on the continent. It has been regularly and uniformly
published from 1745, to the present time (1810), with the exception of a short suspension in 1765, on account of the stamp
act; and there is only one paper printed in the United States
which is of a prior date.

After it had been published several years, the imprint was as
follows: 'Annapolis: Printed by Jonas Green, at his Printing-
Office in Charles-Street; where all persons may be supplied

with this Gazette, at 12/6. a year; and Advertisements of a moderate Length are inserted for 5s. the First Week, and 1s. each Time after: And long ones in Proportion.'

When the publication of this Gazette was suspended on account of the stamp act in 1765, its printer occasionally issued a paper called *The Apparition of the Maryland Gazette, which is not Dead but Sleepeth*. At one corner of the sheet of The Apparition was, as a substitute for a stamp, the figure of a death's head, about which the words following were arranged: 'The Times are Dismal, Doleful, Dolorous, Dollar-less.'

The publication of The Maryland Gazette was resumed January 30th, 1766, and it was printed until 1767; completing a period of twenty-two years by Green, the first publisher. From April 1767 to December of that year, it was issued from the press by his widow, Anne Catharine Green; and from January 1768 to August 1770, by Anne Catharine Green and William her son. William died in 1770; and Anne Catharine published it until her death, in March, 1775. It was then continued by her sons, Frederic and Samuel Green.*

THE MARYLAND JOURNAL, *and Baltimore Advertiser* was the third newspaper published in Maryland, and first appeared in August, 1773. It was handsomely printed on a demy sheet, and had a cut of the arms of the colony, or those of

---

* Both Frederic and Samuel Green paid the debt of nature not long after the first edition of this work was published. [The *St. Mary's Gazette* announced in 1848, that it was printed on the press used in printing this *Maryland Gazette*, which had been in constant use for more than a hundred years, and upon which the first edition of the *Laws of Maryland* was printed. M]

lord Baltimore, in the title. At first it was published on Saturdays, afterward on Thursdays. Imprint, 'Baltimore: Printed by William Goddard, at the Printing-Office in Market-street, opposite the Coffee-House, where Subscriptions, at Ten Shillings per Annum, Advertisements and Letters of Intelligence, are gratefully received for this paper; and where all Manner of Printing Work is performed with Care, Fidelity and Expedition. Blanks and Hand-Bills in *particular* are done on the shortest Notice in a neat and correct Manner.'

From 1775, to 1784, Mary Katharine Goddard, in the absence of her brother, published the Journal in her own name. In the year 1784, William Goddard resumed the publication.

During several years Goddard was in habits of intimacy and friendship with the celebrated but eccentric general, Charles Lee, who, in one stage of the American war, was the second in command of the American army; and, it is supposed, contemplated the removal of General Washington from the chief command, with an expectation of occupying his place. Lee having failed in the execution of his orders at the battle of Monmouth, in 1778, was disgraced, and spent the remainder of his days in retirement, chiefly on his large estate in Berkeley county, Va., said to have contained 2752 acres of valuable land. He died at Philadelphia, October 2, 1782; and in his last will and testament, as a token of his esteem, left Goddard, as has been mentioned, a valuable real estate in Virginia.

Lee's papers were deposited in the hands of Goddard with a view to the publication of them; and, in June 1785, a proposal for printing them by subscription, in three volumes octavo, at the price of one guinea, was issued in the *Maryland Journal*. The papers consisted, first, of letters to Lee from persons of distinction, both in Europe and America; secondly, letters from the general to his friends in Europe previous to the war, likewise to the principal characters in America, civil and military, during his command in the American army; and thirdly, essays on various subjects, political and military; to which it was proposed to prefix memoirs of his life.* In the prospectus, the

---

* Major General Charles Lee was the son of Colonel John Lee, and a native of Wales. He was allied to several of the most noble, ancient and respectable families in England; and could trace his genealogy from the Norman conquest. As he possessed a military spirit, he entered the army early in life; but the profession of arms did not damp his ardor in the pursuits of literature. He possessed a competent knowledge of Greek and Latin; and, in his travels, formed an acquaintance with the Italian, Spanish, German and French languages. He served against the French in America, anno 1756; and, when General Abercrombie was defeated at the French lines of Ticonderoga in July, 1758, Lee was severely wounded at the head of his grenadiers. He served with great reputation under General Burgoyne in Portugal; and was a volunteer against the Turks in the Russian army, commanded by General Romanzow, where he had some 'hair breath 'scapes.' He was made a major general in the army of the king of Poland; after which he returned to England, but meeting with disappointments, he retired with some disgust to America, where he became an enthusiast in the cause of liberty. In the contest which ensued between England and her colonies, he took up arms in favor of the latter; by which proceeding he risked his very considerable estate in England, which however escaped confiscation; yet he was deprived of its profits, and was thereby subjected to many difficulties and mortifying privations. He lost also his rank of a major general in the British army, with a very fair chance of becoming a lieutenant general, and, perhaps, of being made a peer of the realm. He was eminently useful in forming and disciplining the American armies, and rendered essential service on many other important occasions. He 'adventured his life far,' in 'many a well fought field;' and did much toward infusing a martial spirit into the American troops. If General Washington was considered as the Fabius, he was called the Marcellus, of the American army; and as he exchanged a life of opulence, wealth and ease, for the toils, dangers and privations of war, we cannot doubt that the affections of his soul were honestly and nobly engaged in the cause of freedom, distinctly and independently of all the principles and motives of ambition.

The principal part of the estate which he possessed at the time of his death, he bequeathed to his sister Miss Sidney Lee, who was a lady of exquisite accomplishments, and treated the Americans who were captured, and imprisoned by the British in England, with great humanity. She remitted four thousand

publishers observed, 'That the greatest task they met with in collecting and arranging these posthumous papers, arose from their desire of not giving offence to such characters as had been the objects of the general's aversion and resentment. Unhappily, his disappointments had soured his temper; the affair of Monmouth, several pieces of scurrility from the press, and numerous instances of private slander and defamation, so far got the better of his philosophy as to provoke him in the highest degree, and he became as it were, angry with all mankind.

'To this exasperated disposition we may impute the origin of his *Political Queries*, and a number of satirical hints, thrown out both in his conversation and writing, against the commander in chief. Humanity will draw a veil over the involuntary errors of sensibility, and pardon the sallies of a suffering mind, as its presages did not meet with an accomplishment. General Washington, by his retirement, demonstrated to the world that power was not his object; that America had nothing to fear from his ambition; but that she was honored with a specimen of such exalted patriotism as could not fail to attract the attention and admiration of the most distant nations.

'The reader then will not wonder that General Lee, disappointed in his career of glory, should be continually inculcating an idea of the extreme danger of trusting too much to the

---

five hundred pounds sterling to America, in order to discharge her brother's debts, lest his legatees in this country should be deprived of what his friendship and gratitude induced him to bequeath to them.

Goddard did not publish the work he had projected; as [Edward Langworthy] whom he had engaged as an associate in the publication, and who was entrusted with the manuscripts, betrayed his trust; for instead of preparing them for the press, he sent them to England, where they were printed and sold for his sole benefit, and formed the imperfect work, which is entitled *Memoirs of the Life of the late Charles Lee* (London, 1792).

wisdom of *one*, for the safety of the *whole*; that he should consider it as repugnant to the principles of freedom and republicanism to continue for years one man as commander in chief; that there should be a rotation of office, military as well as civil; and though the commander of an army possessed all the virtues of Cato, and the talents of Julius Cesar, it could not alter the nature of the thing, since by habituating the people to look up to one man, all true republican spirit became enervated, and a visible propensity to monarchical government was created and fostered; that there was a charm in the long possession of high office, and in the pomp and influence that attended it, which might corrupt the best dispositions.

'Indeed it was the opinion of Marcus Aurelius, whose virtues not only honored the throne but human nature, that to have the power of doing much, and to confine that power to doing good, was a prodigy in nature. Such sentiments of this divine prince, who was not only trained up in the schools of austere philosophy, but whose elevated situation rendered him the most able judge of the difficulty there is in not abusing extensive power, when we have it in our hands, furnish substantial arguments for not entrusting it to any mortal whatsoever. But while we are convinced of the justness of these sentiments, we are led the more to respect and reverence our most disinterested commander in chief, who stands conspicuous with unrivalled glory, superior to the fascinations which have overthrown many a great and noble mind.'

Before any further steps were taken toward the publication of this work, Goddard addressed General Washington, in the most respectful manner, giving him the outline of the plan, with assurances that every possible precaution would be taken to avoid injuring either his reputation or his feelings. To this letter the general returned the following answer, which, I believe, has not before been published.

Mount Vernon, 11th June, 1785.

'Sir,

'On the 8th inst. I received the favour of your letter of the 30th of May. In answer to it I can only say, that your own good judgment must direct you in the publication of the manuscript papers of General Lee. I can have no request to make concerning the work. I never had a difference with that gentleman, but on public ground; and my conduct towards him upon this occasion, was only such as I conceived myself indispensably bound to adopt in discharge of the public trust reposed in me. If this produced in him unfavourable sentiments of me, I yet can never consider the conduct I pursued with respect to him, either wrong or improper, however I may regret that it may have been differently viewed by him, and that it excited his censure and animadversions.

'Should there appear in General Lee's writings any thing injurious or unfriendly to me, the impartial and dispassionate world must decide how far I deserved it from the general tenor of my conduct. I am gliding down the stream of life, and wish, as is natural, that my remaining days may be undisturbed and tranquil; and, conscious of my integrity, I would willingly hope that nothing will occur to give me anxiety; but should any thing present itself in this or in any other publication, I shall never undertake the painful task of recrimination, nor do I know that I shall even enter upon my justification.

'I consider the communication you have made, as a mark of great attention, and the whole of your letter as a proof of your esteem.

'I am, Sir, Your most obed^t. humble servant,

'*Mr. Goddard.* G^o. WASHINGTON.'

Goddard continued the Journal, and published it twice a week until August, 1792, and then sold his right to James Angell, who for three years had been his partner. Angell did not publish the Journal a long time, but sold the establishment to Philip Edwards, and soon after died of the yellow fever in Philadelphia.

Before 1786, Edward Langworthy was, for a few months, a partner with Goddard in the Journal.

NOTES TO CHAPTER X

MARYLAND   Students of Maryland printing are fortunate in having at their disposal an outstanding series of volumes which admirably cover the subject. L. C. Wroth, *A History of Printing in Colonial Maryland, 1686–1776* (Typothetæ of Baltimore, 1922); J. T. Wheeler, *The Maryland Press, 1777–1790* (Maryland Historical Society, 1938); A. R. Minick, *A History of Printing in Maryland, 1791–1800* (Enoch Pratt Library, 1949); D. C. McMurtrie, *History of Printing in the United States,* II, 99–131.

ANNAPOLIS   1. Mr. J. Sabin sends the following title: The | Declaration | of the | Reasons and Motives | For the Present | Appearing in Arms | of | Their Majesties | Protestant Subjects | In the Province of | Maryland. | Licens'd, November 28th, 1689. J. F. | [Colophon:] *Maryland, Printed by*

William Nuthead at the City of St. | *Maries.* | *Reprinted in London, and Sold by Randal Tay-* | *lor, near Stationers Hall,* 1689. | Folio, pp. 8. No clue has been found to any press in Maryland so early as this. M. Thomas says, first at Annapolis, by Green, about 1726; should be 1700. Example: *The Necessity of an Early Religion,* by Thomas Bray, D.D. (Annapolis: Tho: Reading for Evan Jones, 1700). Brinley's note.

2. *Dictionary of American Biography,* XIV, 250–251.

3. *Dictionary of American Biography,* VII, 552–553.

★ XI ★

VIRGINIA

THIS colony was the first British settlement in America; but it is not the oldest in printing. Printing was not courted, and it would seem not desired, till many years after the establishment of the province.

Sir William Berkeley, who was governor of the colony thirty-eight years, in his twenty-third answer to the inquiries of the lords of the committee for the colonies in 1671, sixty-four years after the settlement of Virginia, says, 'I thank God we have not free schools nor printing; and I hope we shall not have these hundred years. For learning has brought disobedience and heresy, and sects into the world; and printing has divulged them and libels against the government. God keep us from both.'*

I had heard many years since, that printing, at an early period after the settlement of the colony, had been prohibited. I made many inquiries respecting this fact, which led to a strict search among the ancient records of the colony, by several of the first law characters, but no trace of any act of government for that purpose was discovered. For this reason some of the most intelligent Virginians were led into the opinion that no such despotic regulation had been made. But the fact is now ascertained. The

* Geo. Chalmers, *Political Annals of the Present United Colonies ... to the Peace of 1763* (New York, 1968), II, 328; Wm. Gordan, *The History of the Rise, Progress, and Establishment of the Independence of the U.S.A.*, 3rd Am. edn. (New York, 1801) I, 53.

discovery was made by William W. Hening, a very respectable lawyer of Richmond, who, on the 21st of July, 1810, favored me with a letter on the subject, of which the following is an extract.

'I am now, and have been for some time past, engaged in publishing the statutes at large of Virginia, from the first session of the legislature, under the colonial government, in the year 1619; and I have in my possession not only all the manuscripts of Mr. Jefferson, late president of the United States, but several of my own collection, which contain the laws, and other public documents relating to Virginia, till the period when the art of printing was generally diffused among us.

'These manuscripts are so void of method, that I am compelled to read them page by page, in order to select matter proper for my publication. In perusing one of them yesterday, which contains minutes of the proceedings of the governor and council, in their executive character, I found the following entry, which is here transcribed verbatim, from the manuscript.

' "Feb. 21st, 1682. John Buckner called before the Ld. Culpeper and his council for printing the laws of 1680, without his excellency's license, and he and the printer ordered to enter into bond in 100£. *not to print any thing* hereafter, until his majesty's pleasure shall be known."

'I am induced to give you this information the earlier, because, although it had been handed down by tradition, that the use of the press had, at some period of our colonial subjugation, been prohibited in Virginia, the evidence of the fact had eluded all my researches till this time.'[1]

This information makes it sufficiently evident, that there was a press in Virginia as early as 1681; but the name of the printer does not appear; and the record shows, that the press was speedily prohibited. Lord Culpeper was appointed governor of Virginia in November, 1682;* the old style was then used, which placed February at the end of the year. In 1683, Lord Effingham received a commission as governor of the colony† and he was ordered expressly, 'to allow no person to use a printing press on any occasion whatsoever.' ‡ And it does not appear that any printing was performed in Virginia from the year 1682 till about the year 1729. Until 1766, there was but one printing house in the colony, and this was thought to be too much under the control of the governor.

BY the foregoing it is evident there was a printing press in Virginia, in or near Williamsburg, as early as 1681, and that it was discontinued in 1682. The printer's name is not known, or if known, I have not been able to ascertain it. The first permanent printing establishment in the colony was made in Williamsburg by WILLIAM PARKS,[2] who at that time, had a press at Annapolis, as already mentioned. He was, by the appointment of each government, printer to both colonies, and received 200*l.* currency, per annum, from Virginia, and the same sum from Maryland. Accommodations of this sort were not unusual in provinces south of Connecticut, during the infancy of printing.

Parks, it has been said, was born and bred to printing in

* Thomas Jefferson, *Notes on the State of Virginia* (Institute of Early American History and Culture, 1955), p. 190.
† Jefferson's *Notes on Virginia*, p. 191.
‡ Chalmers's *Annals*, I, 345.

England. About the year 1733, he left Annapolis and made
Williamsburg the place of his permanent abode. His appointment as printer to the government was continued, and his
salary enlarged. Soon after he became a resident of that city he
published a newspaper;[3] and, for many years, his press was the
only one in Virginia.

Parks was prosecuted by a member of the house of burgesses,
for publishing a libel, as appears by the following anecdote,
extracted from the newspapers printed more than forty years
ago. This was inserted in the journals of that time, as a striking
instance of the influence and effect which the press has on public
men and officers of government.

'Some few years ago, a man was convicted of stealing sheep,
at Williamsburg, in Virginia, for which crime he was prosecuted; and, on answering the demands of public justice, retired
into what was called the back woods of that dominion, in
order to avoid the reproaches of his neighbors. Several years
passed away; during which time he acquired considerable
property, and that part of the country where he took up his
residence being made a new county he was by his neighbors
chosen to represent them in the house of burgesses, which then
met at Williamsburg. A mischievous *libeller*, who remembered
the crime formerly committed by the burgess, published an
account of it in the *Gazette*, and although he did not mention
the name, he clearly pointed out the transgressor, who, it
seems, had defended some measures in the government that
were considered as arbitrary, and who was highly offended
with the freedom of the printer. The house was also displeased
that one of their honorable body should be accused in a public
paper of being guilty of such a base transaction.

'Parks was prosecuted for printing and publishing a *libel* against Mr. ****, an honorable and worthy burgess; and many members of the honorable house would no doubt have been highly gratified, if, on that occasion, they could have introduced the Star chamber doctrine of libels, and punished Parks for daring to publish an article which, as they observed, scandalized the government by reflecting on those who are intrusted with the administration of public affairs. But Parks begged that the records of the court might be produced, which would prove the truth of the libel. This was allowed, and the records were examined, though contrary to the doctrine of some men, who would impose on the community as law, that a libel is not less a libel for being true, and that its being true is an aggravation of the offence; and, such men observe, no one must speak ill of rulers, or those who are intrusted with power or authority, be they ever so base and oppressive, and daily abuse that power. Now, mark the sequel: the prosecutor stood recorded for sheep stealing; a circumstance which he supposed time had fully obliterated, both from the records of the court, and from the minds of the people; and he withdrew, overwhelmed with disgrace, from public life, and never more ventured to obtrude himself into a conspicuous situation, or to trouble printers with prosecutions for libels. Thus, it is obvious that a free press is, of all things, the best check and restraint on wicked men and arbitrary magistrates.'

Parks was well acquainted with the art of printing, and his work was both neat and correct. He acquired a handsome property, was a respectable member of the community, extensively known in Virginia and Maryland, and much esteemed by his acquaintances in both provinces.

On the 23d of March, 1750, he embarked in one of the trading ships for England. Soon after the vessel sailed, he was seized with pleurisy, which terminated his life on the first of April of that year. His remains were carried to England, and interred at Gosport.

WILLIAM HUNTER was born in Virginia, and probably served his apprenticeship with Parks, whom he succeeded in 1751. He printed for the house of burgesses, and published a newspaper. He had a relation who was paymaster to the king's troops in America, by whose influence he was appointed deputy postmaster general, with Franklin, for the colonies; which office he held during life. He died in August, 1761.

JOSEPH ROYLE succeeded Hunter in 1761. He was bred to printing in England, and had for several years been a foreman in Hunter's printing house. He printed for the government, and continued the Gazette.

Hunter at his death left an infant son, and he bequeathed Royle 1000*l.* currency, on condition that he would continue the business for the joint interest of himself and this son, whose name was William. Royle, who married a sister of Hunter, died before his nephew became of age.

Young Hunter attained to his majority about the time the revolutionary struggle commenced. He began business, but being a royalist, he soon joined the British standard, and eventually left the country.

ALEXANDER PURDIE was born in Scotland, and there brought up to printing. He continued the business at Williamsburg after the death of Royle, for the benefit of the widow of Royle, young Hunter and himself. Purdie died in 1779, of the dropsy. He possessed talents and integrity.

JOHN DIXON, who married the widow of Royle, was not a printer. After his marriage a partnership was formed between him and Purdie. The firm was PURDIE & DIXON. They remained together until the commencement of the war. Purdie was appointed postmaster, and continued to print at Williamsburg until he died. Dixon removed to Richmond, and died there in May, 1791. He was greatly esteemed.

WILLIAM RIND opened a second printing house in Williamsburg in 1766. He served his apprenticeship with Jonas Green of Annapolis, and it appears was a short time his partner.

As there was but one newspaper published in Virginia in 1765; and but one press in the province, which was judged to have an undue bias from the officers of government, a number of gentlemen who were desirous of having a free and uninfluenced Gazette, gave an invitation to Rind to settle in Williamsburg, with a promise of support; he accordingly opened a printing house in that city, and received satisfactory encouragement.* Rind published a newspaper, and was, soon after his

---

* This fact is corroborated by the following extract of a letter to the author from Thomas Jefferson, late president of the United States, dated July, 1809.

'I do not know that the publication of newspapers was ever prohibited in Virginia. Until the beginning of our revolutionary disputes, we had but one press, and that having the whole business of the government, and no competitor for public favor, nothing disagreeable to the governor could be got into it. We procured Rind to come from Maryland to publish a free paper.'

establishment, appointed by the legislature printer to the government. This office was at that time lucrative.

October 16, 1766, Rind, and Purdie & Dixon, the printers of the two Virginia Gazettes, were presented for publishing libels, at the instance of John Wayles, and the Hon. William Bird, respecting the bailment of Col. Chiswell; but the grand jury found no bills. Chiswell was supposed to have been under such anxiety of mind, on this account, as occasioned his death.*

Rind died August 19, 1773.

CLEMENTINA RIND was born in Maryland. She was the widow of William Rind, and succeeded to his business in 1773, and printed the Gazette, etc. She died within two years after the death of her husband.

JOHN PINKNEY was the successor of Clementina Rind; and, probably, was previously her partner. He continued the Gazette in 1775, and did other printing after the war began, but died at Williamsburg, soon after that event.

JOHN CLARKSON & AUGUSTINE DAVIS were printers and copartners, in Williamsburg, in 1778. They commenced the publication of a newspaper in April of that year. They were printers to the state in 1779, and, probably, before that time.

Clarkson was nephew to Alexander Purdie. Davis was born in Yorktown, and was taught printing by Purdie. He published a newspaper several years in Williamsburg; then removed to Richmond; and was a respectable printer in that place.

* Rind's *Virginia Gazette*, Oct. 17, 1766.

ONLY two newspapers were published in Virginia before 1775. They were both printed at Williamsburg. The first, which was under the influence of the governor, commenced August, 1736. The second in 1766.*

The first public journal printed in the colony was entitled

THE VIRGINIA GAZETTE, which appeared as early as the year 1736, on a half sheet foolscap, and, occasionally, on a whole sheet, printed by William Parks, who continued it until he died, in 1750. Some months after his death the paper was discontinued.

THE VIRGINIA GAZETTE in fact was but a renewal of the first Gazette, which had been a short time suspended, but it commenced with No. 1. It was published weekly, on Monday, on a crown sheet, folio, neatly printed, and had a cut of the Virginia arms in the title. The first number was published in February, 1751. Imprint, 'Williamsburg: Printed by William Hunter, at the Post-Office, by whom persons may be supplied with this paper. Advertisements of a moderate length for *Three shillings* the first week, and *Two* shillings each week after.' In this Gazette were published, in 1757, many well written essays, under the signature of *The Virginia Centinel.*

Hunter died in 1761. The Gazette was enlarged to a demy size, and published by Joseph Royle; after whose death it was carried on by Purdie and Dixon; who continued it until the commencement of the war; and Purdie alone published it several years during the revolutionary contest.

* See notes on p. 552.

THE VIRGINIA GAZETTE was first published in May, 1766, and continued weekly, on Thursday. A cut of the arms of the colony was in the title. It was well printed with new types, on a demy sheet, folio. Imprint, 'Williamsburgh: Printed by William Rind, at the New Printing-Office, on the Main Street. All Persons may be supplied with this Gazette at 12/6. per Year.' At the end of the first year, 'Published by Authority' was omitted in the head of the Gazette.

This paper was published by Rind until his death, which happened on the 19th of August, 1773. Clementina Rind, who was his widow, continued it after he died; and to her succeeded John Pinkney, who also died soon after, and the Gazette was discontinued.

VIRGINIA GAZETTE was first published in April, 1775, and continued weekly, on Saturday, by John Clarkson and Augustine Davis, at Williamsburg, several years.[4]

NOTES TO CHAPTER XI

For a brief history of the craft in Virginia, see D. C. McMurtrie, *History of Printing in the United States*, II, 276–306; E. G. Swem, *A Bibliography of Virginia* (Virginia State Library, 1916–1932), 4 parts; C. C. Samford and J. M. Hemphill, *Bookbinding in Colonial Virginia* (Colonial Williamsburg, 1966). VIRGINIA

1. See *The New-England Historical & Genealogical Register*, XXVI, 30–36 (Jan. 1872), for the article 'Early Printing in Virginia,' communicated by Col. A. H. Hoyt. It contains the correspondence which grew out of Mr. Thomas's application for information on the subject. H

2. August Klapper, *The Printer in Eighteenth-Century Williamsburg* (Colonial Williamsburg, 1958); R. Goodwin, 'The Williamsburg Paper WILLIAMSBURG

Mill of William Parks,' in *Papers of the Bibliographical Society of America*, XXI, 21–44 (1st qtr. 1937); L. C. Wroth, *William Parks, Printer and Journalist of England and Colonial America* (William Parks Club, 1926).

3. It was claimed by the *Williamsburg Gazette* in 1870, that it was the oldest paper published in the United States, having been commenced in 1736. It was rejoined that the *Gazette* had been often suspended, at one time for six years. M

4. A paper was printed at Norfolk in 1775, by John Hunter Holt, whose press was carried off by a British force landed from war ships, in harbor, Sept. 30. See Force's *American Archives*, 4th ser., III, 847, 923, 1031. M

✴ XII ✴

NORTH CAROLINA

PRINTING was introduced into this colony about 1755; before that time, the necessary printing for the public was principally done at Williamsburg, Virginia, and at Charleston, South Carolina. There were only two presses in North Carolina before 1755.

THE first press established in the colony was set up at NEWBERN Newbern, about twenty years before the revolution commenced. Until that time, there was only one press in both the Carolinas.

JAMES DAVIS[1] was the first printer in this colony. He began his establishment in 1754, or 1755. He was, I believe, from Virginia.

In December of the year last mentioned, he published a newspaper. He received some encouragement from government, and was appointed post master by Franklin and Hunter.

Davis printed for the colony, and, in 1773, completed an edition of the Laws of North Carolina. The volume is in folio, and contains five hundred and eighty pages.

His printing appears to have been well executed; but there was not much employment for his press before the declaration of Independence.

He was a respectable man, and held a commission as a mag-

561

istrate, which I believe he received during the administration of Governor Tryon.

THE second press established in this colony, was set up at Wilmington, near the close of the year 1763, or the beginning of 1764, by

ANDREW STEUART, who was from Ireland, as was mentioned when he was taken notice of as a printer in Philadelphia, where he had resided and printed several years. He commenced the publication of a newspaper, but it was soon discontinued. Although he had but few printing materials, his printing shows tokens of a good workman.

On settling at Wilmington he was encouraged with a share of the printing for government, and was patronized by gentlemen of the first respectability in the colony; but he soon lost their confidence, and fell into discredit. It was said that he intercepted and opened some private letters to a gentleman of distinction in the colony, and made their contents known. Be this as it may, he no longer received encouragement, and the work of the government was taken from him, so that he was obliged to discontinue his newspaper for the want of customers.

The end of Steuart was tragical. In 1769, he was drowned in the river near his own residence, where he went to bathe.

ADAM BOYD was born in Great Britain. He was not brought up to printing. In 1769 he purchased the press and types which had been used by Steuart. Boyd was the second person who printed in Wilmington; he published a newspaper. It has been said that he possessed some classical knowledge, which is not improbable; but his printing was, certainly, that of an unskilful workman. In 1776, he exchanged the press for the pulpit.

THE establishment of three newspapers had been attempt-ed in North Carolina before the revolution. One of these, after the first trial, was discontinued for several years, and then revived. Another was published only three years, between 1763 and 1768, and dropped. The third was begun about 1770, and this, as well as the first, was published when the war commenced.[2]

THE NORTH CAROLINA GAZETTE, the first paper published in the colony, was printed at Newbern. No. 1 appeared in December, 1755, printed on a sheet of pot size, folio, but often on half a sheet. It was published weekly, on Thursday. Imprint, 'Newbern: Printed by James Davis, at the Printing-Office in Front-Street; where all persons may be sup-plied with this paper at Sixteen Shillings per Annum: And where Advertisements of a moderate length are inserted for Three Shillings the first Week, and Two Shillings for every week after. And where also Book-Binding is done reasonably.'

This paper was published about six years, after which it was discontinued.

On the 27th of May, 1768, it again appeared, numbered one, and enlarged to a crown sheet, folio; the imprint, after the title, was: 'Printed by James Davis, at the Post-Office in Newbern.' The price of Advertisements, and the paper per annum, the same as in 1755. It was continued after the commencement of the war.

A NEWSPAPER was published in this place about the year 1764. I am not certain respecting the title of it, but if I recollect aright, it was

THE CAPE-FEAR GAZETTE *and Wilmington Advertiser*.[3] A small cut of the king's arms was in the title. This Gazette was printed on a sheet of pot, on pica and long primer types, by Andrew Steuart, who styled himself 'Printer to the King's Most Excellent Majesty.' It was discontinued before or during the year 1767.

THE CAPE-FEAR MERCURY was first published October 13, 1769.[4] It was printed weekly, on Friday, on paper of crown size, with pica and long primer types. A cut of the king's arms was in the title. The imprint was long and singular, viz: 'Boyd's Printing-Office in Wilmington, Cape-Fear, where this Paper may be had every Friday at the Rate of 16 s. a year, one half to be paid at the time of Subscribing, or at 8 s. every six months. Subscriptions for this Paper are taken in by Gentlemen in most of the adjacent Counties, and by A. Boyd, who has for sale sundry Pamphlets and Blanks; Also: Epsom and Glauber Salts by the lb. or larger quantity. N.B. Advertisements of a moderate length will be inserted at 4 s. Entrance, and 1 s. a Week

Continuance: Those of an immoderate Length to pay in proportion.'

This paper was badly printed; and although destitute of
system in the arrangement of its contents, it was, I believe,
continued until 1775.

NOTES TO CHAPTER XII

See G. W. Paschal, *A History of Printing in North Carolina* (Raleigh, NORTH CAROLINA
1946) and D. C. McMurtrie, *History of Printing in the United States*, II,
337–365.

   1. R. N. Elliott, Jr., 'James Davis and the Beginning of the News- NEWBERN
paper in North Carolina,' in *North Carolina Historical Review*, XLII, 1–20
(Jan. 1965).

   2. In B. J. Lossing, *The Pictorial Field Book of the Revolution* (New NEWSPAPERS
York, 1860), II, 360, we read that James Davis brought the first press
into this state from Virginia, in 1749, and printed the first edition of the
acts of the assembly; that the first periodical paper was called the *North
Carolina Magazine, or Universal Intelligencer*, which was printed on a
demy sheet, in quarto pages, and was filled with long extracts from
theological works and British magazines. Mr. Lossing's account of early
printing in this state differs materially from that of Mr. Thomas. M

   3. Mr. Lossing says it was called the *North Carolina Gazette and Weekly Post Boy*; that the first number was printed in September 1764. M

   4. Lossing says Oct. 1767. M

★ XIII ★

SOUTH CAROLINA

P RINTING was introduced into South Carolina as early as 1730. The government is said to have offered a liberal encouragement to any printer who would settle in Charleston;* and that, in consequence of this offer, three printers arrived there in 1730, and 1731, one of whom was appointed printer to the province; another in the year following, published a newspaper.

CHARLESTON T HE first press introduced into the Carolinas was established in this city.

ELEAZAR PHILLIPS was born in Boston, and served his apprenticeship with Thomas Fleet of that town. He was the son of Eleazar Phillips, bookseller and binder, who lived at Charlestown, near Boston.

Phillips opened a printing house in 1730, and executed the printing for the colony. He was but a short time in business,

---

* I am informed that a record of this offer cannot now be found, but the fact can, I believe, be fully authenticated. It was usual for the colonial governments in the new settlements to make such offers. *The Barbadoes Mercury* of October 16th, 1732, and the *Weekly Rehearsal* printed at Boston, of December 25, 1732, contain the following paragraph. 'We hear from South Carolina, that there has been such a sickness, that near twenty on a day have been buried there; that of the three Printers that arrived there, for the sake of the 1000*l.* Carolina Currency offered by the government, there is but one left; and he that received the *premium* is one that is lately dead.'

A similar paragraph appeared in other newspapers, printed on the continent at that time.

when he was seized by the sickness which prevailed in that city
in 1731, and became one of its numerous victims. The following
words are a part of the inscription engraven on his tomb stone—
'He was first printer to his majesty.'

THOMAS WHITMARSH arrived with a press soon after
Phillips, and began the publication of a newspaper, the first
printed in either of the Carolinas. After Phillips died, Whitmarsh was appointed printer to the government, but was very
soon arrested by death. He died in 1733.

LOUIS TIMOTHÉE was the son of a French protestant refugee,
who left France in consequence of the revocation of the edict of
Nantz, and went to Holland. Timothée came from Holland,
where he had acquired the art of printing, to Philadelphia. He
was employed some time in the printing house of Franklin; and
was the first who was appointed librarian of the Philadelphia
library company.* That office he resigned in December 1733,
and removed to Charleston, where he arrived soon after the
death of Whitmarsh, succeeded to his business, and accommodated his name to the English language by changing it to
Lewis Timothy. In February, 1734, he published a newspaper,
which, although not the earliest printed in the colony, was the
first which gained permanency.

Timothy did the work for government, which with his
newspaper formed his principal employment. His course was
short, as he died in December, 1738.

* The Philadelphia library company was established in 1731; there was no
librarian till November 1732 when Timothée was chosen.

ELIZABETH TIMOTHY,[1] the widow of Lewis Timothy, with the aid of her son, conducted the press for a year or two, and then the son, being of age, carried on the concern in his own name. She died in April 1757.

PETER TIMOTHY, the son of Lewis, went into business on his own account in 1740; and, in January 1741, he was arrested for publishing a letter written by Hugh Bryan, in which it was asserted, that 'the clergy of South Carolina broke their canons daily.' The celebrated George Whitefield and Hugh Bryan were arrested at the same time, by a warrant from Chief Justice Whitaker: Timothy for publishing, Bryan for writing, and Whitefield for correcting Bryan's letter for the press. They were all admitted to bail. Whitefield was then bound to England;* he confessed the charge, and entered into a recognizance to appear by his attorney, at the next general session.

Timothy succeeded his father as printer to the colony, and was, after the revolution, printer to the state. He remained in Charleston during the time that city was besieged; and in 1780, when it was surrendered, he was taken prisoner by the British.

---

* This celebrated itinerant preacher, when he visited America, like a comet drew the attention of all classes of people. The blaze of his ministration was extended through the continent, and he became the common topic of conversation from Georgia to New Hampshire. All the newspapers were filled with paragraphs of information respecting him, or with pieces of animated disputation pro or con; and the press groaned with pamphlets written in favor of, or against, his person and ministry. In short, his early visits to America excited a great and general agitation throughout the country, which did not wholly subside when he returned to Europe. Each succeeding visit occasioned a renewal of zeal and ardor in his advocates and opponents; and, it has been said, that from his example American preachers became more animated in their manner. Whitefield died very suddenly in Newburyport, Mass., Sept. 30, 1770, of an asthmatic fit. His remains were deposited under the pulpit of the Presbyterian church in that town. He was on his seventh visit to that town.

In August, 1780, he was sent as a prisoner to St. Augustine. In 1781, he was exchanged and delivered at Philadelphia, where he remained until the autumn of the next year, and then embarked with two daughters and a grandchild for St. Domingo. His ultimate object was to reach Antigua, where his widowed daughter, Mrs. Marchant, had some property; but, soon after he left the capes of Delaware, the vessel in which he was a passenger foundered in a violent gale of wind, and every soul on board perished.

Timothy was a decided and active friend of his country. He was a very intelligent and good printer and editor, and was for several years clerk of the general assembly. As a citizen he was much respected.

ANNE TIMOTHY, the widow of the before mentioned Peter Timothy, after the war ceased, revived the *Gazette*, which had been established by the elder Timothy, but was discontinued while the British troops were in possession of Charleston. She was appointed printer to the state, and held the appointment until September, 1792, when she died. Her printing house was at the corner of Broad and King streets.

ROBERT WELLS[2] was born in Scotland, and there educated as a bookseller. He opened a bookstore and printing house at Charleston in 1758, and published a newspaper. His *Gazette* was the second established in the colony. Wells had a partner in the printing establishment, by the name of George Bruce, who managed the concerns of the printing house. His name appeared after Wells's in the imprint of their works. Wells was the owner of the press and types, and the business was under his sole control. Bruce remained with Wells several years, and when they separated Wells conducted his printing house by the aid of journeymen.

Wells kept a large book and stationery store, well supplied. For many years he was the principal bookseller for both the Carolinas. His business was extensive, and he acquired property. He was marshal of the court of admiralty, and one of the principal auctioneers in the city. This last business was very lucrative, especially the sale of cargoes of slaves. He owned a number of negroes; two or three of whom were taught to work at press. It was a common custom in the Carolinas, and in the West Indies, to have blacks for pressmen. Wells's slaves were frequently intoxicated, and unfit for work when they were wanted at press; at such times, he adopted a singular method to render them sober. The water in the city is unfit to drink; and, as on many it operates medicinally, he would take his drunken negroes to the pump, and pour water down their throats until they began to sicken; then shut them up for an hour or two; and, the operation being there completed, they were taken out and put to press.

His printing house and bookstore were on the bay, near Tradd street. He was a staunch royalist, but a good editor, active in business, and just and punctual in his dealings. About the time when the revolutionary war commenced, he resigned his establishment to his son, went to Europe, and never returned.

GEORGE BRUCE was born in Scotland, learned printing there, whence he came to Robert Wells in Charleston. He managed, several years, the concerns of Wells's printing house, and his name, as has been mentioned, appeared after Wells's in their imprints. When they parted, he opened a printing house on his own account. He lived in Church street, where he commenced a trade in English goods, and paid but little attention to typographical concerns. His printing house was furnished with new types; but he had only those founts which were most in use. He remained in the city, in 1775, after the war began.

CHARLES CROUCH was born in Charleston; he was brother-in-law to Peter Timothy, with whom he served an apprenticeship. In 1765, he opened the fourth printing house in the colony. He was encouraged to set up a press, and to print a newspaper in opposition to the stamp act, at the time the act was to have taken effect. He was a sound whig.

Crouch printed but little excepting his paper, which was lucrative. He was in business when the war commenced; soon after which, he took passage in a vessel bound to New York, and was drowned. He lived in Eliott street, and his printing house was in Gadsden's alley.

THOMAS POWELL was an Englishman, and served his apprenticeship in London. He came to Charleston in 1769, and was employed by Timothy as foreman in his printing house. Powell was a correct printer, his education had been good, and in his manners he was a gentleman. In 1772, Timothy admitted Powell as a partner. The firm was, THOMAS POWELL & COMPANY. Their printing house was near the Exchange. Timothy, as a silent partner, edited the *Gazette*, and directed the general concerns of the firm.

On the 31st of August, 1773, in consequence of a motion

made by the chief justice in the council, or upper house of assembly, it was ordered, that Powell should immediately attend that house. Powell accordingly attended, and 'was examined if he was the printer and publisher of the *South Carolina Gazette*,' then shown to him. He answered that he was. He was then asked, 'by what authority he presumed to print as an article of news in his paper, a matter purporting to be a part of the proceedings of this house, on the 26th of August instant?' To which he replied, 'That the copy of the matter there printed was delivered to him by the Hon. William Henry Drayton, one of the members of that house, who desired him to print the same.' The house '*Resolved*,' That as he acknowledged himself to be the printer of a part of their proceedings, without their order or leave, he was 'thereby guilty of a high breach of the privileges, and a contempt of the house.'

Powell was told to ask pardon; he declined. The house then ordered him to be taken into the custody of the sergeant at arms, and brought to the bar. This was done; and, when at the bar, he was again informed of the charge against him; and that the house desired to hear what he could say in exculpation of said charge. Powell declared that 'he did not know that he had committed any offence.' It was again demanded of him, if he would ask pardon; he answered, he would not.

The Hon. Mr. Drayton, in his place, acknowledged that he was the person who sent the copy of that part of the journals printed by Powell, to the press; but, without intention to offend the house, etc. The house then

'*Resolved*, That Thomas Powell, who hath this day been adjudged, by this house, to have been guilty of a high breach of privilege, and a contempt of this house, be for his said offence committed to the common gaol of Charleston; and that his honor, the president of this house, do issue his warrant accordingly.' Before putting the question, Mr. Drayton claimed leave to enter his protest and dissent; which he did accordingly. The president, the Hon. Egerton Leigh, agreeably to the resolution of the house, issued his warrant. Powell was imprisoned, and remained in confinement until the morning of the second of September following.

On the second of September, the Hon. Rawlins Lowndes, speaker of the lower house, or 'commons house of assembly,' and George Gabriel Powell, one of its members, justices of the peace, etc., had Powell brought before them by a writ of *habeas corpus*, and discharged him.

On the same day, Powell published a *Gazette* extraordinary, in which Drayton's dissent and protest were inserted. The council resolved, that the protest, as published that day, was materially different from that on their journals, and was therefore 'false, scandalous and malicious, tending to reflect upon the honor and justice of the house;' and, 'that William Henry Drayton was instrumental to the publication.' Before putting the question, Mr. Drayton claimed leave to enter his dissent and protest; which he accordingly did. In this protest Mr. Drayton asserted, that the protest as published, excepting some misspelling in copying by the clerk, and the misprinting the word *fulfilled* for *published*, was expressly the same as the original.

The next day the council, styling themselves, 'the upper house of assembly,' resolved, 'That Mr. Drayton had been guilty of a breach of privilege and contempt of that house, in being instrumental to the publication of the protest,' etc. Before putting the question, Mr. Drayton entered his dissent and protest. The resolve was passed, and Mr. Drayton directed to withdraw. He withdrew accordingly. The council then passed the following resolve.

'That when T. Powell was before this house, his whole deportment and behavior manifested the most insolent disrespect; and, so far was he from discovering any contrition for his offence, that he flatly declared that he did not know that he had committed any, and therefore thought it hard to ask pardon; and, being informed by the president, that the house was of a different opinion, he still obstinately persisted that he could not ask pardon.'

In the afternoon of the same day, Mr. Drayton, in consideration that the house had not proceeded with him 'to the last extremity,' informed that body, 'that he neither sent the protest to the press, nor ordered any person to carry it, or even desired the printer, or any person to publish it; that Mr. Edward Rutledge sent the copy to the printer.' On this information, the house resolved, that Mr. Drayton 'had purged himself of the contempt and breach of privilege with which he stood charged.'

On the fourth of September, the sheriff of Charleston district, having attended the council agreeably to order, was directed by the president to make out a copy of the writ of *habeas corpus*, issued by the Justices Lowndes and G. G. Powell, Esquires, by virtue of which he had two days before removed T. Powell from prison and carried him before said justices, with his return thereon. A committee was appointed to 'take under their consideration the nature of the discharge of T. Powell, printer, to report such resolutions as may be necessary for the house to enter into; and to prepare an humble address on the subject to his majesty, and another to his honor the lieutenant governor.'

The chief justice, and two other members were of this committee, who reported the following resolutions, which were
agreed to by the house.

'*Resolved*, That the power of commitment is so necessarily
incident to each house of assembly, that without it neither their
authority nor dignity can, in any degree whatsoever, be maintained or supported.

'*Resolved*, That Rawlins Lowndes, Esquire, speaker of the
commons house of assembly, and George Gabriel Powell, Esq.,
member of said house, being two justices of the peace, *unus
quorum*, lately assistant judges and justices of his majesty's court
of common pleas, have, by virtue of *habeas corpus* by them
issued, caused the body of T. Powell to be brought before them,
on the second of this instant September, and the said justices,
disregarding the commitment of this house, did presumptu-
ously discharge said T. Powell out of the custody of the sheriff
under the commitment of this house.

'*Resolved*, That the said justices have been guilty of the most
atrocious contempt of this house, by their public avowal and
declaration, made by them in pronouncing judgment, that this
house is no upper house of assembly; on which principle alone
they did discharge the said T. Powell; they have, as far as in
them lay, absolutely and actually abolished one of the branches
of the legislature; and, in so doing, have subverted the constitution of this government, and have expressly sounded the most
dangerous alarm to the good subjects of this province.

'*Resolved*, That a copy of these resolutions be sent to the
commons house of assembly, together with a message, com-
plaining of such conduct and breach of our privilege, by their
members; and, setting forth, that, as this house has always been

careful to support its own just rights and privileges, so it has always been cautious not to infringe the rights and privileges of the commons house; and, that this house, relying on the justice of the commons house, does expect they will direct Rawlins Lowndes and George Gabriel Powell, Esqrs., two of their members, to waive their privilege, in order that this house may proceed to the cognizance of their said breach of privilege and contempt.'

The committee reported, also, according to order, a message to the commons house of assembly; an address to the king, and another to the lieutenant governor;* with all which the council agreed, and presented and forwarded them according to their respective destinations.

The commons house of assembly did not comply with the requisition of the upper house; on the contrary, they justified the conduct of their speaker and Judge Powell, and directed the agent of the province in London, 'to make the most humble representations to his majesty of the conduct of his council [upper house] and to implore their removal; or, such marks of his royal displeasure to them, as may prevent, for the future, such an encroachment on the liberties of his people.' The commons house, at the same time, addressed the lieutenant governor, informing him of the conduct of the council, and that they had directed the agent of the province to represent it to the king, etc., and concluded with earnestly requesting his honor,

* The upper house of assembly, in their address to the lieutenant governor, observe, that Powell was discharged by the justices, 'by virtue of a power given by a provincial act, passed December 12, 1712, to two justices, one being of the quorum, to put in execution the *habeas corpus* act, to such intents and purposes, as the said act can be put in execution in the kingdom of England; upon the sole and avowed principle that we are not an upper house of legislature.'

that, as a considerable time must elapse, before their complaint to the king could be heard, etc., he would 'be pleased to suspend such members of the council as ordered the said commitment, until his majesty's royal pleasure should be known; and to appoint in their stead men who really have at heart the service of his majesty, and the interest of the province.' The governor, as was expected, declined complying with the request of the commons, and in this situation the affair rested, until the pleasure of his majesty should be known.

The business remained before the king and council, I presume in an unsettled state, at the commencement of the war, which event, probably, stayed all proceedings upon it, and it was never more agitated. As to what became of Powell, or respecting the part he took in the war, or whether he returned to England, I have not been able to obtain any information. The *Gazette* was discontinued some time after the war commenced, but was revived by Timothy.

MARY CROUCH was born in Providence, Rhode Island. She was the wife of Charles Crouch, and continued the business of printing in Charleston some time after his death. In 1780, she removed with her press and types to Salem, Massachusetts.

JOHN WELLS, the eldest son of Robert Wells, was born in Charleston, and served an apprenticeship at Donaldson's printing house in Edinburgh. He succeeded his father as a printer and bookseller at Charleston, in 1775. Although the father was a zealous royalist, the son took a decided part in favor of the country. He printed and fought in its defence, until the city fell into the hands of the British in 1780.

Wells belonged to a military company in Charleston which marched to assist in the siege of Savannah, by the allied American and French armies, in 1779, and during this unsuccessful campaign, he acquired the reputation of a brave and vigilant soldier. When Charleston fell into the possession of the British, he, with many others, to save his property, signed an address to the British commander, and he printed a royal *Gazette*, which he continued until December 1782. For these offences he was proscribed by the state government, at the close of the war. Apprehending that he could not safely remain in Charleston when the British surrendered the place to the American government, he left the city, and went with his press to Nassau, New Providence, published the *Bahama Gazette*, and never more returned to the United States. [See pp. 609–610.]

Except in Charleston, there was no printer in South Carolina before the revolution.

BOOKSELLERS IN
CHARLESTON

1758. ROBERT WELLS, 'at the Great Stationery and Book-Store, on the Bay.' He was from Scotland, dealt largely in imported books, and printed a newspaper.

1764. —— WOODS, binder and bookseller from Scotland.

1771. JAMES TAYLOR, binder, and an inconsiderable dealer in books; he also was from Scotland.

NEWSPAPERS IN
CHARLESTON

THE SOUTH-CAROLINA GAZETTE, the first newspaper published in the Carolinas, made its appearance in this city January 8, 1731–2, printed by Thomas Whitmarsh.[3] It was published on Saturdays, through that year, and, as circumstances required, on a sheet or half sheet of paper, pot size, but soon after was discontinued, on account of the sickness and death of its publisher.

Imprint: 'Charles-Town: Printed by T. Whitmarsh, at the Sign of the Table Clock on the Bay. Where Advertisements are taken in, and all Persons may be supplied with this Paper at *Three* Pounds* a Year.'

THE SOUTH CAROLINA GAZETTE. After the Gazette published by Whitmarsh had been discontinued some months, another paper with the same title was, in February 1734, begun by Lewis Timothy. This gained a permanency. It was published weekly, on Saturdays, printed on a half sheet of paper of pot size, but sometimes on a whole sheet, and often on a type as large as english, and at other times on long primer. Price 15s. currency, per quarter.

Timothy died about the year 1738, and the paper was continued by his widow for a short time, with the aid of her son. The son, in 1740, published it on his own account. His imprint was, 'Charles-Town: Printed by Peter Timothy, in King-street, where Advertisements are taken in. Price 15s. a Quarter.' Some years after, it was printed 'in Broad-Street.'

The size of this Gazette was enlarged from time to time, until the year 1760, when it was printed on a sheet of the size of medium, four columns in a page; and a cut of the king's arms was added to the title. The day of publication was changed to

* Equal to two dollars.

Monday; but it seldom made its appearance on that day. No mail was then established between the southern and northern colonies, and the Gazette depended on the arrival of vessels from distant ports for supplies of intelligence. The publisher often waited several days for arrivals; but the Gazette dated Monday was always issued within the week.

The publication was interrupted a few weeks in 1765, at the time the British stamp act was to take place. The Gazette had a large number of advertising customers; and it was ably conducted. It supported the cause of the country, and energetically opposed the measures of the British administration.

In 1772, this Gazette was printed by Thomas Powell, who continued it two or three years, at Timothy's printing house. Powell, during this time, accounted to Timothy, the proprietor, for a certain proportion of the proceeds.

About May, 1775, the Gazette was discontinued; but it was revived by Timothy in April, 1777, when the title was altered to *The Gazette of the State of South-Carolina.* Timothy conducted this paper until the city was about to be surrendered to the British in 1780, when it was again suspended, and the publisher became a prisoner of war.

After the restoration of the city, Timothy being dead, his widow, Anne Timothy, revived the Gazette, and from December, 1782, published it twice a week, on Monday and Thursday, until her death, which took place in 1792.

On the death of Anne Timothy, the Gazette was published by her son, Benjamin Franklin Timothy, who soon took a partner, and the Gazette appeared under the title of *The South-Carolina State Gazette, and Timothy and Mason's Daily Advertiser.* 'Printed at the corner of Bay and Broad Streets.' When the partnership

of Timothy and Mason was dissolved, the Gazette was printed
by B. F. Timothy until 1800. In that year the publication of it
finally ceased. B. F. Timothy died in 1804.*

THE SOUTH-CAROLINA AND AMERICAN GENERAL GA-
ZETTE was first published in 1758, by Robert Wells. It was
printed on a medium sheet, four columns in a page; the day
assigned for the publication was Friday, but although so dated,
it did not regularly appear, but was at times delayed several
days; it was published, however, without intermission once in a
week. It had a cut of the king's arms in the title; and, some time
after its first publication, the following motto from Horace was
adopted: 'Nullius addictus jurare in verba magistri.' Imprint,
'Charlestown: Printed by R. Wells and G. Bruce, for Robert
Wells, at the Great Stationery and Book-Store on the Bay.'

After this Gazette had been printed a few years by Wells and
Bruce, the connection between them was dissolved, and Wells
printed and published the paper in his own name, a short intermission excepted when the stamp act of 1765 was to have taken
effect, until 1775. Wells being a royalist he went to England
soon after the war commenced, and this Gazette was continued
by his son John Wells until 1780, when the city fell into the
possession of the British; on which event the paper was discontinued, and John printed a *Royal Gazette*. Very few original
essays appeared in *The South Carolina and American General
Gazette*; but while it was published by the senior Wells, the

* Peter Timothy Marchant, great grandson of Lewis Timothy, was in 1807
and 1808, one of the members of the house of Marchant, Willington & Co.,
editors of *The Charleston Courier*.

intelligence it contained was judiciously selected, and methodically arranged, and it had a large share of advertisements; for which reason it was often accompanied by an additional half sheet.

After the younger Wells became the editor, it supported the cause of the country until about the period when it was discontinued.

THE SOUTH CAROLINA GAZETTE, *and Country Journal* was established in opposition to the British American stamp act, November, 1765, and was published without stamps about the time the act was to have taken effect. The title bore a cut of the king's arms. Tuesday was the day of publication, and it was printed on a sheet of demy, folio, from a new bourgeois type. It was often accompanied by a half sheet supplement. Imprint, 'Charles-Town: Printed by Charles Crouch at his Office in Eliott-Street, Corner of Gadsden's Alley.'

The general opposition of the colonies to the stamp act induced the public to patronize this Gazette. It immediately gained a large list of respectable subscribers, and a full proportion of advertising customers.

Of the three newspapers printed at that time in Charlestown, this only appeared regularly, on the day it was dated. These papers were all entitled Gazettes, in order to secure certain advertisements, directed by law to be 'inserted in the South Carolina Gazette.'

Crouch published his Gazette till he died in 1775. His widow continued it a short time, but it finally ceased.

NOTES TO CHAPTER XIII

See D. C. McMurtrie, *History of Printing in the United States*, II, 307–336;   SOUTH CAROLINA
R. J. Turnbull, *Bibliography of South Carolina, 1563–1950* (Bibliographical
Society of the University of Virginia, 1956–1960), 6 vols.

1. See E. M. Oldham, *op. cit.*, note 34 to Chapter II.   CHARLESTON
2. *Dictionary of American Biography*, XIX, 644–645.

3. There is an indication that Eleazer Phillips, Jr., printed the first   NEWSPAPERS
paper in Charleston. We learn from W. L. King's *Newspaper Press of
Charleston* (Charleston, 1872), that Phillips died in July 1732 and that
his father advertised nearly two years after for settlement of debts due
the former for six months subscriptions to the *South Carolina Weekly
Journal*, a paper which is not named in any of the early records of the
press and of which no other trace can be found. Phillips was the first
printer in the colony. M.   See also Henig Cohen, *The South Carolina
Gazette, 1732–1775* (Univeristy of South Carolina Press, 1953).

✶ XIV ✶

GEORGIA

THE settlement of this province, named after George II, king of Great Britain, did not begin until the year 1732. The public printing, till 1762, was done in Charleston, South Carolina. There was only one press established in Georgia before the revolution.

SAVANNAH PRINTING was introduced into this colony at this place, and a printing house was opened early in 1762, by JAMES JOHNSTON,[1] who was born in Scotland, and there served a regular apprenticeship. After his establishment in Savannah, he printed for the government.

The government of the colony gave Johnston a handsome pecuniary consideration for settling in that place. He printed an edition of the laws; and, in 1763, began the publication of a newspaper. This newspaper, and printing for the colony, was the chief employment of his press. He did some business as a bookseller; was a very honest, reputable man, acquainted with the art he professed to practice; and in his general conduct was a good and useful member of society. He died in October, 1808, aged seventy years, leaving a widow and six children.

THE GEORGIA GAZETTE was first published on the 17th of April, 1763, printed on a new long primer type, on a foolscap sheet, folio, two columns in a page, and continued weekly, on Wednesday. Imprint, 'Savannah: Printed by *James Johnston*, at the Printing-Office in Broughton-Street, where Advertisements, Letters of Intelligence, and Subscriptions for this Paper, are taken in.—Hand-Bills, Advertisements, &c., printed on the shortest Notice.' After a few years, it was enlarged and printed on a sheet of crown size.

The publication of this Gazette was for some time suspended, like that of several others on the continent, when the British American stamp act was to take place in 1765; but it was, at the end of seven months, revived. It reappeared in May, 1766; and, in September of that year, a cut of the king's arms was introduced into the title. It was again suspended for some time during the war. The Gazette was published twenty-seven years by Johnston, and continued by his successors. It was the first and only newspaper published in the colony, before the revolution.

NOTES TO CHAPTER XIV

See L. T. Griffith, *Georgia Journalism, 1763–1950* (University of Georgia Press, 1951); D. C. McMurtrie, *History of Printing in the United States*, II, 366–399.   GEORGIA

1. A. A. Lawrence, *James Johnston, Georgia's First Printer* (Savannah, 1956).   SAVANNAH

NEW STATES

AS states founded, and admitted into the Union, since the Revolution, and Territories of the United States, were not settled, or were not located as distinct governments, before 1775, I shall only take notice of the period when the art was introduced into them.[1]

VERMONT   THIS district became a state after the revolution; no press had previously been established in it.[2]

JUDAH PADDOCK SPOONER and TIMOTHY GREEN, who have been mentioned as printers at Norwich, in Connecticut, removed from that place to Hanover in New Hampshire, then claimed, with other towns on the east side of Connecticut river, by the people inhabiting Vermont, where, for a short time, they published a newspaper. They then carried their press to Westminster, and were the first who introduced printing into Vermont. In Westminster they published *The Vermont Gazette; or, Green Mountain Post Boy*. This paper made its first appearance in February, 1781.

Spooner had the whole management of their printing house, as Green still prosecuted the printing business in New London. The firm continued only a short time. Green relinquished his interest in it; and the press and types which were owned by him were sold, after the lapse of four or five years. George Hough was the purchaser. He removed them to Windsor in 1783, and there formed a partnership with Alden Spooner. Alden was the brother of Judah.

In February, 1781, the first newspaper printed in Vermont was published at Westminster; it was entitled, *The Vermont Gazette or Green Mountain Post-Boy.* Motto: 'Pliant as Reeds, where streams of Freedom glide; Firm as the Hills, to stem Oppression's Tide.'

It was printed on a sheet of pot size, and published weekly, on Monday, by Judah Paddock Spooner and Timothy Green. Green resided in New London, and Spooner conducted the Gazette, which was continued only two or three years.

In 1810 there were not less than fourteen newspapers in this state, which forty years before was' an uncultivated wilderness.

After the establishment of peace, the settlement of the uncultivated country progressed with a rapidity unparalleled, perhaps, in history. The press seems to have followed the axe of the husbandman; forests were cleared, settlements made, new states were formed, and gazettes were published.

A GAZETTE was first published in this state in September, 1786, by John Bradford,[3] in Lexington. Another newspaper was soon after printed at Frankfort. Others speedily followed in various towns.

IN 1793, G. Roulstone, from Massachusetts, settled at Knoxville; and, in that year, first published *The Knoxville Gazette.*

OHIO

588

PRINTING was introduced into this state at Cincinnati in 1795, by S. Freeman & Son;[5] and they published a newspaper. A second newspaper was published at that place in 1799. Then a press was established at Marietta, from which was issued *The Ohio Gazette*; and, there are now [1810], other newspapers published in the state; particularly two or three at Chillicothe.*

MISSISSIPPI TERRITORY

A PRESS was established at Natchez in 1815, and a newspaper published.[6]

MICHIGAN TERRITORY

PRINTING is said to have been introduced into Detroit in 1815.[7]

LOUISIANA

SEVERAL printing houses were opened at New Orleans, as soon as that country came under the government of the United States.[8]

Several newspapers were published in the city of New Orleans, immediately after the country was purchased by the government of the United States.

There is now [1810], a press at St. Louis, in Upper Louisiana, at the confluence of the Missouri and Mississippi rivers, at which a newspaper is printed.[9]

Most of these new states and settlements, at the time of the war were but little known. The white inhabitants were but few, and they were scattered in solitary settlements, or in a few

---

* *The Ohio Patriot*, a newspaper published in 1811, contains the following remark, 'The progress of population in the state of Ohio is truly astonishing. Large districts of country, extending hundreds of miles, over which one of the editors wandered thirteen years ago, amid the gloom of the groves, without viewing "the human face divine," except in the persons of his military companions, or the solitary Indian hunter, are now covered with populous towns, in several of which newspapers are published.'

straggling towns and villages through a vast tract of country, where the art of printing had not extended.

NOTES TO CHAPTER XV

1. MAINE. The first paper printed in this state is said to have been established at Falmouth in 1785 for the purpose of advocating a separation from Massachusetts. It was about the size of a sheet of foolscap, and was made up principally of extracts from other papers, giving dates a fortnight or three weeks old from Boston and New York as the latest intelligence. The printer, whose name is not mentioned, was living in 1842.

MICHIGAN. It is stated in the Catholic Almanac of 1871 that Gabriel Richard, a French Catholic priest, was the first person that undertook printing west of the Alleghanies. He printed a paper called the *Essai du Michigan* in 1809, which seems to have given offense to the British authorities, by whom he was imprisoned. There were undoubtedly earlier printers west of the Alleghanies.

ILLINOIS. The *Illinois Herald*, the first paper in that state, was begun at or before 1809, by Matthew Duncan, at Kaskaskia. It passed soon after under the name of *Illinois Intelligencer*, and was removed to Vandalia.

MISSISSIPPI. A paper is said to have been established at Natchez in 1808, but nothing authentic is found concerning it.

MISSOURI. A paper is reported to have been printed at St. Louis, called the *Gazette* in 1806.

INDIANA. The *Western Sun*, the first paper in this territory, was begun at Vincennes in 1808.

WISCONSIN. The *Green Bay Republican* was printed by W. Shoals in 1831 or 1832.

ARKANSAS. The first paper in this state is supposed to have been issued in 1834, at Little Rock.

IOWA had a paper at Burlington in 1836.

TEXAS. The *Galveston Star* was commenced in 1834.

CALIFORNIA. It was not till 1848 that a paper was begun on a small sheet at San Francisco, called *Alta California*.

OREGON. A paper called *The Freeman* was begun at Columbia in 1847.

MINNESOTA. S. Randall began to publish *The Register* at St. Paul in 1849. M

VERMONT 2. The Vermonters had their printing done at Hartford, and before and during the revolution, were dependent upon the columns of the *Connecticut Courant* to carry on their warfare with the citizens and authorities of New York, respecting their title to the present territory of Vermont. M See also M. A. McCorison, *Vermont Imprints, 1778–1820* (American Antiquarian Society, 1963, 1968).

KENTUCKY 3. *Dictionary of American Biography*, II, 557–558; J. W. Coleman, *John Bradford, Esq.* (Lexington, Ky., 1950); W. R. Jillson, *The First Printing in Kentucky* (Louisville, 1936); D. C. McMurtrie, *Check List of Kentucky Imprints, 1787–1810* (American Imprints Inventory, no. 5).

TENNESSEE 4. D. C. McMurtrie, *Early Printing in Tennessee* (Chicago, 1933); *A Check List of Tennessee Imprints, 1793–1840* (American Imprints Inventory, no. 32); J. H. Sears, *Tennessee Printers, 1791–1945* (Kingsport, Tenn., 1945); S. C. Williams, 'George Roulstone, Father of the Tennessee Press,' in East Tennessee Historical Society *Publication* no. 17, pp. 51–60 (1945).

OHIO 5. *A Check List of Ohio Imprints, 1796–1820* (American Imprints Inventory, no. 17); D. E. Agner, *William Maxwell, Ohio's First Printer* (Continental, Ohio, 1960); P. G. Thomson, *A Bibliography of Ohio* (Cincinnati, 1880).

MISSISSIPPI TERRITORY 6. D. C. McMurtrie, *A Bibliography of Mississippi Imprints, 1798–1830* (Brook Farm, 1945).

MICHIGAN TERRITORY 7. D. C. McMurtrie, *Early Printing in Michigan* (Chicago, 1931); A. H. Greenly, *A Bibliography of Father Richard's Press in Detroit* (William L. Clements Library, 1955) and *A Selective Bibliography of Important Books, Pamphlets, and Broadsides Relating to Michigan History* (Lunenburg, Vt., 1958).

LOUISIANA 8. D. C. McMurtrie, *Early Printing in New Orleans, 1764–1810* (New Orleans, 1929).
9. David Kaser, *Joseph Charless, Printer in the Western Country* (University of Pennsylvania Press, 1963).

★ XVI ★

BRITISH COLONIES

PRINTING was introduced into Nova Scotia in 1751; but, at that time, there was but little encouragement for the press. The first press was established at Halifax, and there was not a second in the province until 1766.

BARTHOLOMEW GREEN, JUNIOR, has already been mentioned. He was the grandson of Samuel Green, of Cambridge, and was of the firm of Green, Bushell & Allen, of Boston. He removed to Halifax with a press and types in August, 1751. He died in about six weeks after his arrival, aged fifty-two years.

JOHN BUSHELL, who had been the partner of Green in Boston, immediately succeeded him in Halifax. He printed for government, and in the first week of January, 1752, published the first newspaper printed in Nova Scotia. The work for government was inconsiderable, but was the chief support of Bushell. He was a good workman, but had not the art of acquiring property; nor did he make the most economical use of the little which fell into his hands.

Bushell died in February, 1761. He left one son and a daughter. The son was sent to New England, and served an apprenticeship with Daniel Fowle, printer in Portsmouth, New Hampshire. When of age, he worked as a journeyman in Philadelphia, and at the same time kept a tavern at the Cross Keys in Front street. He died February 4, 1797.

The daughter, whose name was Elizabeth, had been accustomed to assist her father in the printing house. She could work both at case and press; and was, in the language of printers, a swift and correct compositor.* Bushell left little, if any, property to his family. His daughter was handsome, but unfortunate.

ANTHONY HENRY succeeded Bushell as a printer at Halifax. He was a German, and had lived some time with a printer, but had left his master, and became a fifer in one of the British regiments. With this regiment he came to America. In 1758, the time for which Henry had enlisted being ended, he was discharged from the regiment, which was then stationed in Perth Amboy, New Jersey. He then went to Woodbridge, and was employed some months in the printing house of James Parker; after which he went to Nova Scotia. There was then no printer

* There have been many instances of women performing the work of the printing house. The nieces of Dr. Franklin, in Newport, [See Newport] were expert compositors; and so were, it is said, the daughters of Mr. D. H. of Philadelphia. Mr. William McCulloch, of Philadelphia, informs me that he saw in a printing house near Philadelphia, two women at the press, who could perform their week's work with as much fidelity as most of the journeymen. As compositors, women and girls have not unfrequently been employed, not only in America, but in Europe. Some printers from Scotland have assured us that the daughter of the celebrated typographer of Glasgow, Foulis, was an adept at the business. Foulis & Son flourished as printers about 1765.

These remarks apply to the year 1815.

in the province, and his pretensions to skill in this art greatly facilitated his introduction to business in Halifax. He began with the press and types which had been used by Bushell. He published the Gazette; and government, through necessity, gave him some work, which was badly executed.

In 1766, a printer with a new and good apparatus, came from London, and opened another printing house in Halifax. He published a newspaper, and was employed to print for government.

Henry, who had been indolent, and inattentive to his affairs, did not despond at the establishment of a formidable rival; but, much to his credit, exerted himself and did better than he had done before. After a few years trial, his rival, not finding his business so profitable, nor the place so agreeable as he expected, returned to England, and Henry was again the only printer in the province. He procured new types and a workman better skilled than himself. Henry's printing from this period was executed in a more workmanlike manner than formerly; he having employed a good workman in his printing house as a journeyman.

He remained without another rival until the British army evacuated Boston in March, 1776, when the printers in that town, who adhered to the royal cause, were obliged to leave that place; and they, with other refugees, went to Halifax. Henry continued printing until his death. He possessed a fund of good nature, and was of a very cheerful disposition. Although not skillful as a printer, he was otherwise ingenious. In 1787, Henry having procured German types from the foundery of Justus Fox, in Germantown, Pa., published a newspaper in the German language, of the same title with that which he continued to publish in English. This German paper was conducted by the journeyman* before mentioned.

When Henry arrived in Halifax, he became acquainted with a woman of African extraction, who was a pastry cook, and possessed a small property, the fruit of her industry. To acquire this property, Henry consented to a connection with this sable female. The property which he acquired by this negotiation enabled him to purchase the few printing materials which had belonged to Bushell, and to build a house in which he afterward lived. His companion died, in two or three years, without issue by him. Desdemona, in another case of particolored nuptials, wished 'That Heaven had made her such a man.' Henry's consort had probably a like desire, for it is said the proffer of marriage came from her.

In 1773, Henry married a countrywoman of his, who had been his housekeeper for ten years.†

He died December, 1800, aged sixty-six.

* This journeyman, named Henry Steiner, arrived at Halifax, in 1782, with the last detachment of Hessian troops that came as auxiliaries to the British in our revolutionary war. He was a corporal. He had been regularly bred to printing. As hostilities ceased soon after his arrival, he obtained a furlough, to work with Henry. When the detachment to which Steiner belonged was about to return to Europe, his officers, according to his account, contracted to sell him to Henry for the term of eighteen months, for thirty-six guineas. Steiner, supposing this sale to be legal, continued with Henry the time stipulated; after which, receiving good wages, he remained with him till 1789. Steiner then went to Philadelphia. When Steiner left Henry, his German paper was discontinued.

† On the occasion, the following paragraph appeared, February, 1774, in the *Boston Evening Post*. 'Married at Halifax, Nova Scotia, Mr. Anthony Henry, aged about 30, to Mrs. Barbary Springhoff, aged about 96; it is said she has two husbands now living, seven children, ten grand children, and fifty great grand children.'

This statement is not correct. Henry was then forty years old, and Barbary not more than fifty-five. She had several children and grand-children; but not near the number mentioned.

ROBERT FLETCHER arrived at Halifax from London, in 1766, with new printing materials, and a valuable collection of books and stationery. He opened a printing house and bookstore near the parade; published a newspaper, and printed for government. Until this time there had been no bookstore in the province. Fletcher executed his printing with neatness, and raised the reputation of the art in Nova Scotia. He remained at Halifax until 1770, then sent his printing materials to Boston for sale, and returned himself to England.

JOHN HOWE began printing in Halifax, in 1776.[1]

After the peace, in 1784, printing found its way into the province of New Brunswick.

THE HALIFAX GAZETTE first appeared in January, 1752, and was printed weekly, on half a sheet of foolscap paper, by John Bushell, from Boston. The circulation of the Gazette was in a great measure confined to the town, which was then a mere garrison. After a trial of some months the publication of it was for a long time suspended; at length it was revived, but not issued at regular periods till about the autumn of 1760; which was soon after Bushell died.

Anthony Henry commenced the republication of this Gazette in 1761. His first paper was marked No. 1, and a cut was placed at each end of the title; the one on the right appeared to be designed for a fowler pursuing game; that on the left was a ship. He continued to print it weekly, on Thursday, in a very indifferent manner, and with few customers, until 1765, when the British stamp act was enforced in the colony.* It was then

* The stamp act took effect in Nova Scotia, Canada and the Floridas, on the continent; and in the islands of Jamaica, Barbadoes, Antigua and Grenada.

printed on stamped paper. Not more than seventy copies were issued weekly from the press. The subscribers did not amount to that number. The Gazette had been printed on a half sheet; but after the stamp act went into operation, it appeared on a whole one, because there was only one stamp on a sheet. Not more than six or eight reams of stamped paper, of the sort appropriated to newspapers, had been sent from England for the colony; the whole of which came into the possession of Henry, and in a few weeks it was expended; or rather the stamps were, unknown to him, by the assistance of a binder's press and plough, cut from the paper; and the Gazette appeared without the obnoxious stamp, and was again reduced to half a sheet. The imprint when printed on a stamped sheet, was—'Halifax, (in Nova-Scotia); Printed and Sold by A. Henry, at his Printing-Office in Sackville-Street, where all persons may be supplied with a whole Sheet Gazette, at Eighteen Shillings [three dollars and sixty cents] a year, until the publisher has 150 Subscribers, when it will be no more than Twelve Shillings, Advertisements are taken in and inserted as cheap as the Stamp-Act will allow.'

In 1766, another newspaper was published in the place, handsomely printed and well edited; but Henry, after a short suspension, continued his Gazette. In 1770, the other paper was discontinued; and, in consequence thereof, Henry obtained an accession of customers. He placed the king's arms in the title of the Gazette, which he altered to *The Nova Scotia Gazette and the Weekly Chronicle*. The size of the paper was enlarged, and the typography was much improved. The publication ceased in 1800, on the death of the printer.

THE NOVA SCOTIA GAZETTE was first published August 15, 1766. It was handsomely printed, weekly, on a crown sheet, folio, on a new long primer type. The day of publication was Thursday. Imprint, 'Halifax: Printed by Robert Fletcher, and Sold by him at his Shop near the Parade; where all Sorts of Printing is executed neatly, correctly and expeditiously. Subscriptions received at Twelve Shillings* a Year, or Three Pence a Paper. Advertisements of a moderate Length inserted at Three Shillings† each.'

This Gazette was printed until 1770, when the publisher who came from England, returned to that country, and the paper was discontinued.

No other newspaper was published in Nova Scotia till after the war commenced.

THE art was introduced into Canada soon after its conquest by the British. There was, however, but one press established there before 1775.

Soon after the organization of the government of the province by the British, a printing house was established in Quebec by William Brown and Thomas Gilmore, under the firm of BROWN & GILMORE. They were the first who introduced the art into Canada. They printed in both English and French; and their work was executed in a very handsome manner. Brown, I am informed, was a Scotchman, and had been

* Two dollars and forty cents.
† Sixty cents.

employed some years in the printing house of William Hunter, in Williamsburg, Va. Gilmore was a native of Pennsylvania, and served an apprenticeship with William Dunlap, in Philadelphia.* Their partnership continued till 1774. From that time, Brown, the senior partner, carried on the business for himself.

Only one newspaper was published in Canada before 1775. In 1791, this territory was divided, and another province formed, distinguished by the name of Upper Canada. There are now (1810) several newspapers printed in that part which is called Lower Canada, and one or more in the new province.

THE QUEBEC GAZETTE, *La Gazette de Quebec* was first published in January, 1765, printed in English and French, on a sheet of foolscap, folio, but afterwards enlarged to a crown size, two columns to a page, the first in English, the second, containing the same matter, in French. A very handsome cut of the king's arms appeared in the title. It was published weekly, on Thursday. Imprint, 'Quebec; Printed by Brown & Gilmore, at the Printing-Office in Parlour-Street, in the Upper Town, a little above the Bishop's Palace. Advertisements of a moderate Length (in one Language) inserted at five Shillings, Halifax, the first Week, and one Shilling each Week after; if in both Languages, Seven Shillings and Six Pence, Halifax,† the first Week, and half a Dollar each Week after.' Then followed an imprint in French of the same import.

---

* The intelligence sent to me from Canada respecting the country where these printers were born, as published in the first edition, I find was erroneous. I have since received more correct information respecting them.

† One shilling equal to twenty cents.

The Gazette was discontinued a short time on account of the stamp act, in 1765.

In 1774, this paper was published by William Brown only, the senior partner, at his printing house 'behind the Cathedral Church.' After the death of Brown, it was continued by his nephew Samuel Neilson, who died, and was succeeded by John Neilson, 'in Mountain-street,' who now (1810), continues the Gazette.

A NEWSPAPER in the French language entitled *Gazette du Commerce et Litteraire, Pour la Ville et District de Montreal*, was first published in that city, June 3, 1778, by Fleury Mesplet & Charles Berger. It was printed on half a sheet of crown, quarto, with a new bourgeois type. Imprint, 'Montreal, Chas. F. Mesplet & C. Berger, Imprimeurs et Libraires.' The partnership did not long exist; in September following, the title was altered to '*Gazette Litteraire, pour la Ville, &c.,*' and published by Mesplet only, who continued it until he died. Le Roi succeeded Mesplet, and published a paper a short time. Edward Edwards, after the death of Le Roi, conducted it until the year 1808, when it was discontinued.

Other newspapers have been published since 1775, in Quebec and in Montreal; some of which have attained a permanent establishment.

A Gazette has lately been established at York, in Upper Canada.[2]

NEWSPAPERS were not printed in this province until the year 1783; two or three then issued from the presses of those printers who, during the war, were with the British army in New York, &c., but who, when peace was established, left the United States and settled at St. John, the chief town of New Brunswick. I do not know of more than one Gazette now [1810] published in the province.

NOTES TO CHAPTER XVI

BRITISH
COLONIES

The bibliography of Canadian imprints has been ably compiled by Marie Tremaine in *A Bibliography of Canadian Imprints, 1751–1800* (University of Toronto Press, 1952), which includes appendices on early Canadian newspapers and printers. The enquirer is directed to her book for additional information on this topic. He should also look into Ægidius Fauteaux's *The Introduction of Printing into Canada* (Montreal, 1930, and reprinted by the original publisher, the Roland Paper Company, ca. 1950).

NOVA SCOTIA

1. See *ante*, p. 176, also Lorenzo Sabine's *Biographical Sketches of Loyalists of the American Revolution* (Boston, 1864), 2 vols., I, 548–551. M

MONTREAL

2. *The Canadian Antiquarian & Numismatic Journal* of October, 1872, has an article on 'The First Printing Establishment of Montreal,' by Alfred Sandham (I, 58–62), in which the first newspaper is called *La Gazette de Montreal*. H

★ XVII ★

BRITISH ISLANDS

A PRINTING PRESS was established on this island about 1720; and within one or two years after a newspaper was published at Kingston.[1]

THE WEEKLY JAMAICA COURANT was published at Kingston as early as August, 1722, and as late as 1755, on a sheet of demy folio; but the exact time at which the publication commenced or closed, I cannot ascertain.

THE KINGSTON JOURNAL was published weekly, on Saturday. In 1756, it was printed on a sheet of medium, folio, by Woolhead; and, in 1761, by Woolhead, Gad and Bennett, 'Printers to the Hon. Council in Harbour-Street.'

THE JAMAICA GAZETTE made its appearance as early as 1745. In 1760, it was printed weekly, on Saturday, on medium, folio. John Walker, one of the proprietors, died in 1786.

C. S. Woodham had a printing house in Kingston in 1756, and published an Almanac and Register annually.

THE ST. JAGO INTELLIGENCER was first 'printed at St. Jago de la Vega,'* about 1756, and was published weekly on Satur-

---

* Columbus was created duke of St. Jago, and marquis of the island of Jamaica. M. L. E. Moreau de Saint-Méry, *A Topographical and Descriptive History of the Spanish Port of Saint-Domingo* (Philadelphia, 1796), 2 vols.

day. In 1768, Larwy and Sherlock were the printers of it, the size medium, folio. 'Price per annum Thirty Shillings, currency, and Two Pistoles sent by post to any part of the island.'

THE CORNWALL CHRONICLE, *and Jamaica General Advertiser* first issued from the press May 29, 1773; and was published weekly, on Saturday, 'at Montego-Bay,' by Sherlock & Co. The size was medium, folio. In 1781, and from that time to 1806, it was printed by James Fannin; who died in England in 1808.

THE ROYAL GAZETTE first came before the public in 1778. It was published by Douglas & Aikman until 1784, when it was 'Printed by Alexander Aikman, Printer to the King's Most Excellent Majesty, at the King's Printing-Office in Harbour-Street, Kingston.' The royal arms were in the centre of the title, and it was very handsomely printed on a medium sheet, quarto.

I have mentioned this paper although the publication commenced after 1775, in order to mark the devotion of it to royalty; the printer was no republican. In May, 1786, he advertised in *The Royal Gazette*, *The Royal Almanack*, *The Royal Register*, and *The Royal Sheet Almanack*; 'all printed at the royal press, and sold at the King's Printing-Office in Kingston.'

David Douglas, a Scotchman, was manager of the American theatre before the revolution;* and after the commencement of

---

* The revolutionary war closed the theatres on this part of the continent. The players were few in number, and formed only two companies under the management of Douglas and Hallam. Douglas was for some years the principal manager both on the continent and in the West Indies. In 1758, he, with his company, called The American Company of Comedians, performed for the

hostilities, he came to Jamaica. He was a scholar, and a man of talents and integrity. Here he was patronized by the governor, and appointed with Aikman printer to the king, in Jamaica, a lucrative office; he was also appointed master in chancery, and commissioned as a magistrate. It has been said, that in a few years he acquired, with reputation, by these offices, a fortune of twenty-five thousand pounds sterling. He died in Spanish-town in 1786.

PRINTING was introduced to this island as early as 1730,[2] and a newspaper was first published in 1731. There was no other press in the Caribbee islands for several years subsequent to that period.

DAVID HARRY. It is supposed that David Harry was the first who opened a printing house on the island. He served his apprenticeship, as we have elsewhere mentioned, with Keimer at Philadelphia, and succeeded him in business; but he left that city, and removed to Barbadoes with his press about the year 1730. At Bridgetown, Harry found Keimer, and obtained his assistance in the printing house; so that, as Dr. Franklin remarks, 'the master became the journeyman of his former apprentice.'

Business, it seems, did not suit Harry better in Barbadoes than

---

first time at New York in a sail loft, on Cruger's wharf, to an audience said to have been very brilliant. The theatres before 1775, were temporary wooden buildings, little better than barns. The first play publicly performed in New England, was by Douglas and his company at Providence, Rhode Island, in 1762.

in Philadelphia; on the contrary, he became more dissipated, and his profits from printing were not equal to his expenditures. In a few months he sold his printing materials, and returned to Philadelphia.

SAMUEL KEIMER, to whom Benjamin Franklin was several years a journeyman in Philadelphia, removed from that city to this island. He sold his press and types to Harry before he left Philadelphia. Harry then sold them to Keimer, as has been stated, who resumed business, and published a newspaper at Bridgetown in 1731, entitled

THE BARBADOES GAZETTE, the first newspaper published in the Caribbee islands, and the first known to have been published twice a week, for any considerable time, in any part of America. This, however, finally became a weekly journal. It was continued by Keimer until the end of 1738; and he soon after died. The Gazette was published many years after his death by those who succeeded to his business.

In 1733 Keimer was presented by the grand jury of the island for publishing, in the Barbadoes Gazette, a defamatory libel on Mr. Adams, one of the king's council. The attorney general, on that occasion, declared that there was not anything in the publication complained of, which could justify a prosecution under the criminal law, yet Keimer was bound to keep the peace during six months.*

A work was published in London in 1741, in two volumes quarto, chiefly selected from this Gazette, entitled, *Caribbeana;*

---

* John Poyer, *The History of the Barbadoes* (London, 1808).

Franklin has informed us that Keimer was a poet. I have met with one of his poetical essays in the Barbadoes Mercury, and insert it as a specimen of his poetical talents, and for the information it contains respecting the encouragement given in his time to the typographic art by the colonial government on this continent. It is as follows:

From the Barbadoes Gazette of May 4, 1734.

TO THOSE WOU'D-BE THOUGHT GENTLEMEN, WHO HAVE LONG TAKEN THIS PAPER, AND NEVER PAID FOR IT, AND SEEM NEVER TO DESIGN TO PAY FOR IT.

The Sorrowful Lamentation of SAMUEL KEIMER, *Printer of the Barbadoes Gazette.*

What a pity it is that *some* modern Bravadoes,
Who dub themselves Gentlemen here in Barbadoes.
Should, Time after Time, run in Debt to their Printer,
And care not to pay him in Summer or Winter!
A Saint by the Hairs of his Beard, had he got 'em,
Might be tempted to swear [instead of P—x rot 'em.]
He ne'er found before such a Parcel of Wretches,
With their Flams, and such Shuffles, Put-offs and odd Fetches.
If *This* is their *Honesty, That* be their *Honour,*
Amendment seize *One;* for the *Last,—Fie upon her.*
In *Penn's** Wooden Country, *Type* feels no disaster,
Their Printer is rich, and is made their Post-master;†
His Father, ‡ a Printer, is paid for his Work,
And wallows in Plenty, just now at *New-York,*
Tho' quite past his Labour, and old as my Grannum,

* Pennsylvania.
† Andrew Bradford, of Philadelphia.
‡ William Bradford of New-York.

The Government pays him Pounds Sixty *per Annum*.
In Maryland's Province, as well as Virginia
To Justice and Honour, I am, Sirs to win ye,
Their Printer* Im sure can make it appear,
Each Province allows two Hundred a Year,
By Laws they have made for *Typograph's* Use,
He's paid 50 Thousand Weight Country Produce.
And if you inquire but at *South Carolina,* †
[*O! Methinks in that Name, there is something-Divine-Ah!*]
Like Patriots they've done what to Honor redounds,
They gave him (their Currency) 50 Score Pounds.
E'en *Type* at *Jamaica*, our Island's reproach,
Is able to ride in her Chariot or Coach; ‡
But alas your poor *Type* prints no Figure;—like *Nullo*,
Curs'd, cheated, abus'd by each pitiful Fellow.
Tho' working like Slave, with Zeal and true Courage,
He can scarce get as yet ev'n Salt to his Porridge.
The Reason is plain; Those *act by just Rules*—
But here *knaves have bit him, all* MAC-*abite* Fools.

GEORGE ESMAND & COMPANY. This firm in 1762 opened a
second printing house at Bridgetown, and began the Publication ot

THE BARBADOES MERCURY. It was published weekly, on
Saturday; printed with long primer types, on a crown sheet,
folio. Imprint, 'Bridge-Town, Printed by George Esmand and
Comp. at the new Printing-Office, in Back-Church-Street.
Price one Pistole per Annum.'

* William Parks, who printed for both colonies.
† Lewis Timothy then printed for the government of South Carolina.
‡ This expression seems to imply that the printer in Jamaica at that time was
a female.

The memorable stamp act took effect in this island in 1765, and the Mercury was printed on stamped paper.

In 1771, the firm was Esmand & Walker.

George Esmand died in November, 1771, and William Walker in February, 1773.

The Mercury was continued after the year, 1794.

PRINTING was brought to this island as early as 1746, and may have been introduced two or three years sooner. There were two printing houses established before 1775.

THOMAS HOWE probably was the first printer, and settled at Basseterre. Howe printed the laws, and did other work for government; and, in 1747, published

THE ST. CHRISTOPHER GAZETTE. This paper was continued until after the year 1775. Howe was a native of Ireland, and lived to old age.

SAMUEL JONES was a printer and postmaster at Basseterre before 1757, and published a newspaper. He died in London in 1762, after an illness of eight days, of inflammation of the lungs.

EDWARD DUBSON, printed after Jones, and was in business after 1767, at Basseterre.

DANIEL THIBOU, had a printing house on this island in 1769, and in that year printed the acts of assembly, from 1711 to 1769. He printed several other works.

THE ST. CHRISTOPHER GAZETTE. A second newspaper
bearing this title was published at Basseterre. The Gazette printed November 19, 1785, is numbered 693, vol. VII. It then had
this imprint, 'Basseterre, Saint Christopher, Printed by Edward
L. Low in Cayon-Street, No. 84.'

ANTIGUA

I CANNOT determine the year when printing was introduced to Antigua, but believe it was about 1748.[3]

I have not discovered that any press was erected on this island
prior to the time when BENJAMIN MECOM opened a printing
house, about 1748. He has been taken notice of in the course of
this work, as a printer in Boston, New Haven and Philadelphia.
It was at St. John that he first began business, and published a
newspaper, entitled

THE ANTIGUA GAZETTE. Mecom continued this publication
six or seven years, and then removed to Boston, Massachusetts,
his native place.

ALEXANDER SHIPTON, published the Gazette, before and
after 1767, which was by him printed weekly, on Wednesday,
on a crown sheet, folio, chiefly with small pica types; and had,
in the title, a small cut of a basket of flowers.

THE ANTIGUA MERCURY was published in 1769; but how
long it was printed before or after that time, I am not able to
say.*

DOMINICA

THE FREEPORT GAZETTE; or, the Dominica Advertiser was
first published in 1765, at Roseau, by William Smith. It had the

---

* John Mears printed a well conducted newspaper in St. Johns in 1779, and
I am inclined to believe it was the *Mercury*.

king's arms in the title; and was printed weekly, on Saturday, on a fools-cap sheet, and with new long primer and small pica types.[4]

In 1767, Smith printed *The Shipwreck*, 'a poem in three parts: By a Sailor, addressed to his Royal Highness the Duke of York. Price Two Dollars.'

In 1775, a newspaper was published in English and French, by Jones.

THE ROYAL GRANADA GAZETTE first appeared at George-town in January, 1765, on a crown sheet, folio, printed with new small pica and long primer types, by William Weyland, 'at the New Printing-Office.' It was published on Saturday and had a cut of the king's arms in the title.

There were two printing houses on this island, and one of them was established some years before Weyland's.

THE ROYAL DANISH AMERICAN GAZETTE was issued from the press at Christiansted before 1770. Printing was not introduced into this island long before the publication of the paper.

THE BERMUDA GAZETTE was not published until July 1784; but a printing house had a short time before been established at St. George, by J. Stockdale.

THE ROYAL BAHAMA GAZETTE. I have introduced this paper, although it was not established till after peace took place on the American continent, in 1783, in order to conclude the account of John Wells, the editor of it, who has been mentioned as a printer in South Carolina, who fled from Charleston when the British army evacuated that city.

This paper was printed at Nassau, New Providence.

Wells was not contented to remain on the island; but had a strong desire to return to the continent, and had attempted several schemes to effect that purpose which proved unsuccessful. He was still endeavoring to arrange his business in such a manner as to permit him to revisit his native country, which he had left with great reluctance, when he was summoned to the world of spirits.

He married at Nassau, and was highly esteemed for his many amiable qualities.

NOTES TO CHAPTER XVII

JAMAICA   1. Frank Cundall, *A History of Printing in Jamaica from 1717 to 1834* (Kingston, 1935) and his 'The Press and Printers of Jamaica prior to 1820,' in *Proceedings of the American Antiquarian Society*, XXVI, 290–412 (Oct. 1916); Waldo Lincoln, 'List of Newspapers of the West Indies and Bermuda in the Library of the A.A.S.,' in *Proceedings of the American Antiquarian Society*, XXXVI, 130–155 (April 1926).

BARBADOES   2. D. C. McMurtrie, *Early Printing in Barbados* (London, 1933); E. M. Shilstone, 'Some Notes on Early Printing Presses and Newspapers in Barbados,' in *Journal of the Barbados Museum and Historical Society*, XXVI, 19–33 (Nov. 1958).

ANTIGUA   3. W. Eames, 'The Antigua Press and Benjamin Mecom, 1748–1765,' in *Proceedings of the American Antiquarian Society*, XXXVIII, 303–348 (April 1928); B. F. Swan, 'A Checklist of Early Printing on the Island of Antigua, 1748–1800,' in *Papers of the Bibliographical Society of America*, L, 285–292 (3rd qtr. 1956); *Dictionary of American Biography*, XII, 488–489.

DOMINICA   4. D. C. McMurtrie, *The First Printing in Dominica* (London, 1932).

INDEX

Index

650